COMPUTER LITERACY

CONCEPTS AND APPLICATIONS

Cover: This computer generated art is an application of today's computer technology (Courtesy Ramtek Corporation)

COMPUTER LITERACY
CONCEPTS AND APPLICATIONS

TIMOTHY N. TRAINOR

MITCHELL PUBLISHING, INC.
Santa Cruz, California

Book produced by Ex Libris □ Julie Kranhold

Production coordination: Susan Defosset
Design: Janet Bollow
Manuscript editor: Janet Greenblatt
Illustrations: Michael Abbey, Barbara Ravizza
Photo essay layout: Michael and Pat Rogondino
Color illustrations for "The Chip": Dave Pauly
Composition: Graphic Typesetting Service

10   9   8   7   6   5   4   3   2

Printed in the United States of America

Library of Congress Cataloging in Publication Data

Trainor, Timothy N., 1953-
    Computer literacy—concepts and applications.

    Includes index.
    1. Computer literacy. 2. Computers—Study and teaching.
3. Microcomputers—Study and teaching.   I. Title.
QA76.9.C64T73   1984   001.64′07′1   83–25105
ISBN 0–938188–18–6 (cloth)
ISBN 0–938188–25–9 (ppbk)

To Diane (my better half)
whose support and insight
made this book possible

Contents

UNIT F
BASIC on
Microcomputers
Step-by-Step 427

APPENDIXES 487

Preface

Computer literacy is a widely used term that is often misused. In writing *Computer Literacy: Concepts and Applications*, I wanted to create a book with a balance between concepts, applications, and programming. To me computer literacy means:

- An appreciation of the impact computers have and will have on society and chosen careers.
- The knowledge of how the components of a computer system interact to produce useful information.
- A familiarity with the functions and limitations of a computer system.
- The ability to operate a computer and attached equipment.
- The capacity to evaluate applications packages to determine if they satisfy a specific need.
- The ability to communicate with computer professionals.

I have emphasized that people do not have to be computer professionals to understand the impact of computers on our world.

Career Orientation Through Fictional Characters

One unique feature of this book is the five fictional characters introduced in the first chapter. They emphasize the career-oriented material and lighten the reading.

These characters are first introduced as students. They reappear throughout the text as they mature and take on new jobs and/or new responsibilities. Two of them become computer professionals; the others become professionals using computers. Their career paths are summarized in the last chapter. This final chapter also discusses educational opportunities and summarizes the computer-oriented jobs highlighted throughout the text.

Flexible Design

As you read through the Table of Contents you will notice that this text is broken into six units. Each unit has three related chapters. After unit A, the units can be assigned in any order. Unit F, "BASIC on Microcomputers Step-by-Step," was designed to be used in parallel with the other units.

Programmed Text Format for BASIC

The BASIC material has been organized for self-pacing. New material and questions are presented on the left side of the page. The answers or results displayed by the computer appear on the right. By covering the right side of the page, the material can be worked through and then checked by uncovering the answers.

In addition, differences in the BASIC language used by four popular microcomputers (Apple, Commodore, IBM, and Radio Shack) are highlighted and discussed. Editing and start-up procedures for each of these microcomputers also appear in the appendixes.

Photo Essays

The photo essays are designed to be instructional as well as visually interesting. Each photo essay comes complete with its own review questions. The color photographs and text highlight important concepts and provide a visually pleasing presentation of the material.

Detailed Study Objectives

Each chapter has a detailed set of study objectives. Great care has been taken to ensure that the answer to each study objective can be clearly identified in the readings. And they have been placed within the text close to the area of introduction, rather than at the chapter's end.

Support Material

The study objectives dovetail with an extensive package of supplementary materials. These materials include an instructor's guide, student workbook, overhead transparencies, a computerized test bank, a videocourse, microcomputer lab manual (Apple and IBM PC versions), and a tutorial disk on BASIC.

The student workbook, by Diane Krasnewich, leads students through the material. It provides thought questions and worksheets to support the study objectives. These materials along with the text have been field tested with a variety of students.

The documentary-style videocourse consists of fifteen 30-minute lessons, which illustrate many of the concepts in the text. Hal Calbom, a professional television journalist, hosts each lesson. An excellent video manual and instructor's guide for the videocourse was prepared by Joe Kinzer of Central State University.

Meeting Different Course Structures

I tried to prepare this manuscript for a wide variety of classroom needs. It can be used as a comprehensive textbook for a computer literacy course. It can support a few weeks of class time dedicated to computer literacy. It can also be used as a supplementary text in business, accounting, secretarial skills, or mathematics classes that touch upon the need for computer literacy.

Special Acknowledgments

Many people played important roles in the creation and production of this book. I have identified those people I owe a great deal of thanks to in the following acknowledgments. But, there are always a select few who help you through the hard times by their tough questions and gentle pats on the back.

First, a great deal of credit and thanks goes to Dave Kroenke. He graciously allowed me to use large portions of his book *Business Computer Systems*. The chapters on the History of Data Processing, Advanced Computer Systems, and Computer Crime and Security are primarily Dave's. In addition, I have borrowed liberally from Dave whenever he said it better then I could. Dave was also one of my best technical reviewers.

The hardest hitting technical reviewers were also the best. Whenever I received a review from Marilyn Bohl I had to steel myself before reading the letter. Marilyn was always right and her reviews have made me a better teacher and writer. Thank you, Marilyn.

My sounding board here in Muskegon was Diane Krasnewich, she spent countless hours with me discussing ideas and reviewing preliminary drafts. Her patience and helpful hints were invaluable.

Lou Meisch also receives a great deal of thanks for his patience with the "amateur photographer." Lou developed and printed the various photographs I took for the book. He always maintained a smile (or was that a snicker) when I brought him that "last" roll of film.

Not just any "thank you" is right for Julie Kranhold. Not even one in bold or in the second color! As the production manager, Julie worked under a grueling schedule. I left this project with a great deal of admiration for her creative instincts.

Finally, Steve Mitchell, Susan Defosset, and everyone at Mitchell Publishing deserve a very special thank you. Steve for having the faith to back me on this project. Susan for holding my hand and guiding me through the publication jungle. The people you work with can make the tough deadlines and hard work easier. All the people at Mitchell Publishing through their professionalism and good natures enabled me to walk away from this project with a good feeling inside.

Timothy N. Trainor
Muskegon, Michigan

Acknowledgments

Thanks to the following people who have provided helpful comments and other assistance in the preparation of the book.

June Atkinson
North Carolina
Department of Public Education

Mike Bradford
Muskegon Mercy Hospital

Betty Boyer
Ponca City High School

Melissa Brown
Herman Miller

Milford Chisum
El Reno Junior College

Roberta Cool
Norfolk Technical Vocational School

Scott Cutting
Muskegon Community College

Luther Dease
Muskegon Area Intermediate
School District

Paul Deffenbaugh
Fremont City Schools

Harley Dyk
Mona Shores High School

Mary Egan
Grand Haven High School

Lori Engler
Computer Process Utility

R. K. Ferrell
United States Navy

Gail Flanagan
Norfolk Technical Vocational School

Linda Flynn
Kimball High School

Winnie Ford
Indiana State University

Bill Fortune
National Weather Service

Katheryn Fouche
Vanguard High School

Jana Frame
Carl Albert High School

Lael Fuqua
Putnam City High School

Terry Fuss
Ponca City High School

Colleen Giddings
Muskegon Community College

Diane Graf
Rockford Vocational Center

Gladys Harris
Malcolm X College

Len Harrison
First of America Banks

H. P. Haiduk
Amarillo College

Romona Holloway
DeValls Bluff High School

Delores Honey
Missouri Southern State College

Joyce Ignatz
Elyria High School

Carol Ann Jennings
Parkview High School

Suzanne Jessup
Grimsley High School

Randy Johnson
PDS Incorporated

Edna Kass
University of Toledo

George Keefe
Keefe's North Muskegon Pharmacy

Margaret King
Oak Park and
River Forest High School

Joe Kinzer
Central State University

Lyle Langlois
Glendale Community College

Jessie Linyear
Cradock High School

Greg Luckey
Cooperative Extension Service
Muskegon State University

Karen McNeill
Putnam City North High School

Nancy Melesco
Franklin County High School

Dodie Miller
SE Senior High School

Karen Miller
Mt. Vernon High School

Robert Morse
The Muskegon Chronicle

Rob Ober
University of Kansas

Chris Oman
V and O Computer Instruction

Pete Oakes
Muskegon Community College

Randy Pidhayny
Calcomp/Sanders

Sandra Price
Hilton-Frost Business Equipment

Ken Pontius
Sealed Power Corporation

Jan Eskew Powell
Belle Isle
School of Business

Ron Rademacher
Fritz-The Druggist

Elwin Randall
Ringwood Public Schools

Eric Richards
White Lake Christian

Bob Sheardy
Kendall School of Design

Larry Sherry
Muskegon High School

Joe Shemanski
Woodbridge Senior High School

Glenn Smith
James Madison University

Jesse Sprayberry and others
Muskegon Skill Training Center

Jeff Stipes
Child and Family Services

Jean Stover
Western Oaks Junior High School

Jeanne Sweany
Muskegon General Hospital

Arthur Tenney
Whitman High School

Frank Thomas
Muskegon Community College

Thomas Trainor
Chrysler Corporation

Val Trainor
Royal Oak Public Schools

Pat VanderSys
Muskegon Community College

Nancy Wardinski
Mt. Vernon High School

Dave Wenk
Martin-Marietta

Eva Williams
Westover Senior High School

Kenneth Williams
Western Michigan University

Elroy Zentner
Tooele High School

Dorothy Zmolek
Auburn High School

Photo Essays

The six color sections in this book are unique. Today, you will find many computer textbooks that are full of color photographs. This book contains exciting color photos, too. What makes these photos unique, however, is the way in which they are presented.

Each of the 200 photos was carefully selected to illustrate the content of six essays—essays written on topics of special interest and importance to today's introductory computer student. Thus, the resulting six *photo essays* both entertain *and* instruct. Each photo essay concludes with review questions and enhances the content covered in the text. They may be used in any order or as optional assignments.

The mystery of today's silicon chip is explained simply, with colorful illustrations and photographs by award-winning *National Geographic* photographer Chuck O'Rear.

THE CHIP:
The Heart of the Computer

This photo essay organizes a look at today's computer hardware into an easy-to-understand format: input, processing, output, storage. It teaches the distinctions between micro, mini, and mainframe environments.

HARDWARE:
More and More for Less
and Less

Graphics is one of the hottest areas of today's computer technology, and this photo essay shows why. It shows graphics as providing something for everyone—from business to the arts and sciences. Illustrations of how simple graphics are generated provide a basis for understanding more complex applications.

COMPUTER GRAPHICS:
An Art, A Science, A Tool

COMPUTERS AND SOCIETY:
More Uses, More Users,
More Questions

This extension to unit C of the text looks at a range of interesting computer applications and asks the reader/viewer to think about their impact—good and bad.

MICROS:
Selecting Your Own
Computer

This extension of Chapter D1 is unique and practical. It illustrates the value of the systems development process, even at the personal level. The photo essay follows student Jennifer Anderson as she learns the correct process of selecting her own micro software and hardware and developing a personal word processing *system*.

THE COMPUTER INDUSTRY
AND CAREERS:
Gold Rush of the 1980s

This photo essay offers a current, practical look at a subject of great importance to every student. It includes statistics on salaries and the computer industry that will be updated annually in text reprints. Many useful tips on career planning, both for the future computer professional *and* the computer-literate user, are provided.

PHOTO ESSAY CREDITS
(clockwise by page)

THE CHIP

Opener: Chuck O'Rear. Pages 2–3: Chuck O'Rear. Pages 4–5: Chuck O'Rear, Intel Corporation, Intel Corporation, Chuck O'Rear. Pages 6–7: Chuck O'Rear, Chuck O'Rear, Chuck O'Rear, Honeywell, Inc. Pages 8–9: Intel Corporation, Intel Corporation, Chuck O'Rear, Intel Corporation, Chuck O'Rear. Pages 10–11: Intel Corporation, Intel Corporation, Chuck O'Rear, Intel Corporation. Page 12: Intel Corporation. Page 13: Apple Computer, Inc., Intel Corporation. Page 14: IBM Corporation, Intel Corporation. Page 15: National Semiconductor Corporation. Page 16: Chuck O'Rear.

HARDWARE

Opener: Xerox Corporation. Pages 2–3: Hewlett-Packard, Anacomp, Inc., 3M Corporation, Digital Equipment Corporation. Pages 4–5: Inforex, Inc., American Airlines, IBM Corporation, Anacomp, Inc., Hewlett-Packard. Pages 6–7: Apple Computer, Inc., Interdesign, Inc., IBM Corporation, Hewlett-Packard. Pages 8–9: Apple Computer, Inc., Wang Laboratories, Inc., Apple Computer, Inc. Pages 10–11: Digital Equipment Corporation, Amdahl Corporation, IBM Corporation, Paradyne Corporation. Pages 12–13: Anacomp, Inc., IBM Corporation, Hewlett-Packard, RCA. Pages 14–15: Carol Lee/BASF Wyandette Corporation, IBM Corporation, Verbatim Corporation, Memorex Corporation, AT&T Company.

COMPUTER GRAPHICS

Opener: Digital Equipment Corporation. Pages 2–3: Hewlett-Packard, Ramtek Corporation, Ramtek Corporation, Ramtek Corporation, Tetronix, Inc. Page 4: AT&T Company. Page 5: Chuck O'Rear. Pages 6–7: Intergraph Corporation, Intergraph Corporation, Hewlett-Packard, Chuck O'Rear, Ramtek Corporation. Page 10: NASA. Page 11: Ramtek Corporation. Page 12: Ramtek Corporation, Aurora Imaging Systems. Page 13: Chuck O'Rear. Page 14: © Walt Disney Productions, AT&T Company, Ramtek Corporation. Page 15: Ramtek Corporation, Digital Productions, Ramtek Corporation. Page 16: Chuck O'Rear, Ford Motor Company.

Opener: Chuck O'Rear. Pages 2–3: Chuck O'Rear, Unimation, Chuck O'Rear, Ford Motor Company, Chuck O'Rear. Pages 4–5: IBM Corporation, Chuck O'Rear, Chuck O'Rear, Hewlett-Packard. Pages 6–7: Anacomp, Inc., IBM Corporation, Ramtek Corporation, Federal Express Corporation. Pages 8–9: Ramtek Corporation, Chuck O'Rear, Wang Laboratories, Inc., Intel Corporation. Page 10: Fairchild Industries, Gannett Company, Gannett Company. Page 11: Computer Sciences Corporation, Xerox Corporation, AT&T Company, Fairchild Industries. Pages 12–13: Chuck O'Rear, Ramtek Corporation/ Digital Productions, NASA, NASA, AT&T Company. Pages 14–15: Chuck O'Rear, IBM Corporation, Chuck O'Rear, General Instrument Corporation. Page 16: Chuck O'Rear.

Opener: Chuck O'Rear. Page 2: Syndia Smith. Page 3: Shelly McComas. Pages 4–5: Syndia Smith, Shelly McComas, Chuck O'Rear, Apple Computer, Inc. Pages 6–7: Syndia Smith, Intel Corporation, Shelly McComas, Shelly McComas, Shelly McComas. Pages 8–9: Apple Computer, Inc., Syndia Smith, Syndia Smith. Pages 10–11: Apple Computer, Inc., Syndia Smith, Hewlett-Packard. Pages 12–13: Roland Compu Music/Apple Computer, Inc., Chuck O'Rear, Chuck O'Rear, Apple Computer Inc. Pages 14–15: Chuck O'Rear, Apple Computer, Inc., Apple Computer, Inc.

Opener: Hewlett-Packard. Pages 2–3: Honeywell, Inc., Intel Corporation, Honeywell, Inc. Pages 4–5: Xerox Corporation, RCA, IBM Corporation, IBM Corporation, Hewlett-Packard. Pages 6–7: Hewlett-Packard, IBM Corporation, Intel Corporation, Apple Computer, Inc., Infocom, Inc. Pages 8–9: Hewlett-Packard, Intel Corporation, Hewlett-Packard. Pages 10–11: Hewlett-Packard, Hewlett-Packard, Wang Laboratories, Inc., AT&T Company. Pages 12–13: IBM Corporation, Digital Equipment Corporation, Honeywell, Inc., Walt Robinson. Pages 14–15: AT&T Company, American Airlines, IBM Corporation, Intel Corporation. Page 16: Apple Computer, Inc., Hewlett-Packard.

U N I T   A

Welcome to the Computer Age

In this unit you are introduced to computer systems. The first part of the unit discusses reasons for studying computers. The story of how computers will affect the careers of five students begins as they all meet for the first time in a computer class.

The five components of a computer system are described in the second part of the unit. You learn how these components fit together to perform a variety of jobs. These jobs are initially categorized as data processing, word processing, or process control systems.

Unit A concludes with the history of data processing. You are taken to the roots from which computerized data processing systems developed and grew. This chapter allows you to put new computer-related developments into historical perspective.

1

CHAPTER A1

The Computer's Impact on Society

This book is about computer systems—about how computers are used, the people who use them, and how computers are put together. When you finish you will not be an expert, but you will have the background necessary to talk intelligently about computers. More importantly, you will have a feel for the awesome impact computers and related technology will have on your life, no matter where you are, what you do, or how you do it.

This may sound like a bold statement! It is! The first computer was built in 1946. In over three decades many industries have been revolutionized by computers. Look around and you will see the effect of computers everywhere.

F I G U R E A 1 . 1

Computers can be used by anyone almost anywhere (Courtesy Gannet Company, *top left*; Steve Potter, *top right*; Wang Laboratories, Inc., *middle*; IBM Corporation, *bottom left*; Hewlett-Packard, *bottom right*)

Computers are used in cars, toys, and appliances. They are used by musicians, waitresses, bank tellers, and teachers. They forecast today's weather, track the migration of reindeer across the arctic tundra, and identify stolen cars. They help organize, write, and edit manuscripts like this text and then send the information across the country to be printed in the blink of an eye.

You haven't seen anything yet! Computers get less expensive and more powerful each year. Every day a new or better computer-based product is announced that costs less than the model before. As computers get cheaper, products using them become more affordable. As people gain more experience working with computers, they increase the computer's capabilities and make them easier to use.

In school today you have the opportunity to learn about computers and to learn how to use them in areas that interest you. Remember, computers are very sophisticated tools—but tools nevertheless.

Why Learn About Computers?

There will always be computer professionals. These people operate computers, design computer systems, and manage these powerful resources. However, most computers do not have to be stuffed into air-conditioned rooms or given special attention.

The use of computers is no longer limited to computer professionals. Doctors, lawyers, pilots, auto mechanics, and salespeople all use computers on a day-to-day basis.

You will find that computers are not very different from other tools. Calculators, typewriters, dishwashers, and ovens are tools that help us work with and change our environment. Computers help us process and sometimes store facts and figures. Common to all of these tools is a simple three-step process:

1. You put something into the device.
2. The device changes it in some way.
3. You get results out.

If the tool happens to be a dishwasher, then the three-step process looks like this:

1. You put dirty dishes and soap into the dishwasher.
2. The dishwasher washes and rinses the dishes.
3. You get clean dishes ready for the next meal as a result.

When working with computers, we call this three-step process the input/processing/output cycle or **IPO cycle.**

In one way or another, you will find that every computer system conforms to the IPO cycle. The facts and figures—called **data**—are input into the computer. The data is then processed and the results are output. This cycle is repeated until all the data is processed.

Computers get more powerful and cost
less every year

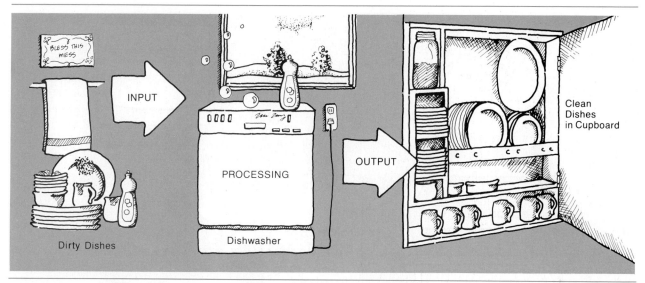

The input/processing/output (IPO) cycle:
a noncomputer example

Sometimes you have to stop and think about the IPO cycle before you can identify each step. The input step could be typing data into the computer through a keyboard, dialing a telephone, or activating a monitor with a bright light or sound.

Most often you will find computers processing letters and numbers. The processing step might involve sorting names into alphabetical order or performing calculations needed to answer a mathematics problem.

The final output may be a printed report or a display on a television screen. It could also be the action of a mechanical arm as it swings into place to tighten a bolt on a new motorcycle.

Identifying the IPO cycle is very important in understanding how computer systems are designed and operate. If you become confused while trying to figure out the operations of a computer system, think about this cycle. Consider what activity is needed for input, what processing must be done, and what results will be output. Breaking down the process in this way is very helpful in organizing your thoughts.

Identifying the IPO Cycle

1. Briefly describe the input/processing/output cycle using computer and non-computer examples.

STUDY OBJECTIVE

To illustrate the impact computers will have on your future, we will follow a group of students through their first computer class and into the job market.

It was hot and humid, summer's last hurrah before cooler fall days arrived. Students gathered in small clusters. As groups passed, hands waved and greet-

MRS. DINGMAN'S COMPUTER CLASS

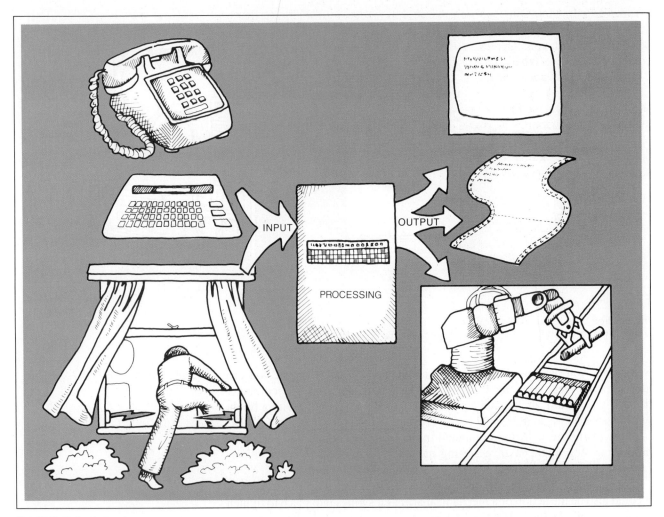

The IPO Cycle: computer examples

ings flew back and forth. New students were easy to spot as they wandered the halls with their trusty maps.

As always, an excitement filled the air the first days of school. The good news in Mrs. Dingman's class was the 10 new computers the school had purchased over the summer. Added to the other computers the school already owned, this represented an impressive collection of equipment.

The first day back, computers were the furthest thing from anyone's thoughts. There were new people to meet, tall tales from the summer to tell, and the latest gossip to hear. A few students, like Harold Johnson, had worked with a computer before and knew what to expect. The others were new to computers. Everyone had heard that Mrs. Dingman's class would be a lot of hard work.

The students in Mrs. Dingman's class had different reasons for being there. Sitting by the door was long and lanky Martha Baker, who had just started a part-time job as a computer operator. She wanted to know more about how computers worked. What's more, she was supposed to graduate in June and was a little uneasy about having no career plans.

Martha was looking for something interesting enough to do full-time when she left school. At one time basketball had been her life and she had planned to play after graduation. This dream had come to an abrupt halt when she was placed on academic probation last year. At the very least, working as a computer operator was going to help her forget basketball as well as fill the time after school. She hoped it would turn out to be more than that.

FIGURE A1.5

Martha Baker

In the desk behind Martha was the "whiz kid" Harold Johnson. Harold was going to program computers. He knew this because he had enjoyed working with his friend's personal computer over the summer. They had mastered all the games and were now going to write some themselves.

Unfortunately, they found that learning how to program on their own was a slow process. Many questions came up, and the only way to find the answers was to read the thick manuals that came with the computer.

Mrs. Dingman taught computer programming so Harold had signed up. You probably know people like Harold. When something catches his attention, he locks on to it and does not let go. He was like that in math. Video games had also caught his attention, and he was the terror of the local arcade. Now it was computers and computer programming; Harold ignored everything else. However, he did manage to pull passing grades in his other classes.

FIGURE A1.6

Harold Johnson

Peter Clark

As it turns out, Martha was not the only one in class without a career plan. Sitting in the next row was Peter Clark. Pete had just come from a rather long meeting with the career counselor. He was really in Mrs. Dingman's class because of the counselor's prodding. You could tell he had left the meeting with a negative attitude by the way he slouched in his chair.

Pete was good with his hands. If it was mechanical, Pete could fix it. He had been taking things apart and putting them back together for as long as anyone could remember. It had started with Tinker Toys and progressed to cars and stereo systems. Tinkering in the garage was how Pete liked to spend his time.

But his teachers complained that Pete did not bring this energy to school with him. They said he only went through the motions. Pete was the first to agree that schoolwork was something to get out of the way so he could work on his latest project. This is not to say he did poorly in school. Pete loafed along getting B's, which aggravated his teachers and the career counselor even more.

Sue McKnight

On the other side of the room, sitting with friends, was Sue McKnight. Sue had the motivation to excel in school that Pete lacked. Self-assured, she came across as being very relaxed and friendly. It was an attitude that came from having a goal in life.

Her father owned the local drugstore. This may account for Sue's desire to be a doctor. Everything she did was focused on this career goal. An A student since elementary school, Sue was taking Mrs. Dingman's class because she had heard that computers were being used everywhere in medicine.

Luckily for Sue, she didn't take herself seriously all the time. She was easygoing and always ready to help someone. Years later, they would call it "good bedside manner."

John LaFriend

At the back of the class was a new face. John LaFriend had recently moved into town from mid-state New York. Still a little stunned from having to move away from old friends and school, he signed up for Mrs. Dingman's course because there was an opening when he transferred.

FIGURE A1.8

Sue McKnight

John LaFriend

John had always been rather neutral about school even before he moved. He would say "school is just the refrain in the ballad of my life." John was a musician and poet.

One of his first objectives since moving to town was to find a new band to join. He had played a very "hot" piano with his old band and hoped to find another as soon as possible. As for Mrs. Dingman's computer class, well, it was as good a place as any to meet people.

Little did John or the others know the effect this class and computers were going to have on their lives. Only two would work as professional computer people. But the others would work with computers in the course of their day's work. One would misuse the technology and pay the penalty, as anyone does when caught committing a crime.

Looking Ahead

Mrs. Dingman's computer class

These people are fictional characters, but the jobs they do and the impact computers are having on these and other occupations are not fiction. The world is going through a transition. The industrial revolution has created the computer age. We can ride this new wave of technology into the future or be drowned by it. As always, the choice is ours.

MIKE DILWORTH
STUDENT/COMPUTER CONSULTANT

RESPONSIBILITIES

My business card says "programming and consulting." I do computer maintenance and programming on microcomputers. I work with a couple of companies, trying to get their computers to do what they want them to do. One business is the publisher of this book. I don't know anything about publishing or much about business, but if they are trying to print labels with customers and addresses, and it won't print what they want, I find out why.

MY BACKGROUND

Two years ago in 11th grade, my Dad brought home a micro. At the same time I was taking a course in BASIC at school. It was a new toy, something to play with. What kind of a student was I? Ha! Not so good. My aptitude tests said I should be a hairdresser or an architect. In my senior year I had to get my act together just to graduate. Actually I think the micro helped. For instance, word processing got me through senior English. My writing is not what you would call clear and legible. Just being able to see what I had written on the screen and read it again helped a lot.

Now I'm taking general education courses at the community college. In my part-time consulting, my confidence is better and so is my communication. Now, I'm not so afraid to do something wrong or to make a mistake, because I know I can figure it out eventually.

SKILLS REQUIRED

You really need to be *interested* in computers. You have to get into it.

Last summer I had an assembly-line job working on printed circuit boards. I wasn't doing any programming, but what really helped was being around a lot of computer people. Just hearing them talk, I began to pick up information.

My little brother John is a jock and isn't interested in becoming a computernik, but he has learned what a micro can do for him. He uses word processing on his reports, and tries to stay eligible for football.

I think any hands-on course will help you to understand computers. It should at least teach you the language used to talk to the computer.

MY FUTURE

I plan to go to a state university. I'm interested in computer graphics right now, because I've always been interested in design and graphics arts. Last year I was interested in computer hardware. Next year it might be something else, but it will have something to do with computers. What do I like best about my computer career? The money!

CHAPTER A2

Components of a Computer System

The term **computer system** will be used throughout this book. It is one of those terms that is often misunderstood. Listen carefully when people talk about computers. You might overhear someone talking about computer equip-

FIGURE A2.1

The five components of a computer system (Courtesy IBM Corporation and Apple Computer)

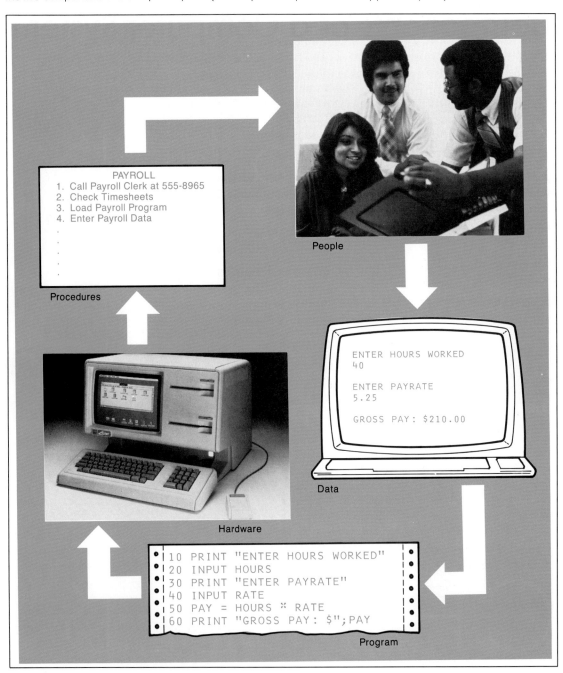

PAYROLL
1. Call Payroll Clerk at 555-8965
2. Check Timesheets
3. Load Payroll Program
4. Enter Payroll Data

Procedures

People

```
ENTER HOURS WORKED
40

ENTER PAYRATE
5.25

GROSS PAY: $210.00
```

Data

Hardware

```
10 PRINT "ENTER HOURS WORKED"
20 INPUT HOURS
30 PRINT "ENTER PAYRATE"
40 INPUT RATE
50 PAY = HOURS * RATE
60 PRINT "GROSS PAY: $";PAY
```

Program

ment when they really mean a computer system. Sometimes people use the words **computer** and **computer system** interchangeably.

The glossary in the back of this text will show you that a computer and a computer system are not the same. The computer by itself is just processing equipment—to use a computer term, **hardware.** It is only one of several parts, or components, of a computer system. What are the other components?

There are five components of a computer system: people, data, hardware, programs and procedures. Each component is needed. Therefore, a computer system is a collection of components, including a computer, that work together to do a job. Take away one component and the system will not work.

Many people are misinformed about computer systems. They think a computer by itself can solve all their problems. Instead, they sometimes find that it can create new problems on top of the old. Buying a computer is easy. Putting all five components to work is the hard part. In this chapter we will take a closer look at the components of a computer system.

1. Define computer and computer system.
2. Identify the five components of a computer system.

STUDY OBJECTIVES

PEOPLE

Computer systems are developed for people. They help us make decisions and solve problems. People create, control, and operate computer systems. You will find that people are responsible for bringing the other four components of a computer system together. People working with computers fall into three general categories: **users, systems development personnel** and **operations personnel.**

Users

A user is anyone who uses information produced by a computer. You are a user when you get a bill from the local telephone company, withdraw money from an automatic teller, or listen to synthesized music. Many times we do not have the choice. We do have a choice as to whether or not we are **informed users.**

Informed users understand how the components of a computer system work together to perform a task. They know what a computer system can and cannot do. They are also able to use the technology to make life better for themselves and others.

Systems Development Personnel

A **computer center** is the physical location of the computer system. At big computer centers, systems development personnel are hired to design and maintain the computer system. Systems development personnel work in the computer center with computer systems. However, you will find their jobs can be either people oriented or equipment oriented.

People-oriented **systems analysts** put together the computer system's components. They help the users understand what the computer system can do for them. In addition, they help identify the user's needs. The systems analyst must

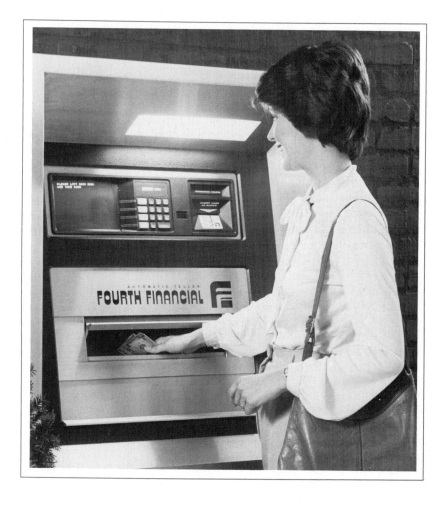

A user withdrawing money from an automatic teller

have good communications skills to decide what the user really needs from the computer system.

Equipment-oriented **programmers** and **engineers** work less with people and more with machines. Programmers write and test instructions for the computer. Each set of instructions—called a **computer program**—is designed to handle only a single job.

Computer centers also employ programmers to maintain programs already in operation. A **maintenance programmer** changes, or modifies, programs as needs, laws, and company policy change. New programmers fresh out of school sometimes start as maintenance programmers. They learn the company's standard procedures and practices "on the job" as they modify working programs.

Engineers work on the cutting edge of technology. They are hired or trained by the computer manufacturers to create new equipment using the latest technological advancements.

FIGURE A2.3

In some organizations, the computer center is a separate work area (Courtesy Wang Laboratories, Inc.)

FIGURE A2.4

Computer programmers write and test the instructions a computer follows (Courtesy IBM Corporation)

There are engineers working today on products that will not be announced for many years to come. In some cases, the engineers must go through very thorough security checks before being hired. The nature of their work and the competition between manufacturers make these security checks necessary.

Programmers and engineers must have a technical knowledge of equipment. They acquire this knowledge through formal schooling and work experience.

Operations Personnel

Operations personnel run the computer and related equipment. **Computer operators** start and stop jobs run by the computer and load special forms into the printer. But their responsibilities go beyond running the computer. They must be familiar with the operation of attached equipment and know what to do in emergencies. Many computer centers are open all day and all night. This means there are operators on duty 24 hours a day.

Data entry operators use typewriter keyboards to enter data into the computer or onto tapes or disks. The tapes or disks store data for later entry into the computer. Typing skills are always a must for data entry operators.

It is interesting to note that both computer operations and data entry operations are considered **entry-level jobs.** This means that most employers are willing to train individuals for the job if they have the basic qualifications. The qualifications for these positions vary from a high school diploma to a four-year bachelor's degree.

Some people, called **data control clerks,** help coordinate and control the flow of information into and out of the computer center. They are the connection between operations and users. The data control clerks accept data from users and check it for completeness. They also deliver the computer-generated reports back to the appropriate user.

Finally, there are **service technicians** who are responsible for keeping the

FIGURE A2.6

An operator mounting a magnetic tape
(Photo by Steve Potter)

equipment in working order. They periodically clean the printer and run checks on the computer's internal circuitry. These routine checks are called **preventive maintenance** procedures and are used to minimize equipment problems.

At most computer centers, service technicians are not part of the permanent staff. Instead, maintenance services are purchased from the computer manufacturer or from a company that specializes in computer maintenance and repair. These companies train the service technicians on the various equipment for which they will be responsible.

All of these people are involved with computers, although not necessarily at the same time. Sometimes one person performs many jobs. In the case of home computers, one person may be responsible for everything.

People Working Together

FIGURE A2.7

Data entry operator (Courtesy Inforex, Inc.)

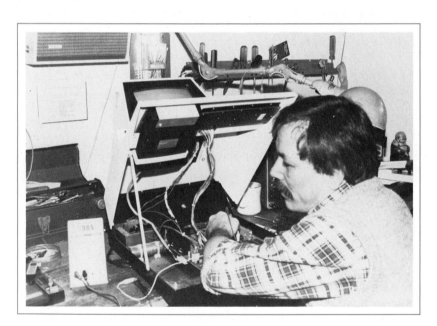

FIGURE A2.8

A service technician repairing computer equipment (Courtesy CalComp)

Programmers or other systems development personnel do not have a role when the system is being used. These people design, develop, and even make changes to the computer system. This last task is referred to as **systems maintenance.** However, they are not part of the day-to-day operations of a well-run computer system. In fact, with large computer systems, there are important security reasons why systems development people should not be involved.

3. Define user, informed user, entry-level job, preventive maintenance, and systems maintenance.

4. Briefly describe how computers can help people.

5. List three groups of people who work with computers.

6. Identify the responsibilities and, when possible, minimum educational requirements and skills for the following jobs: systems analyst, programmer, maintenance programmer, engineer, computer operator, data entry operator, data control clerk, and service technician.

DATA

People have processed data—facts and figures—since the beginning of time to help them make decisions. As time passed, people began to use tools to process important facts and figures. A computer system is just the latest tool to help people process data.

To use a computer, we must have data that is in a machine-readable form. Many machine-readable forms are possible, such as the bar code on canned goods or the strange numbers on the bottom of checks. The data can then be input into the computer for processing. Other options are also available. For example, data can be typed directly into the computer or put onto tape or disk for later use.

Computer data can be grouped together using the IPO cycle. There is **input data** which goes into the computer, the **processing data** used by the computer, and the **output data,** or **information.** People sometimes say that information is knowledge derived from processed data. Information is usually in a people-readable form like a printed report or television display.

Storing Data

Finally, there is **stored data,** which is data saved on **tape** or **disk** for processing later. You may be surprised to learn that the tapes used by the computer operator are like those you use to record music.

On the other hand, the disks used to store data are different from the disks—record albums—played on stereo systems. Instead of grooves, they have a smooth recording surface very similar to tapes.

Disks come in several styles. Computer systems that must store and access huge amounts of information rely on **hard disks** like those shown in figure A2.10. Computer systems like those in homes and schools use the smaller **floppy disks** shown in figure A2.10.

Errorless Data

Complete and correct data is essential for the successful operation of any computer system. Computers are fast, but they have no intuition or judgment. They will work diligently with absolute gibberish and produce output that is also gibberish.

Once in a while you read about "a computer" that sends someone a check for a million dollars. Do the computers really make mistakes like that? No more than your car does when it runs out of gas!

When a check for a million dollars is mistakenly sent out, there could be a variety of people-related mistakes responsible. A common mistake is to have

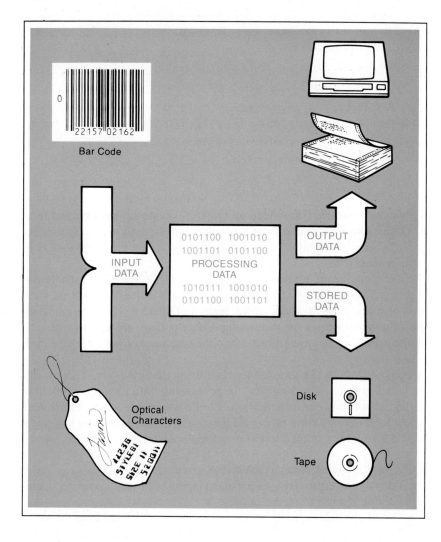

FIGURE A2.9

Different forms of data in the IPO cycle

the data entry operator accidentally put the decimal point in the wrong place. Thus, 10000.00 quickly becomes 1000000.

This is why a good part of any data entry operator's time is spent checking input data for correctness. "Garbage in, garbage out"—**GIGO**—is an old but appropriate saying in the computer business.

STUDY OBJECTIVES

7. Define data, information, and GIGO.

8. Using the IPO cycle, describe how data passes through a computer system.

9. Describe the difference between information and stored data and identify how each is used.

10. List two types of disks.

11. Identify two essential features that data must have for successful processing.

Hard Disk

Floppy Disks
(8 inch and 5¼ inch)

FIGURE A2.10

Different styles of disks (Courtesy BASE
Corporation, *top*; Verbatim Corporation,
bottom)

Hardware is another name for computer equipment. Depending on what the computer system is designed to do, a variety of hardware can be used. Computer hardware can fill several floors of a large office building or fit on top of your desk. We can use the IPO cycle to divide the hardware into four groups: **input hardware, processing hardware, output hardware,** and **storage hardware.**

Input Hardware

Input hardware is used to put data into the computer. Keep your eyes open and you will begin to notice input hardware all around you. The keyboard on the

FIGURE A2.11

Different forms of hardware in the IPO cycle

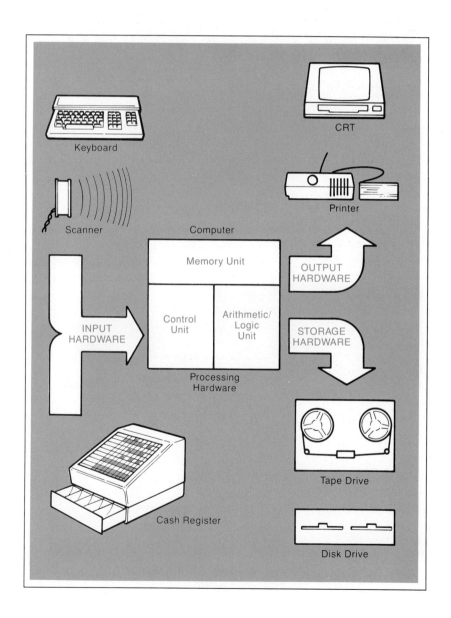

counter of the ticket office could enter data into a computer. The computer would then find you a seat for tomorrow's ball game.

The cashier at the corner market slides your groceries over a scanner that enters the item number into the computer for inventory purposes. The computer also calculates your bill and change.

Even restaurants are using special input devices that allow the waiter or waitress to enter your order directly onto a computer. The computer then coordinates cooking times, checks the inventory, prints the bill, and even orders more stock.

Processing Hardware

Processing hardware—the computer—performs calculations or comparisons on the input data. The computer is composed of a **memory unit, control unit,** and **arithmetic/logic unit.**

Data and instructions must be stored in its memory before the computer can do any work. Once the data and instructions are in the memory, the control unit uses the program to perform the desired calculations and comparisons on the data by directing the arithmetic/logic unit.

The arithmetic/logic unit is really just a supercalculator. Like your pocket calculator, it can add, subtract, multiply, or divide using only two numbers at a time. Unlike your calculator, it can work with the letters of the alphabet and make comparisons on both numbers and letters.

In comparing two numbers, the arithmetic/logic unit can decide if one number is less than, greater than, or equal to the other number. Names and addresses can be sorted into alphabetic order by using the same comparisons.

Since the memory in most computers requires uninterrupted power, it is wiped clean if the power is turned off or fails. You can now see why tapes and disks are used to store programs and data.

A copy, or **backup,** is always kept in case of emergencies. The computer only works with a copy of the program, and all important data is immediately copied to tape or disk hardware as backup. If the power fails, the operator copies the backup into memory and starts again.

The processing hardware comes in many sizes, the smallest being a **microcomputer** that people can use at home or in school. Larger computers used in research or to monitor a specific manufacturing process are called **minicomputers.** The largest computers, found in big business or used by the government, are often referred to as mainframe computers or just **mainframes.**

Output Hardware

Output hardware provides processed information to the user. Traditionally, it is in one of two forms. For permanent records, information is printed on paper by a **printer.** Your report card and bills fall into this category. These printed reports are sometimes called **hard copy.**

When the information is temporary or is needed right away, it is displayed on a television screen or cathode-ray tube—**CRT.** Directory assistance operators working for the telephone company use CRTs. When you ask for a telephone number, the telephone operator enters the request, and the computer searches for the number and displays it on the CRT.

Computers come in different sizes
(Courtesy Data General Corporation)

Microcomputer System

Minicomputer System

Mainframe Computer System

After you hang up, the screen is cleared and the next request is processed. Other specialized output hardware is used in manufacturing and security systems.

Storage Hardware

A fourth and final group of computer hardware is used to store data. This is necessary hardware but not part of the IPO cycle. Since the computer's memory has only a limited capacity to hold data, storage hardware is needed to record data for later use.

Computer systems are a little like stereo systems in this regard. After all, we need a way to store music when the stereo is not in use. The solution in both cases is to store the data or music on tape or disk.

To store data on tape, the computer operator mounts the tape on a device called a **tape drive,** which is something like a tape recorder. A similar device called a **disk drive** is used to store data on disks.

STUDY OBJECTIVES

12. Define hardware, backup, hard copy, and CRT.
13. Name one type of input hardware, processing hardware, output hardware, and storage hardware.
14. Identify a computer's three units and describe the function of each.
15. List three types of decisions the arithmetic/logic unit makes.
16. Identify three sizes of computers.
17. Describe two traditional forms of output.

PROGRAMS

A **program** is a sequence of instructions that a computer follows to perform a specific job. Another term for computer programs is **software.**

Computers are really just general-purpose machines that need special instructions to perform a given task. They can add, subtract, multiply, divide, or make comparisons. The order in which these functions are performed is provided by the software.

Programs, like data, are stored on tape or disk. When the operator runs a particular job, the program written for that purpose is copied into the computer from the storage hardware. The instructions that make up the program are then followed by the computer to produce the needed output.

Programming Languages

Computer programs can be written in a variety of **programming languages.** Like the languages we speak, they differ in vocabulary and structure. However, they all have the same function: to instruct a general-purpose computer.

The programs in figures A2.13, A2.14, and A2.15 all perform the same simple task of accepting two numbers, adding them together, and displaying the result. The program in figure A2.13 is written in the BASIC language. The programs in figures A2.14 and A2.15 are written in PASCAL and COBOL, respectively.

Although there are several hundred programming languages, only about six or seven of them are commonly used. For one reason or another, the rest have not been accepted.

FIGURE A2.13

BASIC program to add two numbers

```
10 PRINT "ENTER FIRST NUMBER"
20 INPUT N1
30 PRINT "ENTER SECOND NUMBER"
40 INPUT N2
50 SUM = N1 + N2
60 PRINT "THE SUM OF"; N1; " + "; N2; " IS "; SUM
```

FIGURE A2.14

PASCAL program to add two numbers

```
PROGRAM ADD-IT;

VAR NUMBER1, NUMBER2, SUM: INTEGER;

BEGIN
  WRITE ('ENTER FIRST NUMBER');
  READLN (NUMBER1);
  WRITE ('ENTER SECOND NUMBER');
  READLN (NUMBER2);
  SUM:= NUMBER1 + NUMBER2;
  WRITE ('THE SUM OF', NUMBER1, '+', NUMBER2);
  WRITELN ('IS', SUM);
END.
```

```
IDENTIFICATION DIVISION.
 PROGRAM-ID. ADDITION.

ENVIRONMENT DIVISION.
 INPUT-OUTPUT SECTION.
    .
    .
    .
DATA DIVISION.
 FILE SECTION.
 FD DATA-IN
    LABEL RECORDS ARE STANDARD.
 01 NUMBERS-TO-BE-PROCESSED.
    05 NUMBER-1-IN        PIC 999.
    05 NUMBER-2-IN        PIC 999.

 FD ANSWER-OUT
    LABEL RECORDS ARE OMITTED.
 01 SUM-TO-BE-PRINTED    PIC X(27).

 WORKING-STORAGE SECTION.
 01 TEMPORARY-WORK-AREA.
    05 FILLER             PIC X(10)    VALUE "THE SUM OF".
    05 NUMBER-1-OUT       PIC 999.
    05 FILLER             PIC XXX      VALUE " + ".
    05 NUMBER-2-OUT       PIC 999.
    05 FILLER             PIC X(4)     VALUE " IS ".
    05 SUM-OUT            PIC 9(4).

PROCEDURE DIVISION.
 PROCESSING-ROUTING.
    OPEN INPUT DATA-IN
         OUTPUT ANSWER-OUT
    READ DATA-IN
    ADD NUMBER-1-IN, NUMBER-2-IN GIVING SUM-OUT.
    MOVE NUMBER-1-IN TO NUMBER-1-OUT.
    MOVE NUMBER-2-IN TO NUMBER-2-OUT.
    WRITE SUM-TO-BE-PRINTED
         FROM TEMPORARY-WORK-AREA.
    CLOSE DATA-IN
         ANSWER-OUT
    STOP RUN.
```

FIGURE A2.15

COBOL program to add two numbers

Since there are a wide variety of programs, they are often divided into two groups according to their function. These groups are **systems programs** and **applications programs.**

Systems programs control the computer. For example, they cause the computer to start or stop jobs or to locate a program on disk and copy it into the computer. Systems programs are usually purchased with a new computer. People rarely spend the time to write their own.

Applications Versus Systems Programs

Applications package with manual, operating instruction, and copy of a program on floppy disk

At a few very large computer centers, programmers are hired to write systems programs. Many systems programmers are hired by computer manufacturers. These programmers either work with engineers in developing systems programs to support new computer hardware or help maintain existing systems programs.

Other systems programs are developed and sold by companies specializing in systems software. Companies that specialize in writing computer programs are called **software houses.** They represent a new and growing industry.

Applications programs are oriented toward a user's needs. For example, they perform payroll calculations, print honor rolls, or forecast tomorrow's weather. An applications program is frequently developed by systems analysts and programmers on the systems development staff.

Lately, there has been an increased demand for ready-made applications programs written by independent software houses. The software house will design an **applications package** that includes a program with manuals and instructions for running it. At an additional cost, many of these companies will modify the programs to meet special needs of the users.

STUDY OBJECTIVES

18. Define computer program, software, and software house.
19. Identify a method to ensure safety for programs and data.
20. Name three frequently used programming languages.
21. Describe the difference between applications programs and systems programs.
22. List three items found in an applications package.

Procedures help people use the other components of a computer system. They identify to everyone what needs to be done and how to do it. Procedures tell newcomers what is expected of them and allow for a smooth transition when people change jobs.

In any organized computer center, you will find procedures for users, service technicians, operators, and systems development personnel. Users need procedures that describe how they are to prepare input data and what to do when errors are found. Using preventive maintenance procedures, service technicians clean the printers and check the computer's circuitry before problems cause a breakdown.

Computer operators follow procedures that outline what programs to run, what data to use, and what to do with the output. They also have a set of emergency procedures to follow when the computer fails, or **crashes** as it is sometimes called.

Don't be fooled into thinking that only the large computer centers need procedures. Anyone owning or operating a microcomputer also needs to follow procedures. There are procedures for turning on the computer, for locating programs on disks, and for operating the computer.

When the computer is used by a group of people at home or at school, procedures need to be defined for storing manuals, tapes, and disks. Special procedures are needed for troubleshooting problems that occur with the equipment.

- What should you do if the computer does not work or is acting funny?
- What should you check?
- Whom should you call?

These are all questions that can be answered with good troubleshooting procedures. You will find preventive maintenance procedures especially important with your own computer because they run only a fraction of the cost of any repair bill.

23. Define computer crash.
24. Briefly describe how procedures are used with a computer system.
25. Identify a financial reason for following preventive maintenance procedures.

Computer systems are used for a variety of applications. These applications often fall into one of three fields: **data processing, word processing,** or **process controls.** There are some applications that belong in more than one field, while others do not fit comfortably in any. These fields represent areas of continued growth for computer technology. New innovations and many new job opportunities will be related to these fields.

An accountant manually entering data
into a ledger

Data Processing

In government, businesses, and service organizations, important decisions are based on accurate records of daily activities. Data processing is the act of converting data into useful information.

People do not necessarily need a computer to process data, but it sure helps. Whether they have a computer, a calculator, or pencil and paper, people need information to run their organizations efficiently. In the past, records of sales, services, payroll, inventory, and other incomes or expenses were entered by hand into large books, or ledgers.

Data processing was also done by hand. People spent hours preparing sales reports or inventory status reports. The accuracy of these reports was often marred by errors in arithmetic.

Today, many businesses have replaced these manual data processing systems with computer systems. The computer systems store data and keep it up-to-date. The computer systems are faster and more reliable record keepers. They also offer an additional advantage of being able to cross-reference related data.

For example, a school administrator might need to know how many students were enrolled in first-hour English during each semester of the last 10 years. To find this information, a secretary could spend several hours going through old reports. But a properly designed computer system would give this information without requiring new programs or extra work by the secretary.

Data processing is a part of any organization. It was also one of the first successful applications of computer systems.

Word Processing

Recently, computer technology has been applied to the office. A computer system's capacity to store large amounts of alphabetic data on disks is especially useful. Using computer technology to prepare letters, memos, and other documents is called word processing.

With a word processing system, the operator uses a typewriter-like keyboard to enter a document. As the operator types, the letters appear on the attached

This text is photographed from the display screen of the new IBM Displaywriter System—an easy-to-use and low-cost text processing system that automatiaclly detects misspelled words. The system analyzes each typed word and then compares it with an electronic dictionery of commonly used words—in English, Dutch, French, German, Italian or Spanish. Unmatched words are highlighted as shown.

The Displaywriter can communicate with other office equipment. It has many features that simplify the typing of correspondance and other documents. The system can automatically indent, justify margins, underscore words, and shift sentences or blocks of text. It can perform mathematical functions—such as verifying arithmetic or rearranging statistics—and also save time in many other ways.

FIGURE A2.18

Memos and letters can be easily changed on a word processor (Courtesy IBM Corporation)

CRT. When word processing operators make typing errors, they simply backspace and type the correction over the error.

Word processing systems allow the operator to **edit** the text on the screen. This means that the operator can move words around, insert words, or delete

FIGURE A2.19

The time needed to prepare business documents is cut in half with word processing systems (Courtesy Wang Laboratories, Inc.)

(erase) words. Word processing systems also automatically center headings and number pages upon request.

Once a document has been prepared, it is saved on disk. At a later time, it can be retrieved, edited again, and printed using a high-speed typewriter. Word processing is particularly useful in organizations where documents go through several drafts before they are finished. Documents do not have to be retyped when a single change is made. Therefore, it is estimated that word processing reduces typing time by half.

The distinction between word processing and data processing is often unclear. The difference usually centers around the need to perform complex calculations. While some word processors add columns of numbers, more complicated calculations are usually considered a part of data processing. Word processing operators primarily work with alphabetic data in the form of letters, memos, reports, and other documents.

Process Controls

An organization's front office is not the only place where you will find computer systems today. Computers now efficiently monitor and control industrial processes. Using computer systems in this way is called process controls.

This term covers a wide variety of applications, from the very complex and dangerous control of a nuclear power plant to monitoring the cooking temperature of the roast in a microwave oven. Process control systems first appeared

FIGURE A2.20

A worker monitoring a process control system (Courtesy Ramtek)

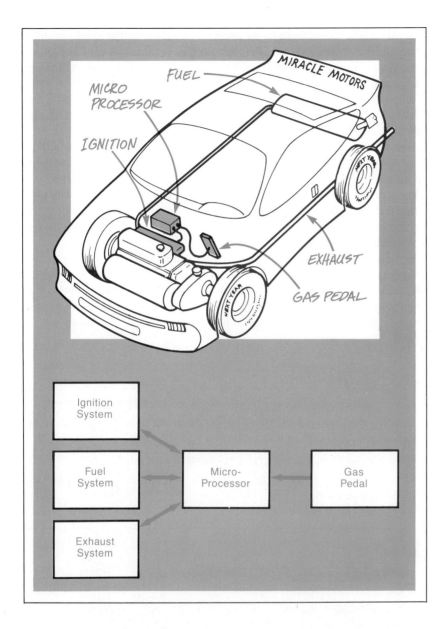

Labels in illustration:
MICRO PROCESSOR
FUEL
MIRACLE MOTORS
IGNITION
EXHAUST
GAS PEDAL

Ignition System

Fuel System

Exhaust System

Micro-Processor

Gas Pedal

FIGURE A2.21

Computer controlled ignition system helps improve car's efficiency

in work environments where people could not survive. Hazardous or undesirable work is now being performed by these systems. In its ultimate form, process control systems use robots to do all production activities in a factory.

Ignition systems in new cars are a good example of a process control application. The gas pedal no longer controls the amount of gas and air fed to the engine. Instead it is connected to a small computer.

Through monitoring devices, the computer senses the engine temperature, fuel-to-air ratios of the air entering the engine, levels of pollutants in exhaust gases, and other operating characteristics. When the driver steps on the gas pedal, the computer calculates the best way to increase speed. The resulting output may cause an increase in air pressure, changes in the spark timing, or the recycling of more exhaust. Perhaps no gas is added at all. The process control system monitors the increase in power and speed, making adjustments as necessary.

Computer systems used in this way can maximize fuel economy while meeting federal automobile pollution standards. Unfortunately, it does make it hard for the average person to tune his or her car.

Some people are rightfully concerned that process control systems will take jobs away from people. While this may be the case in some areas, many new jobs are also created to design, program, and maintain these machines.

Others point out that the lost jobs were relatively boring or physically taxing and that the new jobs will be more interesting. Computers are controlling more and more industrial processes because they are tireless, efficient, and inexpensive over years of operation.

The fields of data processing, word processing, and process controls are experiencing a tremendous growth because computers provide low cost and high performance—sometimes called a low **cost/performance ratio.** Since computer systems are relatively new, only a few of the possible applications have been developed. Many opportunities are available for those who are prepared.

STUDY OBJECTIVES

26. Define data processing, word processing, edit, and process controls.

27. Identify the features that distinguish word processing applications from data processing applications.

28. Give the rationale for using process control systems.

29. Describe what is meant by the statement "Computers provide a low cost/performance ratio."

FIGURE A2.22

Components of a computer system

People	Hardware
Users	Input
Systems Development Personnel	Processing
Operations Personnel	Output
Data	Storage
Input	
Processing	*Procedures*
Output (Information)	Data Entry
Stored	Operating
Programs	Back-up
Systems	Emergency
Applications	

A computer system is a collection of five components working together to satisfy some purpose. People, data, hardware, programs, and procedures are the necessary components. The computer hardware or any other component by itself is not enough to get the job done. The five components are found in all computer systems, from the small microcomputer systems to the larger minicomputer and mainframe systems.

Three groups of people work with computer systems. Users are those who use the processed information from the computer. Behind the scenes, systems development personnel create the computer systems that the operations personnel run. These people run data through the computer to produce useful information for the users. Data and hardware can be grouped together using the IPO cycle as a model. Input data, such as sales figures, is entered into the computer through a variety of input hardware.

The computer, or processing hardware, stores the data in its memory unit along with a computer program. The control unit follows the instructions that make up the program and sends the processing data to an arithmetic/logic unit. This unit acts like a supercalculator. It performs mathematical operations or makes comparisons with the data and returns the results to the memory unit. Once back in memory, the data can be sent to output hardware to be printed or displayed as output data or information. Important data is copied to tape or disk for safekeeping.

The whole processing cycle is controlled by the computer operator. These operators follow detailed procedures that outline how to handle day-to-day operations and special emergencies.

The impact of computer technology is especially apparent in three fields: data processing, word processing, and process controls. In data processing, calculations once done by hand are now being processed with the help of computers. Word processing is an office application where computer systems handle the entry, storage, and printing of letters, memos, and other office communications. Computer systems working in factories are called process control systems. Here the computer systems monitor and control production activity. Each of these fields represents areas of continuing growth with many new job opportunities.

THE CHIP

The Heart of the Computer

At the heart of the computer is the tiny silicon chip, still shrinking in size. It has reduced the cost of computers as well as their size and placed the technology in everyone's hand. How is it done?

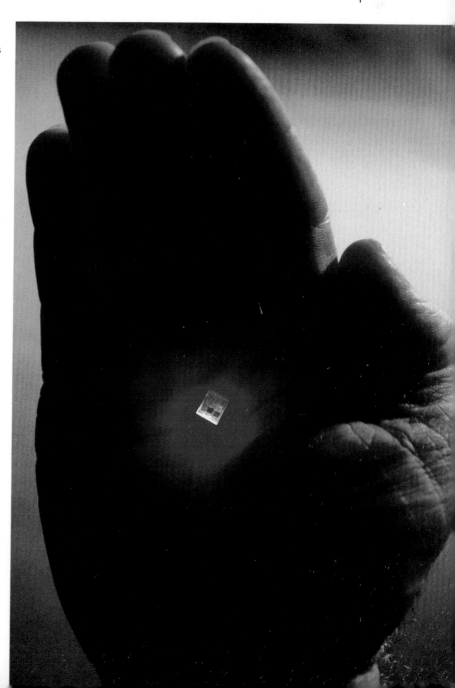

THE CHIP: FROM THE BEGINNING

These rocks are melted into nearly pure silicon.

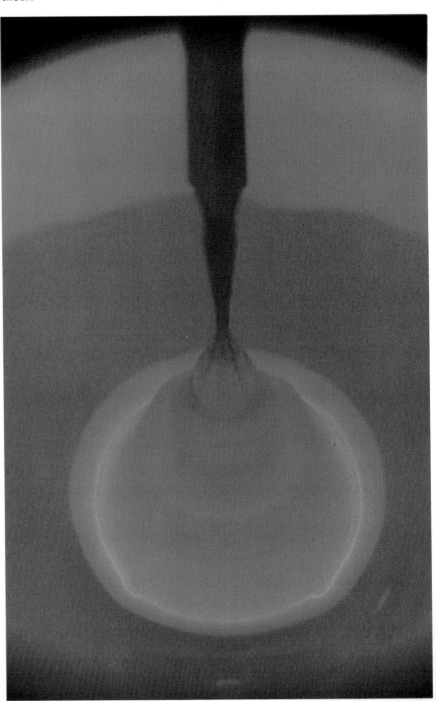

The silicon comes from rocks in the southeastern United States, not from sand as is popularly believed.

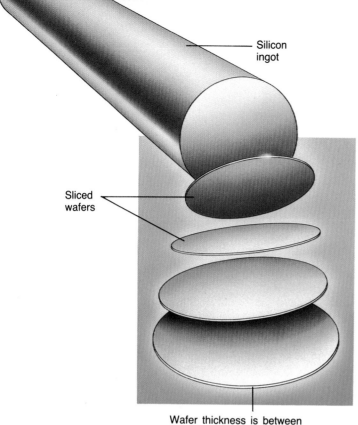

Silicon
ingot

Sliced
wafers

Wafer thickness is between
9 and 20 one-thousandths of an inch.

Wafers are sliced from the ingot and polished.

Ingots, or long silicon crystals, are grown
from the melt.

Enlarged circuit designs are used to
determine the circuitry to be reduced
onto the chip.

THE CHIP:
SILICON WAFER

The design is reduced to a "mask" size that will put a million circuit components on a chip.

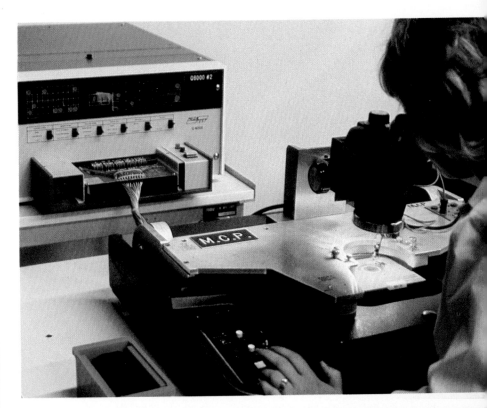

Masking plate with circuit design

Photoresist
Oxide layer
Silicon wafer

Wafer thickness is between 9 and 20 one-thousandths of an inch.

A masking plate is placed on top of the wafer.

A light-sensitive plastic, called *photoresist*, is applied to the wafer.

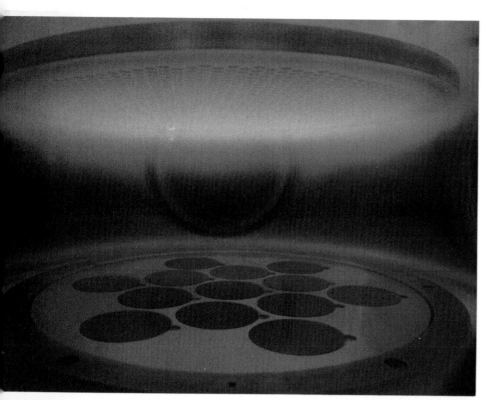

The wafer is flooded with ultraviolet light, which "prints" the mask pattern on the exposed photoresist.

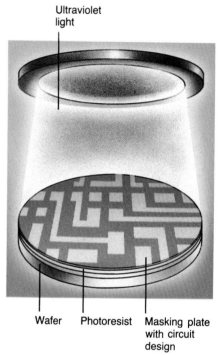

Ultraviolet light

Wafer   Photoresist   Masking plate with circuit design

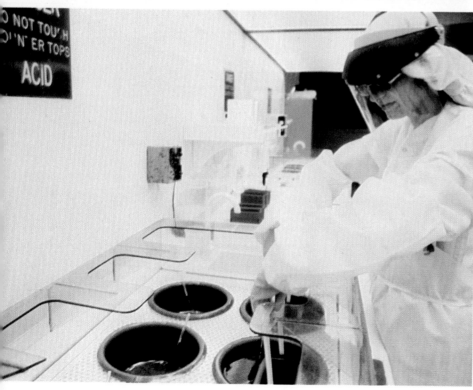

The wafer is then washed in chemicals that remove the resist from the exposed areas, leaving the pattern, or blueprint, for the circuitry.

THE WAFER BECOMES A MICROPROCESSOR

To create the necessary negative and positive zones, chemicals called doplants are embedded on the circuitry.

Mask blueprint imprints on photoresist

Chemical doplants are embedded to create positive and negative zones

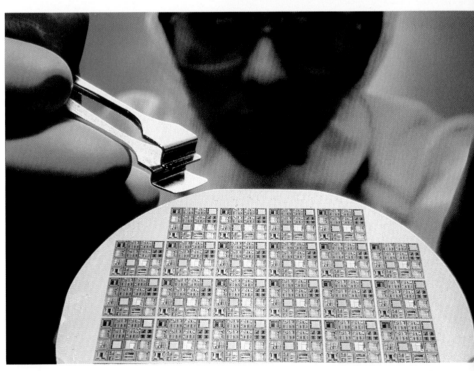

Each wafer is cleaned and carefully inspected.

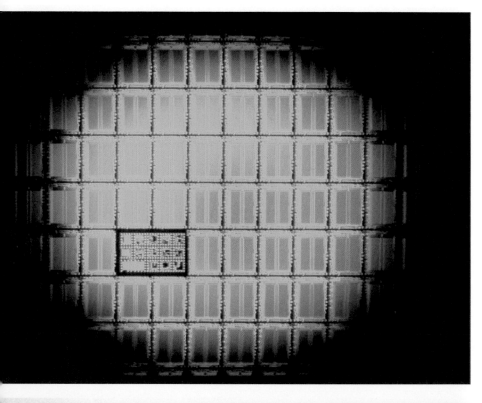

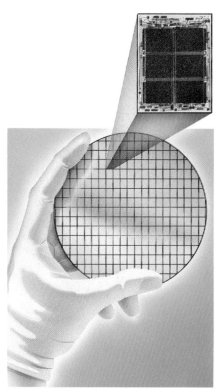

A single wafer thus contains many individual chips, each now a microprocessor.

THE CHIP:
ITS BLUEPRINTS

Each chip is then diced, or cut from the wafer with a diamond saw.

Reflected light can produce a colorful mosaic of the wafer's chips and individual circuitry.

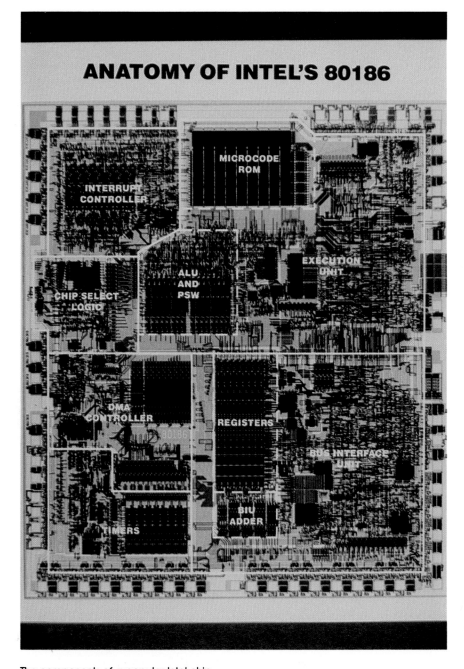

ANATOMY OF INTEL'S 80186

MICROCODE ROM

INTERRUPT CONTROLLER

EXECUTION UNIT

CHIP SELECT LOGIC

ALU AND PSW

DMA CONTROLLER

REGISTERS

BUS INTERFACE UNIT

BIU ADDER

TIMERS

The components of a popular Intel chip design are labeled.

Chips are then bonded, or attached to a lead frame, and sealed.

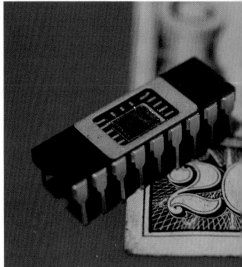

THE CHIP BECOMES
A "BOARD"

Japan is a leader in chip fabrication, and the Japanese approach to teamwork sometimes includes a "seventh-inning stretch."

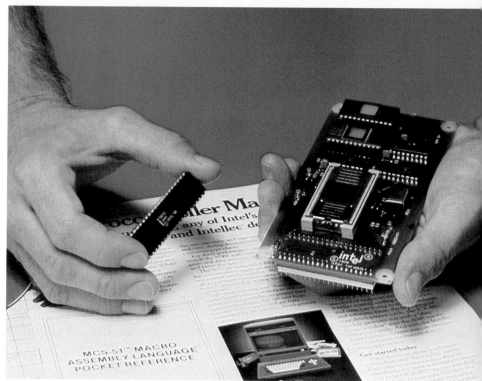

The lead package of chips is assembled into a board.

A board with its microprocessor packages is loaded into a computer.

Intel board components are labeled.

intel
MICROCOMPUTERS

ROM 2048 BYTES

RAM 128 BYTES

PORT I/O

I/O STROBE

PORT I/O

I/O

TIMER AND LOWER ADDR.LATCH

CLOCK ALU

MISC. LOGIC

DATA BUS CONTROL

ALU CONTROL

I/O TIMING AND CONTROL

DATA BUS DRIVERS

1/4"

8049

8085 CPU

CLOCK AND TIMING

I/O DRIVERS AND TERMINATORS

RAM I/O PORTS & TIMER 256 BYTES

ROM/EPROM 4096 BYTES

RS232C DRIVER RECEIVER

SINGLE BOARD COMPUTER 80/05   PWA 1001299   REV.

ADDRESS DECODERS AND MISCELLANEOUS

ADDRESS LATCH

BUS CONTROL

ADDRESS BUS DRIVERS

DATA BUS DRIVERS

RAM 256 BYTES

12"

SBC 80/05 8085

THE CHIP: COMMON APPLICATIONS

This microwave oven is controlled with a microprocessor.

Vehicle microprocessor systems in the 1980s.

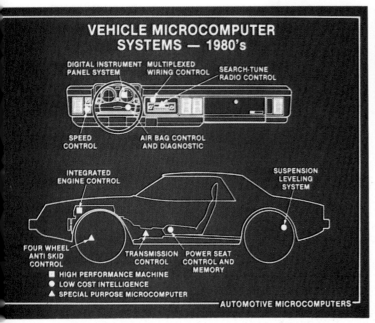

VEHICLE MICROCOMPUTER SYSTEMS — 1980's

DIGITAL INSTRUMENT PANEL SYSTEM

MULTIPLEXED WIRING CONTROL

SEARCH-TUNE RADIO CONTROL

SPEED CONTROL

AIR BAG CONTROL AND DIAGNOSTIC

INTEGRATED ENGINE CONTROL

SUSPENSION LEVELING SYSTEM

FOUR WHEEL ANTI SKID CONTROL

TRANSMISSION CONTROL

POWER SEAT CONTROL AND MEMORY

■ HIGH PERFORMANCE MACHINE
● LOW COST INTELLIGENCE
▲ SPECIAL PURPOSE MICROCOMPUTER

AUTOMOTIVE MICROCOMPUTERS

Sale $

Gallons

Cents Per Gallon
including tax

Microprocessor control of a gas pump.

Microprocessors in a typical kitchen and service area.

An Apple microcomputer *system*, with microprocessors inside and a chip at its heart.

Today's football scoreboard, courtesy of microprocessors.

THE CHIP:
FUTURE
APPLICATIONS

This IBM "super chip" continues to provide more memory on less space: 288,000 bits of data are stored on this ⅜-inch chip.

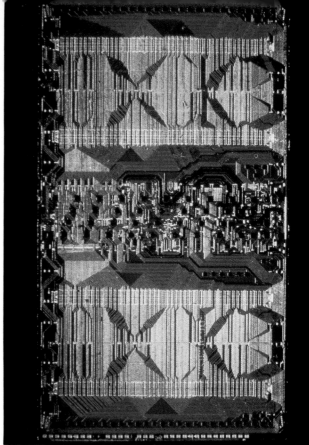

New technology: the bubble chip.

BUBBLES

- Mass Storage—Up to one million bits per chip

- Nonvolatile

- Replacement for mechanical, rotating disk memories

- Excellent for harsh environments (military applications)

- Applications range from small portable data-gathering equipment to crash recorders in aircraft.

- Naturally radiation resistant

Ion beam etching directed by computer.

New technology: ion beam etching of silicon chips may someday replace the masking process.

Japan serves a challenge to the United States for future growth in the chip industry.

The enemy of the chip. Electromagnetic pulse, or EMP, testing emits waves that can shatter silicon chips ... an increasing national defense concern.

QUESTIONS

1. Why are computer memories that are embedded on chips smaller and cheaper than first-generation computer vacuum tubes?

2. Why are "clean rooms" used in chip manufacturing?

3. List ten common applications of microprocessors.

4. What damage to a country's defense could be effected by EMP?

5. Distinguish between a microprocessor and a microcomputer.

6. Name a possible new application for cheaper and more powerful chips.

CHAPTER A3

History of Data Processing

The history of data processing began centuries ago, when people first started to count on their fingers. In fact, fingers and toes were probably—no one knows for sure—the earliest computational devices. As business and commerce developed, a need arose for a device that could count higher than 20.

The **abacus** was an early form of the calculator. It is still used in many areas of the world. Other computational devices have been constructed throughout the centuries. The **numerical wheel calculator** preceded the adding machines that were used before electronic calculators. The **slide rule** was another type of computational device.

FIGURE A 3.1

The abacus (Photo by Steve Potter)

FIGURE A 3.2

The numerical wheel calculator (Courtesy IBM Corporation)

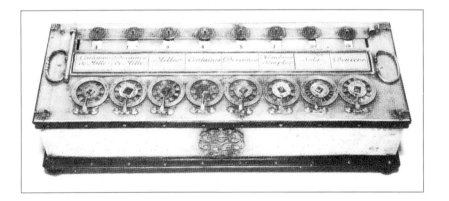

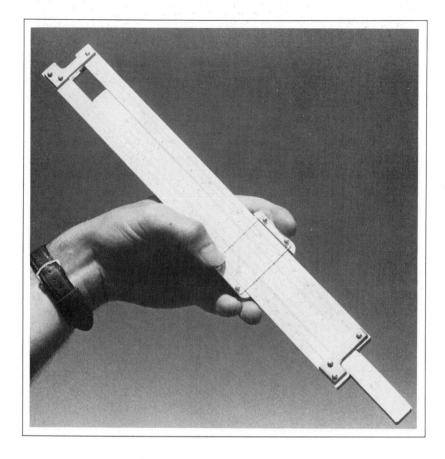

FIGURE A3.3

The slide rule (Photo by Steve Potter)

CHARLES BABBAGE AND HIS MACHINES

As far as we know, Charles Babbage was the father of computing. This amazing man developed the essential ideas for a computer over 100 years before the first computer was constructed. He was so far ahead of his time that few of his peers appreciated him. In addition to his work in computing, Babbage contributed to the fields of mathematics, optics, underwater navigation, railroads, industrial engineering, and mechanics.

Many of the mistakes that Babbage made continue to be made today. Therefore, it is worth considering his life in some detail. George Washington was still alive in 1792 when Babbage was born in England. Babbage's father was a wealthy banker who left him a sizable fortune. Babbage says he suffered from high fevers as a child and was sent to a private tutor "with instructions to attend my health, but not to press too much knowledge upon me: a mission which he faithfully accomplished." Babbage goes on to say, "My invariable question on receiving any new toy was, 'Mama, what is it made of?' "* Apparently, if she couldn't answer, he tore it apart to find out.

---

*From Phillip and Emily Morrison, eds. *Charles Babbage and His Calculating Engines*, New York: Dover Publications, 1961.

Charles Babbage (1792–1871) (Historical Pictures Service)

The Difference Engine

Some time prior to 1822, Babbage and his friend John Herschel were checking data calculated for the Astronomical Society. In frustration, Babbage remarked to Herschel, "I wish to God these calculations had been executed by steam." Steam engines were a common means of power at that time. In 1822, Babbage proposed the design of a **difference engine** composed of gears and wheels. This engine would automatically compute the functions in the form

$$y = a + ax + ax^2 + \ldots + ax^6.$$

In 1823, the British government granted Babbage money to build the engine. The first government-sponsored computer project was on! Like most of those to follow, the project fell behind. By 1833, the government had invested £17,000, but only part of the difference engine was completed.

The Analytical Engine

Meanwhile, Babbage's active mind was extending the possibilities of automated computing. By 1834, he developed the idea of an **analytical engine.** The analytical engine would compute any mathematical function. It had most of the concepts embodied in early computers.

FIGURE A3.5

The difference engine (Courtesy IBM Corporation)

In 1834, Babbage asked the government whether it wanted him to finish the difference engine or start on the analytical engine. After eight years of frustrating correspondence, Prime Minister Robert Peel told Babbage that the government was going to abandon the project.

The analytical engine was designed to have a memory unit, which Babbage called the store. It was to have room for 1000 variables of 50 digits each. It would also have an arithmetic/logic unit, which Babbage called the mill. Programs for the mill were to be written on punched cards. The engine would drive a typesetter. It was designed to have logical capability and would ring a bell or take other action when a variable passed zero or exceeded its capacity. All operations were to work mechanically.

Babbage received more attention outside of England than from within. He had two automated devices at home, a clockwork lady who would dance and a portion of the difference engine. He reported that his English friends would gather around the dancing lady, while an American and a Hollander studied the difference engine. In fact, a Swedish printer, George Scheutz, made the

FIGURE A3.6

Ada Augusta, Countess of Lovelace
(1816–1852)

only complete version of the difference engine except for the one IBM recently made. Babbage was delighted and helped Scheutz explain it.

Ada Augusta, Countess of Lovelace

We know about the analytical engine largely because of a paper written by an Italian, L. F. Menabrea. This paper was written in French and was translated into English by Ada Augusta, the Countess of Lovelace.

Ada Augusta was the daughter of the poet Lord Byron. She was an excellent mathematician and understood Babbage's concepts perhaps better than anyone. In 1842, when she translated Menabrea's paper of 20 pages, she added 50 pages of notes. Babbage wanted to know why she didn't write a paper of her own. "I never thought of it," she replied. In fact, she didn't sign her translation or notes, but used the initials A.A.L. instead.*

*Phillip and Emily Morrison, eds. *Charles Babbage and His Calculating Engines,* New York: Dover Publications, 1961.

The countess loved racing, and it may have been inevitable that she would use the difference engine to determine bets. Apparently, it didn't work too well. She lost the family jewels at the track. Her mother, Lady Byron, had to buy them back.

The countess died of cancer at the age of 36, just 10 years after reading Menabrea's description. This was a big loss to Babbage and perhaps the world. A new programming language, ADA, is named after Ada Augusta Lovelace (see chapter B3: Computer Programs).

Other Sides of Charles Babbage

Babbage was a fascinating person. He was very social; he worked and played hard. Charles Darwin reported lively dinner parties at Babbage's home. Another person complained of barely being able to escape from him at two o'clock in the morning. Babbage once said he would be glad to give up the rest of his life if he could live three days 500 years in the future.

Babbage spent several months riding railroad cars around the United States. He was doing research on railway and train design. It is sad that he could not know that the very tracks he was riding on would someday carry trains controlled by computers having the design he envisioned. Also, he would have been interested to know that those same computers would someday be used to steal over 400 railroad cars (see chapter E1: Computer Crime and Security).

Babbage died in 1871. He never saw his analytical engine developed and he never knew how right he was. At the time of his death, he was bitter about the lack of government support. However, his autobiography does not seem bitter, and he probably was not the frustrated and unhappy man some people report.

Lessons We Can Learn from Babbage

Many of the errors Babbage made have been repeated in the computer industry. First, Babbage began with vague requirements. "Let's compute numbers by steam" sounds all too much like "Let's use a computer to do billing." Much more precise statements of requirements are needed.

Second, it appears that Babbage started production before the design was complete. His engineers and draftspeople often complained that they would finish a project only to be told the work was wrong or not needed because the design had been changed. The very same complaint has been made by countless programmers since then.

Babbage's Mistakes

Vague problem definition and requirements
Implementation started before design was complete
Requirements added during implementation
Working documentation not complete
Dependency on one person
System used for unintended purposes
Grandiose plans that exceeded existing technology

Mistakes Babbage made that are still made today

Another mistake Babbage made was to add more and more capability to his engines before any of them were complete. As his work progressed, he saw new possibilities and tried to use them in his existing projects. Many computer systems have failed to be completed for the same reason.

Work on the difference engine was set back considerably when Babbage and his chief engineer, Joseph Clement, had a crisis over Clement's salary. Clement quit, and Babbage had little documentation to recover that loss. Further, Clement had the rights to all the tools. Who knows how many systems projects have failed because indispensable programmers quit in the middle?

Even Lady Lovelace's losses at the track have a lesson. Systems should not be used for purposes for which they were not designed. The computer industry has suffered much inefficiency because systems are applied to problems they were not originally designed to support.

One reason Babbage failed to complete his analytical engine was that there was no electronics industry to support his ideas. All the concepts had to be implemented with mechanical components. The parts needed to fit so precisely that they could not be manufactured using nineteenth-century technology.

Babbage's plans were also grandiose. Building a computer with 1000 variables of 50 digits each was a large task. He might have been more successful at completing a smaller computer and building credibility with his government. Many government-sponsored projects fail today because of a lack in technology to support grandiose plans. These lessons are summarized in figure A3.7.

We do not know what impact, if any, Babbage's work had on the development of computer systems. One pioneer, Howard Aiken, reported that he worked three years before discovering Babbage's contributions. We do not know about the others.

STUDY OBJECTIVES

1. List five computational devices besides a computer.
2. Briefly describe Babbage's difference and analytical engines.
3. Describe the contributions Charles Babbage and Ada Augusta Lovelace made to the development of computers.
4. Identify seven mistakes made by Babbage that are often repeated in the computer industry today.

HERMAN HOLLERITH

In the late nineteenth century, the U.S. Census Bureau had a problem. The bureau was supposed to produce a census of the U.S. population every 10 years. However, the 1880 census took 7½ years to finish. By the time the census data was processed, it was no longer useful. Furthermore, considering the rate of growth of the U.S. population, the Census Bureau was afraid that the 1890 census would not be finished before the 1900 census was due to begin.

In 1879, the bureau hired Herman Hollerith to help them. He worked for

Herman Hollerith (1860–1929) (Bettmann Archive)

the Census Bureau for five years and then started his own company. While working for the bureau, Hollerith designed and managed the construction of several **punched-card** processing machines.

Data in the form of letters, numbers, and special characters were stored using the punched cards. Each **character** was represented by a unique combination of holes in the card's 12 **rows.** Since there were 80 **columns** on each punched card, the cards could store 80 different characters (see appendix E).

In 1889, the bureau held a contest among Hollerith's system and two other competitors' systems to determine which system was the fastest. Hollerith's system required only one-tenth of the time needed by his nearest competitor. Using this equipment, the first count of the 1890 census took only six weeks! However, the final, official count was not announced until December of 1890.

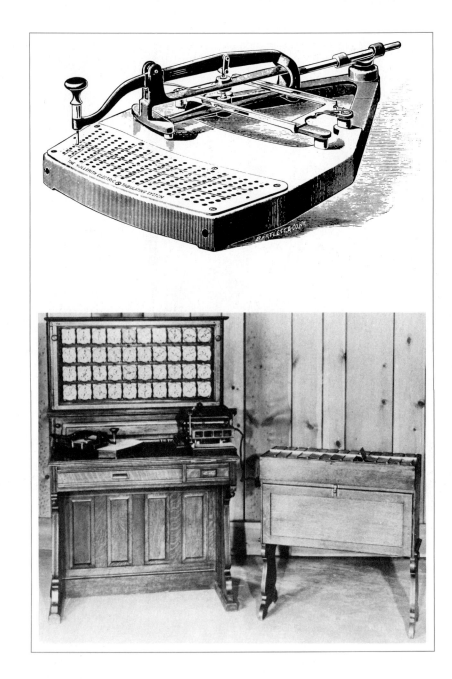

FIGURE A3.9

Hollerith's punched-card machines
(Courtesy IBM Corporation)

Joseph Marie Jacquard's Looms

Hollerith's equipment was an extension of the work of the Frenchman Joseph Marie Jacquard. Jacquard designed looms in which punched cards controlled the pattern of the woven material. In Jacquard's looms, needles fell through the holes in the cards. The needles lifted the threads in a way that produced a pattern. This technique had been used in the weaving industry since 1804.

FIGURE A3.10

Joseph Marie Jacquard (Bettmann
Archive), (1752–1834) and his loom
(Courtesy Ontario Science Centre)

Hollerith extended Jacquard's idea by using the cards to control electric
circuits. Punched cards were fed into a machine that moved the cards over a
group of pins. If there was a hole in a card, the pin would fall through the hole
and touch a pan of mercury. This closed a circuit and registered on a meter.
Apparently, the machine worked so well that the people became exhausted.
There is a story that occasionally someone would pour all the mercury into a
nearby spittoon. The machine would stop and everybody could rest.

Hollerith decided that he had a marketable idea. He sold his equipment to
railroads and other large companies with data processing problems. This was
the start of the punched-card industry. Hollerith built up his business and then
sold it to the company that was later to become International Business Machines—
IBM.

Beginning of the Punched-
Card Industry

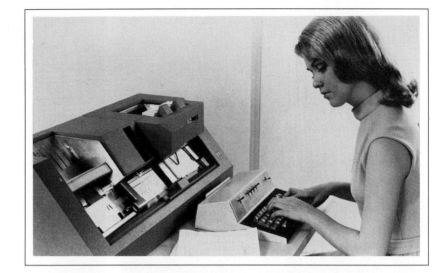

Keypunch and data entry operator
(Courtesy IBM Corporation)

Inside a cardreader (Courtesy IBM
Corporation)

The punched-card industry was the beginning of automated data processing. Many organizations stored and processed data on punched cards using keypunches. A **keypunch** has a regular typewriterlike keyboard. As the operator types on the keyboard, the keypunch punches holes in blank punched cards. This device let businesses store data on cards before the invention of computers.

Because of the heavy use of cards, early computer systems were developed around punched cards. **Cardreaders** input data into the computer from punched cards. They were one of the first types of input hardware. Since cards were used for storage, a **cardpunch** was used to punch output data into the cards. Only recently have cards been replaced by tapes and disks for storing data.

5. Describe how data is stored in a punched card.
6. Briefly describe the contributions Herman Hollerith and Joseph Marie Jacquard made to the development of automated processing.
7. Identify one reason early computer systems used punched cards for storage.
8. Describe the functions of a keypunch, cardreader and cardpunch.

In 1937, Howard G. Aiken proposed the use of electromechanical devices to perform calculations. He was a graduate student at Harvard at the time, and the IBM Corporation gave him a grant to pursue his ideas. IBM was active in the punched card industry. They may have felt that electromechanical calculators would be useful to them.

In 1944, Aiken and IBM completed an electromechanical calculator called the Mark I. This computer had mechanical counters that were manipulated by electrical devices. The Mark I could perform basic arithmetic and could be changed to solve different problems.

Mark I and ENIAC

At the same time, the U.S. government signed a contract with the University of Pennsylvania to develop a computer to aid the military effort during World War II. As a result of this contract, John W. Mauchly and J. Presper Eckert developed the first all-electronic computer, called the Electronic Numerical Integrator and Calculator, or ENIAC. Unlike Mark I, there were no mechanical counters; everything was electronic.

Although Mauchly and Eckert are often given credit for developing the first electronic computer, their work was actually based in part on the work of John V. Atanasoff. Atanasoff was a professor at Iowa State University and by 1939 had developed many ideas for an all-electronic computer. In 1942, he and a

FIGURE A3.13

Mark I computer (Courtesy IBM Corporation)

55

FIGURE A3.14

Members of the Mark I development team with Grace Hopper and Howard Aiken to her right (Courtesy Harvard University)

FIGURE A3.15

The Atanasoff-Berry computer with John V. Atanasoff on the right and Clifford Berry on the left (Courtesy Iowa State University)

FIGURE A3.16

ENIAC (Courtesy University of Pennsylvania)

FIGURE A3.17

Members of the ENIAC development team with J. Presper Eckert on the far left and John W. Mauchly fourth from the right (Courtesy University of Pennsylvania)

graduate student, Clifford Berry, completed an electronic computer that could solve systems of linear equations.

ENIAC—the Mauchly/Eckert computer—was used to perform many different calculations. It had 19,000 vacuum tubes, 70,000 resistors, and 5 million soldered joints. ENIAC could perform 5,000 additions per second. It used 150,000 watt-hours of power a day—so much that when it was turned on, the lights in one section of Philadelphia dimmed.

Unfortunately, ENIAC was inflexible. Changing its program required rewiring and took considerable time and resources. Since it could be changed, it was programmable. However, it was not programmable in the sense we know today.

New Ideas for New Computers

In the mid-1940s, the mathematician John von Neumann joined the Mauchly/Eckert team. Von Neumann proposed the design of a computer that stored programs in memory. He proposed other concepts that were to become the foundation of computer design for the next 30 years.

Two computers evolved from this work: EDVAC—Electronic Discrete Variable Automatic Computer—and EDSAC—Electronic Delay Storage Automatic Calculator. Both machines stored programs. EDSAC was completed in England in 1949 and EDVAC in the United States in 1950.

At the time, the potential of these machines was not understood. Atanasoff could not get support from the university. The administration thought there would be a need for only three or four of these devices throughout the United States. People did not seem to feel that the work was going to be very important.

The first programmers for the Mark I and ENIAC were women. Captain Grace Hopper of the U.S. Navy programmed Mark I, and Adele Goldstine programmed ENIAC. Both of these women were talented mathematicians.

FIGURE A3.18

John von Neumann (1903–1957) (Courtesy Institute of Advanced Studies)

ENIAC master programming unit
(Courtesy University of Pennsylvania)

Their presence undoubtedly helped to establish women's strong position in the computer industry.

Mauchly and Eckert formed their own company, the Eckert-Mauchly Corporation, in 1946. This company was later purchased by the Remington-Rand Corporation. Their first product was the UNIVAC I—Universal Automatic Computer. This was the first computer built to sell. The Census Bureau took

FIGURE A3.20

UNIVAC I (Courtesy Sperry Rand Corporation)

delivery in 1951, and it was used continuously until 1963. It now resides in the Smithsonian Institution. Sperry Rand still manufactures a line of computers under the name UNIVAC. These computers are a far cry from the UNIVAC I.

Meanwhile, other companies were not idle. IBM continued development on the Mark I computer and eventually developed the Mark II through Mark IV as well. Burroughs, General Electric, Honeywell, and RCA were also busy with computer development.

IBM's Successful Marketing Philosophy

IBM took an early lead in applying this new computer technology to business problems. They developed a series of business-oriented computers and sold them to their punched-card customers. Since IBM had a near monopoly on punched cards—they were sued by the U.S. government for this in the 1930s—they were in a strong position to capitalize on the new technology.

Furthermore, IBM had an extremely effective marketing philosophy. They emphasized solving business problems. They developed products that were useful to business people and then showed them how to use those products. IBM provided excellent customer services and good maintenance.

This philosophy paid off. Some other companies had better computers, but their computers were not packaged to provide the total solutions to business problems. IBM was the first company to understand that intelligent business people do not buy the best computers; they buy the best solutions to their problems. Today, many companies have adopted this philosophy. But the fact that IBM understood this principle first has much to do with its strength in today's computer market.

Characteristics of First-Generation Computers

The computers manufactured in the 1950s are often called **first-generation computers.** They had **vacuum tubes** as their major components. Memory units did not exist. Instead, most of them used **magnetic drums** as primary storage devices.

Because of the number and size of vacuum tubes, these computers were huge. They generated tremendous amounts of heat, were expensive to run, and often failed. A large first-generation computer occupied a room the size of a football field. It contained rows upon rows of racks with vacuum tubes. A staff of a half-dozen people was required to change the tubes that were continuously burning out.

STUDY OBJECTIVES

9. Describe the contributions Howard Aiken, John Mauchly, J. Presper Eckert, John Atanasoff, John von Neumann, Grace Hopper, and Adele Goldstine made to the development of computers.
10. Explain IBM's successful marketing philosophy.
11. Describe the features of a first-generation computer.

COMPUTERS: SECOND GENERATION

In the late 1950s and early 1960s, vacuum tubes were replaced by **transistors.** This led to **second-generation computers.** These computers were much smaller and more powerful than vacuum-tube computers.

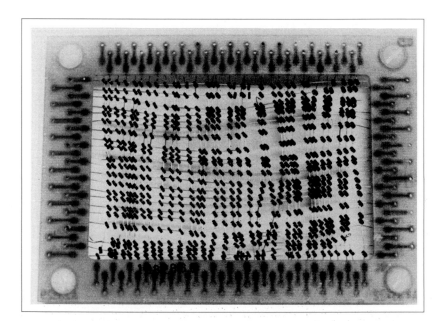

FIGURE A3.21

Core memory from early automatic pin scorer used at bowling centers

Memory units became part of the processing hardware. This new memory was called **core memory** because it used little ring magnets, or cores. Some people still use the term core synonymously with memory. This usage is incorrect, since most memory units today do not contain magnetic cores.

Programming Languages

The first **high-level**—people-oriented—**programming languages** were developed during this time. First-generation computers were programmed in the computer's own language, or **machine language.**

Second-generation computers were programmed in languages like FORTRAN and COBOL. Also, primitive systems programs were installed on second-generation machines. These systems programs were called an **operating system** because they controlled the use of the computer's resources.

Working with Second-Generation Computers

Most computers during this time could run only one program at a time. Therefore, to speed things up, certain input and output operations were done **offline.** Offline means not under the control of the computer. For example, punched cards could be read and the contents copied onto tape without the computer's involvement. After the data on tape had been read into the computer and processed, the tape output could be printed on an independent printer.

The advantage of doing work offline was that the computer did not have to wait for input from the cardreader or for the printer to output the next line. Whenever possible, tapes were used for input and output because they were faster than either a cardreader or printer. Offline processing sure kept the computer operators busy!

The applications being worked on were usually business related. The computer was used to produce checks for payroll, to keep track of inventory, and to perform other business functions. Processing was done in batches to keep the machine as busy as possible. Input data was gathered into batches, processed,

A second-generation computer, the IBM 7094 (Courtesy IBM Corporation)

and then output to a printer or storage medium such as tape. The next batch was then run through and this process repeated throughout the day. Not surprisingly, it is called **batch processing.**

STUDY OBJECTIVES

12. Define core memory, high-level programming language, machine language, operating system, offline, and batch processing.

13. Describe the features of second-generation computers and how they are different from their first-generation counterparts.

14. Identify one advantage to working offline.

COMPUTERS: THIRD GENERATION

In the 1960s, the **third-generation computers** became available. In these machines, **integrated circuits** were used instead of transistors. An integrated circuit is a complete electric circuit on a small chip of silicon. The use of integrated circuits meant that third-generation computers were smaller and faster than their second-generation counterparts. Figure A3.23 compares the sizes of vacuum tubes, transistors, and integrated circuits.

Working with Third-Generation Computers

Vast improvements were made in systems programs during the third generation. Sophisticated operating systems were developed. These operating systems allowed several programs to be in a computer's memory and selectively run. The computer no longer waited for slow input or output operations like card reading or printing. It ran another program instead of waiting.

This capability, called **multiprogramming,** allowed the computer to divide

Vacuum
Tube

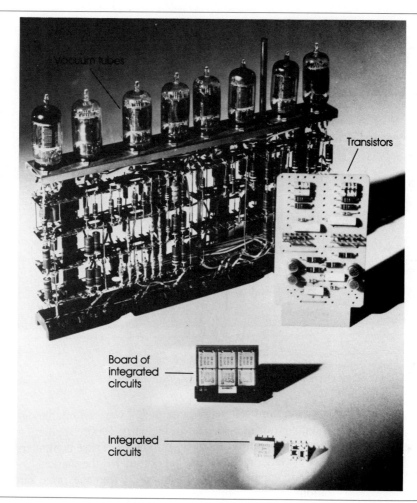

Vacuum tubes

Transistors

Board of
integrated
circuits

Integrated
circuits

Transistor

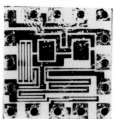

Integrated
Circuit

FIGURE A3.23

Three generations of electronic circuitry
(Courtesy IBM Corporation)

its time between several programs in memory. Third-generation computers with multiprogramming capabilities were able to eliminate offline work typical of second-generation machines. They could process one program while another was being read into memory and the output of a third was being printed.

Third-generation computers supported **online** applications. This meant that instead of grouping data into batches, users could input information directly into the computer for processing.

Online capabilities opened many new applications for third-generation computer systems. With online order entry systems, people could call in to find out if the items they wanted were in stock. The airlines developed complex seat reservation systems that allowed travel agents and ticket counters immediate access to flight information.

FIGURE A3.24

A third-generation computer, the Honeywell 6000 (Courtesy Honeywell Information Systems, Inc.)

The Appearance of Minicomputers

Until the third generation, computers were affordable only to large businesses and government agencies. In the early 1960s, smaller, specialized computers called **minicomputers** were introduced. These computers were less expensive than the large mainframes that dominated the market.

Minicomputers brought computers into the price range of many organizations. The very first minicomputers were designed for limited, special-purpose applications. Gradually, the capability of these machines increased until the more powerful minicomputers and the smaller mainframe computers overlapped in what they could do. It is now difficult to distinguish between minicomputers and mainframes. Some people suggest we just categorize computers as small, medium, and large!

STUDY OBJECTIVES

15. Define integrated circuit, online, and minicomputer.
16. Describe the features of third-generation computers and explain how they are different from second-generation machines.
17. Identify one advantage of computers with multiprogramming capabilities.

COMPUTERS: FOURTH GENERATION

Smallness characterizes **fourth-generation computers.** Today, because of advances in the design of integrated circuits, it is possible to put an entire computer on a small **chip** of silicon.

FIGURE A3.25

Microprocessor (Courtesy AT&T Bell Labs)

Computers on a Chip

The computing power that occupied an entire room in 1952 resides today on a silicon chip smaller than a dime. The processing hardware on a chip is called a **microprocessor.** When the chip is installed with other chips that perform input, output, and additional functions, it is called a **microcomputer.**

Microprocessors were not originally designed with any forethought. They just happened. For example, the Intel 8008 microprocessor was originally intended to be the controller for a CRT. As it turned out, the chip was not used for this purpose and Intel put the chip in their catalog. To their surprise, it sold very well. The company then saw the light, put a design team together, and a year later introduced the Intel 8080 microprocessor.

The Intel 8000 family of microprocessors has become very popular. Different members of the family are the main chips in a number of very successful microcomputers. Other manufacturers quickly followed suit. Today there are dozens of microprocessor products to choose from.

Working with Fourth-Generation Computers

The ability to mass-produce microprocessors means that computers will become less and less expensive. And because the microprocessor can be programmed for a variety of applications, it can be used just about everywhere. In addition to price reductions and greater flexibility in programming, the fourth generation is characterized by increased use of **data communications, distributed data processing,** and **database management systems.**

Data communications is the linking of one computer to another via **communication lines.** These communication lines can be the telephone lines that caught your kite when you were a kid, special microwave transmitters, or even communication satellites. Computers using data communications capabilities make up a computer **network** as they transfer data from one to another. Figure A3.26 shows part of a network of large computers called the ARPA (Advanced Research Project Agency) network.

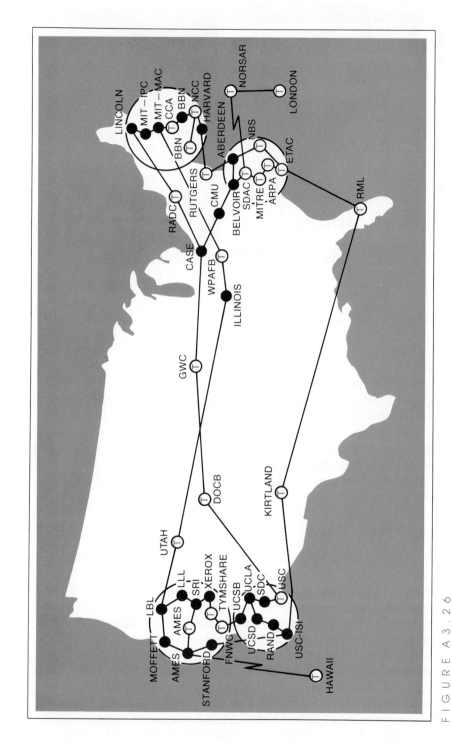

F I G U R E   A 3 . 2 6

Portion of the ARPA network of computers

FIGURE A3.27

Computer connected to another computer by using a telephone (Courtesy Commodore Computer Systems)

Closer to home, many personal microcomputers have special data communications hardware that lets them communicate with larger computers through the home telephone. With this capacity, people can obtain news, specialized magazines, business statistics, and even books or other literature at home. These communications can even take place over cable TV lines. Individuals can also use this service to order goods and services along with receiving information.

The idea of having many computers working together instead of one large computer system doing everything is called distributive data processing. The technological advances of the fourth generation have forced many people to rethink how computer systems can best be put to use.

In the past, people thought that the processing had to be centralized in one large, expensive computer system. The idea behind distributive data processing is that small computers can now be used where the data is collected and the information needed.

Advances in fourth-generation systems programs have led to new software capabilities. One is database technology. Database processing allows data to be combined into large **databases.**

Special systems programs called database management systems—**DBMS**—allow data to be accessed and cross-referenced to other data in the database. Such programs have only been available since 1970 and they will have a significant impact on new technologies. In the future, database management systems may be integrated with microprocessors to form database computers.

Although the cost of hardware has dramatically decreased in the fourth generation, the cost of programming has increased. For this reason, the biggest computing problem in the future is likely to concern programs. The development of more sophisticated database management systems is one solution. When possible, businesses will buy these and other programs from software houses. Both will need to be general purpose and flexible enough to meet varying business needs.

The most successful programs probably will sacrifice speed while being easier to use. Gradually, there will be less need for programmers and a greater need for systems analysts.

STUDY OBJECTIVES

18. Define microprocessor, microcomputer, data communications, network, and distributive data processing.

19. Describe the features of fourth-generation computers.

20. Briefly describe the function of a database management system.

21. Identify what is likely to be the biggest computing problem of the future.

SUMMARY

Although the history of data processing began thousands of years ago, the development of computers is a recent phenomenon. In the early 1800s, Charles Babbage developed many of the design concepts used in today's computers. However, these concepts were not implemented at the time. Many of the mistakes that Babbage made are still being made today.

In the late 1800s, the U.S. Census Bureau hired Herman Hollerith to develop automated ways of computing census data. This effort led to the development of punched-card equipment and started the punched card industry.

Computers were not actually developed until the mid-1940s. Early computers were produced through the cooperation of universities, government, and industry. There have been four generations of computers so far. First-generation computers had vacuum tubes and magnetic drum storage. These computers were huge and very hard to maintain. Programs were written in machine language.

Computers in the second generation were made with transistors and had memory units of magnetic cores. They were smaller than first-generation computers but still very expensive. High-level languages were developed for programming and simple operating systems were invented.

The third-generation computers were composed of integrated circuits on silicon chips. These chips were used for both the arithmetic/logic unit and for memory. Third-generation computers were much smaller and less expensive than first- or second-generation computers.

Today we are in the fourth generation. Computers have become significantly less expensive and more powerful because of advances in integrated circuit design. Processing hardware on a chip, called microprocessors, has led the way. With smaller computers and advances in communication has come data communications. Computers in different places can now work together in communication networks. In addition, some centralized computer systems have been replaced by distributive processing networks.

The fourth generation has also brought advancements in systems software. Database management systems now control vast databases and represent the wave of the future. Clearly, more emphasis will be placed on purchased programs that are easier to use.

U N I T   B

Putting Computer Technology in Its Place

In this unit, you look into a computer center to see how the components of a computer system fit together. The first part of the unit explores ways in which people organize and enter data into a computer. You learn how a computer processes data, then examine different forms of useful output. In addition, the means for storing and retrieving data are discussed.

The second part of the unit examines computer hardware. Computers come in many different sizes to perform a variety of jobs. Input, output, and storage equipment are also found in many shapes and forms to satisfy different needs. Jobs in building, operating, and servicing computer hardware are also reviewed.

Computer programs are the focus of attention for the last part of Unit B. You learn different ways to obtain working programs and what the responsibilities of the computer programmers are. Seven computer programming languages are surveyed. Since computers cannot function without programs, the special programs that all computers use are examined.

CHAPTER B1

Organizing, Entering, Using, and Storing Data

People collect data as a normal part of most jobs. For instance, teachers collect tests and record the scores in their grade books. In other areas, records are kept for everything from the highs and lows in the stock market to the high and low scorers in last night's basketball game. Business people in particular must collect data. The data is then analyzed to order more inventory, pay employees, fill out government reports, and determine if the organization is making or losing money.

Sue McKnight's father is a good example. He was a pharmacist by profession and a businessman out of necessity. In running the pharmacy, he had to keep track of the bills coming in and going out. In addition, he needed to know what drugs to order and the hours each of his employees worked. Also, the government requires special reports when some drugs are prescribed.

If the data itself is unorganized, the job of data processing is difficult. The procedures used to collect data directly affect the success of the organization. Efficient data collection procedures are usually found in well-run and profitable organizations. Companies in financial difficulties are often unorganized at all levels of operation.

Let's take a look at this problem through Sue McKnight's eyes as she helped her father organize data from the pharmacy.

FIGURE B1.1

The broom closet

It always amazed Sue when she walked into her father's office at the pharmacy. Out front, the aisles were brightly lit 24 hours a day. In contrast, the small office in the back—the broom closet, as she called it—was dimly lit and filled by an old desk and small metal table. Piled on top were color-coded shoe boxes that contained her father's business records. During a weak moment last summer she agreed to help him "reorganize things." A month later she was still up to her eyebrows in pharmacy papers.

It was worse than she had originally thought. Sales receipts were mixed in with electric bills and service orders. Just getting this week's papers sorted took several hours. When it was time to finish the entries she pleaded with her father to purchase a computer-supported accounting system.

Sue was convinced that her father needed a computer. But even before that, he needed procedures to help him organize the paperwork. The pharmacy's books would be just as bad off in the future unless they simplified procedures. A computer would certainly help speed up processing once everything was organized again.

The Need for a Computer System

Mr. McKnight and friend discussing computer applications for the pharmacy

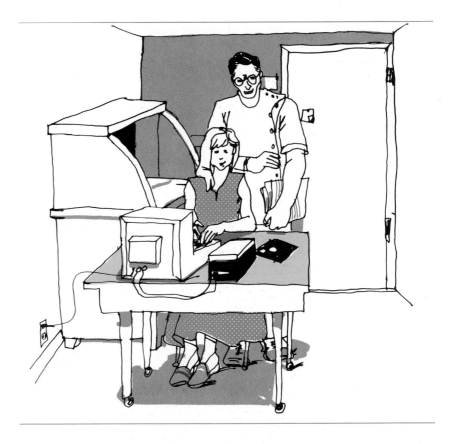

The new computer

Selecting Equipment

Mr. McKnight had an old friend who was a business instructor at the local community college. Together they went over all the potential jobs where a computer system could be used in the pharmacy. After that, they set priorities and identified the IPO cycle for the highest priority jobs.

Her father's friend then helped select applications packages and hardware. Sue was officially hired by her father to be the data entry operator and records management clerk.

The computer had a standard typewriterlike keyboard and stored data on floppy disks—also called **diskettes.** Sue's first job was to organize the data and have the computer store it on disk. The computer program took care of how the data was transferred to disk. All she had to do was organize the paperwork and follow the instructions as they appeared on the CRT.

ORGANIZING DATA

The papers Sue used are called **source documents.** Source documents are forms on which data is collected. Orders, time sheets, and answer sheets are examples of source documents.

Characters, Fields, and Records

To describe data in more detail, we could say that it contains typed or hand-written characters. A **character** is a single letter or digit, like the character Q or 6. A group of related characters is called a **field.** This data usually has a

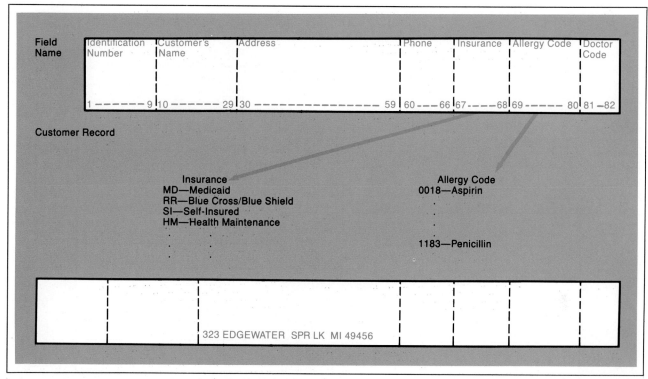

Field Name	Identification Number	Customer's Name	Address		Phone	Insurance	Allergy Code	Doctor Code
	1 ------ 9	10 ------ 29	30 ---------------- 59		60 --- 66	67 ---- 68	69 ----- 80	81 –82

Customer Record

Insurance
MD—Medicaid
RR—Blue Cross/Blue Shield
SI—Self-Insured
HM—Health Maintenance

Allergy Code
0018—Aspirin

1183—Penicillin

		323 EDGEWATER SPR LK MI 49456					

F I G U R E B 1 . 4

Customer record for the pharmacy

logical meaning. For example, it may represent a name or sales price. The nine characters in a postal zip code go into the zip code field. The seven characters in a telephone number go into the telephone number field.

One of Sue's projects was to set up **records** for each of the pharmacy's customers. To start, she collected a name, address, telephone number, and some special identification like a social security number. Each piece of data would fill a separate field. All of the fields related to one customer would be a customer record. In other words, a collection of related fields is called a record.

Figure B1.4 shows this imaginary customer record. The numbers across the bottom of the record refer to the field's location and size in the record. These numbers do not exist on tape or disk; they are shown here for reference. If this record were printed, the customer number would appear in the first nine positions, name in positions 10 through 29, and so forth.

Note the use of abbreviations and special codes. Rather than enter lengthy insurance names, like Medicaid, abbreviations are used. Also, the allergy code field contains one or more numbers that are assigned meanings as shown in the figure. These codes are established when the system is designed. They save space and prevent spelling errors.

An 1183 in the allergy field means that the customer is allergic to penicillin. When codes like these are used, they must be explained in procedures for users; otherwise, people will not know how to interpret the results.

DISPLAY ON PHARMACY'S CRT

```
        ORDER ENTRY
CUSTOMER ID: 364-99-1846
  DRUG CODE: 1183
   QUANTITY: 25

    ***WARNING***
CUSTOMER HAS REPORTED
ALLERGY
```

359254116
360902379
363392702
364991846 Joe Smoe
366514484

CUSTOMER FILE

1074
1183 Penicillin VK 250MG
1267
1298
1301

DRUG USAGE FILE

ID Number	Name	Address				Phone	Insurance	Allergies	Doctor
364991846	Joe Smoe	323 Edgewater	Spr Lk	MI	49456	556 4518	MD	1183	17

Match

		Sales	Total	Total quantity	Average	Rank	Orders
1183	Penicillin VK 250MG	2	1.62	45	.81		1/20, 1/25

FIGURE B1.5

How records and files can relate

Files and Databases

A collection of records is called a **file.** You can remember this by thinking of metal filing cabinets that hold folders, or records. Thus, the records in figure B1.5 would combine into a customer file. This file would be one of many files maintained by the pharmacy's computer system.

Data contained in one file often relates to data in other files. For example, when a prescription is filled, data is needed from the customer file and the drug usage file, as shown in figure B1.6. The drug code from the prescription is checked against the customer's known allergies as a standard precaution. If the customer is found to be allergic to the medicine, a warning flashes on the screen. The pharmacist can then contact the doctor.

When files are often cross-referenced, the files can be integrated and placed under the control of a **database management system.** They are then called a **database.**

Data relationships

Changing to a database management system requires plenty of organization and professional expertise to be successful. Someone—usually a systems analyst—must anticipate all the possible uses of the data before designing the database. This requires an understanding of the application and takes many hours of research and preparation.

STUDY OBJECTIVES

1. Define source document, diskette, field, record, file, and database.
2. Briefly explain why abbreviations and special codes are used as fields.
3. Identify the professional responsible for designing a database and describe when this is usually done.

INPUT DATA

To get the computer ready for her father, Sue had to type all of the important data into the computer. Luckily, she only had to enter the data about each customer once. After that it was stored on floppy disks. Her father could then get any customer record whenever he wanted.

Looking for Errors

As she entered names, addresses, drug codes, and so on, into the computer, Sue could see that the computer distinguished between letters and numbers. Sometimes after making a typing error, a special message would appear on the screen. The message indicated that a data entry error had been made and needed to be corrected. This usually happened when she accidentally typed a letter instead of a number—like typing F9442 for a zip code instead of 49442.

Fields on a source document are often classified as either **numeric** or **alphanumeric.** Numeric fields contain numbers, a plus (+) or minus (−) sign, and a decimal point. Special characters like dollar signs and commas are usually not accepted in a numeric field. Alphanumeric fields can contain any combination of letters, numbers, and special characters.

Verification and Editing

Sue tried to find her own mistakes when possible. The term **verification** is used when the data entry operator takes responsibility for checking data for errors.

Computer programs are also written to check the incoming data for errors. Having the computer program check for data entry errors is called **editing.** The editing routine in figure B1.7 is part of a BASIC program that checks the incoming zip code.

Machine-Readable Source Documents

Sue's father had actually been using computers for several years. The distributor that sold the pharmacy nonprescription items like soap and toothpaste used a computer for orders. They supplied all their customers with hand-held readers and special labels for marking each item and shelf.

Checking Inventory

Each morning, one of the employees at the pharmacy would take the reader down the aisles looking for items that needed to be reordered. When he found one, he would scan the label on the shelf using the reader. In this way, the item

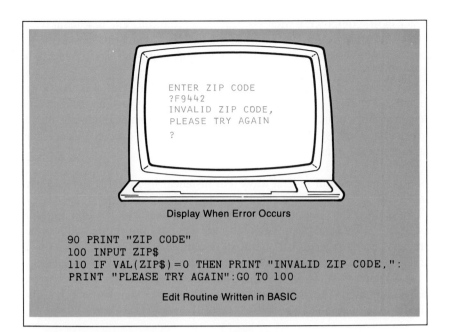

Display When Error Occurs

```
90 PRINT "ZIP CODE"
100 INPUT ZIP$
110 IF VAL(ZIP$)=0 THEN PRINT "INVALID ZIP CODE,":
PRINT "PLEASE TRY AGAIN":GO TO 100
```

Edit Routine Written in BASIC

FIGURE B1.7

Editing data

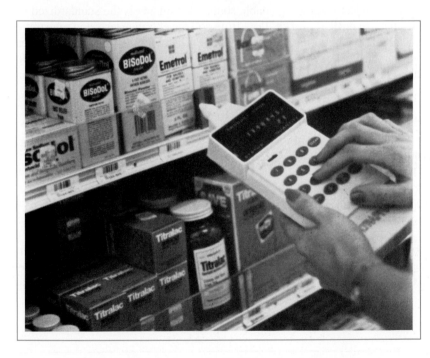

FIGURE B1.8

A clerk scanning a shelf with the reader (Courtesy Bergen-Brunswig Corporation)

code was input and stored in the reader. The employee would then enter the order amount on the reader's numeric keyboard.

After all the orders were entered into the reader, the employee would call a special telephone number provided by the distributor. The reader was attached to the mouthpiece of the telephone. Data was then directly sent to the computer at the distributor's office.

Once in the computer, a shipping order was produced. The new items would arrive at the store within 24 hours. In bigger cities, the items can arrive that same afternoon. Entering orders directly into the computer saved Sue's father and the distributor a lot of time and paperwork.

Many organizations have found that manually entering data is the slowest step in the IPO cycle. To avoid data entry errors and to speed up the data entry process, organizations are converting to machine-readable source documents. In particular, retail stores like the pharmacy are using special readers—also called **scanners**—that can read specially coded labels.

Optical Characters

Labels can be coded in several ways. For instance, figure B1.9 shows **optical characters.** Their shapes are standardized across the country.

Optical characters are used in many business applications. For example, MasterCard, Visa, and gasoline credit card invoices are printed with optical characters. Sales tags in a clothing store can also be printed using optical characters. The customer or a special wand can read the optical characters on the tag. When the wand is run across the sales tag, the item number is read into the computer. The price is matched with the item number and the bill is printed by the computer.

Optical Marks

One of the oldest machine-readable source documents is the standardized test forms that use **optical marks.** Data from college entrance tests and registration forms is input using optical mark scanners. The marks are made by dark lead pencils on designated areas of the answer sheet. If you mark in another location or don't thoroughly erase mistakes, the scanner can pick up the stray mark and may incorrectly spell your name or lower your score on the test.

Bar Codes

A third type of character read from machine-readable source documents is a **bar code.** The bar code on the side of grocery items is called the **Universal Product Code** or **UPC.** Grocery stores can now speed up checking out by having UPC sensing scanners at each checkout counter. Faster service is just one benefit. The stores also justify the equipment's extra cost through improved inventory control. By having more accurate counts of inventory, stores can save money by reducing stock. They also avoid running out of items as often.

Magnetic Ink Characters

Another popular way of reading data directly from a source document is with magnetic-ink character readers. **Magnetic Ink Character Recognition— MICR—** is most frequently used in banks. Check numbers and amounts are

F I G U R E   B 1 . 9

Optical characters

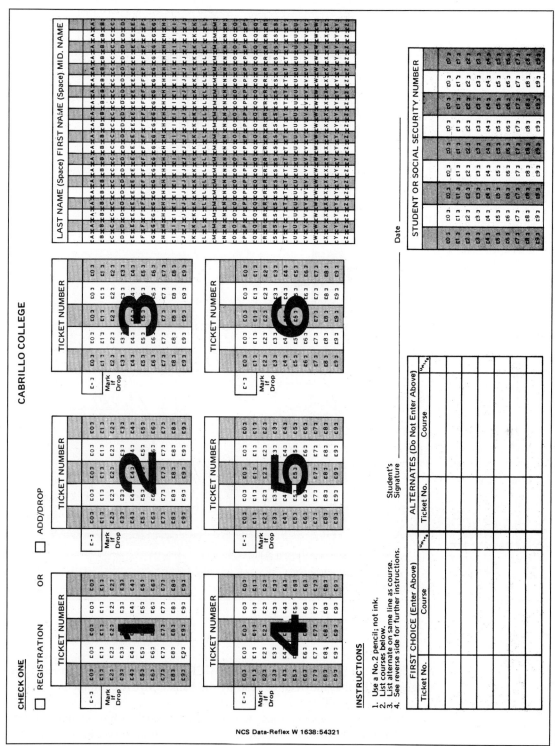

FIGURE B1.10

College registration form using optical marks

UPC bar code

Universal Product Code
(UPC) Bar Code

a. MICR Character Codes

284

DAVID M. KROENKE

MERCER ISLAND, WASHINGTON 98040

1/15 19 80   19-2/1250

Pay to the
order of   Postmaster $ 15.00

Fifteen and 00/100   Dollars

FIRSTLINE
SEATTLE-FIRST NATIONAL BANK
MERCER ISLAND BRANCH/MERCER ISLAND 98040

For

⑆125000024⑆ 93178 000⑆ 0284   ⑈0000001500⑈

Rocky Mountain Bank Note B

MICR Characters

b. Cancelled Check with MICR Printing

FIGURE B1.12

Check with MICR characters

encoded on the bottom of checks with MICR characters. These characters are magnetized so that they can be read by the bank's MICR equipment.

Environmental Data

In process control applications, it is often necessary to bypass manual data entry. The process control systems in a nuclear power plant would be ineffective if they relied on people for the entry of data.

Process control systems continuously monitor production activities by col-

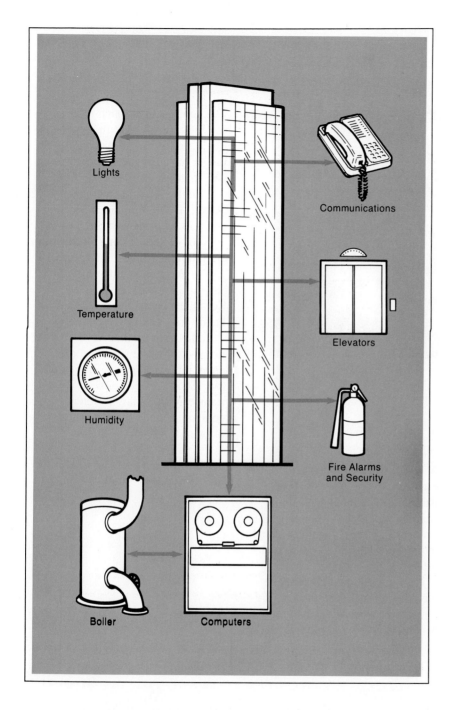

Lights

Communications

Temperature

Elevators

Humidity

Fire Alarms
and Security

Boiler   Computers

FIGURE B1.13

Some environmental data found in a
skyscraper

lecting **environmental data.** Depending on the monitoring device, the data
can be voice, light, temperature, sound, pressure, or dozens of kinds of data.

Commercial and home security systems use infrared light to watch building
entrances. If the infrared signal is interrupted, a special code is sent to an
online computer. The computer identifies the building and area of concern by

ARLENE AMELIA
SENIOR DATA ENTRY/WORD PROCESSING
OPERATOR

RESPONSIBILITIES

Actually, I do very little data entry now. With all of the terminals scattered around the campuses, and the use of such communication devices as modems, much of the data is entered by other people at other locations.

Today, I am more responsible for data output, which means that I see that the computer programs are printed and distributed to the right department.

This isn't a huge computer center, so I have a chance to work with a lot of different departments. This gives my job some variety, which I like.

MY BACKGROUND

A vocational counselor visited my high school and passed out a pamphlet on data entry. I didn't want to wait and go to college; I wanted a job fast! I went to a three-month-long business school that offered keypunching.

Now I teach data entry at the local vocational center, which I really love. Word processing is becoming more and more a part of this skill, and that makes it more interesting and challenging.

SKILLS REQUIRED

The job has changed so much from several years ago when I started.

The equipment is much more sophisticated. I can't imagine what it will be like in five years. We no longer have the mechanical machine jams that we used to have constantly. Also, the computer center has become much less noisy and a nicer place to work.

A lot of people can't sit down for eight hours, which is necessary if you're doing data entry. And you have to like working with machines. Computer operators, on the other hand, are on their feet all day.

Today, I think that word processing is the road into data entry jobs. The pay is very good, too. The skills can also be transferred to many different companies and places if you have to or want to move.

checking the appropriate record in the data file. It then notifies the person designated to be called in emergencies.

Security systems are just one of a number of interrelated process control systems used in many large buildings. These systems use environmental data as input to control temperature and humidity, to turn lights on and off, and to make sure that the pressure in the boiler is kept constant. If, for example, the boiler pressure were to exceed designated safety levels, the proper authorities would be notified through the security system.

STUDY OBJECTIVES

4. Define verification, editing, UPC, and MICR.

5. Identify two types of fields and describe the type of characters in each.

6. Identify four types of machine-readable source documents and give an example of the use of each.

7. Identify five types of environmental data.

PROCESSING DATA

As Sue entered data into the computer she thought back to Mrs. Dingman's lecture the week before. The lecture was about how the computer internally represents data. Until then, Sue had not really given it much thought. She had assumed that the computer stored and processed data just like she typed it in. This is not true.

Bits of Data

The basic building block for representing data electronically is called a **bit,** which is an abbreviation for **binary digit.** You are familiar with decimal digits. They are the digits 0, 1, 2, 3, 4, 5, 6, 7, 8, and 9. A binary digit is similar, but there are only two digits: 0 and 1.

Bits are used as the basic building blocks for processing data because they are easy to represent electronically inside the computer. Bits can be represented by devices that are either on or off. For example, we can say that a light represents a 1 when it is on and a 0 when it is off. Figure B1.14 shows a panel of light switches. If we define up as 1 and down as 0, then this panel represents the bit pattern 1101. While computers are not composed of panels of light switches, they do contain switchlike devices that are either on or off.

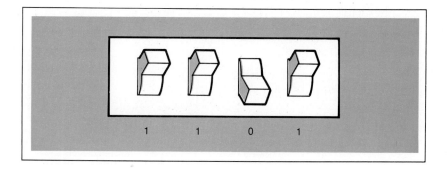

FIGURE B1.14

Panel of light switches representing bit pattern 1101

In the simplest terms, patterns of bits are used to represent characters. For example, the pattern 0100001 might represent an A, the pattern 0100010 a B, and so forth. The word "might" is used here because there is no accepted code. The code varies depending on the type of computer system and equipment. Let's examine two sets of codes used in the computer's memory unit.

ASCII for Microcomputers

Characters are stored in memory in several ways. People talk about a 7-bit or 8-bit code. Most microcomputers use a 7-bit code called the **American Standard Code for Information Interchange** or **ASCII** (pronounced Ask-key). Larger computers traditionally use an 8-bit code called the **Extended Binary Coded Decimal Interchange Code** or **EBCDIC.** Figure B1.15 shows the bit pattern used to represent letters, numbers, and special characters in ASCII.

Computers can hold literally millions of bits in memory. Early memory units were composed of tiny magnetic rings. These were called cores and they could then be magnetized in one of two ways—a binary 1 or 0.

Bubble memory units magnetize microscopic areas of a silicon chip to store bit patterns. Other methods of internally storing data have been used throughout

FIGURE B1.15

ASCII character bit codes

CHARACTER	BIT PATTERN	CHARACTER	BIT PATTERN	CHARACTER	BIT PATTERN
!	0100001	=	0111101	Y	1011001
"	0100010	>	0111110	Z	1011010
#	0100011	?	0111111	[	1011011
$	0100100	@	1000000	\	1011100
%	0100101	A	1000001	]	1011101
&	0100110	B	1000010	↑	1011110
'	0100111	C	1000011	<	1011111
(	0101000	D	1000100	'	1100000
)	0101001	E	1000101		
∷	0101010	F	1000110		
+	0101011	G	1000111		
,	0101100	H	1001000		
–	0101101	I	1001001		
.	0101110	J	1001010		
/	0101111	K	1001011		
0	0110000	L	1001100		
1	0110001	M	1001101		
2	0110010	N	1001110		
3	0110011	O	1001111		
4	0110100	P	1010000		
5	0110101	Q	1010001		
6	0110110	R	1010010		
7	0110111	S	1010011		
8	0111000	T	1010100		
9	0111001	U	1010101		
:	0111010	V	1010110		
;	0111011	W	1010111		
	0111100	X	1011000		

Initial screen display for Commodore Vic 20

the development of computers. The particulars can be very complex. Therefore, only designers and service technicians are ever concerned with working with computers at this level.

Sometimes you will hear the term **byte** used with regard to computer data. A byte is the group of bits required to represent one character. Seven bits are used to represent characters in ASCII, so the byte contains 7 bits. If the computer uses 8 bits for each character, then the byte has 8 bits. Memory is often described by the number of bytes available for use.

8. Define bit, ASCII, and byte.

9. Briefly describe how processing data is stored in a computer using the American Standard Code for Information Interchange.

STUDY OBJECTIVES

OUTPUT DATA

Once the computer system was up and running, Sue's father moved the equipment behind the counter. The keyboard and CRT were on the counter top, and he had the printer on a little cart underneath. From there he entered prescriptions and printed labels.

Mr. McKnight was now primarily responsible for data entry. Instead of typing the labels and writing the bills by hand, the computer system automatically did both after the prescription was entered. This saved him time and vastly improved record keeping. The labels were usually ready before the prescription.

Sue's responsibilities after school were now limited to reviewing the printed reports and checking them against the reports from suppliers. Every four weeks she used the accounting programs to produce end-of-the-month reports.

FIGURE B1.17

Prescription labels on a pharmacy's printer

The distribution of reports in many organizations is a job in itself. An employee called a **data control clerk** is often given this and other responsibilities. He or she would double-check the accuracy of the reports and make sure users received the reports they needed on time.

Keep in mind that the purpose of a computer system is to produce information. People traditionally see this output as a printed report or screen display.

Today, output data is used in a variety of ways. Voice synthesizers have computers actually talking out loud. In other situations, the output can be photographically reduced and placed on film. Output from process control systems results in some type of action. For instance, the computer may turn off the furnace or turn on an exhaust fan.

Reports

Reports, like all output, should be designed to help users. Some reports are very detailed. Others contain summarized or special data. Reports are usually classified as **detailed, summary,** or **exception.** Each has its own use.

Detailed Reports

Detailed reports contain all available data related to a subject. An assistant basketball coach will keep statistics from each game, including the number of shots, baskets, and fouls each player made during the game. The resulting detailed report lists each player's statistics.

At the pharmacy, Sue printed a customer list for her father each month. This detailed report listed each customer by his or her customer number and included name, address, telephone number, and family doctor. Figure B1.18 is an example of such a report.

Summary Reports

When large amounts of data are available, it is usually not practical or necessary to see all of it at one time. In these situations, a summary report is used. Summary reports result from calculations. For example, basketball league standings will show the number of games each team has won or lost—not the scores of each individual game.

|| CUSTOMER LIST FOR APRIL				
CUSTOMER NUMBER	NAME	ADDRESS	PHONE	DOCTOR
359-25-4116	Marvin Douglas	7106 Cherry Ave Muskegon 49442	555-3449	D. Gasharik
360-90-2379	Betty Jo LaRue	327 Neece White Lake 49461	581-6407	R. Morison
363-39-2002	Stanley Baker	582 Glen Oaks Fruitport 49415	555-3175	S. Johanson
364-99-1846	Joe Smoe	323 Edgewater Spring Lake 49456	556-4518	R. Morison
366-51-4484	George Clark	1864 Briarwood Grand Haven 49417	556-0849	J. Getty

FIGURE B1.18

Detailed printed report

FIGURE B1.19

Basketball coach using computer to obtain game statistics

```
                    INSURANCE BILLING SUMMARY

                      SEPTEMBER—PERIOD 1

  COMPANY       NO. PRESCRIPTIONS    COST    MARGIN  MARGIN PCT.  BILLED AMOUNT

Medicaid              37          $222.25  $86.67    28.05%       $308.92

Blue Cross/           13            97.75   40.30    30.06         134.05
   Blue Shield

Self—Insured          42           254.43  122.96    32.04         377.39

Health Maintenance     5            94.52   15.75    14.28         110.27

TOTAL                 97          $664.95 $265.68                 $930.63
```

Figure B1.20 shows an insurance billing summary report. This report is used at the pharmacy to identify the money billed to each insurance company every month. It does not show each order. Instead, orders from customers using the same insurance company are added together and presented as a single figure.

Exception Reports

Exception reports, like summary reports, are the results of processing data. In this case, comparisons are used to produce exception reports. Only special conditions are looked for and reported. For example, our basketball coach may want a list of each player that had more than two fouls midway through the last game. If the data was organized by the period when the foul occurred,

```
                        UNPAID BILLS
                     OVER 30 DAYS OLD

                        SEPTEMBER 1

    CUSTOMER                CUSTOMER
     NUMBER                   NAME

   247—86—1521            Pete Carrier
   296—19—5804            Sara Stanford
   315—93—7736            Mike Townsend
   360—90—2379            Betty Jo La Rue
   364—99—1846            Joe Smoe
   372—01—4997            Lisa Price
```

then a list can be made of only those players having more than two fouls by half-time.

A report listing only unpaid bills over 30 days old would be another example of an exception report. The report in figure B1.21 is produced by checking the date from each billing record. Only customers with bills outstanding longer than a month would have their name and identification number printed.

Screen Displays

When CRTs are used to display output, several options may be available: **highlighting, reverse video, scrolling,** and **paging.**

Highlighting and Reverse Video

Key words or headings can be highlighted by increasing or decreasing the intensity in which the characters are displayed. A special form of highlighting called reverse video actually changes the character's features. If the screen usually displays white characters on a black background, reverse video displays black characters on a white background. Reverse video is used in figure B1.22 to visually separate information on the screen.

Paging and Scrolling

Either paging or scrolling is used to display information on a CRT. With paging, the screen is cleared and a new set of information displayed. Paging is often used when information can be organized into units. Each unit of information is displayed by itself; then the screen is cleared before displaying the next unit.

Scrolling allows one line of information to be added to the bottom of the screen. When this happens, the top line rolls off. This technique is often used with a word processor. As new text is added to the screen, older text rolls up and eventually off the screen. The operator's eyes do not rove the screen looking for the last entry. The last item is always on the bottom of the screen.

Reverse video

FIGURE B1.23

Microfiche viewer (Courtesy Eastman Kodak Company)

Other Types of Output Data

Some organizations must by law keep records for long periods of time. This is a problem because of the space required to store a large number of printed reports.

Microfilm and Microfiche

Banks save space by having output data photographically reduced and placed on film. If the film comes in rolls, it is called **microfilm. Microfiches** are sheets of film with output. Either method provides an inexpensive and space-saving way to hold a lot of output data.

Computer Output on Microfilm, or **COM,** is also very fast. Over 20,000 lines a minute can be recorded on film. One major disadvantage to storing output on microfilm is that the user must have a screen display to see the information.

Computers That Talk Back

Fourth-generation computers are also making use of **sound output.** Computers beep at you when they spot a data entry error. Speech-generating devices talk to you. In your car, they will tell you when you are low on oil or your door is ajar.

Speech-generated output also has tremendous value in safety-related systems. The computer can describe exactly where the problem is without the user having to press a button or look at a screen. Other exciting applications exist in foreign language translators, elementary education, and reading machines for the blind.

10. List two responsibilities of a data control clerk.

11. Briefly describe the difference between detailed, summary, and exception reports and give an example of each.

12. Describe highlighting, reverse video, scrolling, and paging.

13. Define microfilm, microfiche, and COM.

14. List three advantages and a disadvantage to using Computer Output on Microfilm.

15. Briefly explain why speech-generated output can be a valuable safety feature to a user.

STORING DATA

Sue actually performed several jobs at the pharmacy. Besides running the computer and keeping the accounting data up to date, she had to make sure that all important data was transferred to disk, labeled, and properly stored.

Larger computer centers hire a **data librarian** to identify and store tapes and disks. These centers have hundreds of files stored on different media that must be cataloged. Usually the tapes and disks are stored in a fireproof room called the **tape/disk library.**

Many computer applications require data to be stored for processing at a later time. For example, grades from each grading period are saved and later printed on the final report card. Payroll data is saved all year and then used on W-2 forms. Several ways exist to store data; punched cards, tapes, and disks all save data for later use.

FIGURE B1.24

Data librarian in a tape library (Courtesy TRW Inc.)

F I G U R E   B 1 . 2 5

80-column punched card

Using Punched Cards to Store Data

Storing data on cards predates computers. The punched-card technology used by the Census Bureau in 1890 is still being used today. The standard punched card is divided into 80 vertical columns and 12 horizontal rows. Each column is used to represent one character. If you examine figure B1.25, you will see that rows 11 and 12 are at the top of the card, with rows 0 through 9 below.

Each letter of the alphabet, digit, and special character is represented by a special combination of holes. This special combination of holes for each character is called the **Hollerith code.** It was named after Herman Hollerith, who first demonstrated the use of punched cards to the Census Bureau back in the 1880s.

In figure B1.25, the number 1 is represented in column 37 by a single hole only in row 1. The number 2 is represented by a hole only in row 2. The letter A in column 5 of figure B1.25 is signified by holes in rows 12 and 1. You will find that numbers are coded using one hole, letters using two holes, and special characters using up to three holes.

Now, if you think of a hole as a 1 and the absence of a hole as a 0, then you see another example of a bit pattern. Starting from the top of the card, the bit pattern for the character 1 is 000100000000 because the only hole—1—is in row 1 or bit position 4. The pattern for the character 2 is 000010000000, and the pattern 100100000000 represents an A (see appendix E). When the Hollerith code is transferred to memory, it is translated into another bit pattern, such as ASCII, which the computer uses for processing data.

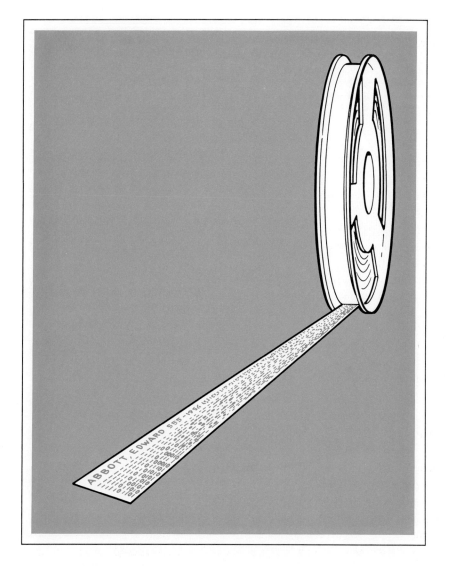

FIGURE B1.26

Storing data on tape

Recording Data on Tape and Disk

Bit patterns are also used to store data on tapes or disks. In both cases, bits are represented by the presence or absence of magnetized spots on the recording surface. Figure B1.26 shows an imaginary section of tape with magnetized areas turned on and off to represent characters. The tape is not limited to storing 80 characters like the punched cards. It can store as many characters as the tape is long.

The disk shown in figure B1.27 has the same advantage as tape. It can hold records with varying numbers of characters. Again, disks are not limited to storing data in sets of 80 characters.

Sequential File Organization

Records on cards, tape, or disk are usually identified by a **key field.** The key field is the basis for organizing and identifying records in a file. When organ-

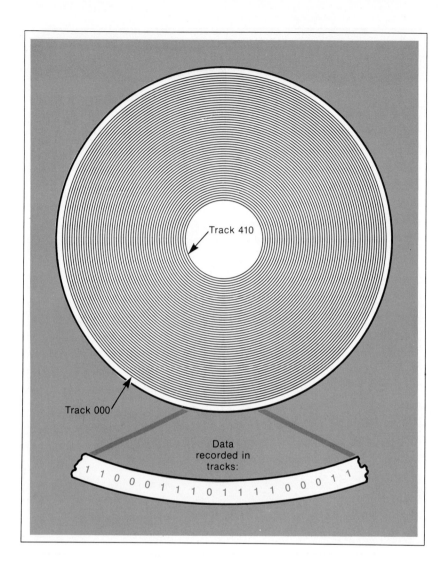

Storing data on disk

izing data, programmers look for a key field that will have different values in each record. The pharmacy used a customer's social security number as the key field. Names are usually not used because two different people can have the same name, causing confusion.

Processing Data Sequentially

The records in a **sequential file** are stored in key field order. These records must be sorted into sequence based on the value of the key field. The computer retrieves a particular record by reading one record at a time from the beginning, which is called **sequential processing.**

Sequential processing means that records are always input from the file in the same order. Files on cards and tapes can only be sequentially processed. There is no way to get the thirty-third card in a card file without first reading the thirty-two records that come before it.

Sequential files all have this special property: the records are processed in order. Think of a stereo tape player. You listen to songs in sequence. If you want to listen to the sixth song, you also listen to the songs before or fast-forward past them. In either case, the first five songs have to be physically run through the tape player.

Processing data from a tape file is the same as playing music from tape. With a tape file, a record is read (played) from the tape in the same order in which it was written (recorded). If you want to get the fifty-fifth record, the tape is placed on the tape drive and one record at a time is read until the desired record is found. One way or another, each record has to be physically run through the tape drive. The fifty-fifth record cannot be read until the fifty-four records that came before it are also read.

Imagine the problem the pharmacy had in keeping records for each customer. What was the best way to store the data? If records were stored on tape, then how could they be changed if some customers moved away or new customers moved in? How could one record be quickly located?

Without some organization, records cannot be quickly located. Take, for example, an unorganized list of phone numbers. Suppose you want to find three telephone numbers: Sue McKnight's, Harold Johnson's, and Martha Baker's, in that order. If you don't know where they are located, you will have to search the list three times.

The searching time can be reduced if you put the names in alphabetic order by last name. You can first search for Martha's telephone number. Then, you search for Harold's number by looking for it after Martha's name. Finally, you find Sue's number, knowing it is on the list somewhere after Harold's name and number. You will only have to search through the list once.

You can also catch mistakes or missing records more easily. Suppose you are searching for John LaFriend's telephone number. You find Harold Johnson's number followed by Sue McKnight's. What does this mean? Since the names

Organizing Sequential Files

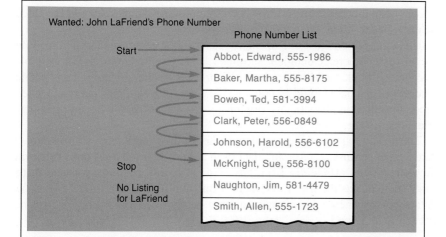

FIGURE B1.28

Sequential search for a telephone number

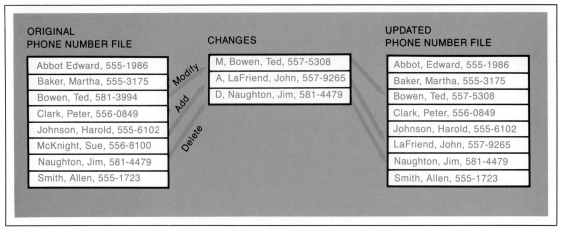

Updating a sequential file

are in alphabetic order, it means that John's number is missing (probably because his number is new or unlisted). If it were listed, LaFriend would be between Johnson and McKnight. Thus, having the names in order by a key field helps you eliminate searching through the whole list only to find that the name in question is not there.

Now consider a customer file with 500 customer records. If the names are in no particular order on the file, then on average, 250 records will have to be searched to find the one you want. Therefore, to find 10 customer records, 2500—10 times 250—records will have to be searched.

On the other hand, if the customer file is sorted by customer number (social security number at the pharmacy) and we also sort all the changes by customer number, then we can find and change all records in one pass through the file. All missing records can also be identified quickly.

Reasons for Accessing Sequential Files

The term **updating** means adding, deleting, or changing records in a file. For example, John LaFriend's name and telephone number would be added to the telephone number file. In addition, other names and numbers would be added, deleted, or modified when the file was updated.

Updating a file is just one of many reasons to access a sequential file. Files are processed to create detailed, summary, and exception reports. For example, a telephone book could be produced by processing the telephone number file. One record at a time would be read and the name and telephone number printed. Since the file is alphabetically organized, the results would be an alphabetic telephone listing.

The ability to process current data is the primary purpose of storing data on cards, tapes, or disks. Accessing data from a file is referred to as **data retrieval.** To retrieve data efficiently from any sequential file, requests must be in the same sequence as the file. Even then, sequential files do not provide very fast data retrieval when a file contains a large number of records and data is only needed from a few.

FIGURE B1.30

Data retrieval from a sequential file

People in direct communication with a computer do not have the luxury of waiting for each record to be searched. Users usually get impatient if they have to wait more than two or three seconds for a response. The problem with sequential processing is that it takes too much time to search through each record in sequence to find data from a single record.

Suppose you want to withdraw money from your bank account using an automatic teller machine on the local street corner. You insert your card and enter your identification number and the amount you want to withdraw. If the bank keeps the balance of your account on a sequential file, you wait while the file is searched to find your account. If there are a lot of people banking there, you could wait several minutes. Clearly, you are going to become impatient. Perhaps you will even find another place to bank. The computer needs to be able to access your account balance directly. The users will not wait for their records to be found by sequentially searching through the file.

The ability to process records in any sequence is called direct access data retrieval or just **direct access.** In general, direct accessing is needed when sequential processing is impractical. The bank cannot ask its customers to line up in order by account number to obtain money. The bank must be able to take withdrawal requests one at a time and in any order.

Since direct access allows records to be processed in any order, it can always substitute for sequential access. When requests happen to arrive in presorted batches, the records still can be directly accessed. The computer system will process them just as if they were unsorted.

The use of direct access automatically eliminates cards and tapes for data storage. These media can only support sequential files and sequential data retrieval. However, data stored on disk can be directly accessed. It can be accessed in any order—including sequential order if it is stored that way. The problem is how to relate the key field to the location of the record on disk.

Direct Access to Data

Reasons for Directly Accessing Records

Limiting Direct Access to Disk Storage

Here's what could happen without direct access capability

There are two ways of organizing records that allow direct access: **indexed sequential file organizations** and **random file organizations.**

Indexed Sequential File Organization

Think about trying to find Harold Johnson's telephone number in a local telephone book. The names and numbers are in the book in alphabetic order. You could sequentially access the number by starting with the A's and proceeding through the book until you found it. But it is doubtful you would start looking at the front of the book. Instead, you would leaf through the book until you found the J's and start looking from there.

Keeping an Index of Key Fields

Indexed sequential files are processed in the same way. The records are organized in a key field order like a sequential file. In addition, an index like the one in the back of this book is also kept. This index may contain only the key field and disk location for some of the records in the file.

For instance, 26 key fields and disk locations might be kept for an indexed sequential telephone number file. The key fields in the index would be the name and storage location of the first person in every alphabetic grouping from A to Z. The index would also be in alphabetic order.

To find Harold's telephone number, you first search the index until you find

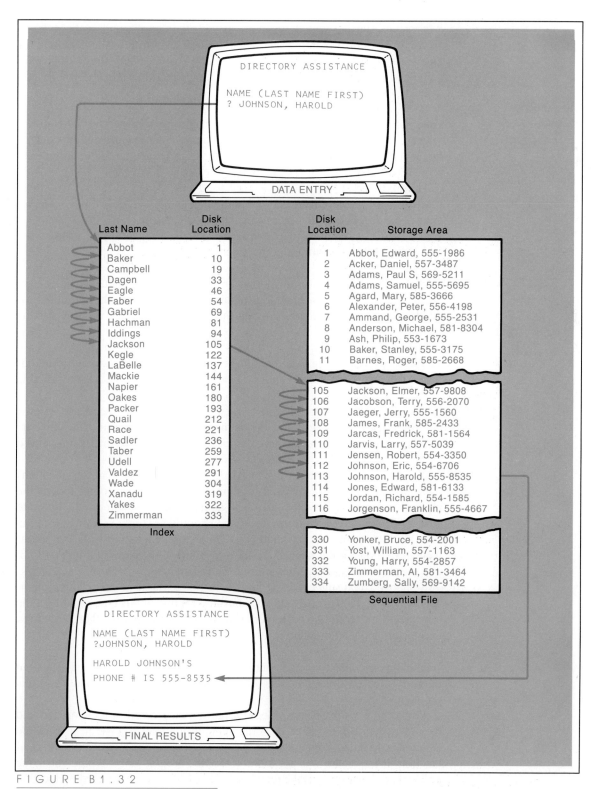

Data retrieval from an indexed sequential file

a last name starting with J. In figure B1.32, the name found in the index is Jackson. The corresponding disk location then takes you to the beginning of the names starting with J. These names are now searched until Harold Johnson's name and telephone number are found. This method has allowed you to skip over all the names from A to I.

The Advantage to Indexed Sequential Files

Only the index and a small part of the file had to be searched to find Harold's telephone number. This method is a vast improvement over having to start at the beginning of the file. Since the records are in sequential order, an indexed sequential file can also be sequentially accessed.

Here lies the primary advantage to using this file organization. It is most useful in applications that need both sequential and direct access. For example, an indexed sequential file used by an automatic teller machine directly updates your record by using the index. But the file can be sequentially accessed at the end of the month to print monthly statements.

Random File Organization

Records in a random file are not in any predetermined sequence. They are located on the disk by means of a **hashing routine.** The hashing routine is a mathematical formula thats converts the key field to a disk location for the record.

A Hashing Routine to Find Records

The hashing routine uses the record's key field to find a disk storage location. When the record is needed, the key field is again used in the hashing routine to find the record.

Random file organization allows for the fastest possible access to records on disk because the record's location is mathematically determined. Computers are at their best when performing computations. Retrieval time is not slowed by having to repeatedly reference an index.

To set up the example in figure B1.33, it was decided that disk locations 000 through 999 would be used to store records in the customer file. If the pharmacy used a three-digit customer number, the problem would be quite simple. The record for customer number 123 could be stored in storage location 123, the record for customer number 125 in storage location 125, and so on. It would eliminate the need for a hashing routine. As in life, things are not this simple. The pharmacy uses a nine-digit key field.

Someone could suggest using just the last three digits of the customer number. This would be a good idea. The hashing routine in this case would get the last three digits from the customer number. The record would then be written in the storage location identified by these three digits.

Two Records for One Disk Location

What happens when two customer numbers have the same last three digits? In figure B1.33, customer numbers 987123456 and 123987456 would cause this problem.

Programmers solve the problem by putting one record in location 456 and the other record in the next available spot. In figure B1.33 the next available location is 458. The computer would start looking for the record at the original location. If the record was not found there, the program logic would check the next storage location until the record was found. A new record needing location 458 would have to be placed in the next available spot.

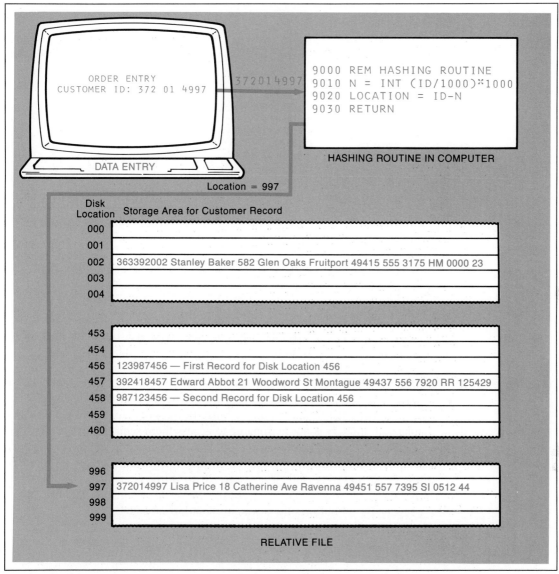

ORDER ENTRY
CUSTOMER ID: 372 01 4997

372014997

DATA ENTRY

```
9000 REM HASHING ROUTINE
9010 N = INT (ID/1000)*1000
9020 LOCATION = ID-N
9030 RETURN
```

HASHING ROUTINE IN COMPUTER

Location = 997

Disk Location	Storage Area for Customer Record
000	
001	
002	363392002 Stanley Baker 582 Glen Oaks Fruitport 49415 555 3175 HM 0000 23
003	
004	
453	
454	
456	123987456 — First Record for Disk Location 456
457	392418457 Edward Abbot 21 Woodword St Montague 49437 556 7920 RR 125429
458	987123456 — Second Record for Disk Location 456
459	
460	
996	
997	372014997 Lisa Price 18 Catherine Ave Ravenna 49451 557 7395 SI 0512 44
998	
999	

RELATIVE FILE

FIGURE B1.33

Data retrieval from a random file

This method of handling duplicate key values could seriously slow down the access time if the file was completely filled. Suppose the only remaining storage location is at position 995. If another key field 012 is entered, a lot of time will be spent checking each storage location between 012 and 995 looking for an empty storage space. For this reason, random files should never be more than 60 to 70 percent full.

Let's walk through all the steps a program would follow to find the record for customer number 372014997. First 372014997 is typed on a keyboard and transferred to the computer. Once there, the hashing routine in the computer program will get the last three digits—997.

File Organization	Advantages/Disadvantages
Sequential	Is simple to use. Is fast and efficient for large batches. Cannot update in middle of file.
Indexed Sequential	Can update in middle of file. Both sequential and direct processing are possible. Processing may be slow.
Random	Can update in middle of file. Processing is very fast. Has wasted file space.

FIGURE B1.34

Comparison of file organizations

The computer then checks disk storage location 997. If customer record 372014997 is located there, the record will be processed. If not, the next record will be read, and so on, until the desired record is found.

Pros and Cons to Random Files

Using a random file allows the fastest possible access to stored data. But it does have three disadvantages worth mentioning. First, records can only be accessed using the hashing routine. Since the records are out on the disk in a haphazard order, it is not reasonable to access them sequentially.

Second, it is hard to expand the file, since the hashing routine is designed around a specific file size. Third, as already mentioned, randomly organized files should never be full. Therefore, 20 to 30 percent of the disk space is wasted.

Figure B1.34 outlines the advantages and disadvantages to each of the file organizations.

STUDY OBJECTIVES

16. Define tape/disk library, Hollerith code, key field, update, data retrieval, direct access, and hashing routine.
17. Identify the responsibilities of a data librarian.
18. Describe how data is stored on cards, tapes, and disks.
19. Name one advantage to storing data on tape or disk instead of on cards.
20. Describe how records are organized in a sequential file.
21. Briefly explain the most efficient way of sequentially processing a data file.
22. Identify a situation in which sequential files do not provide fast data retrieval.

23. Describe a situation where direct accessing is needed.
24. Identify the only medium that allows data to be directly accessed.
25. Briefly describe direct accessing of an indexed sequential file organization using a key field.
26. Identify the primary advantage to using an indexed sequential file.
27. Briefly explain directly accessing a random file.
28. Identify one method for handling two records with duplicate key fields.
29. List the advantages and disadvantages of using random files.

FINDING DATA FILES ON TAPE OR DISK

Sue was angry with herself. She spent three hours at the pharmacy after school entering data but forgot which disk the customer file was stored on. In a hurry to get home, she had not labeled it. Luckily, the manual had a section on looking up files. As it turned out, one simple command to the computer let her display the names of all the files stored on a disk.

FIGURE B1.35

Sue McKnight trying to find the customer file on disk

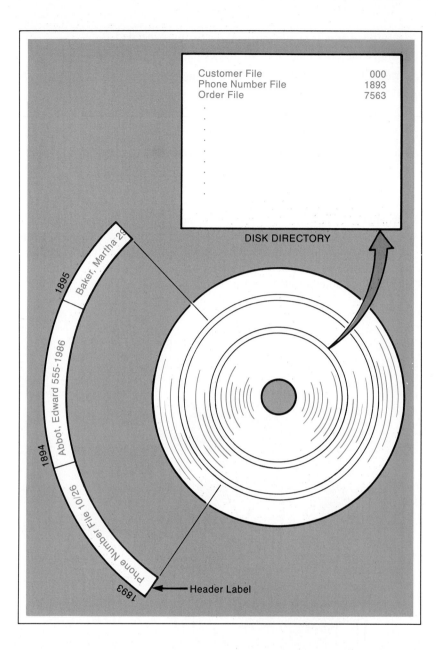

Customer File	000
Phone Number File	1893
Order File	7563

DISK DIRECTORY

Baker, Martha 28

1895

Abbot, Edward 555-1986

1894

Phone Number File 10/26

1893

Header Label

FIGURE B1.36

Finding data on disk using a directory and header label

Disk Directories and Header Labels

The list of files stored on a disk is called the **disk directory.** When a data file is recorded on disk, the computer automatically adds the file's name to the directory.

In addition, a label is placed in front of the file for identification. The label—called a **header label**—contains the file name and the date it was recorded on the disk. It is always placed in front of the file.

The file name and the storage location of the header label are stored in the directory. The directory is used later to find the file. Since the directory has the starting location of each file, files can be directly accessed from the disk.

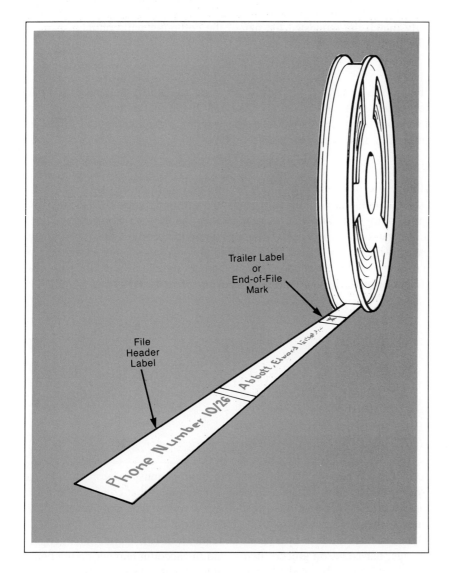

Trailer Label
or
End-of-File
Mark

File
Header
Label

Phone Number 10/26 Abbott, Elvard (what)...

FIGURE B1.37

Tape labels

Sue found another benefit provided by the directory. Every computer system allows the user to display the contents of the directory. This feature helped Sue locate the file she had entered on disk the night before.

A header label also precedes files on tape. For example, the header label shown in figure B1.37 is used by the computer to make sure the correct tape and file are being accessed.

When several files are stored on one tape, the file headers are sequentially accessed to find the requested file. If the name on the file header does not

Header Labels for Tape Files

exactly match the requested file name, the computer will continue searching until it finds an exact match.

Using Trailer Labels

Trailer labels or **end-of-file marks** are used to identify the end of the data. Programmers will write checks for the end-of-file marks into their programs. When the end-of-file mark is found, the program logic assumes that all records from the file have been processed.

Differences Between Manufacturers

While the use of labels is common on all tapes and disks, their format varies between manufacturers. This is one reason a tape or disk recorded using a TRS-80 microcomputer cannot be read by a Commodore microcomputer.

Equipment can be forced to write files without labels, but this is bad practice because it is easy to destroy data accidentally. Even if labels are absent, you still cannot use the Commodore microcomputer to read a TRS-80 tape or disk. Different bit patterns and recording frequencies make them incompatible.

STUDY OBJECTIVES

30. Define disk directory, header label, trailer label, and end-of-file mark.

31. Describe how a header label is used to find data on tape and disk.

32. Briefly explain why tape and disk are incompatible between different makes of computers.

SUMMARY

Before data can be prepared for computer input, it must be properly collected on source documents. These documents contain data that combines to form a record. A collection of records is called a file. When data from several files is frequently cross-referenced, it is combined into a database.

Data sometimes starts in a machine-readable form. Optical characters on sales tags, bar codes on grocery items, and the account number on the bottom of a check are machine-readable data. Environmental data can also be directly entered into a computer.

As data is input into a computer, it is converted to 0's and 1's called bits. The American Standard Code for Information Interchange is the 7-bit pattern used by microcomputers.

Output data is traditionally printed on reports or displayed on a CRT. It can also be photographically reduced and placed on film. Computers are even talking as a form of output.

Important data is stored on tape or disk for processing at a later time. Sequential files have data organized in key field order. This method can be used with cards, tapes, and disks but is slow when a few records are needed from a large file.

Indexed sequential files and random files on disk can have records directly accessed. To support this extra capability, indexes are used with indexed sequential files and a hashing routine is used with random files.

To locate files on tape or disk, a header is placed in front of each file. The end of the file is followed by a trailer label. In addition, disks have a directory of all the files stored on them. The computer uses the directory to find the beginning of the file.

CHAPTER B2

Computer Hardware

Except for people, computer hardware is the most visible part of a computer system. In the early days, hardware filled a large room. It generated enough heat to warm the building. A few years later, a machine just as powerful could sit on top of a desk.

The purchase of computer hardware was once the concern of corporate executives. Its operation was the responsibility of an entire staff of people. Today, computer hardware is sold in local retail stores and many students have access to it at home.

There is a certain mystery about hardware when people are first exposed to it. In the past, this mystery was often due to the fact that computer systems were hidden away in back rooms. Today, computers have come out from these back rooms to become a part of many people's working environment.

Let's explore computer-related hardware and examine the uses of each.

MARTHA BAKER'S PART-TIME JOB

It was a cool fall afternoon when Martha Baker first walked into the Computer Center. The nameplate on the door read DATA PROCESSING. Martha followed the personnel director into a brightly lit room and passed a keyboard-operated device.

FIGURE B2.1

Martha's new job

The computer was located in another room behind a double set of doors. It was bigger than the microcomputers at school, but not impressively large. Martha was introduced to a computer operator who was tearing a report off the printer.

"Well, Miss Baker, this is it," said the personnel director. "It may not be very big, but it does everything we ask it to. I'll leave you in George and Betty's care for now. Please stop by my office before you leave. Enjoy yourself."

Computer/Data Entry Operator

Martha was being trained as the second-shift computer/data entry operator at Jeans and Seams, Inc. A friend of her father's had arranged the job for her when she stopped playing basketball after school.

Jeans and Seams was a local chain of stores that specialized in casual clothes. The minicomputer was housed in the central warehouse downtown. All the data processing was done there. The data entry operator used key-to-disk equipment when preparing data for input.

The Computer System

The minicomputer supported a printer for reports with hard disk and tape for data storage. The data processing department was really just a three-person operation. The chief accountant for the company was in charge of the center. George the computer operator and Betty the data entry operator completed the staff.

The computer system currently handled payroll, updated inventory, and scheduled deliveries. These jobs took most of the day. Martha was hired because several new applications were being considered for the computer system. Right now she was expected to help with the current workload. Later, she would take on expanded duties.

George was going to train her to run the computer during a short second shift. Her work after school would eventually range from some data entry tasks to running reports using the minicomputer—called the mini.

Martha admitted in private that this was more responsibility than she had ever had.

PROCESSING HARDWARE

A minicomputer is processing hardware. Sometimes processing hardware is referred to as the **central processing unit** or **CPU.** Like all computers, it is composed of three units: **memory, control,** and **arithmetic/logic.** Before any processing starts, a program is loaded into the memory.

Loading a program into the computer means a copy of the program from tape or disk is placed into the memory unit. Once there, the control unit follows one instruction at a time. As data enters the computer, it is stored as bit patterns. Programs are stored in the same way.

The Memory Unit

Physically, memory units have stored data in many ways over the years. Figure B2.2 shows how older computers stored data using core storage. The integrated circuits (also shown in figure B2.2) represents newer memory technology. In every case, the internal circuits store characters as bit patterns of 1's and 0's.

The memory is quite limited when compared with disk or tape storage. Therefore, a computer's memory is used for temporary storage. The data and

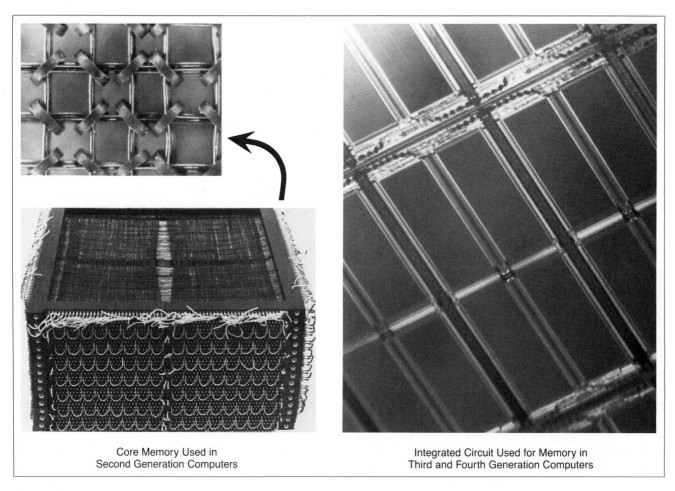

Core Memory Used in
Second Generation Computers

Integrated Circuit Used for Memory in
Third and Fourth Generation Computers

program are only stored there while the computer works with them. Once processing is completed, important data is copied to storage media. The original copy of the program remains on a storage medium, such as tape or disk, for later use.

Part of Martha's job as a computer operator was to make sure the correct programs and data were loaded into the computer's memory. Martha quickly learned that saying the computer had 997K memory meant it could hold about 997,000 characters, or bytes, in memory. To be more specific, a capital K stands for a **kilobyte,** or 1024 bytes of memory.

The Arithmetic/Logic Unit

The arithmetic/logic unit (also called the A/L unit) contains the circuitry that performs calculations and comparisons. Today, the contents of the A/L unit can be placed on part of a small silicon chip as shown in figure B2.3.

The A/L unit is not unlike a calculator in its ability to add, subtract, multiply, and divide. The A/L unit can also work with alphabetic and special characters. It can compare two numbers or letters to see if one is greater than, less than, or equal to the other.

The Control Unit

The control unit is a little like an orchestra conductor. It coordinates the activities of the computer by following a score—the program. One instruction at a time is brought into a limited storage area called a **register.** There the control unit analyzes the instruction and performs the desired action.

The control unit brings data in and out of memory. As data enters the memory, the control unit stores each character in its own memory slot. A 997K machine has approximately 997,000 memory slots.

Each slot is identified by a unique number or **address.** The instruction in the control unit identifies the storage addresses to be used. In this way, data can be located and transferred to the A/L unit or output device.

Example IPO Cycle

Think how you add two numbers using a calculator. You press 101, then +, and then 22. As soon as you press the = key, the result is displayed. To add a series of numbers together, you repeat this process, even though just the numbers change. In each case, they are to be added together.

On the other hand, the computer program in figure B2.4 will repeat the process with less work if the following steps are taken:

1. The program is loaded into memory.
2. The computer operator instructs the control unit to follow the instructions. This is done on a microcomputer by entering RUN.
3. The control unit now takes over and accepts the data—101 and 22—from the keyboard or storage medium. The data is first stored in memory.
4. The numbers are then transferred to the A/L unit with the instruction to add the two numbers.
5. The answer—123—is transferred back to memory.
6. Finally, the control unit sends the results to the screen, where the answer is displayed.

This process can be repeated many times. Our part as users is minor. At the most, we enter the data through the keyboard. If the data is already on disk, the operator just loads the program, checks that the correct disk is ready for input, and types RUN.

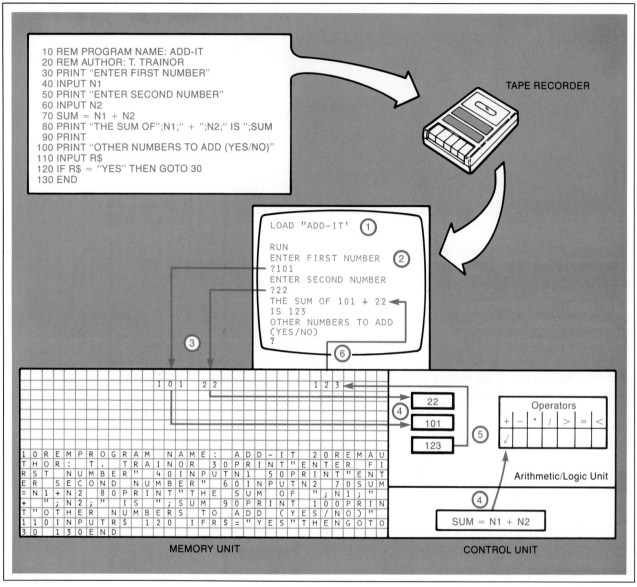

```
10 REM PROGRAM NAME: ADD-IT
20 REM AUTHOR: T. TRAINOR
30 PRINT "ENTER FIRST NUMBER"
40 INPUT N1
50 PRINT "ENTER SECOND NUMBER"
60 INPUT N2
70 SUM = N1 + N2
80 PRINT "THE SUM OF";N1;" + ";N2;" IS ";SUM
90 PRINT
100 PRINT "OTHER NUMBERS TO ADD (YES/NO)"
110 INPUT R$
120 IF R$ = "YES" THEN GOTO 30
130 END
```

TAPE RECORDER

```
LOAD "ADD-IT'   (1)

RUN
ENTER FIRST NUMBER   (2)
?101
ENTER SECOND NUMBER
?22
THE SUM OF 101 + 22
IS 123
OTHER NUMBERS TO ADD
(YES/NO)
?
```

(3)   (6)

| 101 | 22 | | 123 |

(4) 22
(4) 101
     123

Operators

+	−	*	/	>	=	<
√						

(5)

Arithmetic/Logic Unit

```
10REMPROGRAM  NAME:  ADD-IT  20REMAU
THOR:  T.  TRAINOR  30PRINT"ENTER  FI
RST  NUMBER"  40INPUTN1  50PRINT"ENT
ER  SECOND  NUMBER"  60INPUTN2  70SUM
=N1+N2  80PRINT"THE  SUM  OF";N1;"
+";N2;"  IS  ";SUM  90PRINT  100PRIN
T"OTHER  NUMBERS  TO  ADD  (YES/NO)"
110INPUTR$  120  IFR$="YES"THENGOTO
30  130END
```

(4) SUM = N1 + N2

MEMORY UNIT   CONTROL UNIT

FIGURE B2.4

Loading and running a simple BASIC program

STUDY OBJECTIVES

1. Define CPU, K, kilobyte, register, and address.
2. Identify what must happen before any computer processing starts.
3. Briefly describe the function of the three units within a computer.

COMPUTER SIZE

The Jeans and Seams job was Martha's first contact with a minicomputer. Up until now, she had only used the microcomputers—micros—at school. Certain

FIGURE B2.5

Martha using microcomputer in school

differences between the computers were easy to see. The minicomputer was larger. It also relied on different equipment for input and output. The micro at school entered data right into the machine through a keyboard and used a floppy disk for permanent storage. Jeans and Seams used floppy disks for input.

On the other hand, many things were similar. Martha found that it was easy to learn how to put paper on the printer. The floppy disk drives here and at school worked the same way. Running programs on the minicomputer was also the same, except that there were a few extra commands she had to know.

The microcomputers Martha used at school are relatively new to the industry. Sometimes called home or personal computers, they can be very inexpensive. As a matter of fact, micros are purchased by many businesses.

While microcomputers are relatively inexpensive, they are capable of performing many tasks that were once handled by bigger and more expensive computer systems. Microcomputers continue to expand in capacity, narrowing the difference between themselves, minicomputers, and mainframes.

Microcomputers

Apple III

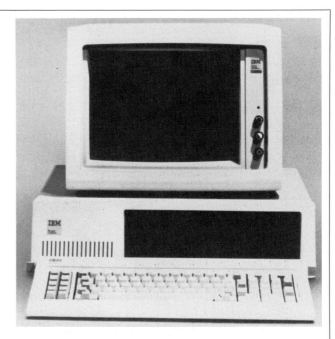

IBM Personal Computer

Commodore VIC 64

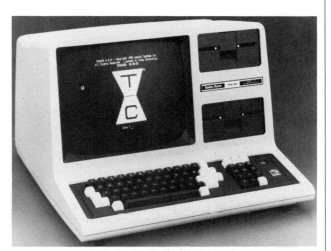

Radio Shack TRS-80 Model 4

FIGURE B2.6

Popular microcomputers (Courtesy Apple Computer, Inc.; IBM Corporation; Commodore Computer Systems; and Radio Shack, a division of Tandy Corporation)

Micros usually have a keyboard for data entry, a CRT to display output, and a tape drive to store data. A floppy disk drive is often used instead of a tape drive because of its ability to directly access data from disk. Some microcomputer systems even use hard disk drives when large amounts of data need to be stored.

Microcomputers are sometimes dedicated to one job. Word processors, cash registers, and even navigational computers can be micros. In other situations, they can perform a variety of jobs, depending on the applications program loaded into the memory. Usually, microcomputers finish running one program before another program is started.

As users have become more experienced with microcomputers, they have demanded more from the computers and supporting software. This demand in turn has promoted the development of more powerful microcomputers.

Minicomputers

Minicomputers have become much more than an inexpensive alternative to larger computers. Today, the amount of memory available in many minicomputers is measured in millions of characters instead of thousands. A capital M represents one **megabyte** or 1 million characters of storage.

This additional memory, together with special systems programs, lets a minicomputer handle more than one job at a time. This capability is referred to as **multiprogramming.** With multiprogramming, the computer still works on one program at a time. However, if the computer must wait for data when

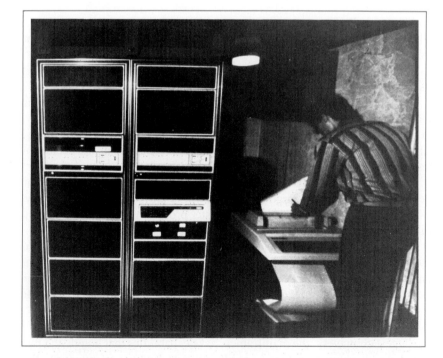

DEC minicomputer system (Courtesy Digital Equipment Corporation)

FIGURE B2.8

Minicomputer and computer operator
Martha Baker

working with the first program, it can switch processing to a second program. When the data for the first is received, it then switches back and continues processing.

Not all minicomputers have multiprogramming capabilities. However, the faster processing speeds of these machines make it useful when available.

It is not uncommon to find floppy and hard disk drives attached to a minicomputer along with a couple of tape drives. Tapes and floppy disks provide an inexpensive way of copying important programs and data. These copies are called backup. The backup copies are used when the originals are accidentally destroyed.

Many medium-sized businesses use minicomputers. Sometimes, several minis are used instead of one large computer. Minis are also used extensively in research and by draftspeople. Here the faster processing speeds help to handle millions of calculations or data manipulations.

Increased memory size, faster processing speeds, and multiprogramming make minis more expensive than micros. Their prices range from a little more than a microcomputer to several hundred thousand dollars. Many companies prefer to lease minicomputers rather than buy them. Few individuals can afford to own one.

Mainframe Computers

The largest computers, the mainframes, have capabilities that boggle the mind. They have superfast processing speeds and vast amounts of memory. These features allow mainframes to handle input and output from banks of disk drives.

Also, communications capabilities allow them to be in contact with other remote **terminals** and computers. A terminal has a keyboard and either a CRT or a typewriter mechanism for output. It may have a memory but no A/L unit or control unit.

Transferring data between terminals or computers using telephone lines is called **teleprocessing.** A ticket reservation system for an airline uses a mainframe's teleprocessing ability and large storage capacity. Computers and terminals from hundreds of different travel agencies call into one mainframe. The mainframe must then keep track of each request and update flight information kept in files on disk.

The U.S Weather Bureau also uses the mainframe's fast processing speeds for forecasting the weather. In analyzing the data from satellites and hundreds of weather stations, forecasters need computers that can process millions of instructions per second. The machine in figure B2.9 is like the computer used by the U.S. Weather Bureau. Some people even call it a supercomputer.

Multiprogramming can be taken one step further with mainframes and some minis. Sophisticated systems programs allow a computer to share its time between different programs in memory. This is called **timesharing.** Each program in memory is given a portion of the computer's time.

With multiprogramming, one program has priority over the others. In a timesharing system, the computer quickly alternates between the programs. It appears to the user that his or her program is being worked on all the time.

Timesharing is effective when the computer has enough memory and

FIGURE B2.9

Cray mainframe computer similar to the one used for weather forecasting by the U.S. Weather Bureau (Courtesy Cray Research, Inc.)

processing speed to support all the users' terminals. If not, the time it takes to get results back—**response time**—slows down and the users are unhappy.

Mainframes and their supporting hardware and software are very expensive. They are so expensive that they are usually obsolete before they are paid for. Since most organizations want to keep up with the latest technology, mainframes are usually leased instead of purchased. The organization then has the option of getting newer equipment when renewing the lease.

STUDY OBJECTIVES

4. Define M, megabyte, backup, terminal, teleprocessing, and response time.

5. Identify one feature that distinguishes each of the three sizes of computers.

6. Describe the difference between multiprogramming and timesharing.

INPUT HARDWARE

"Now, this is fun and easy," thought Martha as her fingers punched the keys. The typing class she took during her freshman year was really paying off now. The data entry part of her new job was a breeze.

The first-shift data entry operator would leave Martha a note whenever she

FIGURE B2.10

Typing class pays off for Martha when working as a data entry operator

needed help. The note outlined any special procedures Martha might have to follow. These procedures were usually straightforward. For instance, certain data might have to be verified to make sure it contained only numbers. Other items could not exceed a certain length. Usually, she was instructed to use a special file name with a new floppy disk.

Martha was preparing data for entry offline. Offline means away from the computer. There was a time when all data was prepared offline. With early computers, data was placed on machine-readable media such as punched cards. Then a card-reading device called a card reader input the data into the computer's memory for processing.

Cards and tapes are still used in some centers for data entry. Data is prepared on keypunches or **key-to-tape equipment.** A Key-to-tape machine like the one in figure B2.11 uses a keyboard to enter data. A keypunch punches the Hollerith code onto the card columns as the keys are struck. Key-to-tape equipment magnetizes spots on cassettes or reels of tape.

Cards, keypunches, and card readers are being phased out in many places for several reasons. First, it is easy to lose or destroy a single card from a card deck. Second, cards are bulky and inefficient when compared with storing the same amount of data on tape or disk. Finally, card readers are slower than tape or disk drives.

The **key-to-disk equipment** Martha was using at Jeans and Seams served the same purpose. As Martha typed on the keyboard, data was magnetized on

Using Card, Tape, and Disk Equipment

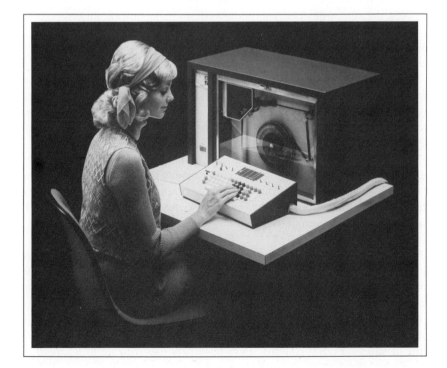

A data entry operator using a key-to-tape machine (Courtesy Mohawk Data Sciences)

Data Entry at Jeans and Seams

a disk. When things got rushed during the day, Martha was asked to enter data during her shift.

A truckload of jeans arrived late one Wednesday. The company wanted to deliver to the stores as soon as possible. First, data about the new shipment had to be added to the inventory file. To do this, Martha keyed the style, size, fabric, and color of each group of jeans onto a floppy disk. She was able to use the key-to-disk device while another program was running on the computer.

When done, Martha left the floppy disk and original shipping documents for the day operator. The day operator would verify that Martha had correctly entered the shipment by entering the data into the key-to-disk device a second time. The key-to-disk equipment would check the entry with the data Martha placed on the disk. If it did not match, the device would indicate that a mismatch existed. After verification, the floppy disk would be put into a floppy disk drive by a computer operator. A program would then update the inventory file and the jeans would be sent to the stores.

Tapes and disks provide an easy way to store data. Still, many organizations are looking for ways to minimize their use of key-operated devices. The manual process of entering data through a keyboard is usually the slowest step in the IPO cycle. Take Jeans and Seams, for example. First they had to wait for Martha to enter the data on disk. Then the day operator had to verify the work. If the data could be entered as it arrives at the warehouse, a lot of work could be avoided.

Avoiding Data Entry Delays

The problem that Jeans and Seams had with data entry delays is a common one. New data entry devices and online systems make other solutions possible.

Voice Input

Voice input is now possible. With these devices, an employee working on the loading dock could tell the computer what items were being unloaded.

Some word processors are also using voice input along with traditional keyboard entries. The operator speaks into the machine as data is entered. Right now, the operator is limited to a small number of words. Only one- or two-word commands like "center," "left justify," or "new page" are currently used.

Systems like these must be programmed to an individual's voice. To do this, the operator must first read to the computer the list of key words he or she will be using. The computer then matches these commands to the desired actions. The problem is that another worker cannot use the system until that worker has also read in all the commands.

Scanners and Readers

Other systems use light-sensitive scanners to input data directly. Answer sheets for college entrance exams are read by **optical scanners.** These scanners shine a bright light on the sheets. Marks made by pencils are found and input into the computer.

Cash registers are often computer terminals. By placing terminals in the store, data is input into a computer as sales are made. These systems are called **point of sales—POS**—systems. POS terminals like the one in figure B2.12

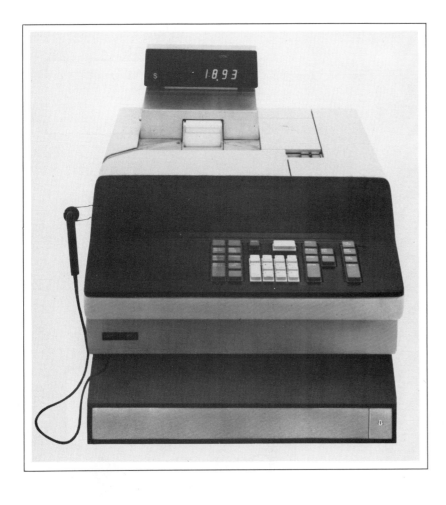

POS terminal with scanner (Courtesy IBM Corporation)

have scanners for machine-readable source documents. Using the scanner speeds up checking out while reducing errors.

In most cases, the scanner does not pick up the price. Instead, the optical characters or bar code contain an item identification number. This number is then used as the key field for the inventory file.

Figure B2.13 shows the steps used to print your bill.

1. The bar code identifying the key field—in this case the inventory number— is input into the system using a scanner.

2. The computer accesses the inventory file, looking for the record with a matching key field.

3. When a match is found, the description and unit price are transferred back to the computer.

4. From the computer, the data is transferred back to the POS terminal.

5. The sales price and tax are figured.

6. The sales price, tax, and description are then printed on the customer's bill.

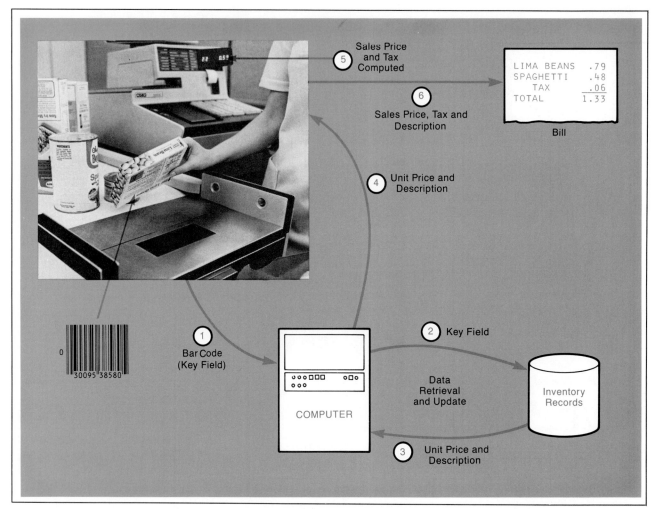

Data entry using a bar code scanner

This method allows the stores to offer special sale prices without having to change each price tag. The record is also updated to take into account the sale in progress.

Figure B2.14 shows an MICR reader used by banks to pick up the magnetic patterns of the characters found at the bottom of checks. A checking account number is one of the numbers found there. The amount of the check is also found on canceled checks. The account number is used to find the current checking balance on disk.

Other Data Entry Options

A push-button telephone also allows direct access to a computer. Credit checks are now made by using a telephone in this way. A special telephone number is dialed, followed by a credit card number. Each button on the telephone makes a different sound, and these sounds can be identified as the numbers of the credit card. The sound generated by the telephone is then used as input. The record is found and the current credit limit identified.

FIGURE B2.14

This MICR reader can process up to 100,000 checks an hour (Courtesy Bank of Montreal)

Scanners and telephones are used to get data directly into the computer. They can do it without having to first put data on a disk or tape.

There are other times when people want to avoid data entry delays. Do you think computer games would be very popular if each move had to be put on disk before it could be entered? Instead, video games use a **joystick** or **mouse**

FIGURE B2.15

Authorization of credit card purchase using the telephone (Courtesy First Interstate Bancorp)

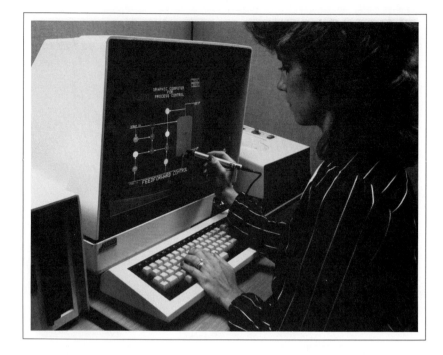

to move items around the screen. These devices allow direct input into the computer. They are also used in other areas besides games. Draftspeople and architects use them to sketch drawings on CRTs.

Figure B2.16 shows a person with a device called a **light pen.** Light pens allow the user to identify items on a screen by touching the screen where the item is located. This eliminates the need to use the keyboard.

Using Environmental Data

You can see that data can be put straight into the computer by using light-sensitive, magnetic, or sound-sensitive devices. People working with visual data, like drawings or photographs, often have problems converting it into alphabetic or numeric input. One picture is worth a thousand words!

Digitizers

Digitizers have been developed to turn drawings and other visual data into machine-readable input. The input is often drawn—or traced—on a writing surface called a **tablet.**

A special pen is used to draw on the tablet's surface. Wires under the surface identify the location of the pen on the tablet. This data is then converted into mathematical locations and sent to the computer. In some cases, the image appears on the CRT as it is drawn on the tablet.

Figure B2.17 shows a tablet and pen attached to a computer for input. The digitizer is used by graphic artists, designers, draftspeople, and architects. After the original image has been digitized, changes can be made to the original without having to redraw it. As a matter of fact, each variation can be stored separately and compared later.

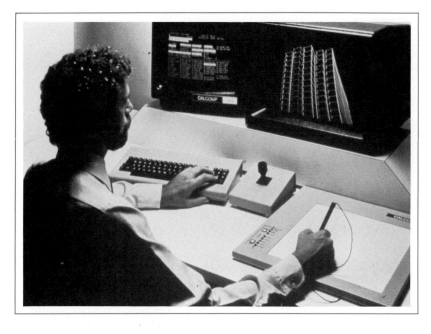

FIGURE B2.17

Draftsperson using a tablet for data entry. Note the joystick in the center of the picture (Courtesy Calcomp, Inc., Anaheim, California)

Digitizers have also been attached to cameras. Pictures are then digitized and sent to a computer. Weather satellites digitize pictures in order to send the data to land-based computers. Carnivals have sideshow attractions that take your picture, digitize it, and then place the image on a T-shirt.

Other environmental data is used by process control systems. The input may be to a lathe, a drill press, a blast furnace, machinery for an oil refinery, and so on. Measurements such as temperature, speed, or weight are taken by monitoring devices. The data is then analyzed by a computer system. If the results indicate that some type of adjustment is needed, a signal is sent to the machine and the change is made without human intervention.

The microwave oven in figure B2.18 is an example of a simple process control machine. It could be set to maintain a cooking temperature of 170°. A temperature probe—monitoring device—is slipped inside the food to measure the heat there. When the temperature falls below 170°, the microwave is turned on. It will stay on until the temperature again reaches 170°.

Monitoring devices can be sensitive to light, sound, pressure, and other environmental data. These devices continuously monitor conditions, and the computer constantly checks for changes.

Monitoring Devices

STUDY OBJECTIVES

7. Define offline, POS, and digitizer.
8. Describe the functions of a card reader, keypunch, key-to-tape equipment and key-to-disk equipment.
9. List three reasons why cards are being replaced as a way to store data.

Microwave oven and its process control circuitry (Courtesy Amana Refrigeration, Inc.)

10. Briefly describe why organizations are trying to minimize data entry with key-operated equipment.

11. Describe how voice input works and identify two limitations to using it.

12. Identify three types of machine-readable characters that are read by light scanners and give a use for each.

13. Briefly describe the steps used to print a bill using a point-of-sale system.

14. Explain how MICR readers and push-button telephones are used to input data.

15. Identify three methods of moving images around a screen besides using a keyboard.

16. Briefly describe how data is input using a digitizer and give two uses.

17. Identify two other input devices that use environmental data.

PETER CLARK'S FIRST FULL-TIME JOB

The obnoxious noise annoying everyone in the movie was Pete's beeper. He quickly left and called his service number from the lobby.

Two years out of high school, Peter Clark was making a good living as a **service technician** for a large computer manufacturer. Emergency calls like this were a part of the job. When a computer broke down in his territory, he was responsible for getting it back up and running.

Working as a Service Technician

This time a printer was the culprit. The night operator at Powers Electronics tried all the recommended troubleshooting procedures in the printer manual before calling. Several important reports still needed to be printed, but not tonight. Powers' service contract did not call for 24-hour service. If it did, Pete would have left immediately. Instead, he made plans to be there in the morning and went back to the movie.

Pete worked out of one of the company's branch offices. He was responsible for preventive maintenance and repairs to hardware in a region assigned to him by the branch manager.

The company required a high school diploma and trained him to repair their computers, disk drives, printers, and other hardware. His first six months on the job were spent in southern California at a training school. He would periodically go back for refresher courses and training on new equipment.

Being a service technician required him to be on the road a lot, but he did not mind the driving. They paid him well for time and mileage and it gave him an opportunity to relax between jobs.

Troubleshooting Problems

Pete walked into a madhouse the next morning. The unprinted reports were for a meeting with the president of the company. All morning he had the Data Processing Manager looking over his shoulder.

Various secretaries hustled in and out, asking if the printer was working yet. This type of excitement was not new to Pete. He was used to the uproar that surrounded the computer when it wasn't working.

Fortunately, most of his job was not like this. He usually scheduled visits to each center to perform routine maintenance checks on the equipment. The operators always knew in advance that he was coming and scheduled their work around maintenance.

But days like this were inevitable. Still, Pete had the printer up and running by 10 o'clock, and the reports were ready for the afternoon meeting.

Pete liked his job. It let him work on the newest equipment around. In addition, people appreciated what he did for them. It is ironic that so many equipment difficulties are due to mechanical rather than electronic problems.

STUDY OBJECTIVES

18. Describe two responsibilities of a service technician.

19. Identify the minimum educational requirements for a service technician.

OUTPUT HARDWARE: PRINTERS

Printers, like computers, range in size and capability. They are usually classified by print image, speed, and printing method. As always, cost is a factor when selecting a printer. At a minimum, they must be able to print the letters of the alphabet, numbers, and special characters.

Dot-Matrix Versus Letter-Quality Printers

The look of a report produced by a **dot-matrix printer** is quite different from that produced by a **letter-quality printer.** Letter-quality printers print a whole character like a typewriter. The characters printed by a dot-matrix printer are an array of dots—like the display on a scoreboard.

Some letter-quality printers used for word processing have a **daisy wheel** print mechanism. One character is attached to the end of each petal. Figure B2.20 shows a 96-petal daisy wheel capable of printing 96 characters. The wheels are removable. The operator selects the daisy wheel with the characters appropriate for the job.

FIGURE B2.20

Daisy wheel print mechanism (Courtesy Qume Corporation)

Print from a Letter-Quality Printer

Standard Print from a Dot-Matrix Printer

Correspondence Quality Print from a Dot-Matrix Printer

Dot-matrix printers are faster and less expensive than letter-quality printers. Figure B2.21 compares characters printed on a letter-quality printer with characters printed on a dot-matrix printer. The print of a dot-matrix printer is generally not considered professional quality.

To overcome this difference, several dot-matrix printers have **correspondence print modes.** In this mode, the printer types each line twice. The dots are printed just a little higher in the second pass, which fills the characters in. Figure B2.21 also shows characters printed using the correspondence mode. As you might suspect, the correspondence mode is slower.

Dot-matrix printers are often used with personal computer systems, where people are willing to sacrifice print quality for price.

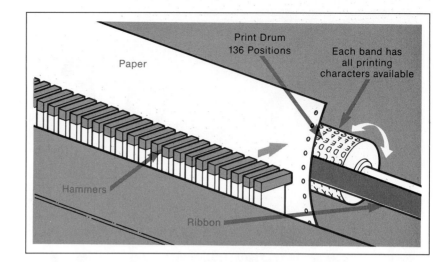

F I G U R E   B 2 . 2 2

Print drum of line printer

Serial Versus Line Printers

Printers are often classified by the amount of information they print at a time. When they print one character at a time like a typewriter, they are called **serial printers.** The daisy wheel printer is one example.

Serial printers operate at speeds from 15 to 200 characters per second. Some print in both directions so that time is not wasted in returning to the beginning of the line.

Line printers print a full line at a time. Figure B2.22 shows a sketch of a line printer that uses a print drum with 136 print positions. At each position is a band containing a complete set of characters.

When a line is printed, the band rotates to expose the correct character. The characters are then struck by hammers, causing the line to be printed. A printer like this operates at 300 to 2000 lines per minute. They are frequently used with minicomputers and mainframes, which need reliable and continuous operation from the printer.

Impact Versus Nonimpact Printers

Impact printers work by striking the paper through a ribbon. They can be very noisy and often have noise covers to quiet them. Daisy wheel printers and the line printer just described are impact printers.

When noise is a problem, **nonimpact printers** are used. Some nonimpact printers write on specially coated paper. This paper reacts to either heat (as with thermal paper) or electric impulses (electrostatic paper).

Other types of nonimpact printers spray the ink on paper (ink jet) or use xerography, which uses the same techniques as copy machines. The fastest printers are nonimpact printers using lasers.

Impact and nonimpact printing methods have their advantages and disadvantages. Impact printers can make several carbon copies along with the original, but they are noisy. Nonimpact printers are quiet, and some are much faster than impact printers. But they cannot make more than one copy at a time.

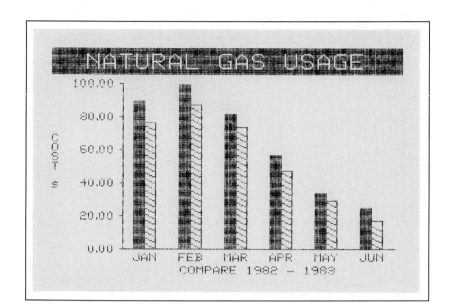

FIGURE B2.23

Bar graph from a dot-matrix printer

Speeds as high as 21,000 lines per minute are possible with laser printers. Because of their faster speeds, it is likely that nonimpact printers will be used more and more in the future.

Special printers are available to print graphic output. A few dot-matrix printers can print simple charts and diagrams and some even print in color.

These graphics printers are still limited to images that can be represented by rows and columns of dots. They can do a fine job reproducing a bar graph like the one in figure B2.23. Unfortunately, as shown in figure B2.24, they have a difficult time printing images with rounded shapes.

Graphics Printers Versus Plotters

FIGURE B2.24

Rounded surfaces on a dot-matrix printer

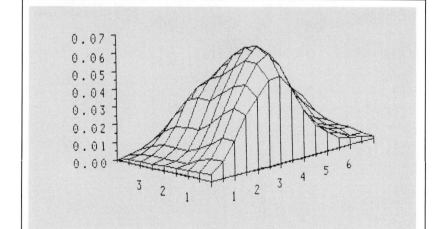

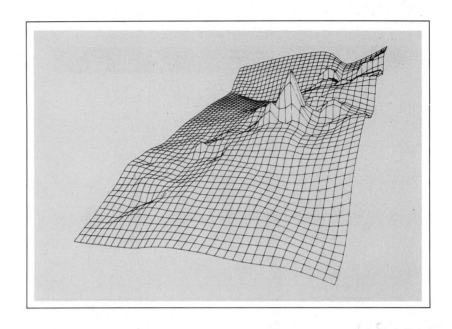

FIGURE B2.25

Three-dimensional image produced by plotter (Courtesy Calcomp, Inc., Anaheim, California)

FIGURE B2.26

Three-pen drawing mechanism for a plotter (Courtesy Calcomp, Inc., Anaheim, California)

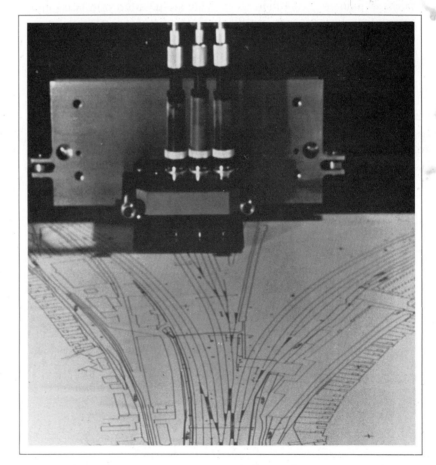

HARDWARE

More and More for Less and Less

Today's fastest printers use laser technology to print over a hundred *pages* a minute.

THE INPUT-PROCESS-OUTPUT/STORE CYCLE

For most systems, the processing of data involves four fundamental functions. Data is *input* to the computer, it is *processed*, results are *output*, and data is *stored* in computer-sensible form. Computer hardware can be classified according to these four primary functions.

Input hardware transforms data from a physical (often human-readable) form into a magnetic or electronic form. *Processing hardware* transforms data into desired results. *Output hardware* transforms results from an electronic form into human-readable form. Finally, *storage hardware* saves data, in magnetic form, for subsequent processing. Do not confuse storage hardware with input and output hardware. Although storage hardware performs both input and output functions, it does not transform the data into a physical, human-readable form. Rather, it saves the data in *magnetic* form.

As the following pages illustrate, there is an incredible variety of hardware, much of which serves the same function. Why? Hardware varies in speed, capacity, quality, and cost. When selecting hardware, the purchaser needs to know the system's requirements in order to buy sufficient (but not excessive) speed, capacity, and quality.

Data **Input** using a terminal and modem.

Processing by a popular Hewlett-Packard minicomputer.

The Input, process, output/store cycle.

Store

Input

Process

Output

Repeat Cycle

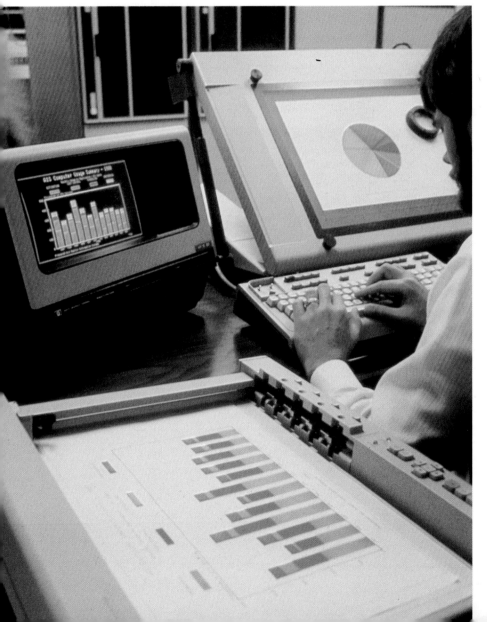

Storage in multiple disk units can accommodate large amounts of data.

Output in several forms is viewed by a user as he enters data.

KEYBOARD INPUT

Keyboard input hardware requires a person to key the data. Generally, the keyboard is similar to that of a typewriter. A cathode-ray tube (CRT) is usually used for displaying data.

Keyboard hardware can be online or offline. If it is *online*, the keyboard is connected directly to a computer. Data flows from the key device straight to the processing computer. If it is *offline*, the keyboard device produces a magnetic tape or disk. The tape or disk is later read by a tape or disk unit that is connected to the processing computer.

Some keyboard terminals contain a microprocessor. If so, they are called *smart* or *intelligent* terminals. There is a wide range in intelligence, depending on the power of the microprocessor contained in the terminal. The advantage of an intelligent terminal is that it lessens the communication between the terminal and the processing computer, as well as reducing the computer's workload. The disadvantage is that smart terminals are more expensive.

There are two types of keyboard operators. A *production data entry operator* works full time keying data. Such operators enter data for many different applications. Generally, data to be input arrives in large batches according to a schedule. Production data entry operators work in the data entry department, which is usually part of computer operations.

This "intelligent" terminal displays a graph of an acoustical signal.

Today's banks utilize online data entry for accurate and current information.

The second type of keyboard operator is the *end-user* operator. An end user generally does not work full time keying data. Rather, keying data is only part of the end user's job. A bank teller using an online terminal is an example of an end-user operator. Although end users employ computer equipment in their jobs, they are not assigned to the data processing department. Rather, end users work for another part of the organization. Bank tellers report to the head teller, not to the manager of data processing.

Many organizations prefer end-user data entry. The end users feel that they have greater control when they do their own data entry. They also must live with their own mistakes, and, consequently, some companies find that the accuracy of data is higher when it is entered by end users.

Data entry using keyboards is very error prone. A production data entry operator may key hundreds of documents in a single day. Unfortunately, correct computer processing requires accurate input data: "garbage in, garbage out." Therefore, procedures to verify the accuracy of data input are crucial. Such procedures might involve, for example, manually counting the number of documents processed and comparing this count with a computer-calculated count, or adding, by hand, the amounts of all orders and comparing this sum to a computer-produced sum.

Key-to-disk data entry.

An end user inputs data from his desk.

Production data entry clerks are employed by companies with continuous data entry needs.

Keyboard input devices are too slow for some applications. A variety of other, special-purpose devices has been developed.

Terminals have a *cursor* that shows the user's position on the screen. The cursor might be a blinking underscore, a highlighted square, or some other, similar character. Moving the cursor around the screen takes time. Most terminals have special keys for up/down, left/right movement, but, even with these keys, cursor movement can be slow and cumbersome. A *mouse* is a hand-held device for moving the cursor more quickly. The user moves the mouse around on a level surface, and the cursor moves correspondingly. Moving the mouse left causes the cursor to move left, moving it back (away from the user) causes the cursor to move up the screen, and so forth.

A *light pen* is another device that reduces cursor movement and keystrokes. Using a light pen, the user simply points the pen to the desired spot on a screen and pushes a button. The terminal senses where the light pen is located and responds accordingly. Light pens are often used to select options from a menu on a screen. The user points the pen to the menu item desired. With some terminals, the user can actually draw on the screen using the light pen.

Data entry using a light pen.

UPC (uniform product code) *bar codes* are used on grocery products. The pattern of bars corresponds to an item number. The sensing device sends the number to a computer for processing. UPC codes save time not only for the clerk, but also for the people who would otherwise mark prices on the items. Further, the grocery store can change prices with minimal effort.

Digitizers sense marks on a document and convert those marks to digital data (whole numbers). Digitizers are used in the medical profession for storing X-ray pictures magnetically.

Other, similar devices are *mark-sense form readers*, which read the exams that you mark with a number 2 pencil, and *MICR* (magnetic-ink character recognition) *devices*. MICR characters are printed with magnetic ink. The magnetism is sensed by the MICR equipment when the document is read. MICR documents are used primarily in the banking industry.

The "mouse" in the lower corner controls the movement of a cursor on the screen.

A scanner uses a low-grade laser to sense UPC bar codes in this grocery store.

A digitizer transforms graphic input into a digital format.

PROCESSISNG, HARDWARE, AND ENVIRONMENTS

Processing equipment includes the central processing unit (CPU) and main memory. There are three common types of CPUs: microcomputers, minicomputers, and mainframes. The characteristics of the three types of processors are summarized in the chart at the end of this essay.

Main memory consists of thousands of on/off devices. Each on/off device represents one *binary digit* or *bit*. A *byte* is a group of bits that represents a single character, such as *A* or *7*. Most computers have 8 bits per byte, although a few have 6 bits per byte. The size of main memory is usually stated in bytes— for example, 64K bytes. Although people often say that 64K equals 64,000, in actuality, the letter *K* represents 1024. Thus, a 64K-byte memory actually has 65,536 bytes. Common memory sizes are 64K, 128K, 256K, 512K, 1024K, and multiples of 1024K.

In recent years, the distinction among the physical characteristics of micros, minis, and mainframes has become blurred. In fact, the mini category may disappear. Smaller minis have become indistinguishable from micros, and larger minis have become indistinguishable from mainframes. Even though the differences in physical characteristics of CPU types are disappearing, major differences remain in applications and environments.

Processing in a microcomputer is occurring within one small hardware unit.

Microcomputers tend to be used for two purposes. As personal assistants, micros are used for word processing, electronic spreadsheets, personal databases, simple graphics, and education. As communications devices, micros are used to connect users to a data source, such as a company's mainframe computer, or to a data utility (a company providing data, such as stock prices, for a fee). A majority of micro programs are acquired off-the-shelf. Most micros are single-user systems.

Minicomputers are used for online, interactive applications. They perform general business functions, such as order entry, general ledger, and the like. Minis are also used in the science and engineering fields for applications like the control and monitoring of scientific equipment and computer-assisted design and manufacturing (CAD/CAM). Minicomputers are also used in specialized applications, such as circuit switching in the telephone system.

A microcomputer environment—this Apple computer sits on a desk top.

A minicomputer environment—this Wang mini resides in secretarial office space.

Mainframe computers generally process large, massive jobs. They do batch processing for large companies, such as billing for credit cards and policy processing for insurance companies. Mainframes also handle large-scale online applications, such as airline reservations, where there may be thousands of terminals active at the same time. In science and engineering, mainframes are used to process computer jobs requiring very large amounts of memory or exceedingly fast computing. Weather forecasting is an example of a science application requiring mainframes.

Micros, minis, and mainframes also differ in the environment in which they reside. Micros are desk-top computers; they can sit on the desk of the end user. The operation and control of micros is informal. Micros are generally single-user systems.

Minicomputers are used in many different environments. Minis used for business applications usually reside in small computer rooms with controlled access. The terminals connected to the mini are usually in the same building, in close proximity to the CPU. When used for science, engineering, architectural, and similar applications, minis are located in the user's work area. They reside in a back room or other out-of-the way space. When used for special-purpose applications, such as circuit switching, the minicomputer may be packaged with other electronic equipment in a common cabinet.

Mainframes are showcase computers, although for security reasons they have disappeared from ground-floor window locations. Mainframes are locked into special-purpose rooms that have extra air conditioning and even water supplies for water-cooled CPUs. Terminals for mainframes may reside thousands of miles away from the computer.

Another minicomputer environment—this mini is within an engineering office environment.

A well-organized and highly trained operations staff runs a mainframe computer and related equipment. The workload of the computer is controlled by a preauthorized schedule. Mainframes are characterized by a formal and controlled operating environment.

The Digital Equipment VAX—a minicomputer with mainframe power—blurring the definition of processor types.

An Amdahl Computer in a mainframe environment—tended by professional operators in a locked room.

IBM's System 370 in a mainframe environment.

OUTPUT

Output equipment transforms results from electronic to physical form. One common output device is the CRT screen discussed under input devices. CRTs are used both to display data being input and to display results.

Printers are a common output device. *Line printers* print a line at a time. *Serial printers* print only a single character at a time. *Full-character printers* print a complete letter the way a typewriter does. *Dot-matrix printers* print letters composed of small dots. *Impact printers* press the character to be printed onto a ribbon and then onto the paper. *Nonimpact printers* do not touch the paper; ink is sprayed onto the paper or printed using a process like that of a copy machine.

How should a company choose among all of these alternatives? The answer depends on requirements. Each of these types of printers has advantages and disadvantages. Line printers are faster than serial printers, but the quality of print is usually not as good. The characters produced by a line printer are often uneven across the bottom. Full-character printers (sometimes called *letter-quality printers*) produce very attractive output, but they are expensive. Dot-matrix printers produce less attractive output, but they are cheaper. Nonimpact printers are quiet and very fast; they are also expensive. Impact printers are noisy, but they are cheaper than nonimpact printers. Impact printers can also produce carbon copies, whereas nonimpact printers cannot.

Line printers produce output at a very high speed.

This graphics plotter displays building floor plans.

Computer paper is bulky and expensive. As an alternative, some companies produce reports on microfilm and microfiche. Generally, this procedure is done *offline*. In this mode, the computer program produces a magnetic tape containing the desired report. The tape is removed from the processing computer and mounted on a special-purpose machine. This machine reads the tape and photographs the report onto microfilm or microfiche. The special-purpose machine is expensive, and some companies use a service bureau for microphotography. They send the magnetic tape to the service bureau and receive the microfilm or microfiche back.

Voice output is emerging as a form of computer output. In its simplest form, a prerecorded message is selected and played. Examples are automobiles that instruct drivers to turn off the lights or inform them that the fuel level is low.

Microfiche imaging displays microfilm data, making it easier and less costly to store and retrieve.

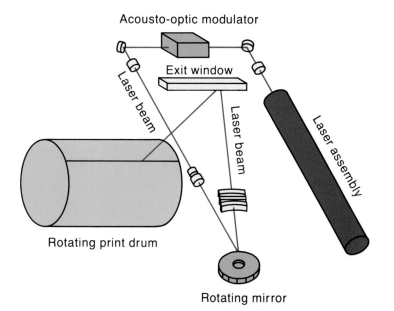

Acousto-optic modulator

Exit window

Laser beam

Laser beam

Laser beam

Laser assembly

Rotating print drum

Rotating mirror

A laser printer. Software turns the laser beam on and off and provides "bit maps"—dot-by-dot instructions for the laser, telling it to create a dark spot or leave it blank. The rotating 18-sided mirror spins at thousands of revolutions per minute and reflects the beam onto a rotating print drum.

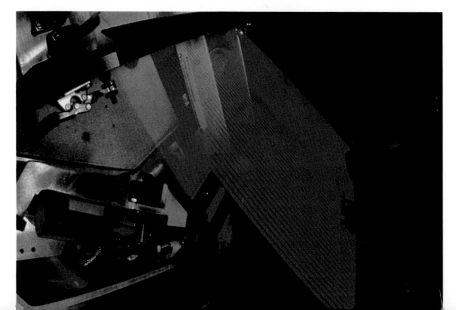

Laser beams scan across a print drum to create text and graphics at speeds up to 20,000 lines per minute.

Some data must be stored because it is needed more than once. For example, for a payroll system, employee name, address, pay rate, and other data are needed every pay period. Such data cannot be left in the computer's main memory for several reasons. First, main memory is very expensive and, for the largest computers, is limited to 32 million bytes (which may sound large, but even small companies need more than that). Further, main memory is volatile. When the power is shut off, the contents of main memory are lost. Thus, computers need *secondary storage* that is less expensive and larger than main memory, as well as nonvolatile.

There are two fundamental types of secondary storage equipment. Sequential devices allow only sequential access to the data. To access the 50th record in a file, the first 49 records must first be read. Furthermore, additions can only be made to the end of a sequential file.

Magnetic tape is the most common sequential storage device. A variety of tape devices is available. The most common device uses tape that is similar to stereo tape but is ½ inch wide. Some microcomputer systems do use stereo tape, however. Tape is inexpensive; a 2400-foot reel of ½-inch tape can be purchased for $15. Because tape is cheap, it is often used for backup storage. Data that resides on other types of secondary storage is off-loaded onto tape until it is needed.

Multiple disk storage at a large computer center.

Magnetic tapes provide an inexpensive method of storing data.

The second type of secondary storage is direct-access storage. Direct-access data can be accessed in any order. The 50th record can be obtained directly, without reading the first 49 records.

There are two common types of direct-access devices. Hard, or conventional, disks consist of several circular recording surfaces mounted on a spindle. The surfaces rotate under read/write heads. Data is recorded in concentric circles called *tracks*. Floppy disks, or diskettes, are single, flexible recording surfaces. Data is written in similar tracks on either one or both sides of the floppy.

A mass storage system is a combination of direct-access and sequential storage. Data is stored on rolls of magnetic tape. When the data is needed, it is staged to direct-access devices for processing. Later the data is destaged to the rolls of magnetic tape.

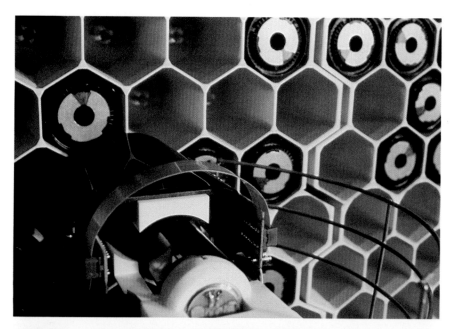

The manufacturing of a disk surface.

Mass storage can resemble a honeycomb.

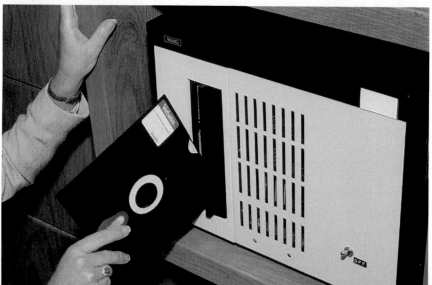

A cleaning disk is inserted into a disk drive.

COMPARISON OF MICRO, MINI, AND MAINFRAME COMPUTERS

	Microcomputer	Minicomputer	Mainframe Computer
Main Memory (1000 bytes)	32–1000	2000–8000	8000–32,000
Instruction Speed (millions per second)	0.25	1–4	8–16
Disk Storage (bytes)	5–20 million	up to 1 billion	up to 20 billion
Cost	$1000–$10,000	$50,000–$250,000	$500,000–$10 million +
Notes	Usually single-user Minimum vendor support	Single-or Multi-user Often sold by OEMs	Multi-user Sold by vendor Extensive support

QUESTIONS

1. Name and describe the four fundamental functions of processing data.
2. Describe the difference between online and offline data entry.
3. Describe the difference between production data entry and end-user data entry.
4. What steps can be taken to compensate for the error-prone nature of data entry?
5. Explain the use of *cursor*, *mouse*, and *light pen*.
6. Describe two keyboard data entry devices.
7. Describe two nonkey data entry devices.
8. Distinguish among the hardware characteristics of micros, minis, and mainframes.
9 Distinguish among the processing environments of micros, minis, and mainframes.
10. Explain the difference between:
    a. Line and serial printers
    b. Full-character and dot-matrix printers
    c. Impact and nonimpact printers
11. Describe the two fundamental types of storage hardware.
12. What is a mass storage system?

Plotters are used when the graphic output must be crisp and continuous. Pens are used to draw the images. Often, different colored pens are used to make drawings. Spectacular three-dimensional images, like the one in figure B2.25, can also be printed.

In figure B2.26, the pens on a plotter are suspended over the paper. They can then move back and forth along the track to draw a straight line. The paper also moves. Circles and other complex images are created by coordinating the movement of the pen and the paper underneath.

20. Define daisy wheel, serial printer, and line printer.
21. Identify three ways of classifying printers and the minimum requirements for a printer.
22. Describe how letter-quality and dot-matrix printers work, and give an advantage to buying either one.
23. Explain how a correspondence print mode works.
24. List and describe five nonimpact printing methods.
25. Identify advantages and disadvantages to using impact and nonimpact printers.
26. Briefly describe the difference between images produced with a dot-matrix graphics printer and images produced with a plotter.

OUTPUT HARDWARE: SCREEN DISPLAYS

The screen display of CRT terminals comes in many sizes and capabilities. A few are limited to one line of display. The standard screen used in businesses has 80 columns and 24 or 25 lines. At a minimum, a screen must be able to display the letters of the alphabet, digits from 0 through 9, and common special characters.

CRT terminals are also used for graphic displays. When you watch television you are looking at graphic images designed for screen displays. These terminals often use color to accent images.

Pixel Graphics

Physically, display terminals work either like a dot-matrix printer or like a plotter. The most frequently used displays will divide the screen into picture elements called **pixels.** The pixel makes up a dot matrix in which characters are formed by turning different dots on or off.

Pixel graphics work nicely on images that are easily represented by rows and columns of dots. As with dot-matrix printers, drawing clear, round images is difficult with pixel graphics. Therefore, the screen displays used in computer-assisted design systems and some arcade games use another method—**vector graphics.**

Vector Graphics

Drawing images on the screen using vector graphics is not limited to rows and columns. Lines can be drawn between any points on the screen. Like pen lines drawn by a plotter, the display is crisp and continuous.

F I G U R E   B 2 . 2 7

Letters on CRT are made up of dots—pixels (Courtesy Conrac Corporation)

F I G U R E   B 2 . 2 8

A drawing on tablet transformed into pixel graphics (Courtesy Conrac Corporation)

This graphic technique also lends itself to **dynamic displays** that allow movement. A graphic artist can design a chair and then rotate the image to view it from different sides. Advertisements on television make extensive use of dynamic displays. Cars spin out at you and tires roll across the screen.

STUDY OBJECTIVES

27. Define pixel and dynamic display.

28. Identify the dimensions of a standard screen display and the minimum display requirements.

29. Briefly describe the difference between pixel graphics and vector graphics.

ACTION HARDWARE

The industrial revolution placed people and machines side by side in the workplace. Computers now direct machines that broaden our control over the environment. These programmable machines perform many labor-intensive jobs. This trend will continue as hardware costs come down.

Robots

The ultimate in action hardware is the **robot.** Robots are not the human-looking machines of science fiction stories. Instead, they are often one or two multijointed arms controlled by a computer. Sometimes they can move from one place to another. Most often they stay in the same place.

Robots, like computers, can be programmed to perform many jobs. Cameras can be attached to robots to let them "see." Other robots use temperature, pressure, and other environmental data for input.

F I G U R E   B 2 . 3 0

Robots welding cars (Courtesy Chrysler Corporation)

Cars coming down the assembly line in figure B2.30 are being spot welded by robots. The same machines could be reprogrammed to paint the cars. This flexibility has a lot of people excited about using robots in manufacturing and other areas.

Robots are currently sheering sheep, delivering mail, and mining coal. They are used in underwater and space exploration. Each space shuttle is equipped with a robotlike arm that enables the astronauts to place research projects in space or to remove them.

Robots have the potential for becoming a standard tool in many factories. They represent the latest of a series of process control systems that have slowly revolutionized the way we manufacture things.

NC Machines

The metalworking industry has been using programmable tools for some time. Drill presses, lathes, and cutting machines can be under process controls known as **numerical control** or **NC.** An NC machine can be programmed to produce parts according to predefined measurements.

The output from NC machines is the action of the drill bit or cutting tool. The machinist who used to operate the machine now programs it. Once programmed, these machines are far more accurate than their human counterparts.

Medical Research

Computer-controlled output can range from welding a car on the assembly line to regulating a patient's heartbeat. The health fields are using computers to keep patient records, monitor patients, and even implant microprocessors inside patients. A pacemaker with a microprocessor could be considered a process control system.

Medical researchers are also experimenting with computers in artificial limbs. They are working to help paralyzed people walk again by having a computer stimulate leg muscles with small electrical shocks.

FIGURE B2.32

Medical researchers seeking ways to help paralyzed people walk by using computer technology (Courtesy Wright State University, Dayton, Ohio)

STUDY OBJECTIVES

30. Define NC machine.
31. Describe one feature of a robot that provides it with so much flexibility.
32. Identify three machines that can be numerically controlled and give one advantage to using them.
33. Identify two medically related applications for process control hardware.

FIGURE B2.33

Disaster strikes

STORAGE HARDWARE: NEED FOR BACKUP AND RECOVERY

Recovery Procedures

Disaster struck when Martha least expected it. She had removed disk packs from the disk drive dozens of times before. This time one slipped out of the dustcover, caught the corner of the table, and slammed onto the floor. The disk contained the employee master file along with other data. At first she thought nothing had happened, but luck was not on her side today. The top platter had bent when it hit the table.

One emotion after another crushed down on her. Finally, she composed herself and called George, the day operator. All he said at first was "Ho, ho, ho— that's a good one!" In the end, George saved the day. He came in and together they went over the necessary recovery procedures to get things back to normal.

First they identified the programs run since the last backup. They found that only the program to update the employee master file had been run. That is the job Martha had just finished when the accident occurred. They carefully copied the tape backup onto another disk and updated the employee master file again.

It was late in the evening when they finally finished. Everything was back to normal, except for Martha. She had a greater appreciation for the nightly backup procedures. Now she realized that it was one of her most important jobs. It used to bother her because it took so long to do every night. It would never bother her again!

Martha's slip could have caused big problems for Jeans and Seams. As it turned out, it only cost her and George a little extra time. Thanks to procedures, damaging the disk did not create more of a problem. Part of Martha's nightly shutdown procedures was to backup important disks on tape.

Tapes are often used to backup data on disk. Some computer systems are now using videotape as backup. Sometimes an organization will backup files and programs on another disk because disks have faster access speeds.

You can now see that tape and disk have several uses in a computer system. First, they permanently store the original data and programs. In addition, they store copies to make sure important data and programs are not accidentally lost.

Backup Procedures

---

34. Describe two reasons for storing data on tape and disk.

STUDY OBJECTIVE

STORAGE HARDWARE: TAPE DRIVES

A tape drive is just another name for a tape recorder/player used to store data. Microcomputer systems often use cassette tape drives.

These machines record on the same cassette tapes used in home and car stereo systems. They are inexpensive and therefore the easiest way to provide permanent storage. Larger computer systems use tape drives with reels of tape that hold more data.

Input and Output Using Tapes

Figure B2.34 shows a simple diagram of a tape drive for reels of tape. As the tape passes under the **read/write heads,** the magnetic spots are either sensed (read) or created (written). Typically, a tape unit will read or write one record at a time and then stop. This means that the tape moves forward in quick jerks. It reads one record and then stops; reads another record and then stops; and so on.

To give the machine time to stop, a gap is left between each record, just the way people leave gaps between songs when recording music on tape. The gap between records is called the **interrecord gap.** This gap may be half an inch or more in size.

You may have seen pictures of tape drives in movies or on television. Typically, the tape reels are shown whirling at great speed. That's because they are being rewound. Tape drives that are actually reading or writing data move in jerks—but apparently this is not dramatic enough for television.

Blocking Records

The tapes waste a lot of time stopping at each interrecord gap before continuing to the next record. To increase the reading and writing speeds, the number of gaps is reduced by grouping records together in **blocks.** This means that a block of records is read or written together as a unit.

Figure B2.35 shows a tape with eight records to a block, or a **blocking factor** of 8. The number of records in a block is the blocking factor. The interrecord gap is now called an **interblock gap.** It still remains the same size.

You might be wondering why there are any gaps at all. Why not compress the data into one long block? The reason is that a block is read into memory in its entirety. A portion of the memory for temporary storage—called a **buffer—**

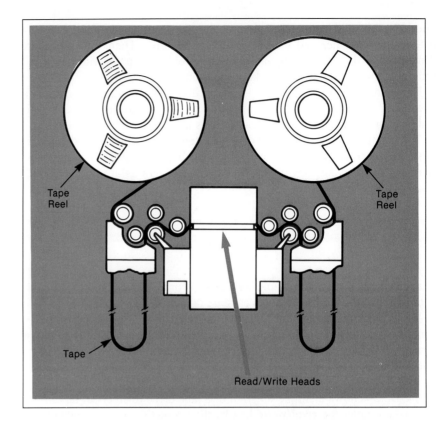

Diagram of a tape drive

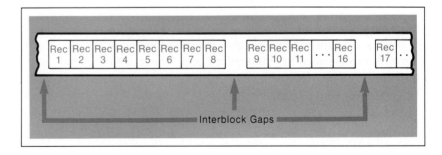

Diagram of tape with a blocking factor
of 8

must be set aside. The buffer stores the block as it comes from tape. If the block contained a file with 200,000 records, each with 120 characters, a buffer for 24 million bytes would have to be set aside.

Even the largest mainframes do not have that much memory for a buffer. Therefore, records are usually blocked into more manageable units, such as 1000 or 2000 bytes.

35. Define interrecord gap, block, blocking factor, interblock gap, and buffer.

36. Identify two types of tape drives.

37. Briefly explain how records are stored on tape, and give an advantage to blocking records.

When data or programs need to be directly accessed, disk drives are used. Disk drives, like disks, come in two basic styles: **floppy disk drives** and **hard disk drives.**

Each disk drive has a different purpose. Floppy disk drives are used for permanent storage with microcomputer systems. They allow an inexpensive method of directly accessing data. In addition, they are used with larger computer systems for data entry. Floppy disk drives are slowly replacing card readers in this function.

Hard disk drives are primarily used for storing and directly accessing data with minicomputer and mainframe systems. However, they are becoming more popular with microcomputer systems as their price comes down.

Floppy Disk Drives

Floppy disk drives are designed to access the floppy disk through a window in its outside cover (see figure B2.36). The surface of the disks is coated with an easily magnetized substance. They come in three sizes: 8 inch, $5\frac{1}{4}$ inch, and 3 inch.

Data is recorded as a read/write head passes over the surface of the disk. The read/write head travels in concentric circles around the disk, as shown in figure B2.36. These circles are called **tracks.**

A single track on a floppy disk can hold several thousand bytes of data. For convenience, tracks are subdivided into storage areas called **sectors.** A single record or a block of records can be stored in a sector. Each sector has its own number. Data is directly accessed from the disk by identifying the sector number.

Hard-Sectored Versus Soft-Sectored Floppy Disks

Sectors are placed on the floppy disk by one of two methods. The method used to define the sectors is determined by the type of floppy disk drive used.

One method is to define the sectors by a series of sensing holes on the inside of the floppy disk. These disks are said to be **hard sectored.** The floppy disk in figure B2.36 is hard sectored.

A second method has the disk drive create the sectors. These are **soft-sectored** floppy disks. They have only a single sensing hole on the inside of the disk. Figure B2.37 shows a soft-sectored disk without its protective cover. The sensing hole identifies the beginning of the tracks.

Before newly purchased disks can be used, they must be **formatted** by the disk drive. A single command and a few minutes are all that are needed. During this time, the computer-controlled disk drive establishes each track and sector.

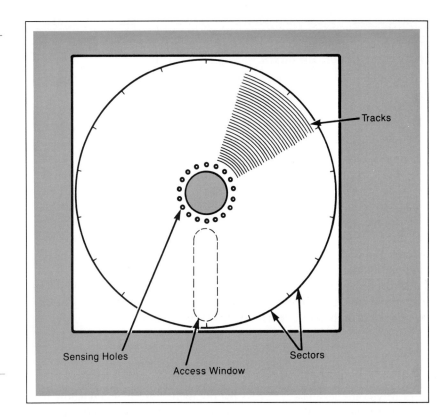

FIGURE B2.36

Hard-sectored floppy disk (inside protective cover)

FIGURE B2.37

Soft-sectored floppy disk (without protective cover)

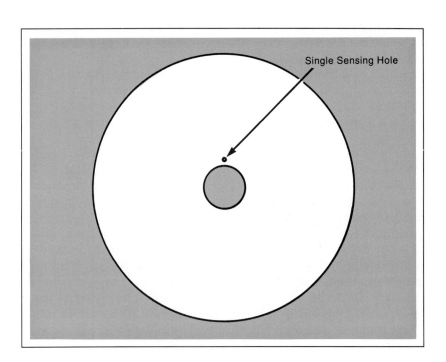

Both hard-sectored and soft-sectored floppy disks have a disk directory. The directory is created on the disk when it is formatted. The directory contains the name of each data file or program stored on the disk.

The starting sector number for each file or program is stored in the directory. The header label is stored in this sector. For example, when a user loads "sample program," the computer goes to the directory, looks up "sample program," and finds the starting sector number. It then goes directly to the sector, checks the label, and copies the program into memory one sector at a time.

Hard disk drives provide the fastest and most extensive data storage capability of any storage device discussed.

A collection of hard disks stacked one on top of another is sometimes called a **disk pack.** The disk pack can be mounted in the disk drive or fixed permanently within the drive. In either case, disk packs revolve at high speeds; 50 to 75 revolutions per second is typical.

Hard Disk Drives

When the disk is fixed permanently inside the disk drive, it has the fastest possible access time. This is because a read/write head is available for each track. The disadvantage to **fixed disk drives** is that the disk pack cannot be removed. Therefore, only one disk pack can ever be used.

Other disk drives allow disk packs to be removed and others mounted in their place. Since the disk can be removed, the read/write heads must move out of the way. Having the read/write heads on a moving access mechanism means access speeds are a little slower. The access mechanism must first position the heads over one set of tracks before data can be read or written.

Figure B2.39 shows a diagram of an access mechanism with read/write heads for a **removable disk drive.** The heads at the end of each arm are used

FIGURE B2.38

Disk pack

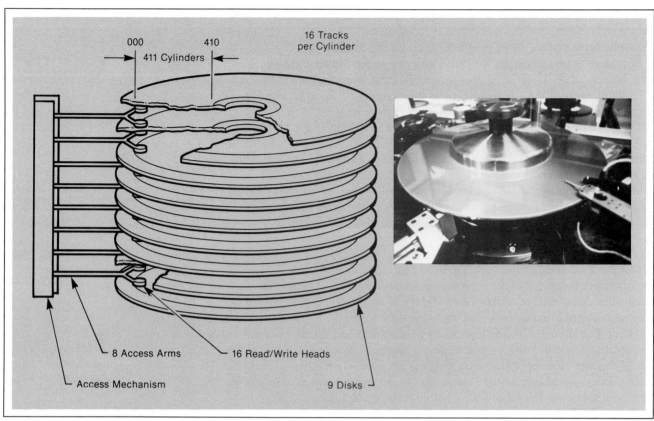

FIGURE B2.39

Disk drive access mechanism and disk
(Photo courtesy of IBM Corporation)

FIGURE B2.40

Sealed data module containing hard disk
and access mechanism (Courtesy IBM
Corporation)

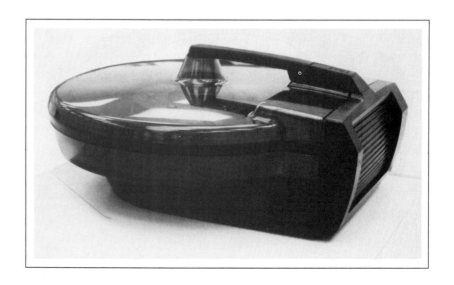

to read data from or write data to one surface. Hard disks have to be formatted, just like floppy disks.

Suppose a disk pack has 10 recording surfaces. When the access arms are in a fixed position over a set of tracks, 10 tracks can be read—one on each surface. When the arms are moved to another position, another 10 tracks can be read. The collection of tracks that can be read when the access mechanism is stationed in one place is called a **cylinder.**

A third type of hard disk drive, called a **Winchester disk drive,** uses a sealed **data module** with the hard disk, access mechanism, and read/write heads inside. The data module shown in figure B2.40 keeps dust and other dirt away from the recording surface where it could cause problems. In some disk drives, the data module is fixed inside; in others, the data module can be removed.

Locating Programs and Data

Hard disks do not have sensing holes to locate the beginning of a track. Instead, a special mark, shown in figure B2.41, identifies the beginning of the track.

Locating a program—or data—on a hard disk is similar to locating it on floppy disk. First the computer searches the directory. If the program name is matched, then the starting location of the program is also found in the directory.

The access mechanism first moves to the correct cylinder. Then the access arm for the correct track is activated and the starting point of the track is found. The program is then located and copied into memory.

STUDY OBJECTIVES

38. Define track, sector, hard-sectored floppy disk, soft-sectored floppy disk, disk directory, disk pack, cylinder, and data module.
39. Describe what happens when formatting a disk.
40. Briefly explain how a directory and sector number are used to find a program or file on disk.
41. Identify three types of hard disk drives.

HARDWARE PROFESSIONALS

There are currently many entry-level jobs working with computer hardware. Computer operator Martha Baker and service technician Peter Clark were both able to get computer-related jobs with their high school education. Further job advancement will be determined by how well they perform these jobs and the additional education they obtain.

Entry-Level Jobs

The future looks good for Martha and Pete. While they will not stay in these jobs for the rest of their working lives, it's a start. There will be a number of careers in computer technology to choose from. Many people make a good living running, assembling, servicing, or selling computer hardware.

At the manufacturing end, there will be a continuing need for **electronic technicians** to assemble hardware. To start, most electronic technicians need a high school degree. In addition, they must be willing to devote time to on-the-job training.

Layout of data on a hard disk track

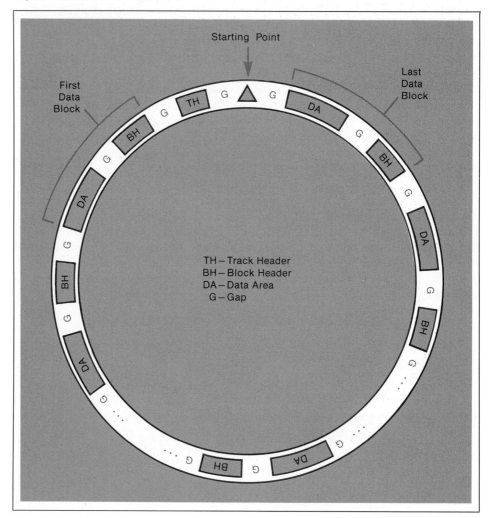

Positions as a data entry operator are also considered entry level. If you can type around 60 words per minute along with having some experience on a word processor or other key-operated device, you may find jobs right out of high school.

To apply for an entry-level job as a computer operator or service technician, you will need a high school diploma and possibly a two-year degree. These positions also require extensive on-the-job training, sometimes at schools run by the company.

It cannot be emphasized enough that you must continue your education once you get your first job. The fields of data processing, word processing, and process controls are always changing. The commitment to keep up with new advancements in your field is as important as your high school or college degree.

CAREER PROFILE

DARRELL MILLICH
COMPUTER OPERATOR

EDIE LAZZERONI
CUSTOMER SUPPORT

RESPONSIBILITIES—DARRELL

I work in the computer center as a computer tape operator. I mount and retrieve magnetic tapes from the tape drives and work with our customer's tape libraries. In a service bureau company such as this, I often get involved with our customers by phone and in person, and I like that.

RESPONSIBILITIES—EDIE

EDS is one of the largest computer service companies in the country. When a customer has a problem, they call. Or if they're local, they come by. I'm in the marketing department, and if I can't help them, my job is to find someone who can. I have to know enough about the problem and about computers to get the right kind of help for a customer.

MY BACKGROUND—DARRELL

Originally I applied for a courier position with EDS, carrying tapes to and from customers. But when an opening as an operator occurred, it was an opportunity. With only eight months experience, I have a long way to go.

Money isn't what attracted me, it was the idea of getting somewhere in life. Working with computers sounded exciting.

MY BACKGROUND—EDIE

After high school I got a job as a receptionist. I had been an average student. The company trained me to do data entry while I was a receptionist. At the beginning I was not really interested in computers. I wasn't afraid of them or anything, I just wasn't that interested. But after a few months you really get caught up in them.

SKILLS REQUIRED—DARRELL

I don't see math as being necessary for an operator, although I've heard that it is needed for programmers and other positions. In high school I didn't like to read, and I was in the learning disability classes. I think you need patience, and you need to want to learn.

SKILLS REQUIRED—EDIE

In customer support you obviously need to like contact with people. Customer and product support jobs are great places to learn. You learn about sales, business, accounting, and computers. It's a good place to start for a woman. The pay is relatively good, and the position is a terrific stepping stone.

I don't have any strong technical skills background. You need to be people-oriented and have a good sense of humor. The next position I want is in sales.

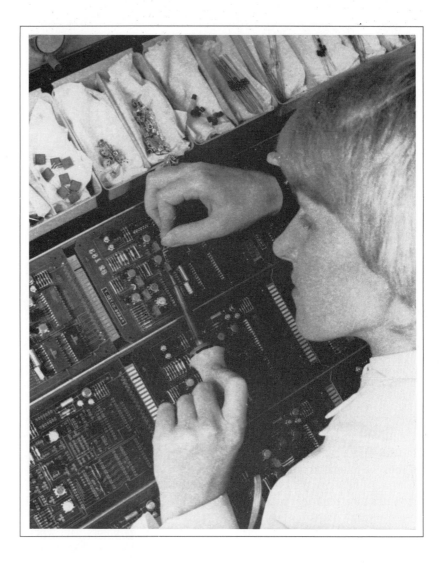

F I G U R E   B 2 . 4 2

Electronics technician (Courtesy Bank of Montreal)

Management-Level Jobs

Many jobs eventually lead to a management position. Individuals in programming, operations, and data entry may be asked to manage others in that area. Larger data processing departments may have more than one level of managers. Shift supervisors are also considered management-level positions.

Some organizations have their own management-training programs. To qualify as a **management trainee,** applicants usually need to have a college degree in management, information systems, electronics, or a related field. However, these companies often accept employees into the management-training program without a college degree if they have proved themselves on the job with good work habits and a positive attitude.

42. Identify the minimum educational requirements and possible exceptions for the following jobs: electronic technician, data entry operator, computer operator, and management trainee.

43. Briefly describe why a commitment to continuing education is important in computer-related fields.

SUMMARY

Computer hardware is one of the most visible components of a computer system. The computer, or processing hardware, contains three units: memory, control, and arithmetic/logic. Computers range in size from small microcomputers to medium-sized minicomputers all the way to large mainframes.

Input hardware has traditionally been key-operated devices that place data on cards, tapes, or disks. Many organizations are now bypassing manual data entry in favor of machine-readable source documents. Special characters, marks, and bars are input into the computer by scanners. Other specialized input devices are being used to input a wide variety of environmental data.

People use output hardware for computer-generated reports and screen displays. Printers are classified by their speed, printing method, and print images. Robots and numerical control machines represent the latest trend in action hardware. Medical researchers are experimenting with computer-controlled devices in pacemakers and artificial limbs.

Important programs and data are stored using tape or disk drives. These storage devices come in many styles to meet varying user needs.

Students entering the job market today will find a variety of entry-level jobs related to computer hardware. Those who dedicate themselves to staying abreast of new technological developments will find many career opportunities awaiting them.

CHAPTER B3

Computer Programs

Working with every computer system is a set of instructions telling the computer what to do. These instructions—a computer program—control the computer's resources for a period of time. When the program is finished, another program can be loaded into the memory.

In this way, a computer performs many jobs. A payroll program has the computer calculate and print paychecks. The same computer with a different computer program could track the flight path of the space shuttle as it orbits the earth. On closer examination, you will find that computer programs are written for an awesome array of jobs. In addition, there is a wide variety of programming languages. In this chapter, computer programs and the programming languages used to write them will be examined.

COMPUTER PROGRAMMER HAROLD JOHNSON

True to his word, Harold Johnson became a computer programmer. Mrs. Dingman's class had been just the beginning. After graduation from high school, Harold continued his training at State University, where he majored in information systems. In college, he learned new computer programming languages and took other computer-related classes.

As in high school, Harold excelled at whatever he set his mind to. His grades at State University were good, and businesses actively recruited him at graduation. He finally decided on a job at Miracle Motors.

FIGURE B3.1

Harold Johnson on tour of Miracle Motors' computer center.

Miracle Motors had a policy that new programmers work as maintenance programmers for at least six months. Maintenance programmers modify existing programs to conform to new laws or new company policies.

At first Harold thought it was a waste of time. But he quickly found out that real-life programming was very different from what he had experienced at school. For one thing, the company had a set of standards that all programmers had to follow. Harold found that by having to modify working programs, he had a better understanding of the use and need for these standards.

Harold was also shocked to find that several of the programs broke all the rules he had learned at school. He found out later that these programs had been written years earlier. Harold spent a good part of the first six months converting a few of these older programs to the company standards. It was like no other project he had ever done.

In a few months, Harold would be promoted to an **applications programmer.** This meant that he would write new computer programs to solve users' needs at Miracle Motors. As a high school student he had also written applications programs. These were game programs for the most part, although he had also written a billing program for his paper route.

An applications program is designed to control a specific IPO cycle. Applications programs do not have to be written from scratch every time. Other sources are usually explored before a new program is designed and written.

1. Define computer program.
2. Describe what maintenance and applications programmers do.

The source of new programs varies from application to application. The choice of programs depends on what is available for a particular computer system.

Games and programs for the home are often found in magazines. Hundreds of magazines and newsletters contain interesting articles and applications programs. Many of the magazines specialize in articles about one or two brands of computers. Since program instructions vary from computer to computer, it is helpful to find programs written for the computer in which you are interested.

You should be very careful when typing a program from a magazine. One typing error can lead to many frustrating hours trying to find out why the program doesn't work. Every once in a while, the typing error is made in preparing the magazine for publication. If this happens, the error will be found and corrected in an article a few months later.

Magazines are an inexpensive source of many simple programs. These programs are usually geared to personal applications. Therefore, businesses must seek other sources of applications programs.

Computing magazines are a possible source of programs

Computer Manufacturers

Computers are purchased with a limited set of systems programs. The manufacturer also provides applications programs to interested users. These applications programs are often a selling feature. Organizations that do not have a systems development staff often buy computers from manufacturers who can provide the needed applications programs as well.

Software Stores

Stores that specialize in selling software are now open in many cities. These stores do not sell computers. Instead, they sell computer programs, related magazines, and supplies. Computers are available in the stores so that customers can try the programs before purchasing them.

Software stores are very popular because they provide users with a way to evaluate software through personal experience. The salespeople provide assistance and manuals on how the software works. Customers then spend the necessary time to familiarize themselves with the programs. Thus, they can accurately judge whether a particular program would be of use to them or not.

User Groups

People who purchase popular models of computers will find groups of people with the same machine getting together to discuss problems and new ideas. User groups are a good way to come into contact with applications programs. They also offer new users a way to learn about the latest developments for that computer.

User groups are not limited to any type or size of computer. There are local user groups for microcomputers as well as national user groups for mainframe systems.

Members of the user groups sometimes sell other users applications programs. Also, they can provide unbiased information on the effectiveness of a program and the type of support that comes with it.

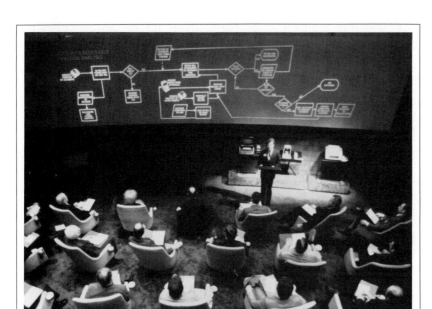

FIGURE B3.3

User groups foster the sharing of computer information (Courtesy AT&T)

Software Houses

A software house is a company that specializes in writing programs. These companies have their own systems development staff to design and write new applications packages. Along with the computer program, these applications packages contain manuals and operating procedures.

Software houses can take one of two approaches to program development. The first approach is to design and develop an applications package to meet the needs of a particular customer.

The other approach is to design and develop applications packages that are as versatile as possible. The idea is to create a package that has a large potential market. Development cost can then be spread across many sales, which brings the purchase price down. Game programs are a good example of this marketing approach. They can cost thousands of dollars to develop, but sell for $20 or $30 because thousands are sold.

Buying an off-the-shelf applications package can cause problems if the organization has a specific need. When this happens, the company can ask the software house to modify the program—at an additional cost—or they can have someone else modify it.

Contract Programmers

When a suitable applications package cannot be found or when a package has to be modified, a company may hire a **contract programmer.** Contract programmers are not permanent employees of the company like Harold Johnson. They are hired to do a specific job.

This arrangement often works out very well for both the programmer and the organization. The programmer is free to move to projects of his or her choice. And the organization can hire someone who has experience in writing the specialized programs it needs. Furthermore, if the company is in a hurry to get the program completed, a contract programmer can be brought in to get the job done right away.

In-house Programming Staff

Many computer centers support their own systems development staff. This staff is made up of systems analysts and programmers.

Usually, a programming project starts with a user's request for help. A systems analyst will be asked to talk to the user to find out what is needed. The user's needs are then summarized in a preliminary report. A group of managers sitting on a steering committee then decide whether or not to go ahead with the project.

Project Specifications

If the steering committee decides the project has merit, the preliminary report becomes the first step in preparing the **project specifications.** The specifications will eventually include a description of the project, charts illustrating what will happen, and cost estimates in terms of people, time, and equipment.

The project specifications become part of a systems proposal that is reviewed before any programming is done. The steering committee makes the final decision about whether the project will be started or not. If the reviewers give the project the go-ahead, they then set a job priority. High-priority jobs get immediate attention. Lower priority jobs are worked into the development schedule at the data processing manager's discretion.

Program Design

When a project is under way, the project specifications are given to the programmers. The applications programmers take the specifications and review them.

They then sit down and design the program by identifying each step the computer must go through to complete the job. This is done before any programming is started so that errors can be avoided.

Figure B3.4 shows two design techniques used by programmers. The first is called a **program flowchart,** where each step in the program is represented by a special symbol with a brief description inside.

The other example shows the program design using **pseudocode.** Pseudocode is an outline of the program in English instead of in symbols or a specific computer language. Flowcharts and pseudocode are also used for program documentation after the programming project is completed.

STUDY OBJECTIVES

3. List seven sources of applications programs.

4. Briefly explain why the arrangement of hiring contract programmers benefits both the company and the programmer.

5. Describe the steps needed to get project specifications ready for a programmer, and identify the parts of the project specifications.

6. Identify two design techniques used by programmers.

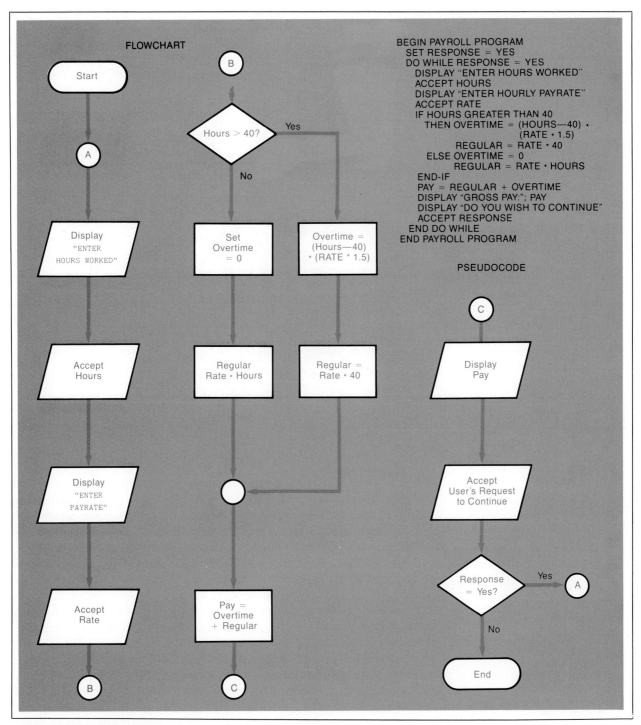

FLOWCHART

Start

A

Display "ENTER HOURS WORKED"

Accept Hours

Display "ENTER PAYRATE"

Accept Rate

B

B

Hours > 40?

No → Set Overtime = 0

Yes → Overtime = (Hours—40) * (RATE * 1.5)

Regular Rate * Hours

Regular = Rate * 40

Pay = Overtime + Regular

C

PSEUDOCODE

BEGIN PAYROLL PROGRAM
  SET RESPONSE = YES
  DO WHILE RESPONSE = YES
    DISPLAY "ENTER HOURS WORKED"
    ACCEPT HOURS
    DISPLAY "ENTER HOURLY PAYRATE"
    ACCEPT RATE
    IF HOURS GREATER THAN 40
      THEN OVERTIME = (HOURS—40) *
                      (RATE * 1.5)
        REGULAR = RATE * 40
      ELSE OVERTIME = 0
        REGULAR = RATE * HOURS
    END-IF
    PAY = REGULAR + OVERTIME
    DISPLAY "GROSS PAY:"; PAY
    DISPLAY "DO YOU WISH TO CONTINUE"
    ACCEPT RESPONSE
  END DO WHILE
END PAYROLL PROGRAM

C

Display Pay

Accept User's Request to Continue

Response = Yes?

Yes → A

No

End

FIGURE B3.4

Flowchart and pseudocode of payroll program

163

APPLICATIONS PROGRAMMING AS A PROFESSION

Harold proved himself to be a very capable programmer in his first six months at Miracle Motors. The programs he modified worked correctly when placed into production. This earned him high marks at his first employee review with the data processing manager. Toward the end of the review, the manager told him that he was going to be placed on an applications development team.

Harold was elated with this news. The review continued, but Harold couldn't remember what was said later. At the end of the review, he floated out of the manager's office and back to his desk.

The applications development team was composed of a systems analyst, a senior programmer, a lead programmer, and Harold. At their first meeting, they discussed a system they were developing for the engineering staff.

The system had to run independently of Miracle Motor's mainframe because the engineering staff had their own minicomputer. Since the mini could communicate with the mainframe, the program had to allow data to be passed back and forth when needed.

This was what Harold had been waiting for. He knew it would require long, hard days of work, maybe even a couple of weekends. But this was where the action was. It meant working with the latest technology, using programming concepts he had been taught at school.

Applications programmers can find work in a wide variety of job settings. With large projects, programmers will work in teams that include other programmers and systems analysts. On smaller projects, the job of analyzing the user's needs and writing the program may be given to a single person—a **programmer/ analyst.**

Programmers must have extensive knowledge of at least one computer language and usually know several languages. Most applications programmers hired today have a four-year college degree in information systems. Often they have a background in business or science. In some special cases, students graduating from community colleges with two-year associate degrees in information systems are finding positions as entry-level programmers.

Career path in computer programming

```
        2-Year Degree              4-Year Degree

        Programmer Trainee

        Junior Programmer
   (Sometimes Maintenance Programmer)

        Applications Programmer
                 or
        Systems Programmer
                                    to System
                                    Analysis Work

        Lead Programmer

        Senior Programmer

        Programming Manager
```

With good programmers so hard to find and keep, some organizations are training employees from other areas to be programmers. It is considered a reward to a good employee to be given a chance to make more money as a computer programmer. These programmers have the title of **programmer trainee** while they are in the training program. They learn about the organization's computer system and improve their programming skills as part of the training program.

Unfortunately, training new programmers is usually an informal process. A new employee is often assigned to a more experienced programmer who shows the new arrival the ins and outs of the computer system.

A Programmer's Future

Programmers can be given several job titles as they gain experience. Successful trainees become **junior programmers** or maintenance programmers. The next step can be to **staff programmer** or applications programmer.

As with any profession, programmers take on more responsibility as they gain experience. There comes a point in many programmers' careers when they become either a systems analyst or a **lead programmer.** When programmers become lead programmers they take on the responsibility of overseeing the work of other programmers. They watch not only their own work, but the work of others.

If an individual stays in the programming profession long enough, that person can become a **senior programmer.** Programmers in this position are responsible for an applications project. They no longer write programs. Instead, they coordinate the activities of the development team and review programs written by other programmers.

The senior programmer in charge of Harold's development project had several very important decisions to make. Since the engineers who would be using the program were not computer professionals, great care had to be taken in designing and documenting the programs. In addition, other users and their potential need for the data needed to be considered. Finally, the programming team had to help the users decide on the best procedures for data entry and processing.

STUDY OBJECTIVES

7. Identify the educational background that most computer programmers have when hired.

8. Describe the responsibilities for the following jobs: programmer/analyst, programmer trainee, lead programmer, and senior programmer.

APPLICATIONS PROGRAMS

Harold's applications development team would be working with the timing and control engineers. The engineers wanted a system that would trace the development cycle of new cars. This would mean keeping track of data starting with the initial drawings and ending when the first car rolled off the production line. They wanted the system to help them schedule production activities and government tests.

Although the engineers were not computer professionals, they would be responsible for data entry and for operating the department's minicomputer. They needed an easy-to-use system that produced accurate reports.

Turnkey Systems

A **turnkey system** consists of a ready-to-use applications program, procedures, and hardware. It implies that the applications program has been carefully designed for people who are not computer professionals. The users just load the program into the computer. It should do the job with a minimum amount of supervision, like turning the key in your car and driving away.

Turnkey systems work on computers dedicated to one application. Since the minicomputer used by the timing and control engineers performed other jobs, the new system could not be considered a turnkey system. However, it had features common to turnkey systems. It needed to be carefully designed and easy to use, since the system would be operated by users who were not computer professionals.

Integrated Software Versus Independent Software

Much of the data processed by the engineers would be used by Miracle Motor's managers to make important decisions. Therefore, the programs—or at least the data—needed to be available to other users. The system had to be integrated with the software on the company's mainframe.

Programs are rarely independent of one another, although programming projects at school sometimes give this impression. In many computer systems, data is first input, processed, and stored by one program. After that, the data can be picked up and processed by another program.

When purchasing or designing new programs, users must be aware of the difference between **integrated software** and **independent software.** For example, if you buy a program to print mailing labels, can the names and addresses stored on disk be used with your word processing program? It would save a lot of time if you could use the addresses from the mailing labels in your letters.

The applications development team had to consider the same question for the Engineering Department's system. Would this be an independent system that would not share data? Or would others outside of the Engineering Department need to use this data? Since the latter case was true, the new system had to be integrated with the mainframe.

The people who design or buy computer programs make very important decisions. They determine whether a program is independent or integrated with other systems. This decision can have a profound impact on how valuable programs and data will be in the future.

Online Versus Offline

The way data flows to and from the computer system is also important to the overall design. When users are offline, they are not directly connected to the computer. Data is placed on cards, tapes, or disks and then input into the computer. Information is printed on reports and then delivered to the users.

In other cases, users are online. This means they are directly connected to the computer system. Data can be input through keyboards for immediate processing or storage. Information is printed or displayed where it is needed.

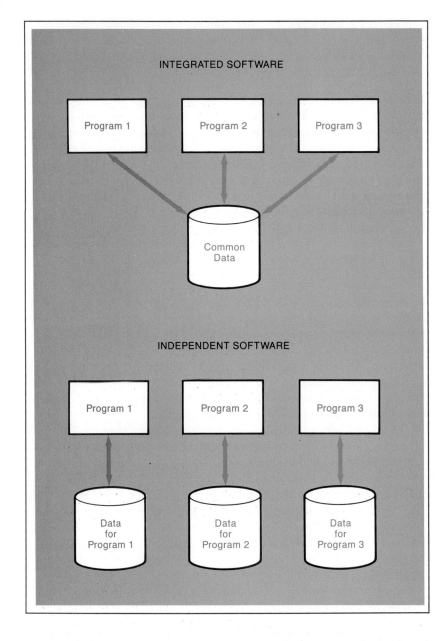

Since the minicomputer at Miracle Motors was located in the engineering department, data entry would most likely be online. However, if data and reports were required from out of town, the system would have to handle offline needs as well.

Transaction Processing Versus Batch Processing

Another important programming decision relates to how the data will be processed. If a **transaction** is defined as updating data related to an application, then one option is **transaction processing.** This is processing data as the transaction takes place. To the engineers at Miracle Motors, this would mean processing production data as it was collected.

Usually, programs that use transaction processing are developed because users need updated information immediately. Airline reservation systems are an excellent example of transaction processing. As people request seats on flights, the travel agent can reserve seats and tell customers when the flight leaves.

Noncritical applications or reports that require a lot of data retrieval are candidates for batch processing. Data is processed as a group with batch processing. Payroll programs are traditionally written for this kind of system. Time sheets are collected into groups. Then the data is keyed onto floppy disks and sent to the computer for processing. The operator mounts blank paychecks on the printer and sees that all the paychecks for the week are printed.

Online systems also support batch processing. The engineers at Miracle Motors could enter data online but have the computer store all the data on disk. At a later time the data could be batch processed.

STUDY OBJECTIVES

9. Define turnkey system and transaction.

10. Describe why the decision to develop—or buy—independent software instead of integrated software can have a profound impact on its usefulness over the long run.

11. Briefly explain the difference between online and offline and between transaction processing and batch processing.

SURVEY OF COMPUTER PROGRAMMING LANGUAGES

By the time Harold was hired by Miracle Motors, he was able to write programs in several computer languages. He had first learned to program using the BASIC language in Mrs. Dingman's class. The microcomputers at the high school could all understand BASIC. In college he had taken classes in COBOL, PASCAL, and FORTRAN. There were things he liked and didn't like about each language.

Each of these languages is considered a high-level programming language. They all use English-like phrases. The first high-level languages were developed in the mid-1950s. The people who developed these early languages were truly pioneers. They had no examples to follow, so they developed languages by intuition. When a language could not do something, they added new features so it could. Because of this, these early languages grew in capability and structure in a haphazard manner.

Some of the languages never worked correctly. Others were hard to use or were inefficient. In still other cases, the programs were hard to understand. All in all, over 1000 languages have been developed in the last 30 years. Of those, no more than six or seven are in popular use today.

Structured Programming

At first, programs just happened. A programmer would sit down with a project and through trial and error get the computer program to work. Unfortunately, these programs were not very well organized. Other programmers often found them hard to read. And even simple modification created more work than needed. Harold Johnson found this to be the case when he was modifying older programs to meet the company's new programming standards.

Miracle Motors' standards were based on the fact that any program could be written using three patterns or **structures:** sequence, selection, and repetition.

Sequence means that a group of instructions is performed in order. The following program segment would be one example:

```
10 PRINT "ENTER THE HOURS WORKED THIS WEEK"
20 INPUT HOURS
30 PRINT "ENTER HOURLY PAY RATE"
40 INPUT RATE
50 PAY = HOURS * RATE
60 PRINT "GROSS PAY: ";PAY
```

Selection means that the sequence of instructions is chosen based on some condition. For example, the following program segment compares hours to 40. It selects the overtime and regular pay calculations when hours are greater than 40. Otherwise, it selects just the regular pay calculation.

```
50 IF HOURS > 40
      THEN OVERTIME = ( HOURS - 40 ) * ( RATE * 1.5)
            REGULAR = RATE * 40
    *ELSE OVERTIME = 0.00
            REGULAR = HOURS * RATE
55 PAY = REGULAR + OVERTIME
```

Repetition means that a sequence of instructions is repeated while some condition is true. In the following example, the pay is calculated and printed while the user enters "yes". This process is repeated until the condition—RESPONSE$ = "yes"—is no longer true.

```
10 PRINT "ENTER THE HOURS WORKED THIS WEEK"
20 INPUT HOURS
30 PRINT "ENTER HOURLY PAY RATE"
40 INPUT RATE
50 IF HOURS > 40
      THEN OVERTIME = ( HOURS - 40 ) * ( RATE * 1.5)
            REGULAR = RATE * 40
    *ELSE OVERTIME = 0.00
            REGULAR = RATE * HOURS
55 PAY = REGULAR + OVERTIME
60 PRINT "GROSS PAY: ";PAY
70 PRINT
80 INPUT "DO YOU WISH TO CONTINUE (YES/
   NO)";RESPONSE$
90 IF RESPONSE$ = "YES" THEN GO TO 10
100 END
```

A program using these principles is called a **structured program.** Some programming languages can easily handle all three structures; others cannot.

You would think that programmers would use languages that lend themselves to structured programming. Unfortunately, by the time structured programming came along, others languages were in wide use. Each language had been developed for a different kind of programming application. These older

---

*ELSE option is not available with all BASICs.

languages had some good points, but they also had many bad ones. Keep this in mind when you read about the following computer programming languages.

BASIC

BASIC stands for Beginner's All-purpose Symbolic Instruction Code. The faculty at Dartmouth College developed BASIC in the early 1960s as an introductory computer language. The college required all students to take a computer class before graduation. Other languages available at this time were complex and geared to either business or scientific use. Since students at Dartmouth were from many academic areas, BASIC was not designed for any specific application. Instead, it was designed to be easy to learn and use.

For years, BASIC was popular only at colleges. Students in first-year college courses were taught to program using BASIC. If these students went on into computer programming, an understanding of BASIC gave them a head start when learning new programming languages.

The rise in BASIC's popularity is directly related to the success of microcomputers. Since microcomputers are purchased by a wide variety of people who have no prior training or experience, an easy-to-use programming language is needed. BASIC was the obvious choice. Today, most microcomputers come ready to handle programs written in BASIC.

The program used in the examples of program structures was a BASIC program. It also highlighted several problems with BASIC. Since BASIC was designed before the idea of structured programming, it does not handle repetition as easily as other languages.

In addition, the selection—IF—structure in the original Dartmouth BASIC did not have an ELSE option as shown in the example. To get around this limitation, programmers had to have two selection statements, like the ones in figure B3.8.

FIGURE B3.8

Two variations of the BASIC IF statement

```
                        IF/THEN/ELSE STATEMENT

    50 IF HOURS > 40
         THEN OVERTIME = (HOURS-40) * (RATE * 1.5)
            REGULAR = RATE * 40
         ELSE OVERTIME = 0.00
            REGULAR = HOURS * RATE

                           IF/THEN STATEMENT

    50 IF HOURS > 40
         THEN OVERTIME = (HOURS - 40) * (RATE * 1.5):REGULAR = RATE * 40


    52 IF HOURS < |=40
         THEN OVERTIME = 0.00:REGULAR = HOURS * RATE
```

To make up for the lack of easy-to-use selection and repetition structures, each microcomputer has its own variations to the BASIC language. Programmers constantly find differences in the BASIC languages used by different makes of computers.

Programmers also run into difficulty when writing complex programs using BASIC. Writing or reading data on disk can be tricky. Each microcomputer has a different way to do it. In addition, great care must be taken to make the programs easy to read. BASIC programs can be difficult to read and even harder to modify.

To summarize, BASIC is an easy-to-learn programming language. Each computer manufacturer has modified the language to make up for some limitations in program structures and input/output capability. As a result, many variations to the original Dartmouth BASIC exist. Complex programs must be carefully written because they can be hard to understand.

LOGO

A more recent programming language designed for educational use is **LOGO.** The design of LOGO is based on work by Seymour Papert. His interest in psychology and computers led him to new ideas about how to use computers for learning. He helped develop this programming language, which allows students to explore geometric principles. This is done not as some abstract process but through the hands-on use of computers. The name LOGO was used to suggest that the language was meant to be symbolic in nature. These concepts are discussed in more detail in Papert's book *Mindstorms*.

Unlike programming languages used for business or scientific applications, LOGO is an end in itself. This language was not designed to create reports or to track an airplane's flight path. It is to be used only as a learning tool. With LOGO, students can use computers for problem solving. They can explore mathematical concepts with the results graphically displayed.

A sample LOGO program is highlighted in the photo essay on Computer Graphics: an Art, a Science, a Tool.

COBOL

COBOL stands for COmmon Business Oriented Language. It was designed in the mid-1950s by a group of people representing businesses and the government. Their objective was to design a language suited for business problems.

If there is a business programming language, COBOL is it. It is one of the oldest and most established languages. It has been standardized by the **American National Standards Institute,** or **ANSI.** Every major mainframe manufactured supports COBOL. Between 60 and 80 percent of all business applications programs are COBOL programs.

Because COBOL was designed with business applications in mind, it has been very successful in business environments. It has an extensive vocabulary for defining files, records, and fields. It easily handles disk or tape input/output and has selection and repetition structures that are much better than BASIC.

In addition, COBOL was designed to be self-documenting. Many lines must be written even for simple programs. Some people say that you can tell that a COBOL program is ready to go when the weight of the program exceeds the weight of the computer. This can also be considered one disadvantage to using COBOL.

```
IDENTIFICATION DIVISION.
 PROGRAM-ID. ADDITION.

ENVIRONMENT DIVISION.
 INPUT-OUTPUT SECTION.
        .
        .
        .
DATA DIVISION.
 FILE SECTION.
 FD DATA-IN
     LABEL RECORDS ARE STANDARD.
 01 NUMBERS-TO-BE-PROCESSED.
     05 NUMBER-1-IN       PIC 999.
     05 NUMBER-2-IN       PIC 999.

 FD ANSWER-OUT
     LABEL RECORDS ARE OMITTED.
 01 SUM-TO-BE-PRINTED     PIC X(27).

 WORKING-STORAGE SECTION.
 01 TEMPORARY-WORK-AREA.
     05 FILLER            PIC X(10)     VALUE "THE SUM OF"
     05 NUMBER-1-OUT      PIC 999.
     05 FILLER            PIC XXX       VALUE " + ".
     05 NUMBER-2-OUT      PIC 999.
     05 FILLER            PIC X(4)      VALUE " IS ".
     05 SUM-OUT           PIC 9(4).

PROCEDURE DIVISION.
 PROCESSING-ROUTINE.
    OPEN INPUT DATA-IN
         OUTPUT ANSWER-OUT.
    READ DATA-IN.
    ADD NUMBER-1-IN, NUMBER-2-IN GIVING SUM-OUT.
    MOVE NUMBER-1-IN TO NUMBER-1-OUT.
    MOVE NUMBER-2-IN TO NUMBER-2-OUT.
    WRITE SUM-TO-BE-PRINTED
         FROM TEMPORARY-WORK-AREA.
    CLOSE DATA-IN
         ANSWER-OUT.
    STOP RUN.
```

FIGURE B3.9

COBOL program to add two numbers

COBOL was designed to solve larger business problems. It is time-consuming and frustrating to write small COBOL programs. Leave those to BASIC.

When it comes to online processing, COBOL has a problem similar to BASIC. Since COBOL was designed before transaction processing became practical, the original COBOL standards did not take this processing method into account. Therefore, each manufacturer has developed different ways to write online programs for transaction processing in COBOL. COBOL programmers who move from one type of computer to another are forced to learn a new variation of COBOL to handle transaction processing.

```
                    FILE DESCRIPTION SPECIFICATIONS
NUMBIN   IP  F      80            DISK          S
NUMOUT   O   F      132    OF     PRINTER
                    INPUT FORMAT SPECIFICATIONS
FILEIN   NS  01
                                              1      30NUM1
                                              4      60NUM2
                    CALCULATION SPECIFICATIONS
    01           NUM1     ADD   NUM2        SUM        42


                    OUTPUT FORMAT SPECIFICATIONS

NUMOUT   H   207   1P
         OR        OF
                                      34 'THE SUM OF 2 NUMBERS'
         D   1     01
                                      20 'THE SUM OF'
                           NUM1   3   24
                                      26 '+'
                           NUM2   3   30
                                      33 'IS'
                           SUM    3   38
```

RPG program to add two numbers

RPG

RPG stands for Report Program Generator. It was first introduced in 1964 to run on minicomputers with limited memory capacity. As the name implies, RPG was designed to produce business reports.

To use RPG, a programmer defines the format of input files by naming fields and specifying their lengths and types—numeric, character, and so forth. Then the programmer defines operations to be performed on certain fields. Adding all the regular pay results together to find the total pay would be one example.

When RPG was first introduced, it could not handle any type of selections. It contained only fixed logic, which meant that the same sequence of instructions were always used. Many detailed reports were easily handled by RPG and its fixed logic. However, when complex logic required the program to select between a set of instructions, another language, like COBOL, was used.

The program logic in an RPG program is not developed in a sequence of steps. Instead, specifications for the file description, input, calculations, and output are developed separately. Other special specifications are also used as the need arises. The RPG program in figure B3.10 shows the four specifications needed to add two numbers together.

While the RPG program in figure B3.10 does not demonstrate all the RPG capabilities, it does show how each entry for one of the specifications must be written in a designated column. This feature, along with its fixed logic format, makes RPG unlike the other programming languages discussed in this chapter.

```
      INTEGER NUM1, NUM2, SUM
      READ (5,10) NUM1, NUM2
  10  FORMAT (I4,I4)
      SUM = NUM1 + NUM2
      WRITE (6,20) NUM1, NUM2, SUM
  20  FORMAT (10X,'THE SUM OF', I4, '+', I4, 'IS', I5)
      STOP
      END
```

FIGURE B3.11

FORTRAN program to add two numbers

To meet the ever-changing demands for business reports, RPG has also changed. More powerful versions labeled RPGII and RPGIII have been introduced to handle selections and transaction processing.

FORTRAN stands for FORmula TRANslator. One of the earliest languages, it was developed primarily for scientific programming. FORTRAN is a prime example of a language that just kept growing. Originally, it was used to perform very complex calculations. As people kept adding to its capability, it became a general-purpose language by accident.

This language has limited input/output capacity. Its selection structure is awkward and the repetition structures are similar to BASIC. Programs written in FORTRAN tend to be hard to read and understand unless they are well documented. Consequently, they are hard to change.

Amazingly, in spite of these disadvantages, more scientific programs are written in FORTRAN than in any other language. There are several reasons for this situation. One is that many other languages do not adequately handle mathematical applications. Another reason is economics. It is expensive to change programs and to retrain programmers in newer languages.

The **PASCAL** language is named after Blaise Pascal, the French mathematician and philosopher. It is one of the new generation of programming languages that was developed for structured programming.

PASCAL is a very powerful language that is now part of the high school Advanced Placement tests. It is an excellent language for scientific applications, but has very limited input/output capability to support business appli-

FORTRAN

PASCAL

FIGURE B3.12

PASCAL program to add two numbers

```
PROGRAM ADD-IT (INPUT, OUTPUT);
VAR NUM1, NUM2, SUM: INTEGER;
BEGIN
   READLN (INPUT, NUM1, NUM2);
   SUM:= NUM1 + NUM2;
   WRITELN (OUTPUT, 'THE SUM OF', NUM1:4, '+', NUM2:4, 'IS', SUM:5);
END.
```

```
USE TEXT_IO;

PROCEDURE MAIN IS
    TYPE NUMBER IS INTEGER;
    PACKAGE NUMBER_10 IS NEW INTEGER_10(NUMBER);
    NUM1, NUM2, SUM: NUMBER;

BEGIN
    GET (NUM1); GET (NUM2);
    SUM:= NUM1 + NUM2;
    PUT ('THE SUM OF');
    PUT (NUM1, WIDTH = 4);
    PUT ('+');
    PUT (NUM2, WIDTH = 4);
    PUT ('IS');
    PUT (SUM, WIDTH = 5);

    NEW_LINE;

END MAIN;
```

FIGURE B3.13

ADA program to add two numbers

cations. The structures for selection and repetition are excellent, and complex data formats are easily represented.

This language has been well received in computer science and engineering departments at colleges. Because it is relatively new and has limited input/output capability, it has had only limited acceptance in industry.

ADA

An even newer language called **ADA** is derived from Pascal. ADA was designed with superior input/output capabilities. Therefore, some experts think that ADA has a better chance of being used in industry than PASCAL.

ADA is a programming language born in the 1980s. This language was named after Lady Ada Augusta Lovelace, who was an important figure in nineteenth-century computing history.

The Department of Defense has sponsored the development of ADA. Their goal is to develop a scientific language that would help programmers use good programming techniques. In addition, they would like ADA to become a national standard like COBOL.

Until recently, different branches of the armed forces used a variety of languages. This practice has made it difficult to transfer quality software from one service to another. To stop duplication of effort, the Department of Defense has mandated that all branches start using ADA when it becomes available.

ADA has been modeled after the PASCAL language. The good features of PASCAL have been included with improved input/output capability. If ADA has any fault, it is its complexity. When a programming language can do many things, it takes time for programmers to master each feature.

STUDY OBJECTIVES

12. Define high-level programming language, structured program, and ANSI.

13. Identify the three structures of a structured program.

14. Describe how each of the following programming languages gets its name and identify the applications each was designed to handle: BASIC, LOGO, COBOL, RPG, FORTRAN, PASCAL, and ADA.

PUTTING HIGH-LEVEL LANGUAGES IN MACHINE-READABLE FORM

You may be wondering how instructions like

```
50 PAY = HOURS * RATE
```

are represented in the computer's memory. The answer is that instructions are represented in binary 1's and 0's like data. Multiply may be represented by 0011100, divide by 0011101, and so on. The addresses of the data—HOURS and RATE—are also represented by binary codes. How would you like to program using only 1's and 0's?

Machine Languages

In the early days of data processing, programmers did have to memorize the binary code for each instruction. These programs are said to be in the computer's own machine language. Thus, someone might spend an hour or two to produce the following machine language program:

```
110010000100011111101010101010111001101110100011110
001101010100001010100010101001110010011111000010101 01
101010101010010100010010101001010100001011101010101 0
1010101000111110100001110101010010000011110100101010 100
00011101001010001010111100001010100111000001101010 1
11100000011101001010000101011000110100010100010101 010
0100100000111010000100010001000001100100101111000 11
011110100001101001000010101010100010110010111001101 010
1010101000011111100000110100010010110010101000110101
```

Writing such gibberish might be fun for a few hours, but clearly it is no way to spend a 40-hour workweek. Also, programs produced by this method often had errors. As you can see, any error would be hard to find and fix. Consequently, people looked for a better way to produce programs.

Assembler Languages

The first step away from a machine language is called an **assembler language.** Assembler languages are midway between machine language and high-level languages.

These languages represent each machine language instruction as **mnemonic**—memory-aiding—characters. The machine language instruction 0101101 would be represented by the assembler instruction AD—Add—or MV—Move. This would make the instructions easier for people to remember.

An assembler language program is the machine language instructions written mnemonically. Actually, there is not one assembler language, but an assembler language for every machine. The assembler is just an easier way to write a program. It also represents the first in a series of steps to make programming languages more English-like. Figure B3.14 shows an example of an assembler language program.

A minor advantage to writing a program in assembler—or machine language—is its efficiency. Assembler programs can be tailored to take advantage of a computer's capabilities better than programs written in high-level languages.

Programming using an assembler language has major drawbacks. It takes

177

```
                    PDP II ASSEMBLY                    DOCUMENTATION
;::::::::::::::::::::::::::::::::::::: INITIAL DECLARATIONS :::::::::::::::::::::::::::::::::::::::::
          PRS=177564                 ;  TTY STATUS WORD
          PRB=PRS+2                  ;  TTY BUFFER WORD
          KBS=177560                 ;  KEYBOARD STATUS WORD
          KBB=BKS+2                  ;  KEYBOARD BUFFER WORD
          R0=%0                      ;  REGISTERS
          R1=%1
          R2=%2
          R3=%3
          R4=%4
          P=%7                       ;  PROGRAM COUNTER REGISTER
;::::::::::::::::::::::::::::::::::::::::: MAIN PROGRAM :::::::::::::::::::::::::::::::::::::::::::::
          .=1000                     ;  LOAD PROGRAM @ ADDRESS 1000
START:    MOV      #CRLF,   R1       ;  SET UP A CARRIAGE RETURN / LINE FEED
          JSR      P,       PSTR     ;  "PSTR" EXECUTES THE CR/LF
          MOV      #MSGA,   R1       ;  SET UP "INPUT A?" MESSAGE
          JSR      P,       PSTR     ;  PRINT THE MESSAGE VIA "PSTR"
          MOV      #A,      R4       ;  R4 POINTS TO ASCII OUTPUT BUFFER FOR "A"
          MOV      #MSG1,   R5       ;  R5 IS THE SENTINAL VALUE OF BUFFER
          JSR      P,       RSTR     ;  "RSTR" READS INPUT STRING FOR "A"
          MOV      R3,      TEMP     ;  "TEMP" HOLDS BINARY VALUE FOR "A"
          MOV      #MSGB,   R1       ;  SET UP "INPUT B?" MESSAGE
          JSR      P,       PSTR     ;  PRINT THE MESSAGE VIA "PSTR"
          MOV      #B,      R4       ;  R4 POINTS TO ASCII OUTPUT BUFFER FOR "B"
          MOV      #MSG2,   R5       ;  R5 IS THE SENTINAL VALUE OF BUFFER
          JSR      P,       RSTR     ;  "RSTR" READS INPUT STRING FOR "B"
          ADD      TEMP,    R3       ;  ADD "A" VALUE TO "B" VALUE
          MOV      #CRLF,   R4       ;  R4 POINTS TO ASCII OUTPUT BUFFER FOR SUM
          MOV      #C,      R5       ;  R5 IS THE SENTINAL VALUE OF BUFFER
CONVERT:  DEC      R4                ;  BACK UP 1 CHARACTER IN BUFFER
          CMP      R4,      R5       ;  CHECK TO SEE IF BUFFER IS FULL
          BLT      FINISH            ;  IF FULL, BRANCH TO "FINISH"
          CLR      R2                ;  CLEAR UPPER 16 BITS OF ACCUMULATOR
          DIV      #12,     R2       ;  DIVIDE R2,R3 BY 10 (12 OCTAL)
          ADD      #60,     R3       ;  CONVERT REMAINDER TO ASCII
          MOVB     R3,      (R4)     ;  MOVE DIGIT TO OUTPUT AREA FOR THE SUM
          MOV      R2,      R3       ;  MOVE QUOTIENT TO R3
          BR       CONVERT           ;  LOOP TO "CONVERT" FOR NEXT ITERATION
FINISH:   MOV      #MSGOUT, R1       ;  SET UP FINAL OUTPUT LINE
          JSR      P,       PSTR     ;  PRINT FINAL LINE VIA "PSTR"
          HALT                       ;  STOP PROGRAM EXECUTION
;:::::::::::::::::::::::::::::: RSTR:   READ STRING SUBROUTINE :::::::::::::::::::::::::::::::::::::
RSTR:     CLR      R2                ;  CLEAR UPPER HALF OF ACCUMULATOR
          CLR      R3                ;  CLEAR LOWER HALF OF ACCUMULATOR
LOOP:     JSR      P,       READIN   ;  READ A CHARACTER VIA "READIN"
          CMPB     R0,      #15      ;  IS THIS CHARACTER A CARRIAGE RETURN?
          BEQ      DONE              ;  YES - BRANCH TO "DONE"
          MOVB     R0,      (R4)     ;  MOVE THIS CHARACTER TO OUTPUT AREA
          INC      R4                ;  MOVE BUFFER POINTER TO NEXT POSITION
          BIC      #177760, R0       ;  CONVERT FROM ASCII TO BINARY
          MUL      #12,     R3       ;  MULTIPLY ACCUMULATOR BY 10 (12 OCTAL)
          ADD      R0,      R3       ;  ADD THIS CHARACTER TO ACCUMULATOR
          BR       LOOP              ;  BRANCH TO "LOOP" TO READ NEXT DIGIT
DONE:     MOV      #12,     R0       ;  SET UP A LINE FEED
          JSR      P,       PRNT     ;  "PRNT" EXECUTES THE LINE FEED
FILL:     CMP      R4,      R5       ;  IS THE OUTPUT BUFFER FULL YET?
          BGT      ENDSTR            ;  YES - BRANCH TO "ENDSTR"
          MOV      #40,     (R4)     ;  NO - MOVE A SPACE TO OUTPUT BUFFER
          INC      R4                ;  MOVE BUFFER POINTER TO NEXT CHARACTER
          BR       FILL              ;  LOOP TO "FILL" & CONTINUE SPACE FILLING
ENDSTR:   RTS      P                 ;  RETURN TO CALLING ROUTINE
;:::::::::::::::::::::::::::: READIN: READ IN CHARACTER SUBROUTINE :::::::::::::::::::::::::::::::::
READIN;   TSTB     KBS               ;  TEST KEYBOARD STATUS WORD
          BPL      READIN            ;  BRANCH TO "READIN" IN NO CHARACTER YET
          MOVB     KBB,     R0       ;  MOVE THIS CHARACTER INTO R0
          BIC      #177600, R0       ;  CLEAR ALL NON-ASCII BITS
          JSR      P,       PRNT     ;  ECHO THIS CHARACTER ON THE TTY
          RTS      P                 ;  RETURN TO CALLING ROUTINE
;:::::::::::::::::::::::::::::: PSTR: PRINT STRING SUBROUTINE ::::::::::::::::::::::::::::::::::::::
PSTR:     MOVB     (R1)+,   R0       ;  MOVE CHARACTER TO BE PRINTED TO R0
          BEQ      RETURN            ;  IF CHARACTER IS 0, BRANCH TO "RETURN"
          JSR      P,       PRNT     ;  PRINT THIS CHARACTER VIA "PRINT"
          BR       PSTR              ;  LOOP TO "PSTR" TO PRINT NEXT CHARACTER
RETURN:   RTS      P                 ;  RETURN TO CALLING ROUTINE
;:::::::::::::::::::::::::::: PRNT: PRINT CHARACTER SUBROUTINE :::::::::::::::::::::::::::::::::::::
PRNT:     TSTB     PRS               ;  TEST TTY STATUS
          BPL      PRNT              ;  BRANCH TO "PRNT" IF NOT YET PRINTED
          MOVB     R0,      PRB      ;  MOVE THIS CHARACTER TO TTY BUFFER AREA
          RTS      P                 ;  RETURN TO CALLING ROUTINE
;:::::::::::::::::::::::::::::::::::: BUFFER DECLARATIONS :::::::::::::::::::::::::::::::::::::::::::
TEMP:     .BLKW 1                    ;  RESERVE 1 WORD FOR TEMPORARY ACCUMULATOR
MSGA:     .ASCIZ /INPUT A? /         ;  RESERVE 9 BYTES + A 0 FOR MESSAGE "A"
MSGB:     .ASCIZ /INPUT B? /         ;  RESERVE 9 BYTES + A 0 FOR MESSAGE "B"
MSGOUT:   .ASCII /THE SUM OF /       ;  RESERVE 12 BYTES FOR THIS STRING
A:        .BLKW 2                    ;  RESERVE 4 BYTES AS BUFFER FOR "A"
MSG1:     .ASCII / AND /             ;  RESERVE 6 BYTES FOR THIS STRING
B:        .BLKW 2                    ;  RESERVE 4 BYTES AS BUFFER FOR "B"
MSG2:     .ASCII / IS /              ;  RESERVE 4 BYTES FOR THIS STRING
C:        .BLKW 3                    ;  RESERVE 6 BYTES AS BUFFER FOR SUM
CRLF:     .BYTE 015, 012             ;  RESERVE 2 BYTES FOR CR / LF
ENDMSG:   .WORD 000000               ;  RESERVE 1 WORD FOR TERMINATOR "0"
;::::::::::::::::::::::::::::::::::::::::::::::::::::::::::::::::::::::::::::::::::::::::::::::::::::
```

FIGURE B3.14

Assembler program to add two numbers

longer to program in assembler than it does in any of the high-level languages because there are more instructions. One high-level instruction might represent several machine language instructions. But for every assembler instruction, there is only one machine instruction.

Assembler language programs are also very hard to read and understand. As a result, they are hard to modify. In addition, they are written for a specific computer. If you were to change computers—especially to a different brand—all the assembler programs would have to be rewritten.

Assembler languages led the way to high-level languages. All the languages previously discussed are high-level languages. They use English-like phrases to express instructions. The availability of high-level languages greatly improved programmer productivity because programmers could now think in English-like terms instead of 1's and 0's. A comparison of programming languages is given in figure B3.15.

High-Level Languages

FIGURE B3.15

Comparison of programming languages

Language	Strengths	Weaknesses	Primary Uses
ADA	Easy to structure programs	Complex, so takes time to master	Scientific
Assembler	Efficient	Requires many statements	Systems
BASIC	Easy to learn; found on most microcomputers	Input/output capabilities; difficult to structure programs	Educational, simple scientific and business
COBOL	Self-documenting; relatively easy to structure programs; found on most minis and mainframes	Verbose; can only do simple calculations	Business
FORTRAN	Handles mathematical calculations and graphics	Difficult to structure programs; relatively weak input/output capabilities	Scientific
LOGO	Easy to learn; allows for simple graphics	Little use outside of education	Educational
PASCAL	Easy to structure programs	Weak input/output capabilities	Educational; scientific
RPG	Easy to generate business reports	Can only do simple calculations; difficult to structure programs	Business

The computer still needs machine language instructions to work. Each program written in a high-level language must be translated into machine language before the computer can run it.

STUDY OBJECTIVES

15. Define machine language and mnemonic.

16. Describe how program instructions are represented in memory.

17. Explain why an assembler language program is easier to write than a machine language program.

18. Identify three disadvantages to writing in assembler or machine language.

19. Briefly explain why programmer productivity improved when high-level programming languages were introduced.

TRANSLATING PROGRAMS

Special systems programs are written to translate high-level instructions into a specific computer's machine instructions. These translator programs are either **interpreters** or **compilers.**

FIGURE B3.16

Language interpreter

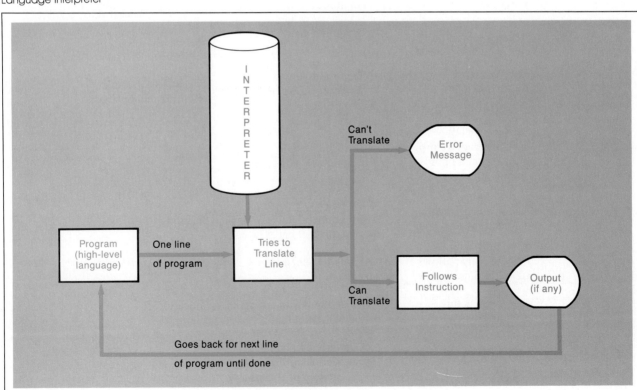

Most microcomputers translate BASIC programs into their machine language by using an interpreter. One instruction at a time is translated and acted upon. The next instruction then takes the place of the completed one; it, too, is then translated and acted upon. This process is repeated until the program comes to its logical conclusion or the interpreter finds a BASIC instruction it cannot translate.

Interpreters

The advantage to using an interpreter is that it uses a minimum amount of memory. The interpreter only needs enough memory to store the instruction it is currently working on. This is also a disadvantage, since the translated version of the program is not saved.

The computer must take the time to translate each instruction as it needs it, even if it has translated the same instruction a dozen times before. Therefore, run time is relatively slow when an interpreter is used because each instruction must be translated before being acted upon.

Larger computer systems and even some microcomputers use compilers when speed is important and memory is not. A compiler program translates the entire high-level program into machine language.

Compilers

A compiler does not run the program, as an interpreter does. It just translates the program into the computer's machine language. The programmer can then save the machine language version on tape or disk.

To use a compiler, the computer must have enough memory to store the compiler and the applications program in both its high-level and machine language forms. The compiler will report any errors it finds.

A word of warning here: a translator program can find some but not all the

FIGURE B3.17

Language compiler

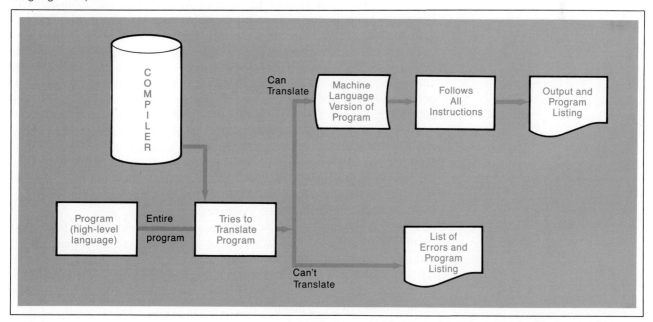

errors in a program. If you spell "print" as PINT, the compiler or interpreter will tell you about it. On the other hand, if you tell it that PAY = HOURS + RATE instead of PAY = HOURS * RATE, it will give you the wrong answer.

When the program has been compiled without any detected errors, the machine language version can be tested. Once the programmer is sure it is working correctly, only the machine language version is used. Therefore, the compiler is only needed while the programmer is developing a program.

A compiler or interpreter is needed for every high-level programming language used on a computer system. If the computer center wants to use COBOL, BASIC, and PASCAL, it can use a BASIC interpreter, a COBOL compiler, and a PASCAL compiler.

STUDY OBJECTIVE

20. Briefly describe the difference between an interpreter and a compiler and identify an advantage and disadvantage to using each.

COMPONENTS OF AN OPERATING SYSTEM

Compilers and interpreters are two types of systems programs that make up a computer's operating system. The operating system is a collection of systems programs used to control the computer's resources. Normally, the manufacturer provides the operating system with the hardware. It helps the computer operator control the IPO cycle through the computer system.

The operating system has two types of systems programs: **control programs** and **processing programs.** The bigger the computer system, the more sophisticated the operating system must be.

Control Programs

The control programs manage the flow of work through the computer. One control program—sometimes called the **supervisor**—is usually the first program loaded into the computer when it is turned on.

As long as the computer is on, the supervisor program takes up a spot in the memory. From there it sets aside memory and processing time for other computer programs. It also coordinates activity between the computer and **peripheral**—attached—devices such as tape and disk drives. With microcomputers, the supervisor handles commands like RUN, LOAD, and SAVE.

The job of the supervisor gets more complicated when computer systems run more than one program at a time. In this situation, the supervisor must keep track of each program. If several programs are waiting to be processed, the supervisor puts them in an input **queue,** or line. The input queue is a list of programs waiting to be run. As space becomes available, the supervisor takes the next program from the input queue.

When processing is complete, the supervisor is responsible for getting the data to the correct output hardware. Since computers work faster than printers and other output hardware, an output queue often accepts the output temporarily. The output is stored in the output queue until the hardware is ready for it. For example, the supervisor will make sure that one program is finished printing before sending another to the printer.

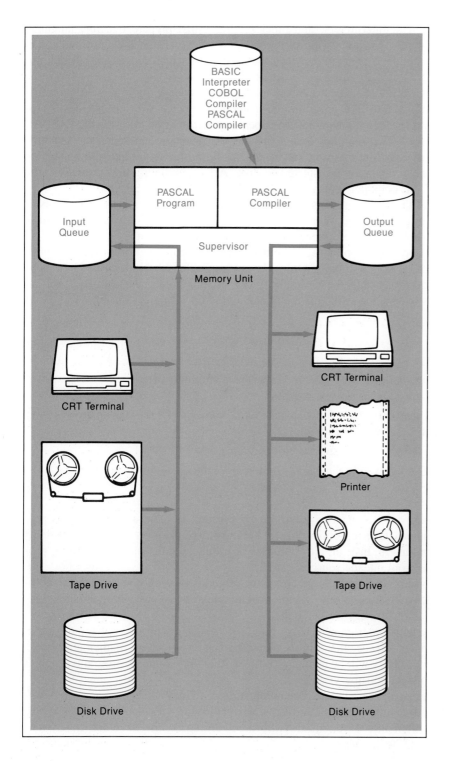

FIGURE B3.18

Job control by supervisor program

Processing Programs

Compilers, interpreters, and other programs that prepare machine language instructions are processing programs. Since several translator programs may be available, a programmer tells the supervisor which processing program to select.

Figure B3.18 shows one way an operating system might handle the translation of a PASCAL program into machine language. After the PASCAL program is loaded into memory, the supervisor is instructed to call in the PASCAL compiler. The compiler then translates the program and sends the machine language translation to the output queue. From the output queue the machine language version is transferred to disk. After completing the translation, the PASCAL compiler returns control back to the supervisor.

Data utility programs are a group of processing programs that help transfer data or programs between equipment. For example, a disk-to-tape data utility program can be used to backup important disk files on tape.

A computer's operating system is actually a combination of many control and processing programs. Only a few examples have been described here. The work performed by the computer system usually dictates the sophistication and types of systems programs that make up the operating system.

STUDY OBJECTIVES

21. Define operating system, supervisor program, peripheral device, queue, and data utility program.
22. Identify the two categories of systems programs that make up an operating system, and give an example of each.
23. Describe how a supervisor program works.
24. Briefly explain the use of input and output queues.

SYSTEMS PROGRAMMING AS A PROFESSION

There are not as many **systems programmers** as there are applications programmers. One reason for this is that most organizations do not hire systems programmers. Instead, they purchase operating systems and other systems programs from outside sources.

Usually, only very large computer centers, software houses, and the computer manufacturers hire systems programmers. In the past, these organizations have trained their own personnel.

Systems programmers being hired today have a four-year college degree in computer science. In addition, they often have very strong mathematics backgrounds. They will be responsible for writing very complex programs, such as compilers and supervisors.

Systems programmers, like applications programmers, often work in development teams. When these teams are employed by computer manufacturers, they often include engineers who are working on the development of new computer technology.

GEORGE BONTECOU
SYSTEMS PROGRAMMER

MY BACKGROUND

One summer, while working toward an economics degree at Southern Methodist University in Dallas, I managed to get a job at IBM as a mailroom clerk. The next summer I went back as both clerk and programmer trainee. During that time, I decided I wanted computer programming as a career.

After graduation, I got a job with the Dallas Planning Commission, again as a programmer trainee. But one day I decided to set out for California. I knocked on the door of every IBM branch office in Los Angeles and San Francisco. I knew they were in a cutback and not hiring anyone at that time, so I was mainly asking for names of their customers who might need help. Eventually, I did go to work for IBM as a systems engineer, and from that position worked my way into systems programming.

RESPONSIBILITIES

I try to see that the software runs and that the users get the results they want. Our computer center runs a number of languages on a new IBM 4331, and the programs are often complex.

SKILLS REQUIRED

To tell the truth, I was never a very good programmer. I really liked designing programs, but I could never get the darn things to run. When you start doing more than just maintenance coding, you find that business and management skills are more important than technical ones. As a systems programmer, in charge of all programming at this computer center, I find that I make more business decisions than technical ones. English communications skills are critical.

The computer industry is actually so diverse that there is room for all kinds of skills. For my career success, it wasn't any particular skill. The most important thing was gaining confidence in myself.

STUDY OBJECTIVES

25. Identify the necessary educational requirements to become a systems
programmer.

26. List three organizations likely to hire a systems programmer.

SUMMARY

Computer programs are a detailed set of instructions that control the computer.
Programs do not have to be written from scratch every time. They can be
obtained from magazines, computer manufacturers, software stores, user groups,
software houses, contract programmers, or in-house programming staffs.

Applications programmers write new programs for users in an organization.
Large projects may require an applications development team made up of a
systems analyst and several computer programmers.

The objective in designing a turnkey system is to make the system easy to
use. Other considerations are whether the program will work by itself or be
integrated with other programs. Finally, users who need immediate access to
information must have online programs using transaction processing. If immediate access to data is not important, then the data can be prepared offline and
processed in batches.

Easy-to-read programs are written according to the principles of structured
programming. These principles are based on the fact that all programs can be
written using three structures: sequence, selection, and repetition.

Several high-level programming languages are used to write computer programs. Business programs are often written in COBOL, RPG, or BASIC.
Scientific programs may be written in FORTRAN, PASCAL, or ADA. LOGO
has been developed as a learning aid.

Programs written in a high-level language must be translated into the computer's own machine language. A systems program does the translation. The translating program can be either an interpreter or a compiler. Interpreters translate one instruction at a time, and the computer acts upon the results. Compilers completely translate the program and save the results.

These translating programs are part of an operating system. The operating system is a collection of systems programs that control the computer's resources. An operating system contains two types of systems programs: control programs and processing programs.

One of the control programs is the supervisor, which stays in the computer's memory. From there it coordinates the flow of data and programs between input devices, output devices, and the memory. Processing programs include interpreters, compilers, and utility programs. All these programs are written by specialized systems programmers.

UNIT C

People Using Computers

Computers have become a common tool used by many people. Unit C explores different computer applications. The first part of the unit takes an in-depth look at how business people use computer technology. Everything from accounting systems to office automation to manufacturing and sales/marketing systems are looked at from the user's point of view.

At one time computers were used only by people in big business and government. This is no longer the case. In the second part of this unit you see that many professionals are now computer users. Doctors, lawyers, teachers, journalists, architects, scientists, and many others work with computers every day.

Unit C concludes with a look at how others use computers on the job for better lives. Artists and musicians with access to computer technology expand visual or sound media. Farmers use computers to improve production by monitoring livestock, inventory, costs, and even the pesticide levels on their fields. Government workers, pilots, athletes, coaches, and blue-collar workers are now working side by side with computers.

CHAPTER C1
People Using Computers in Business

CHAPTER C2
People Using Computers in Other Professions

CHAPTER C3
People Using Computers on the Job for Better Lives

CHAPTER C1

People Using Computers in Business

Computers are one of the few bright spots on the business horizon. In times of rising prices, computers are one resource that is getting both better and less expensive.

One of the biggest roles computer systems play in business is the control and distribution of resources. Giant corporations like IBM, American Telephone and Telegraph, and the Boeing Company could not exist without computers. These companies could not account for their operations, manage their personnel, or control projects without computer systems. The design of the Boeing 747 took 16 million engineering hours. This work could not have been coordinated without computers (see figure C1.1).

A COMPUTER'S PLACE IN THE BUSINESS COMMUNITY

Business people use computer systems to help manage their resources. Consider the chair you are sitting in. The production, distribution, and sale of that chair was most likely controlled by a computer system.

Chair Manufacturer

The chair manufacturer could use a computer system in the following ways:

- To analyze a market survey on the type of chairs consumers want
- To order the raw materials needed to make the chairs
- To control the raw materials inventory
- To accept and process the distributor's orders for chairs
- To schedule and route the production of orders
- To control the inventory of the finished chairs
- To prepare shipping orders to send chairs to the distributor
- To schedule and route the delivery trucks
- To prepare the distributor's bills for the chairs

Distributor

Perhaps the distributor uses another computer system to help keep track of the merchandise. A computer system could be used in the following ways:

- To enter new chairs into the inventory
- To accept and process the retailer's orders for chairs
- To prepare shipping orders to send chairs to the retailer
- To schedule and route the delivery trucks
- To remove delivered chairs from inventory
- To prepare the retailer's bill for the chairs

Retailer

The retailer could then use a computer system in the following ways:

- To enter new chairs into inventory
- To price the chairs
- To remove a chair from inventory when it is sold
- To prepare the customer's bill for the chair
- To order more chairs when inventory is low

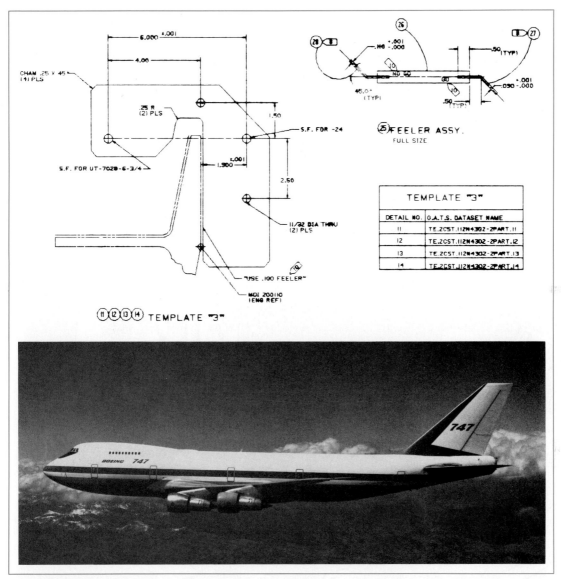

FIGURE C1.1

The Boeing 747 cannot be produced without computers (Courtesy The Boeing Company)

The process is not over yet! If your school purchased the chair from the retailer, it may use a computer system to do the following:

- To keep track of equipment inventory and cost
- To figure taxes from the chair's current value
- To remove the chair from inventory when it is scrapped

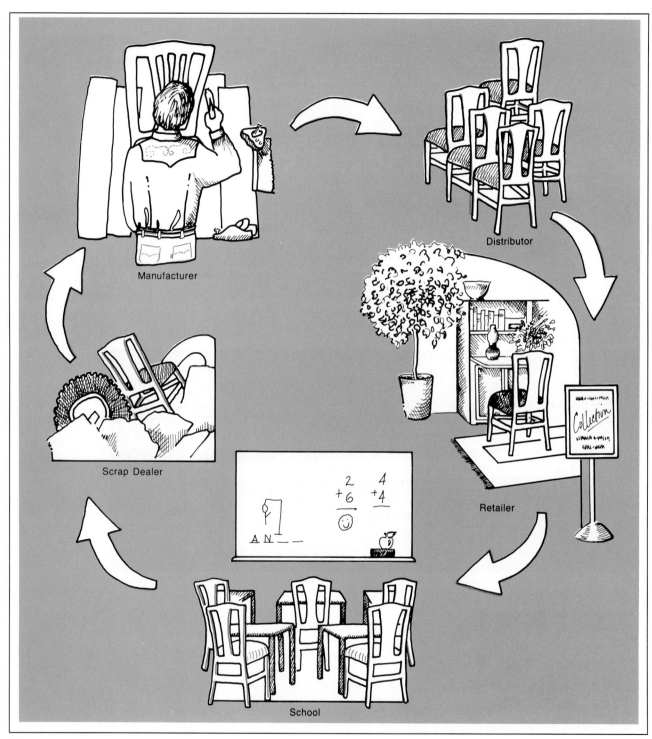

Life cycle of a chair

The process continues. If the chair is made of metal, it may be sent to a scrap dealer who uses a computer system. This system will control the shipment of scrap and the production of new metals. The new metals will be sold, distributed, and stored in inventories using computer systems until the day—you guessed it—they find their way into the production of a new chair! From there the cycle will repeat itself.

There is no escaping computer systems. They are everywhere. Why is this good? It is good because products can be manufactured for less when they are well controlled. There may be six different ways of producing, delivering, and selling a chair. Of the six, we want the least expensive way. Why spend more money than we have to? By improving control, computers help management produce goods for less.

When information is needed about a business, business people use the company's **management information system (MIS)** to find the answer. An MIS is a collection of business systems that provides information to business people.

Every company has an MIS whether they know it or not. The secretary with last year's profit-and-loss statement is part of the MIS. So are the contents of a manager's file drawer. The annual report is part of the MIS, as well as hundreds of other sources of information.

Look again at the definition of MIS. It is a collection of business systems. It does not necessarily include a computer. An MIS can be composed entirely of data, procedures, and personnel. Computer hardware and programs need not be involved.

For years people have recorded business data and processed it into useful information using only hands and head. These management information systems have been around for centuries—long before the computer was invented.

The focus of this chapter is on business computer systems—a subset of all management information systems. As you proceed through the chapter, you will study many types of business computer systems. Remember that the goal of all this sophisticated technology is to provide better information to managers.

FIGURE C1.3

Possible uses of a computer in a management information system

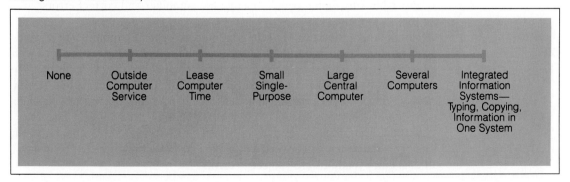

| None | Outside Computer Service | Lease Computer Time | Small Single-Purpose | Large Central Computer | Several Computers | Integrated Information Systems— Typing, Copying, Information in One System |

The proportion of the total MIS that is computer based varies from company to company. Some companies do not have computers at all. One company may purchase computer services from others. Some companies have computers dedicated to one job, like inventory control or billing. At the other extreme, companies have joined their business computer systems with their typing, copying, and communications systems so that the entire MIS is computer based. There are many variations in between.

STUDY OBJECTIVES

1. Identify one advantage to having computer systems help control production.
2. Define MIS.
3. Identify the components common to both computerized and noncomputerized management information systems.

ACCOUNTING

Computerized **accounting systems** have been very successful at satisfying the information needs of business people. There are two major reasons for this success. First, the accounting profession has had years of experience with computers. Second, computers are excellent record keepers. Given accurate data and correct programs, they can work many, many hours without errors.

Accountants identify and record all important facts and figures. They also help create reports that accurately reflect the financial status of the company. Since computers never become bored or complain, they have been given the most tedious, time-consuming tasks in accounting.

Basically, the purpose of an accounting system is to maintain data that accurately represents the financial status of the company. Documented changes in the state of a business, like bills and checks, are called **transactions.** For a computerized accounting system to be useful, accurate data must be collected and records modified whenever a transaction occurs.

To maintain records, a computerized accounting system needs all five components of a computer system:

1. Trained personnel
2. Accurate data
3. Computer hardware of sufficient capacity and speed
4. Programs that instruct the computer to modify data and produce reports
5. Procedures by which people operate the computer and correct errors

Special Properties of Accounting Systems

Several unique properties of accounting impose special requirements on computer programs and procedures. First, accounting systems usually deal with transactions of money. Consequently, errors can have a severe impact. In accounting systems, there is sometimes an opening for computer crime: people can gain financially by making unauthorized changes to programs or data. This is especially true with systems that print negotiable output such as checks.

Second, accounting systems usually deal with a tremendous amount of input data. This data must be converted to a machine-readable form. Unfortunately, all data entry methods are subject to errors.

Consider these two points together. Do you see the dilemma facing the systems analyst designing an accounting system? The system involves money, and the impact of errors or theft can be severe. In addition, there is the possibility of data entry errors. Because of these problems, much of the processing in an accounting system is intended to identify and correct errors.

A final property of accounting systems is the need to generate and save large amounts of data for income tax reporting and audits.

An **audit** is a procedure in which other people—called **auditors**—come in to check on the procedures used by the accountants. Auditors are interested in how accountants identify and record all important transactions. During an audit, the auditors often want to trace a transaction. For example, they might trace an order from the original request to the recording of the final payment.

If the order is processed by a computer system, then the auditors must be familiar with computers. They have to examine computer records. Thus, accounting systems must be designed to save and easily access data of interest to auditors. All of this is part of keeping track of the financial status of the company.

Accountant Martha Baker

Not a day went by on her new job that Martha Baker didn't remember something from her experience as a computer operator. That job could also be credited with interesting her in accounting. And those paychecks provided the seed money for her college education. Now, seven years later, she had her four-year degree in accounting and she was back working with computers.

As an accountant for Midstate Bank, Martha did not have to operate the computer anymore. That job was left to the computer operators. One of her new responsibilities required using reports generated by the computer to keep track of the company's hourly **payroll.**

Using Computers to Prepare Paychecks

Figure C1.4 lists the requirements for processing payroll. It was Martha's job to make sure that everything was done correctly and on time.

The first two functions on the list are self-explanatory. The third function outputs data to the **general ledger** file. Payroll entries to the general ledger store data related to the amount of cash paid out for wages, taxes, and social security. A general ledger is used to keep track of a company's revenues and expenses. Therefore, payroll entries represent just a part of the data stored in this file.

1. Compute pay, taxes, deductions
2. Print paychecks
3. Produce entries for general ledger
4. Account for sick leave and vacation time
5. Print W-2 tax forms at year end
6. Accommodate new employees and changes to employee data
7. Account for ex-employees until year end
8. Minimize risk of error or unauthorized activity

FIGURE C1.4

Hourly payroll specifications

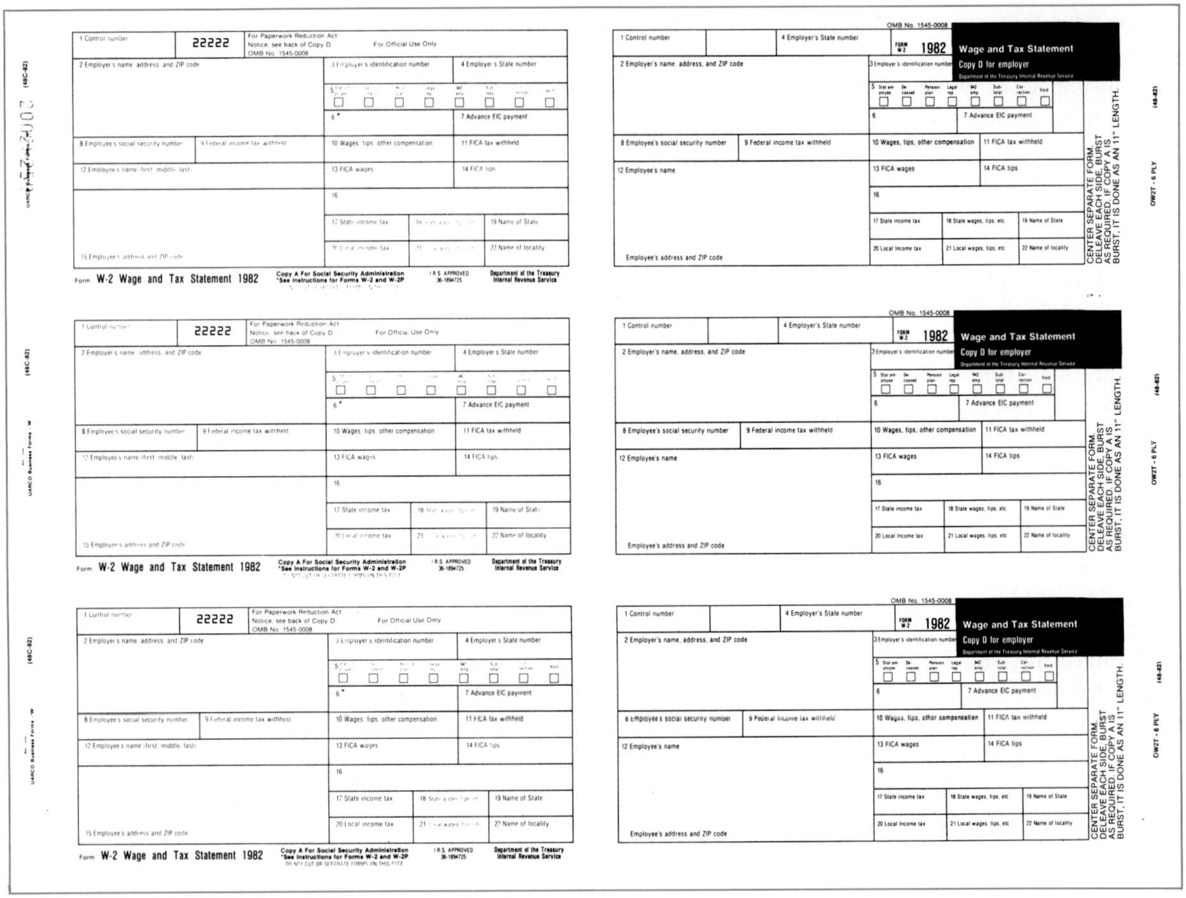

1 Control number | 22222 | For Paperwork Reduction Act Notice, see back of Copy D | OMB No. 1545-0008 | For Official Use Only

2 Employer's name, address, and ZIP code | 3 Employer's identification number | 4 Employer's State number

5 Stat em- ployee | De- ceased | Pension plan | Legal rep. | 942 emp. | Sub- total | Cor- rection | Void

6 | 7 Advance EIC payment

8 Employee's social security number | 9 Federal income tax withheld | 10 Wages, tips, other compensation | 11 FICA tax withheld

12 Employee's name (first, middle, last) | 13 FICA wages | 14 FICA tips

16

17 State income tax | 18 State wages, tips, etc. | 19 Name of State

20 Local income tax | 21 Local wages, tips, etc. | 22 Name of locality

15 Employee's address and ZIP code

Form W-2 Wage and Tax Statement 1982 | Copy A For Social Security Administration *See Instructions for Forms W-2 and W-2P | I.R.S. APPROVED 36-1894725 | Department of the Treasury Internal Revenue Service

DO NOT CUT OR SEPARATE FORMS ON THIS PAGE

1 Control number | 4 Employer's State number | OMB No. 1545-0008 | FORM W-2 1982 | Wage and Tax Statement | Copy D for employer | Department of the Treasury Internal Revenue Service

2 Employer's name, address, and ZIP code | 3 Employer's identification number

5 Stat em- ployee | De- ceased | Pension plan | Legal rep. | 942 emp. | Sub- total | Cor- rection | Void

6 | 7 Advance EIC payment

8 Employee's social security number | 9 Federal income tax withheld | 10 Wages, tips, other compensation | 11 FICA tax withheld

12 Employee's name | 13 FICA wages | 14 FICA tips

16

17 State income tax | 18 State wages, tips, etc. | 19 Name of State

20 Local income tax | 21 Local wages, tips, etc. | 22 Name of locality

Employee's address and ZIP code

CENTER SEPARATE FORM. DELEAVE EACH SIDE, BURST AS REQUIRED. IF COPY A IS BURST, IT IS DONE AS AN 11" LENGTH.

OW2T - 6 PLY (48-82)

UARCO Business Forms (48C-82)

FIGURE C1.5

W-2 forms

Martha also watched over accounting reports that listed sick leave and vacation time. The computer system added time each pay period and deducted time as it was taken. Since she was responsible for these reports, she checked them before her manager authorized any requests.

For the computer to be able to print W-2 tax forms (figure C1.5) at year-end meant that the system had to keep track of total pay to date, taxes to date, social security, and other taxable income. This data had to be kept for all employees, even those who left the company.

The next two functions in figure C1.4 refer to changes that were made to the employee file. As employees were hired, data had to be added to the file. In addition, since pay rates were stored in the file, changes had to be made when employees received pay increases.

When an employee left the company, his or her record had to be marked so that no further checks would be issued. However, the record was not deleted until the W-2 form was printed at the end of the year.

Finally, all these functions were double-checked by Martha's boss and an independent auditor. This procedure minimized the risk of computer error, people error, and unauthorized activity.

A closer look at Martha's responsibilities will show you that running hourly payroll each week was actually a four-phase process:

1. Preparing changes to employee file
2. Making changes to employee file
3. Preparing input data from employee time cards
4. Using employee file and input data to print paychecks

These four phases provided important checks and balances between the accounting department and the data processing department. The checks and balances were reflected in the fact that one individual was not given complete responsibility for preparing paychecks. This provided an easy means of catching errors and preventing unauthorized activities.

Payroll: Phase 1

The personnel department was responsible for hiring new employees and keeping employee information up-to-date as people moved. Every week the personnel department sent Martha a list of new employees and changes to the employee file in the form of a change notice.

Martha would check the change notices and send them to the data processing department. A control clerk received the request, recorded it, and sent the change notices on to a data entry operator.

The data entry operator used the change notices as source documents and keyed the data onto a tape using a key-to-tape machine. The work was verified and any errors corrected. The data entry operator then notified the control clerk that the job was done.

Next, the control clerk passed the tape to the computer operator. The computer operator would load a pre-edit program into the computer and mount the tape on a tape drive. The pre-edit program input each change and printed the data on the printer in the form of a pre-edit report.

The control clerk then returned the pre-edit report to Martha and gave the tape to the librarian. The librarian catalogued and stored the tape. Martha checked the pre-edit report for errors. If any errors were found, the process was repeated.

Figure C1.7 contains a pre-edit report for changes to the employee file. As Martha examined the report, the first two changes appeared to be correct. However, the pre-edit program detected an error in the third entry. In this company, all employee numbers started with 1. Since Joy Johnson's number did not, it was identified as an error. Martha made sure that the errors were corrected.

There was another error on the pre-edit report that was not identified by the

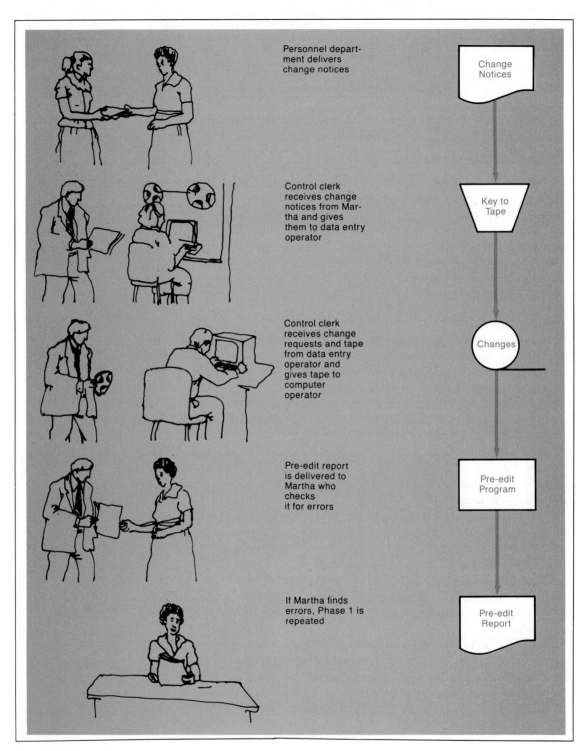

Personnel depart-
ment delivers
change notices

Control clerk
receives change
notices from Mar-
tha and gives
them to data entry
operator

Control clerk
receives change
requests and tape
from data entry
operator and
gives tape to
computer
operator

Pre-edit report
is delivered to
Martha who
checks
it for errors

If Martha finds
errors, Phase 1 is
repeated

Change
Notices

Key to
Tape

Changes

Pre-edit
Program

Pre-edit
Report

FIGURE C1.6

Hourly payroll: phase 1

```
        EMPLOYEE
        NUMBER                           EMPLOYEE NAME            TYPE OF CHANGE

        12481                            FRED PARKS               PAY CHANGE TO 8.73
        14618                            SALLY BATTS              PAY CHANGE TO 7.50
    ::::  ERROR  IN  NEXT  CHANGE--INCORRECT  EMPLOYEE  NUMBER   ::::
        02800                            JOY JOHNSON              NEW EMPLOYEE
                                         ADDRESS                 1418 S. TAMARACK
                                                                 ALEXANDRIA, VA 01042
                                         DATE OF BIRTH           DECEMBER 11, 1944
                                         TITLE                   PRODUCTION ASSISTANT
                                         PAY RATE                7.52
                                         DEPENDENTS              3
                                         SOCIAL SECURITY NUMBER  522-00-1841
        17281                            ELMER NILSON             PAY CHANGE TO 98.70
        16415                            DOROTHY SUHM             PAY CHANGE TO 21.50
```

FIGURE C1.7

Payroll pre-edit report

pre-edit program. The pay change for employee 17281 should have been 9.87—not 98.70. It was Martha's responsibility to find this type of error and correct it. Since two errors were found, phase 1 was repeated after the corrections were made.

Payroll: Phase 2

After verifying that there were no errors on the pre-edit report, Martha had the control clerk ask the computer operator to update the employee file using the changes from phase 1.

The computer operator would load the employee file update program and mount the changes on the tape drive and the employee file on the disk drive. The computer then used the employee number to identify each employee record that needed to be changed. In some cases, new records were added to the file.

As a result of updating the employee file, an edit report was printed. The edit report listed all the additions and changes made to the file. The control clerk returned the edit report to Martha, who checked the edit report against the original change notices. Since Martha had carefully checked the pre-edit report in phase 1, few errors ever appeared on the edit report.

Payroll: Phase 3

The previous week's time cards also went through a pre-edit run, just like the change notices. The control clerk received the time cards from each department. The data entry operators then entered the data onto tape.

The tape was then sent to the computer operator, who ran a pre-edit program. As a result, a preliminary time report was printed. This report was also sent to Martha for checking.

Payroll: Phase 4

After the preliminary time report was double-checked, Martha would inform the control clerk that payroll was ready to be run. The tape with the time card data and the disk with the employee file were mounted and the payroll program loaded into the computer.

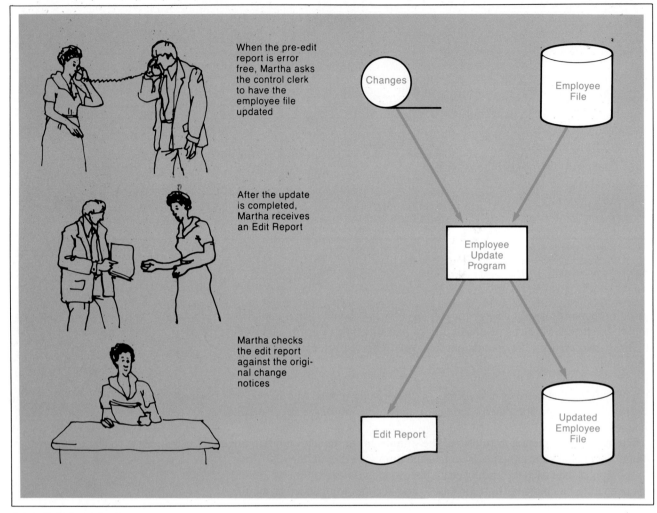

When the pre-edit report is error free, Martha asks the control clerk to have the employee file updated

Changes

Employee File

After the update is completed, Martha receives an Edit Report

Employee Update Program

Martha checks the edit report against the original change notices

Edit Report

Updated Employee File

FIGURE C1.8

Hourly payroll: phase 2

The employee file was then updated with the latest payroll data. In addition, a payroll report, paychecks, and error report were produced. The reports and paychecks were returned to the accounting department for Martha to look over. If everything was in order, she passed the work on to her boss for the final OK. The paychecks were then distributed to the employees.

Systems Flowcharts

Figures C1.6, C1.8, C1.9, and C1.10 illustrate what Martha and the data processing staff did to prepare paychecks. Often, symbols are used to represent

COMPUTERS AND SOCIETY

More Uses, More Users, More Questions

The robots are coming! Or are they? Is this Star Wars setting a myth or reality?

ROBOT MYTHS AND REALITIES

R2D2 and C3PO are fiction. At this time, state-of-the-art robotics does not even include voice recognition and communication in one language, let alone C3PO's claim to over six million forms of communication. Today's mobile robots can do little more than avoid objects, utter a few canned phrases, and wave an arm or two around in the air. Such robots are toys.

Industrial robots, on the other hand, are very much a reality. Although they are unexciting to see, industrial robots are quite useful, performing repetitive, sometimes dangerous, tasks with a high degree of reliability. Industrial robots cut airplane parts, pack candy, drill holes, and remove parts from hot ovens. Further, such robots are cost effective. In 1981, a robot could be operated at $5.50 an hour; during that same year, the average wage and benefit expense for a comparable laborer was $18.10.

Industrial robots have the potential to eliminate drudgery and meaningless labor. They can replace humans in unpleasant environments, such as mines or hot factories. Industrial robots can also work in dangerous environments, such as the bowels of nuclear reactors or in the presence of highly contagious and dangerous diseases.

Robots at a Ford plant are tireless and uncomplaining workers, but 24 million industrial workers are worried about increasing automation.

This new-found friend is actually being controlled by a human being a few feet away.

Japan has emerged as a leader in the practical application of robotics.

Asimov's Three Laws of Robotics

1. A robot may not injure a human being, or, through inaction, allow a human being to come to harm.

2. A robot must obey the orders given it by a human being except where such orders would conflict with the First Law.

3. A robot must protect its own existence as long as such protection does not conflict with either the First or Second Law.

This "Apprentice" robot from Unimation is used for arc welding.

A victim of a power line accident tries out his new electronic arms, activated by motion sensors and electrical signals from the skin.

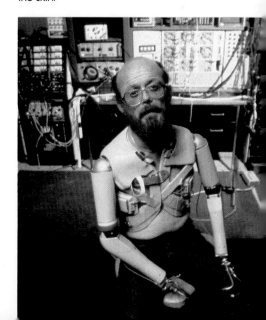

But what are the social consequences? If robots take over spot welding, what will happen to the world's spot welders? If robots take over auto painting, what will happen to the world's auto painters? Although robots will create some new jobs, the ratio of lost jobs to new jobs will not be one to one. Further, today's spot welders are unlikely to be tomorrow's robot mechanics. What will the response of the labor unions be? What *should* the response of the labor unions be?

Futhermore, the use of robots means a loss of control. Who is responsible if a robot accidentally kills someone? If robots can be programmed to produce useful work, they can also be programmed to commit crimes. Who is responsible if a robot intentionally kills someone?

Less dramatically, considering that robots follow standardized procedures, will products become so similar that our environment becomes uniform, sterile, and bland? Will craftsmanship and creativity in workmanship disappear? Does today's laborer have only three choices—to become a technologist, an artisan, or unemployed?

Computers prolong life and reduce pain and suffering. Computers help doctors to detect diseases; they improve diagnoses; they enable surgeons to operate more precisely; they monitor critically ill patients. Computer systems analyze the occurrence of disease and help determine causes and means of prevention.

Computer technology also helps people to compensate for or overcome handicaps. Hearing can be improved; artificial limbs can be made more useful; optical sensors can detect eye movements, thus enabling paraplegics to turn pages or cause other action to occur by moving their eyes.

All of these benefits are possible, but not without social cost. People are confronted with new ethical dilemmas. When is someone really dead? At what point should life-sustaining equipment be removed to allow a person to die? At what point is life no longer worth living? Who pays the cost of maintaining a person who cannot afford to be maintained? Such questions necessitate a new morality. Meanwhile, physicians, relatives, and friends are forced to make life-and-death decisions.

Futhermore, what are the biological consequences of introducing technology into medicine? If the evolution of the human race is governed by the law of the survival of the fittest, what happens when the unfit are maintained? Should people with certain diseases or medical conditions be prohibited from procreating?

By controlling the processes of aging and by using artificial organs, doctors may extend life expectancy to 100 years or more. When it becomes possible, should it be allowed?

Imaging systems help doctors with patient diagnosis.

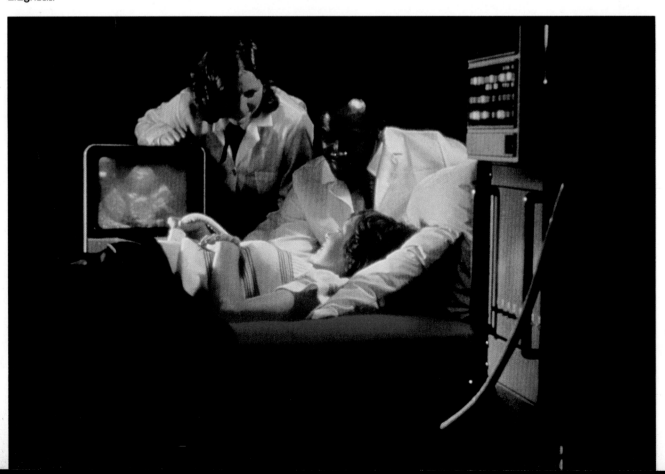

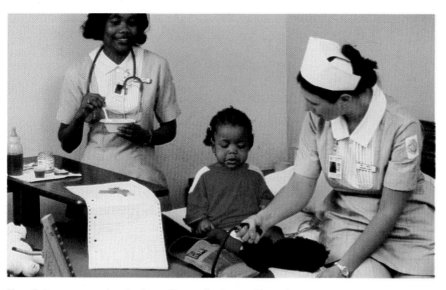

Hospitals use computers to streamline patient record keeping.

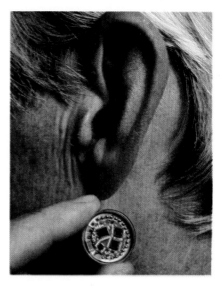

Small hearing devices continue to shrink, with medical research producing circuitry as tiny as nerves and neurons.

Understanding and duplicating human speech integrates medical research with computer technology.

The computer has revolutionized the way we do business. Credit checking, order processing, travel reservations, automated manufacturing, typing, communications—all have been changed by computers. In fact, many services we take for granted would be impossible without computer technology.

Many law firms use computers to organize, store, and retrieve information.

ATMs, or automatic teller machines, are becoming as commonplace as human tellers.

Stockbrokers and investment houses use computers to provide customers with current information.

Warehouses throughout the world use computerized inventory control.

Computers improve productivity and operating efficiency. Product quality can increase, costs can decrease, or both. Consider the telephone: because of the computer, long distance service has improved, while costs have decreased. Computer technology can substantially improve our material well-being.

At the same time, however, computers can create standardized, sterile, and inflexible environments. With computers, warm and friendly offices can become cold and hostile. Decision making can be constrained, and people can lose freedom of action. Computer systems provide new opportunities for crime. Privacy can be invaded, and sometimes the victim is unaware of the invasion.

Worst of all, computer systems contribute to the acceleration of our pace of life. With computers, we can acquire better and cheaper things more and more rapidly. But do we want better and cheaper things, more and more rapidly? Computers do not help us answer that question.

Educational games and drill and practice programs can improve the quality of education and increase teacher productivity. Educational software can make learning easier and more fun, and it can respond to individual differences. For example, computer-assisted instruction (CAI) can respond to each student's level of knowledge. Students who answer all questions correctly can be introduced to new and more difficult material. Students who consistently answer incorrectly can be presented with more basic material or with tutorial discussions.

Even more exciting, computers offer opportunities to teach subjects in entirely new ways. Computer graphics can be used to present mathematical principles, such as the concept of a limit. Students who are exposed to mathematical concepts from a graphical point of view appear to gain improved intuition into mathematical concepts.

Simulation provides another educational possibility. Students can perform chemistry or physics experiments on the computer. For example, students can instruct the computer to combine chemical compounds, and the computer will simulate a chemical reaction. Such simulation can reduce laboratory expenses, as well as allow students to learn from experiments that would be too dangerous to do in reality. High school geometry has been taught in the same fashion for centuries. With the computer language LOGO, however, geometry can be taught using entirely new methods.

Many teachers find that microcomputers stimulate curiosity and learning.

Languages such as LOGO take children beyond the game-playing and into programming.

Unfortunately, there are not enough computers to go around. According to one estimate, there are more than 200 students for every microcomputer. (In contrast, IBM has one computer terminal for every two employees.) The benefits of computer-based education will have little impact until this ratio is drastically reduced.

Even then, what are the social costs? Will computers take the humanness out of teaching? Will students feel more isolated and alone when using computer-based systems? A classroom may be slow and inefficient, but it is social. Will the cost of computer-assisted instruction be less well-developed social skills?

Computer-assisted instruction (CAI) provides a learning system for a wide variety of subjects.

Simulation is used for the training of both pilots and flight controllers.

COMMUNICATIONS

The world gets smaller and smaller. Reporters at remote sites write stories on word processing systems and submit their stories over communications lines to a computer at the newspaper's headquarters. The paper is composed in electronic form and sent via satellite to distributed printing plants. Finally, near the point of sale, the paper is printed.

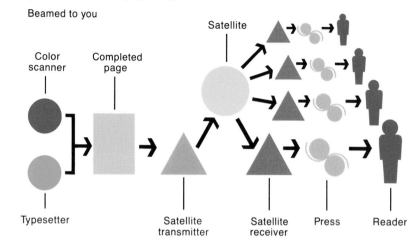

Beamed to you

Color scanner — Completed page — Typesetter — Satellite transmitter — Satellite receiver — Press — Reader — Satellite

Printing presses across the United States receive satellite-transmitted pages for printing and daily local distribution.

Newspaper by satellite. Computer and satellite technology are used to allow *USA Today* to be printed overnight across the United States. Computer-set type and reproduced photographs are laid out as newspaper pages. The pages are converted to electronic impulses and beamed to the WESTAR III satellite 22,300 miles above the earth. The satellite broadcasts the signals back to receiving stations at the print sites.

The *USA Today* newsroom reporters enter their stories using computer terminals.

USA Today provides a practical example of today's computer communications technology.

Using teleconferencing, business people in different locations meet face-to-face without travel. Air traffic controllers instruct pilots whom they never meet to fly airplanes that they never see, except electronically. Airplanes are kept on the ground in Seattle because of crowded airspace in Chicago. A shopper at home in Milwaukee buys a TV from a store located in Phoenix using a credit card from a bank in Memphis. In less than five seconds, computers in Milwaukee, Phoenix, and Memphis communicate to verify credit and inventory levels, to generate the shipping invoice, and to record the sale.

It becomes easier and easier to "reach out, reach out and touch someone," whether that someone is a friend, a business associate, a business, or a computer. What are the consequences of all this reaching out? Closer communication, better understanding among people, a world view instead of a neighborhood view are some consequences. Others are a furious pace of life, confusion and complexity, and more information than we are capable of handling. According to Bell Laboratories, the weekday edition of *The New York Times* contains more information than a person in the sixteenth century received in an entire lifetime. How can we cope? Do we need a computer to say "no thanks" when someone reaches out?

Air traffic controllers "watch" planes electronically.

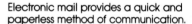

Teleconferencing is used by large companies for face-to-face communication without travel.

Electronic mail provides a quick and paperless method of communication.

CBS and AT&T combine to introduce catalogue shopping by videotext, allowing customers to browse, select, and pay using terminals.

COMMUNICATIONS AND CONTROL

Computers control processes. They run machinery, regulate the speed of production lines, monitor power plants and refineries, and control space probes. Computers instructed a robot on Mars to perform experiments—experiments that, ironically, were concerned with searching for signs of life. Computers assimilate more data than human beings, make decisions in split seconds, and work tirelessly at boring and repetitive jobs. They are ideal for industrial control.

This seventh Space Shuttle launch used computers for communications and control, orbited communication satellites for Canada and Indonesia, and employed a robotic arm to deploy and retrieve a space platform.

User-transparent communications control is effected at the Bell Telephone network center.

NASA's Deep Space Network control center communicates with and controls spacecraft traveling in and exploring deep space.

But should we trust computer control? If surgeons avoid surgery and lawyers avoid lawsuits, will computer programmers avoid automated airplanes? Who is responsible for mishaps? Computers introduce possibilities for crime, sabotage, and blackmail. Are these possibilities being examined, discussed, and controlled?

Control of electricity and water is essential to our society and impossible without the aid of computers, such as those shown here at the Bonneville Power Authority.

Military use of computers can combine computer graphics and computer communications to provide commanders with realistic representations of troop movements as they are occurring.

GENERAL ELECTRIC COMPANY
ADVANCED TERRAIN REPRESENTATION
MILITARY TACTICAL SCENE WITH OVERLAY SHOWING DEPLOYMENT
OF FORCES (KEY CULTURE FEATURES CUED WITH SYMBOLS)

GOVERNMENT AND LAW ENFORCEMENT

Computers facilitate the making, the keeping, and the breaking of the law. Computer systems control the massive flow of paperwork through the U.S. Congress. Computer systems keep congressional schedules, record ballots, send and receive electronic mail, maintain records of correspondence, and help to produce the *Congressional Record*.

Congressman Charles Rose of North Carolina uses a local communication network for status information on legislation.

Today's sheriff with today's gold: recovering $50,000 worth of computer chips.

Computers assist law enforcement by keeping records of crimes and criminals. Using computers and communications, police can check records on a suspected stolen automobile without stopping the vehicle. More information for law enforcement means greater safety for police and less disruption for law-abiding citizens. Computer systems also increase the efficiency of police operations, producing lower costs and better law enforcement.

Unfortunately, computer systems provide new opportunities for crime, necessitating new laws and new law enforcement techniques. If money in a French bank is stolen in the United States through communications with a computer located in Switzerland, which country's laws pertain? Suppose such a crime is suspected. Who investigates it? Where and how?

Suppose someone steals software by copying it. How should the investigating officer proceed? Since no object was stolen, what evidence should be gathered? Clearly, the investigation of computer crime requires special training. Who has this training?

In a police car, computers can access information on suspects immediately.

Law enforcement agencies, such as this one in Louisiana, provide network communication with other agencies throughout the world.

SUMMARY

Computer systems are tools; as such, they are instruments for accomplishing jobs or solving problems. Tools have no conscience. They can be used for good or evil, for creation or destruction, for benefit or harm. Whether a tool is beneficial, on balance, depends on the people who use it.

In the preceding pages, you have seen some of the ways computer systems benefit society. Each of these applications is, in itself, good. The tool behind these applications, however, is ethically neutral. Computers are powerful tools, and the more powerful the tool, the greater the potential danger. To avoid such danger, human beings need to gain awareness and to maintain control.

The Japanese are pioneering the development of a street map navigation display for visitors to a city.

QUESTIONS

1. Describe two benefits and two dangers of robotics. What can you, as a citizen, do to reduce the dangers?

2. Summarize the ethical problems caused by the introduction of computers into the medical field.

3. Consider the consequences to you of obtaining better and cheaper goods, more and more rapidly. At what point does the acquisition of material goods lose value to you? How can you structure your life to reflect this priority?

4. Describe two advantages and two disadvantages of computers in education. On balance, do you think the impact of computers in education will be positive?

5. Summarize the ways in which computer technology has made the world smaller and smaller. On balance, has this change been beneficial? What changes do you expect to see if the world continues to shrink?

6. Suppose a computer-controlled process explodes and kills several people. Subsequent investigation shows that the problem was caused by an error in a computer program. The vendor of the program had detected the error and sent a correction to all users. However, employees of the company in which the explosion occurred had not made the change. Who should be held responsible?

7. Suppose someone steals software by copying it. What evidence do you think is necessary to prove that the crime occurred?

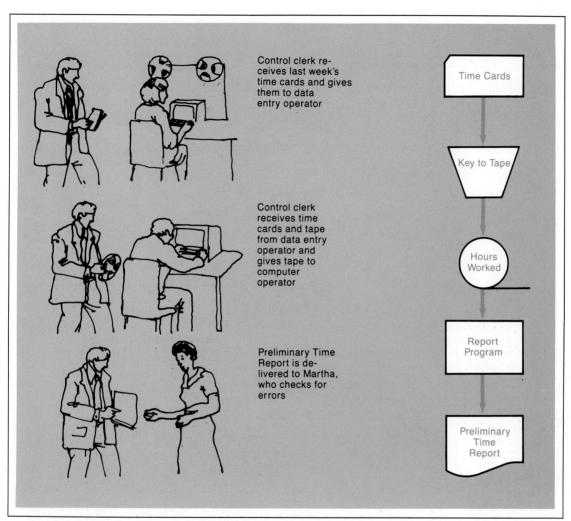

Control clerk receives last week's time cards and gives them to data entry operator

Control clerk receives time cards and tape from data entry operator and gives tape to computer operator

Preliminary Time Report is delivered to Martha, who checks for errors

Time Cards

Key to Tape

Hours Worked

Report Program

Preliminary Time Report

FIGURE C1.9

Hourly payroll: phase 3

the IPO steps for a particular application. These symbols are combined to produce a **system flowchart.** System flowcharts are shown in figures C1.6, C1.8, C1.9, and C1.10 to represent the steps in each phase.

As you compare the illustrations with the system flowchart, you will see that each symbol has a special meaning. Any manual operation like data entry is represented by the symbol $\bigtriangledown$. Processing data using the computer is shown by the symbol $\square$. The symbol $\square$ is used for any report. Data on storage media is represented by $\square$ for cards, $\bigcirc$ for tapes, and $\bigcirc$ for disks.

203

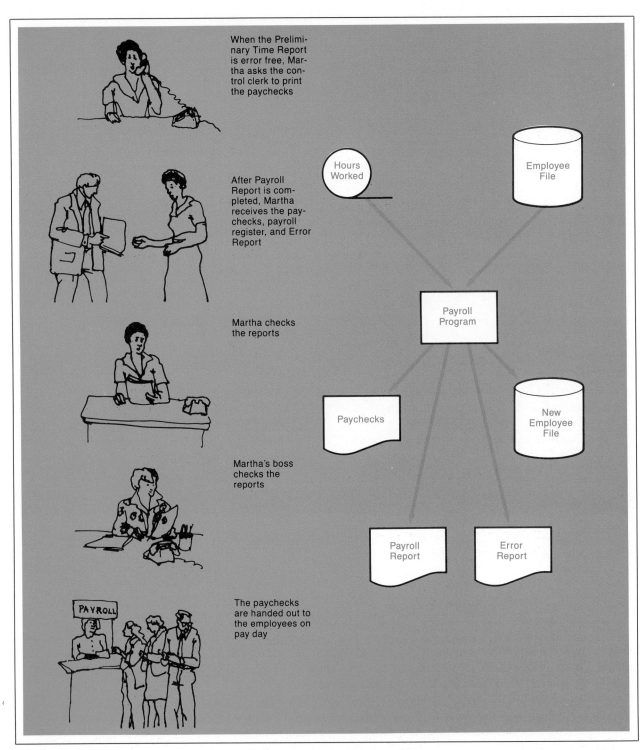

When the Preliminary Time Report is error free, Martha asks the control clerk to print the paychecks

After Payroll Report is completed, Martha receives the paychecks, payroll register, and Error Report

Martha checks the reports

Martha's boss checks the reports

The paychecks are handed out to the employees on pay day

Hours Worked

Employee File

Payroll Program

Paychecks

New Employee File

Payroll Report

Error Report

FIGURE C1.10

Hourly payroll: phase 4

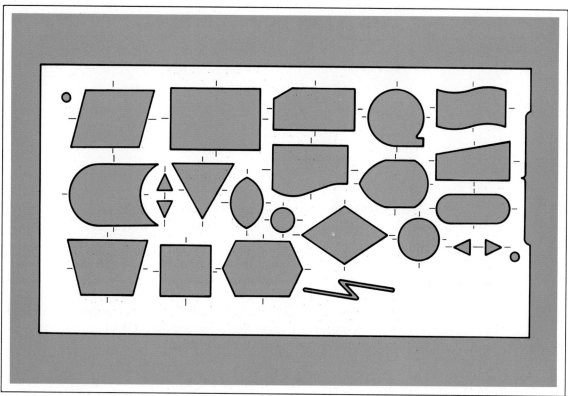

Flowcharting template

A **flowcharting template** like the one in figure C1.11 is used to draw a system flowchart. The template allows people who are not too artistic to prepare a flowchart. People like to use system flowcharts because they can identify each step in an IPO cycle without having to read a lot of words.

STUDY OBJECTIVES

4. Define transaction.

5. Identify two reasons that computer systems have been successfully used in supporting accounting functions.

6. Identify the purpose of an accounting system.

7. Describe three properties of an accounting system that impose special requirements on a computer system.

8. Briefly describe the responsibilities of an accountant and an auditor.

9. List eight requirements of hourly payroll and describe the purpose of each.

10. Briefly explain the reason for breaking hourly payroll into four phases.

11. Describe the purpose of a system flowchart.

12. Describe the function of a flowcharting template and identify the following symbols:

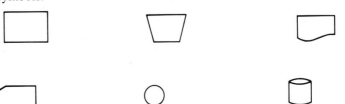

OTHER ACCOUNTING COMPUTER SYSTEMS

Billing

Figure C1.12 lists common accounting systems. These systems are found in most businesses and represent the backbone of their MIS.

Billing systems generate bills, or invoices, to customers. The invoice shows the money the customer owes the company. Figure C1.13 shows a typical billing statement. The information on this output comes from an order and the customer's record.

Besides printing the bill, the computer system also updates an accounts receivable record. The system flowchart in figure C1.14 shows how these business systems interact to use the same data.

FIGURE C1.12

Common accounting computer systems

Payroll
Billing
Accounts Receivable
Accounts Payable
General Ledger
Inventory Control

FIGURE C1.13

Billing statement

CONSOLIDATED INDUSTRIES

STATEMENT OF ACCOUNT WITH

TAYLOR CONSTRUCTION PRODUCTS   DECEMBER 1, 1984

INVOICE	SHIPMENT DATE	DESCRIPTION	COST
11046	10/20/83	ALUMINUM SIDING	$1148.12
11982	11/04/83	FASTENERS	37.15
12257	11/20/83	ROOFING MATERIALS	3894.84
TOTAL DUE			$5080.11

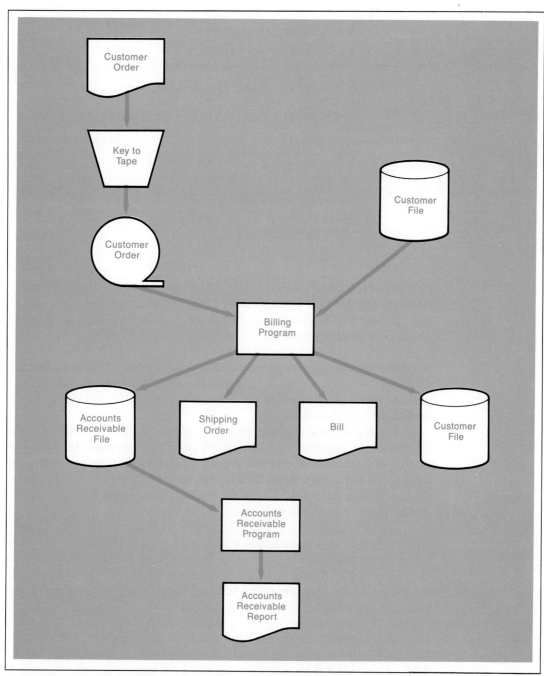

Systems flowchart of billing and accounts receivable

CONSOLIDATED INDUSTRIES

AGED ACCOUNTS RECEIVABLE   DECEMBER 1, 1984

CUSTOMER NUMBER	CUSTOMER NAME	CURRENT BALANCE	BALANCE OVER 30 DAYS LATE	BALANCE OVER 60 DAYS LATE	TOTAL BALANCE
37842	TAYLOR CONST.	$5080.11	$ 0.00	$ 0.00	$5080.11
39148	ABC SUPPLIES	0.00	438.10	300.14	738.24
40418	SHAKEWELL INC	127.13	541.27	1384.17	2052.57
41183	ZAVASKY INC	2312.47	0.00	0.00	2312.47
44817	ABLE ENTERPRISE	1497.12	348.97	0.00	1846.09

FIGURE C1.15

Accounts receivable report

Accounts Receivable

Accounts receivable systems keep track of the money owed to a company. Reports from this system are used for collection purposes, for credit checks, and for watching for potentially bad debts. Figure C1.15 shows a sample accounts receivable report.

Accounts Payable

Accounts payable systems produce checks to pay company bills and keep track of money the company owes its suppliers. Since accounts payable systems generate checks, they usually have the same type of double-checks that Martha used in the payroll system.

A common accounts payable problem concerns discounts. Suppliers often offer savings if payment is made within a certain time period. An accountant may or may not want to take the discount, depending on the cash available, the amount owed, the size of the discount, and other factors. Some accounts payable systems use these factors to produce reports that help accountants decide on the best time to pay debts.

General Ledger

General ledger systems maintain a company's primary records. This system performs the bookkeeping function for the company. Balance sheets, like the one in figure C1.16, and income statements are produced. These reports tell the owners of the company if they are making or losing money. The general ledger system produces other reports as well.

Inventory Control

Inventory control systems maintain records of additions and deletions from stock of finished or unfinished goods. Computer systems are especially useful for inventory control because they can take advantage of complex techniques that minimize taxes. In addition, inventory systems controlled by a computer can tie into point-of-sale (POS) systems that update the inventory records while the bills are being printed.

All of these accounting systems have the same objective. They try to maintain data that accurately reflects the financial state of the company. In turn, this helps people make good business decisions.

```
                      FRONTIER IRONWORKS

                   BALANCE STATEMENT            DECEMBER 31, 1984
                   (THOUSANDS OF DOLLARS)


            ASSETS                              LIABILITIES

CASH                    $  127      ACCOUNTS PAYABLE        $  197
ACCOUNTS RECEIVABLE        583      ACCRUED EXPENSES
INVENTORY                  317        EMPLOYEE BENEFITS        349
PREPAID EXPENSES            53        OTHER                     23
MACHINERY                1,483      PREFERRED STOCK           987
FURNITURE AND FIXTURES     275      COMMON STOCK            2,384
LAND AND BUILDINGS       1,788      RETAINED EARNINGS         686


TOTAL ASSETS            $4,626      TOTAL LIABILITIES       $4,626
```

FIGURE C1.16

Balance sheet

STUDY OBJECTIVE

13. Briefly describe the functions of the following accounting systems: payroll, billing, accounts receivable, accounts payable, general ledger, and inventory control.

SALES AND MARKETING

Sales and marketing are closely related areas involving the selling of goods and services. People who work in these departments have widely varying jobs. They analyze potential sales markets, develop ideas for new products, and devise plans for selling existing products.

People in sales and marketing present products to customers through advertising, telephone calls, and direct contact. When customers have questions or concerns, sales and marketing people provide the answers. As sales are made, these people handle the paperwork, such as contracts and orders. Sales personnel follow up each order to ensure delivery. When necessary, they investigate customer complaints and make corrections.

Sales and marketing systems fall into two categories: operational and analysis. **Operational systems** provide direct support to the business. Processing orders and printing letters for advertising are examples.

Analysis systems work behind the scenes processing sales data. The resulting reports are used for determining marketing plans and relate to business operations only indirectly. For example, customer profiles are reports of customer buying habits (figure C1.17). They can be used to plan marketing approaches, but they cannot be used directly to help produce or market goods.

Analysis systems are usually simpler than operational systems. Since their

```
                    CUSTOMER PROFILES

                    SOUTHWEST REGION

                 PERIOD ENDING MARCH 1984


        CUSTOMER              PRODUCT                 PURCHASES
NAME            NUMBER    NAME           NUMBER     UNITS      AMOUNT

ACE BILLIARD    10043     DISPLAY CASE   P1040        4      $1287.50
                          EXECUTIVE DESK Q3877        1      $1150.99


AJ ARCHITECT    70089     DRAWING TABLES J8897       12      $4588.85
                          72 INCH TABLES J9789        4      $1768.04
                          SECRETARY DESK Q0446        4      $1238.79
                          EXECUTIVE DESK Q3877        3      $3452.97


DR. PAUL A AZURE 33879    EXECUTIVE DESK Q3877        1      $1150.99
```

FIGURE C1.17

Customer profile report

users are within the company, they do not have to be very fancy and need fewer checks and balances.

Operational Systems

Figure C1.18 lists popular sales and marketing computer systems. The most common operational systems involve **order entry.** These systems receive order requests, check inventory, and prepare bills. In retail stores, computer terminals often act as cash registers. These POS systems collect data at the point of sale—sometimes from machine-readable labels. They provide up-to-the-minute information for sales and marketing people.

FIGURE C1.18

Computer systems for sales and marketing

Operational Systems
   Order Entry
   Mail Order Process
   Order Status
   Advertising Products
Analysis Systems
   Customer Profiles
   Product Penetration
   Sales Agent Effectiveness and Commission Calculation
   Market Analysis

Another common operational sales system handles mail-order processing. Orders are received by mail and processed, and customer statements are prepared. Requests for back orders can also be printed. Forms used by a popular mail-order mountaineering and camping equipment company are shown in figure C1.19.

Computer systems are also used to check order status. Some systems are designed so that order entry clerks can check on the status by using CRT terminals. Thus, an order can be monitored from order entry through production, packaging, and shipping. In this way, the customer can be kept informed of its progress.

A final type of operational system provides advertising assistance. Mailing labels, form letters, and advertisements are produced. Many companies create large files with the names and addresses of customers or potential buyers. Mailing labels can be printed easily from these files. These files are used to produce form letters and other types of personalized advertisements.

Analysis Systems

One type of report produced by an analysis system is the customer profile report shown in figure C1.17. Salespeople use customer profile reports when making sales calls. Such reports are easily produced when records are processed by a computer system.

A sales agent effectiveness report (figure C1.20) shows the number of sales made by various sales agents. These reports help salespeople analyze how well they sell different products. These reports also show commissions and bonuses earned. Sometimes they even compare this year's sales with those of previous years.

Microcomputers using special applications packages called **electronic spreadsheets** are especially useful in market analysis. An electronic spreadsheet organizes data into rows and columns. The user can then have the computer process data from selected areas and place the results in a new row or column.

The sales agent effectiveness report in figure C1.20 was prepared using an electronic spread sheet. In addition, the salesperson can use the spread sheet to see the effect of a new sale or sales discount. All the salesperson has to do is change selected data. The computer updates any numbers related to the new entry.

For example, Mary Pitts wants to see the effect on her sales if she sold 50 more pairs of Zansen boots. Mary simply has to change the units sold from 319 to 369. The electronic spread sheet will recalculate the sales amount, commission, and other information based on selling 369 units.

Product penetration reports show how particular products sell in different geographic markets. Using such a report, a marketing manager might decide to increase advertising. This report could also highlight underdeveloped markets. In this case, the manager might assign additional salespeople to these areas.

Market analysis systems using electronic spread sheets can estimate possible sales in different markets, a company's share of each of them, and the distribution of markets across an area. These reports can be used to measure a company's sales against its competitor's sales. This comparison may reveal that the company sales are increasing, but not as fast as those of the competitor.

PLEASE USE REVERSE SIDE FOR SKI PACKAGES

Recreational Equipment, Inc.
P.O. Box C-88125
Seattle, WA. 98188

FOR FAST TOLL FREE SERVICE PHONE:
Wash. Residents 1-800-562-4894
Alaska & Hawaii 800-426-4770
All other states 1-800-426-4840
Greater Seattle 575-4480
For Best Service Phone Between 7:00 am & 3:30 pm Seattle Time
TOLL FREE LINES NOT AVAILABLE FROM CANADA
Canadian Customers Please Call . . . . (206) 575-4480

MEMBER'S PERMANENT MAILING ADDRESS   CO-OP NO. _____

NAME _____

ADDRESS _____

CITY _____ STATE _____ ZIP _____

PHONE _____ AREA CODE _____
Is this an address change? ☐ Yes ☐ No

SHIPPING ADDRESS, IF DIFFERENT FROM PERMANENT MAILING ADDRESS

NAME _____

ADDRESS _____

CITY _____ STATE _____ ZIP _____

PHONE _____ AREA CODE _____

QTY (5)	CATALOG NO.	CATALOG NO. 2nd Color Choice	SIZE	DESCRIPTION	PRICE	TOTAL

Shop R.E.I. by Mail or Telephone

Convenient. Order at your convenience. We are as near as your phone. No running from store to store.

Fast Service. Orders received by 3:00 pm are shipped the next work day.

Our Pledge of Quality. If any item you purchase from us proves to be unsatisfactory, please return it for a replacement or a full refund.

Send Your Friend a Catalog

Help your friend become a Co-op Member
We will send a current catalog

NAME _____

ADDRESS _____

CITY _____ STATE _____

FORM #186 REV. 10-78

SHIP MY ORDER:
(9) ☐ SURFACE   (10) ☐ AIR

SHIPPING, HANDLING & INS. U.S. ONLY

Subtotal & Value	Surface	Air
0- 5.00	.35	.60
5.01- 10.00	.60	1.25
10.01- 25.00	1.00	1.75
25.01- 50.00	1.60	2.75
50.01-100.00	2.70	4.50
Over 100.00	3.20	5.50
Ski Sets @	4.00	10.00

Add $4.00 Per Package surface or $10.00 Per Package air for each ski package on the reverse side.

Total—Ski Packages from other side	
Sub-total (28)	
Current Sales Tax WA. & CA. only	
Shipping Charge	
Membership Fee (11)	
Previous Due (12)	
Total	

Method of Payment

☐ Check (U.S. Funds) (1)
☐ Dividend (3)
☐ COD (25)
☐ Mastercharge (4)
☐ Visa (4)
☐ American Exp. (4)

Credit Card Number

_____

Expiration date _____

Customer Sig. _____

Thank you for your order!

FIGURE C1.19   *a.* Order Entry Form

Typical mail-order form (Courtesy Recreational Equipment, Inc.)

```
REI CASCADE PARKA-MNS-BLUE          HEEL LOCATER
LRG                       0150      PAIR                      9313

M222002404    D03   $164.95         M406600007    D08   >>$9.95


KASTINGER HIGH TOUR DOUBLE          WONDER HEADLIGHT
BOOT   11                 9319      4.5 VOLT                  9345

M354402158    D08   $140.00         M236000006    D02   >>$8.95
```

b. Picking Slip

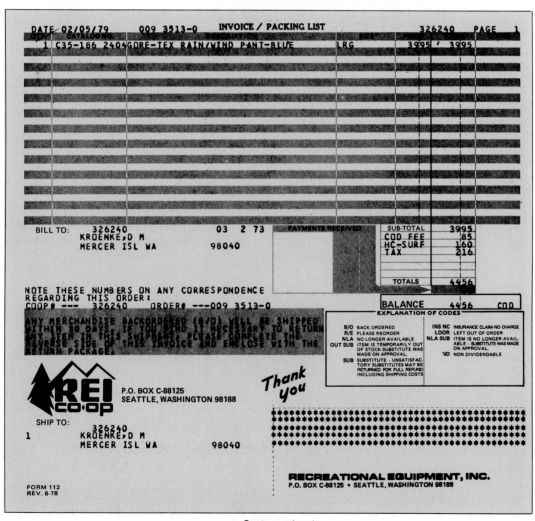

c. Customer Invoice

```
                    SALES AGENT EFFECTIVENESS REPORT

                          FALL QUARTER, 1984


SALES AGENT                PRODUCT           PRODUCT      SALES       SALES
NAME                       NAME              NUMBER       UNITS       AMOUNT

MARY PITTS                 ZANSEN BOOTS      14327        319         $47,340
                           JET IV SKIS       36575        412          38,415
                           LAMBRETH POLES    55478        127           1,270


LENNY PORTZ                ZANSEN BOOTS      14327        450          66,780
                           NORDIC BOOTS      13788        139          27,845
                           JET IV SKIS       36575          7             653
                           K-3 SKIS          37782        539          73,422
```

FIGURE C1.20

Sales report prepared using an electronic
spreadsheet

This type of analysis often involves complex calculation. Computer systems ease the job of a market analyst by allowing more estimations to be prepared. In addition, computer-generated estimates are apt to be more accurate than manually prepared ones.

STUDY OBJECTIVES

14. Identify the responsibilities of sales and marketing personnel and describe how computer systems can be useful to these people.

15. Identify two major categories of computer systems for sales and marketing and describe the function of each.

16. List four computer applications for each major category of sales and marketing systems.

17. Briefly describe an electronic spread sheet.

18. Explain how an electronic spread sheet can be used to prepare reports and analyze data.

OFFICE AUTOMATION

Word processors are essential to the automated office. In chapter A2, word processors were described as computer systems that store and manipulate large amounts of alphabetic data. They are used to prepare letters, memos, and other documents.

FIGURE C1.21

An intelligent copier (Courtesy Xerox Corporation)

Word Processors and Intelligent Copiers

In an **automated office,** word processors are connected to other office equipment. One common connection is between a word processor and an **intelligent copier** like the one in figure C1.21. Some of these copiers are just like any coin-operated copy machine in the way they reproduce printed material. They can also accept electronic input directly from a word processor.

When word processors and intelligent copiers are used together, the copier is able to accept instructions from the word processor. For example, a secretary at a word processing station could issue a command to make 100 copies of a report. The word processor would retrieve the report from disk. It would send the report to the copier with the command to make 100 copies. The copier would then translate the command into the appropriate action. This method is more efficient than using a printer to make multiple copies. The copier is much faster than the letter-quality printer normally attached to a word processor.

Networks for Electronic Mail

Another option is to connect several word processors together into a network (see figure C1.22). This is useful for companies that have offices in several geographic locations. Memos, letters, and reports can be prepared in one place and printed at connected word processors. This approach is faster than mailing these documents.

Sending documents electronically is called **electronic mail.** In elaborate systems, employees are assigned a personal disk file or **electronic mailbox.** When someone writes a memo using a word processor, they also prepare a list of the people who are to receive the memo. The word processor uses the list

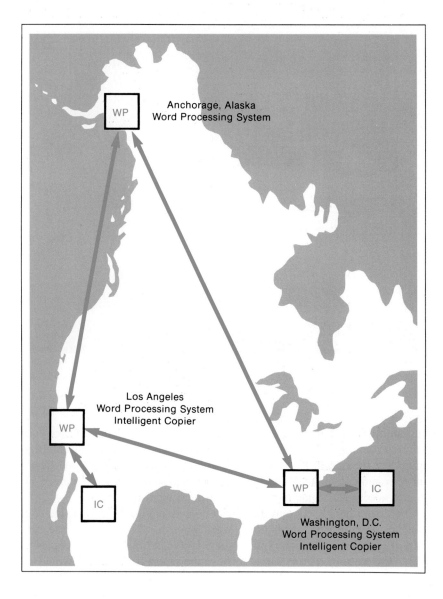

to identify the electronic mailboxes—files—to a central processor. The central processor copies the memo into each file.

When the people who were sent the memo next use their own word processor, terminal, or microcomputer, they can read the memo. Handling memos in this manner is quicker than typing, copying, and routing them through company mail.

There is even talk about "the paperless office." The idea is to combine word processors and online data processing systems. Documents would be stored by a word processor and recalled on any CRT without a paper copy ever being

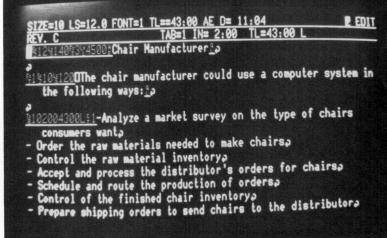

FIGURE C1.23

Computerized typesetting

printed. Reports and other important information would be stored on the system's hard disk. These documents would be online and available to users at any time.

Typesetting

A related application has people using computers to typeset books like this one. Modern typesetting operations insert special commands directly into the text created by a word processor. Figure C1.23 shows the beginning of this chapter with the typesetting commands inserted in the text.

A computer-controlled typesetting machine like the one in figure C1.23 can then lay out the page and photographically reproduce the text. Characters in the text can be of different sizes. They can also be in various styles, such as roman, bold, or italic.

The automated office may sound like something off in the future. But it is being used in businesses today.

STUDY OBJECTIVES

19. Define automated office, electronic mail, and electronic mailbox.

20. Describe three ways in which word processors are used as part of an automated office.

MANUFACTURING

A company's manufacturing department has the job of turning raw materials into finished products. Computers can help in this complex task in four different ways.

First, manufacturing personnel must order enough raw materials to produce the desired quantity of finished goods. This task may seem simple. But consider the great variety and number of parts needed to make a television set, car, or airplane. In many cases, materials need to be ordered six or more months in advance. Therefore, production supervisors must be thinking at least that far ahead.

FIGURE C1.24

Manufacturing computer system

Materials Management
Materials Requirement Planning
Inventory Control
Materials Tracking

Facility Scheduling
Production Scheduling
Operations Research

Engineering
Computer Assisted Design
Simulations

Process Control
Computer Assisted Manufacturing
Quality Control
Environment Control
Security System

```
           BILL OF MATERIALS FOR

           HIKER BACKPACK

           PRODUCT NUMBER 14356


MATERIAL                QUANTITY            DIMENSIONS (INCHES)

CLOTH TOP               1                   20X12
CLOTH SIDES             4                   8X22
LEATHER BOTTOM          1                   8X14
VELCRO HOOK TAPE        1                   6X1/2
LEATHER TIEDOWN         3                   3X2
WEB STRAPS              2                   2X35
PADDED BELT             1                   3X40
THREAD                  1                   400(FEET)
```

FIGURE C1.25

Bill of materials

A second activity is the scheduling of equipment to maximize its use. For example, if a company has only two lathes, management tries to schedule each machine an equal amount of time. Extra costs and time delays occur if one machine is overloaded while the other sits idle.

The third activity is engineering. The design of parts and machines is an engineer's responsibility. When possible, engineers must incorporate new materials and technology into existing products.

A fourth manufacturing activity is the production of parts and the assembly of those parts into finished products. In addition, manufacturing systems inspect goods and provide other quality control procedures.

Computer systems are used to support all four of these manufacturing activities. Figure C1.24 lists common computer systems used in manufacturing.

Materials management supports the purchase of the correct amount of raw materials. In addition, it keeps records for inventory control of these materials and finished goods. This system also tracks materials through the production process.

Figure C1.25 shows a bill of materials for a simple backpack. If the company wants to make 1000 backpacks, someone needs to figure the amount of raw materials required. To make tents, sleeping bags, and other products, the total amount of many different materials must be computed. Materials requirement planning (MRP) systems eliminate the manual effort required to make these calculations.

Inventory control systems are used to minimize the cost of the inventory while avoiding running out of stock. Computers are used to maintain this

Materials Management

delicate balance. Computer systems keep inventory records that identify the stock on hand, the stock on order, and the cost of each piece. In addition, they keep track of the rate at which stock is used, how long it takes to receive stock when ordered, and the name and address of the suppliers. A reorder report uses this data to identify stock that needs to be reordered.

Tracking of materials and finished goods is also accomplished using computer systems. Companies do not want to lose finished goods through accident or theft. In addition, they want to minimize waste on the production line. Keeping track of materials is a major task for large manufacturers. Computers are used to process the large volume of data needed to track materials in production.

Facility Scheduling

Facility scheduling systems are another example of computer applications in manufacturing. These systems are used to maximize the use of machines while minimizing setup time.

Suppose it takes 10 minutes to set up a saw for the cutting of table legs. And suppose 15 minutes are needed for setup to cut the top. If five tables are to be made, it makes sense to cut all the legs and then all the tops. Otherwise, if a set of legs and a top were cut independently, a lot of time would be wasted in setup. Many firms have increased production 20 to 30 percent simply by scheduling machines and people more efficiently.

Special operations research departments are often established to find the best solution to scheduling problems. Computer systems perform the extensive calculations needed to determine the best production schedule.

Engineering

The analysis and design of new products are the responsibilities of an engineer. The development of large and sophisticated products requires coordination, storage, and processing capabilities that only computer systems can provide.

Computer-Assisted Design (CAD) systems are now being used to help engineers design new products. In addition, these systems help individuals coordinate the flow of ideas between one another as they work on the same project.

Computer systems developed for engineering have two properties that are especially useful for design work. First, they contain special programs that allow engineers or draftspeople to draw images on the CRT. These graphic images can be either two-dimensional like the one in figure C1.26 or three-dimensional as shown in figure C1.27. Once the graphic image is stored on disk, engineers can call up the design and make further modifications.

Some CAD systems will even allow the image to be rotated and viewed from different angles. This second property enables the engineer to simulate different conditions for a new design. If a bridge is being built, simulations will test a particular design's ability to withstand strong winds and heavy loads. Designs for cars, airplanes, and boats are placed in simulated wind tunnels to check their aerodynamic properties. Large buildings can even be built on a screen to see if all the walls meet and if it will stand up by itself.

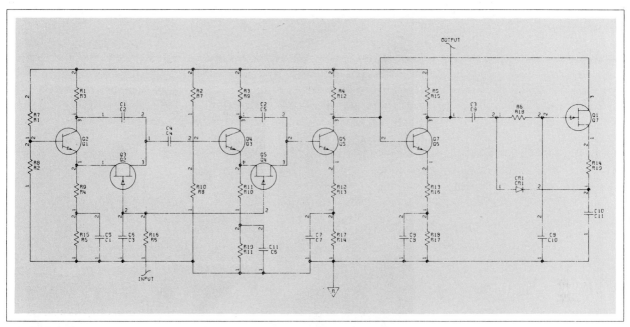

FIGURE C1.26

Two-dimensional drawing (Courtesy
Calcomp, Inc., Anaheim, California)

Finally, data stored on CAD systems can be directly used in production. **Computer-Assisted Manufacturing (CAM) systems** are part of a family of process control systems. The link between engineering and manufacturing is often referred to as **CAD/CAM.** See figure C1.28.

One use of the CAD/CAM connection is the programming of **numerical controlled (NC)** machines. Since the dimensions of a part are contained in the design data, this data can be used to program the lathe, drill press, or cutting tool used to manufacture the part.

Taken one step further, the CAD/CAM connection can be used to program industrial robots for a variety of tasks. These tasks can range from spot welding in the metal shop to painting in the paint department.

Process control systems also monitor manufacturing processes and provide quality control. Using environmental data, they can tirelessly monitor production cycles. For example, they can make sure that chemicals are always mixed in the same proportion or that paper is always rolled at the same thickness. Programmed for quality control, these systems can find flaws in a piece of glass and reject it when a person using the naked eye could not.

Large production complexes are using process controls to maintain the working environment. These systems regulate the temperature and humidity in the building. They also turn lights on and off.

Computer systems can provide backup for security guards. As the guards make their rounds, they stop at certain checkpoints. Stationed there are small

Process Controls

221

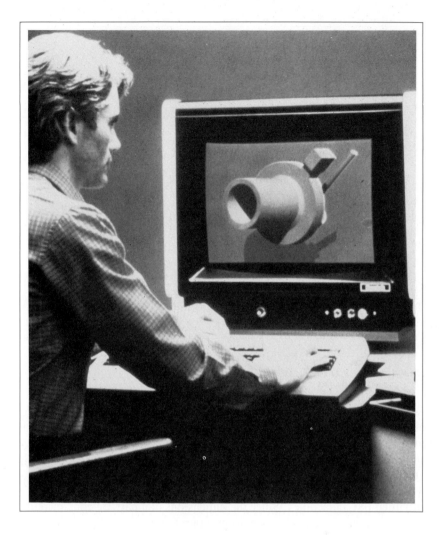

Three-dimensional drawing from CAD system (Courtesy Ramtek)

boxes that accept a key or card. When the card—or key—is slipped into the box, the computer is notified of the guard's present location. If the guard is overdue at a checkpoint, the computer system automatically notifies the proper authorities.

STUDY OBJECTIVES

21. Identify four major categories of computer systems for manufacturing.
22. List eleven computer applications for manufacturing and relate each to one of the four major categories.
23. Define CAD/CAM and NC.

CATHY COYLE
Manager, Information Services

RESPONSIBILITIES

I'm the person that has to make the total computer system work. I'm the link between the user and the computer. Though I really don't need heavy technical skills, I have to listen to the user's problem, communicate that problem to the programmers, and then monitor their progress. I oversee a data processing department with a supervisor and eight operators, and interact with a computer service bureau and their programmers.

MY BACKGROUND

I never graduated from college. I sure went long enough, but I didn't know what I wanted to do and changed majors a lot. I was a microbiology major, then English for several years, then switched to business when I started working full time.

My first job was as a clerk, and I ended up working with some programmers. Computers seemed to be where the fun was. I took a job here at Dominican hospital as a clerk. When they asked for someone to work with an outside computer service bureau for our data processing, I quickly volunteered.

From there I just progressed, learning all I could about the computer. When the hospital decided to buy their own, they put me in charge of the committee. Now we maintain a large effective information system.

SKILLS REQUIRED

Problem solving, written and verbal communication skills, and a lot of diplomacy! You know all those English essays and compositions I hated to write—that was probably the most important course I took. Analytical skills are important, too, and writing teaches those skills. You need to be able to solve problems, but if you can't communicate the solution to someone, then where are you?

Careers in computing for women are wide open. Maybe it's a good field for women because it is so new, and there hasn't been time to develop the same stereotypes for jobs and people.

PROGRAMMERS

Programmers often operate in a vacuum. The user just wants the computer to work, and the best programmers find a way to understand what the user is saying.

Programmers often have a short career life span. They make good money right from the start, but seem to face a change when they're about thirty. People don't realize that programming can be very competitive—there's always a new young hotshot that keeps the pressure on.

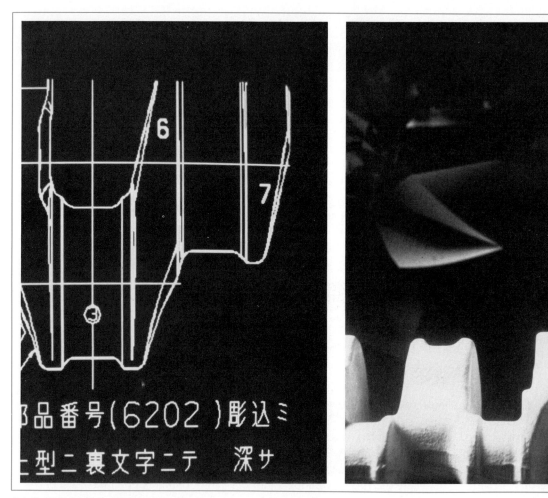

品番号（6202 ）彫込ミ

型二裏文字二テ 深サ

FIGURE C1.28

Designing a crankshaft using CAD/CAM
(Courtesy Computervision)

SUMMARY

Without computers, many big businesses could not operate. Business data stored and processed by computers is part of a company's management information system.

Accounting systems represent one of the most successful applications of computers in business. These systems are responsible for keeping accurate records of the financial status of a company. Various checks and balances are used to eliminate errors and unauthorized activity.

Sales and marketing systems help people analyze sales data and prepare marketing plans for new and old products. Word processors are connected to other office equipment, resulting in an automated office. These systems can be used to transfer memos and reports from the word processor to an intelligent copier or typesetter. In some cases, mail can be sent across the country electronically with the push of a button.

Manufacturing systems use computers to manage material, schedule production activities, and process controls. Engineers use computer-assisted design systems to create and test new products.

While this chapter did not cover all the possible uses of computers in business, it did give you an overview. There are far too many business applications to be covered in a single chapter or even in a single book.

By now you probably realize that a knowledge of computers will be important whether you want to be a manager, salesperson, accountant, or secretary. In fact, a knowledge of computers will be necessary in any business position.

CHAPTER C2

People Using Computers in Other Professions

Business people are not the only ones benefiting from computers today. Other professionals are using computer technology in their daily work. Equipment is less expensive every year, and applications packages are available for a wide range of jobs. As a result, more and more professionals have turned to computer systems for help.

It would be difficult to name a profession not affected by computers today. Therefore, an understanding of computers is no longer limited to computer professionals. Teachers, doctors, lawyers, journalists, scientists, and many others use computers every day.

These people do not program computers. Often they leave computer operations to others. It is a computer system's ability to provide useful information that is of interest to them.

Let's examine how various professionals are using computer systems as a tool.

EDUCATORS

The students in Mrs. Dingman's computer class were exposed to a variety of educational uses of computers. Many of these uses could have been applied to other classes. Mrs. Dingman, because of the subject she taught, used all of them.

In general, computer systems are used in education in three ways. First, they can be used as the object of instruction, as in Mrs. Dingman's class. Second, they can be used as a teaching tool, where students practice with the system's help. And third, they can be used to manage student records. Students, teachers, administrators, counselors, librarians, and resource specialists all have applications that can put the computer to work for them.

Computers as the Object of Instruction

In a class like this, computers are the object of instruction. You learn how to operate them for home or occupational needs. An introduction to computer programming helps you control the computer yourself. In addition, you examine how computers work, analyze the components of a computer system, and explore the impact they are having on society.

A course that concentrates on computers as the object of instruction is often classified as a **vocational class.** This is one way of describing a class that teaches students things they will need in their chosen careers.

Computer-Assisted Instruction

When and how fast to introduce new ideas is one of the problems confronting teachers. Since everyone learns in a different way and at a different speed, a roomful of students represents a real challenge. When transfer students and people who have been absent are added, the class becomes a group with a wide variety of needs.

Computers provide the means to individualize some types of instruction. **Drill and practice** programs available in many subject areas quiz students on important material. Figure C2.2 shows a CRT display with a mathematics question. Students answer the question and the computer tells them if the answer is right or wrong.

A **tutorial** program takes computer-assisted instruction one step further. These programs are used to introduce new material. Instead of reading a book,

FIGURE C2.1

The computer lab

students can load and run a tutorial program that presents the next assignment. The computer then displays questions about the material. After the student answers a question, the computer indicates if the answer is right or wrong. Tutorial programs are especially useful for students who want to get ahead of the class or who need to catch up.

Social science, business, and natural science problems can be presented through computer **simulations.** For example, students can manage imaginary businesses or refight major historical battles. Computer programs mimic var-

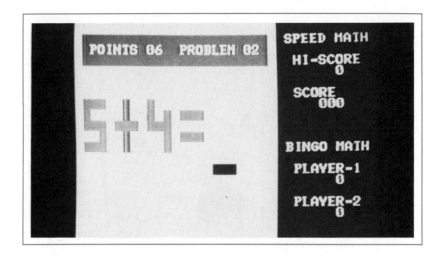

Drill and practice (Courtesy Commodore
Computer Systems)

ious conditions in which the student must make decisions. Dangerous science
experiments can also be simulated with a computer. In this case, the worst
thing that can happen is having to rerun the program instead of accidentally
destroying the lab equipment.

Computers have also found their way into libraries with **reference searches.**
Here they can search through large databases composed of titles, authors, and
subject descriptions by looking for keywords. For example, several library
services would allow students to search a database for any book or article using
the words "computer-assisted instruction" in the title.

Hundreds of hours in research time can be saved by having the computer
do the initial search through the literature. Although this service is expensive,
it can be justified if the right keywords are used. On the other hand, someone

Program to help generate tests

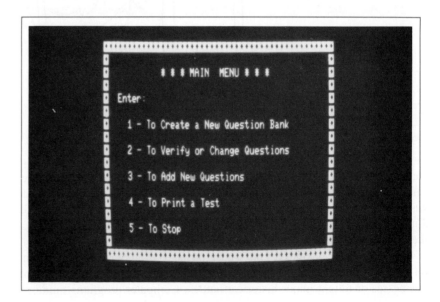

doing a report on computer literacy who uses the keyword "computer" will really be no better off than before. The books and articles using that keyword would fill a small library.

Computers are also working behind the scenes helping teachers and administrators keep student records up to date. Many schools have computer systems running business programs that keep track of inventory, payroll, and other business functions.

Mrs. Dingman uses the computers in the computer lab to store student grades and her test questions. A test-generating program randomly selects questions for each test from a file of questions. By using this program, she can easily make several versions of each test, along with their answer keys. Figure C2.3 shows the main menu of a test-generating program used by the author.

Counselors use computers to help students determine occupational and academic preferences. They can also tie into large databases that provide information about education and experience requirements for various jobs.

Computer-Managed Instruction

STUDY OBJECTIVES

1. Define vocational class.
2. Identify three ways that computer systems can be used in education.
3. Briefly describe five uses for computers as the object of instruction.
4. Explain how computers are used for drill and practice, tutorials, simulations, and reference searches.
5. Identify and describe four applications for computer-managed instruction.

HEALTH PROFESSIONALS

"Dr. McKnight, Dr. McKnight, please come to nursing station three," barked the speaker in the doctors' lounge. Sue was up and out the door before the message was finished. She knew it had to be about her patient in room 309.

It had been a long, hard road for Sue, but becoming a doctor is never easy. High school had been the halfway point in her education to become Dr. McKnight. Computers were still part of her life, although she rarely gave them a thought anymore.

Using Computers to Improve Patient Care

As she walked into room 309, she glanced at the computer printout attached to the front of the bed. A few quick questions to the nurse and a gentle examination of the patient gave her a few clues to the patient's problem.

Many times, clues are all a doctor has to go by. Sue learned through experience some of the questions to ask. Often she felt like Sherlock Holmes as she tossed a few facts around in her head, trying to puzzle out an answer. Her "Dr. Watson" was the hospital's computer system. It helped her put the many mismatched pieces of data together and assisted her by communicating her needs to the other professionals on duty.

After leaving the patient in room 309, Sue went back to the nursing station.

Dr. McKnight uses the computer to retrieve
medical history

She requested a blood test from the lab, a change in the patient's medication,
and a printout of the patient's medical history.

The hospital's computer system was up to the task. First, the CRT terminal
was used to request a copy of the patient's medical history. This one-page
report was immediately printed on the attached printer.

Next, the patient's name and room number and the time the blood test was
needed were entered. This information was transferred down to the lab by the
push of a button. The request then printed out on the lab's printer. The lab
technician used the information to schedule the next set of tests.

The lab had its own minicomputer for analyzing the blood samples that were
collected. The results were then entered into the central computer system and
added to the patient's record. Dr. McKnight had immediate access to the results
as soon as they became part of the patient's record. In addition, the charges
for the test were also added to the patient's record.

A similar procedure was used to change the patient's medication. A nurse

1. Administrative Business Functions
2. Patient Records
3. Pharmacy Records
4. Nursing Stations
5. Radiological Analysis and Process Control
6. Monitoring of Patient Health
7. Diagnosing Illnesses
8. Monitoring Public Health

FIGURE C2.5

Computer applications in medicine

entered a drug code and drug administration schedule along with a cancellation code for the other medication. The patient's name and room number were also entered in the terminal. The computer system transferred the request down to the pharmacy.

The pharmacist then used the computer to check the request against the patient's record. In a few cases, this check would show that the medication might interact with other drugs the patient was currently using. It could also show that the patient had a history of being sensitive to that type of medication or needed to avoid eating certain foods with it.

Another check was made of the formulary, again using the computer. The formulary is data about drugs and compounds stocked in the hospital. Since the needed drug was in stock, the prescription was filled and the label printed on the pharmacy's printer. The patient record was also updated to include the new medication, the dosage, and the charge for filling the prescription. The medication was then delivered to the nursing station.

In the hospital where Sue worked, doctors, nurses, pharmacists, radiologists, administrators, clerks, and other support personnel used the computer to improve services and reduce costs. The computer handled typical business functions—payroll, billing, inventory, and so on. But it was also used for problems unique to health care.

Patient Record Keeping

Common to all these functions are the patient records. Data is added to the patient record from many areas. Initially, the people at admitting establish the record and enter historical and physical data. Figure C2.6 shows patient data being entered at admission. Later, other data is added as the patient undergoes tests and receives medication.

In the Pharmacy

The pharmacy system is used to record the drugs taken by the patient. Such systems can assist the doctor in planning treatment courses. Furthermore, these systems can notify the pharmacist if harmful combinations of drugs have been prescribed.

Control of drug inventory in the formulary is an additional advantage. What's more, some pharmacists use computers to provide income tax records for their patients. These systems keep track of the cost of each prescription and print a receipt for the total at the end of the year. This way, the patients don't have to keep their own records.

FIGURE C2.6

Hospital admissions using a computer

FIGURE C2.7

The computer can be used to analyze
and plan orthodontic treatment (Courtesy
Rocky Mountain Data Systems)

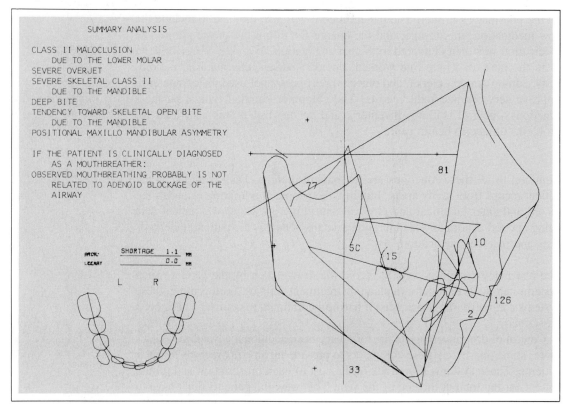

Computer systems help nurses by eliminating some of the paperwork. The nursing station can display or print patient drug histories and treatment plans. The nurse also records the patient's vital signs—pulse, blood pressure, and so on—at scheduled times via this station.

At the Nursing Station

Computers are used in radiology to analyze X-rays and to control equipment. The analysis of X-rays can be particularly helpful to orthodontists. The patient's dentist sends the X-rays to a computer service. These X-rays are input to a computer, where the effect of different treatment plans is then simulated. From the results—like those in figure C2.7—the orthodontist can plan the best treatment.

    Radiologists now have other tools besides X-ray machines. Equipment like **computerized axial tomography (CAT)** scanners uses computers to control radiation and to analyze the results. CAT scanners are just one of a series of new machines using computers for diagnostic help.

In the Medical Lab

In special cases, computers are used to monitor patients. Seriously ill patients, such as those having heart problems, can be connected to computerized monitoring systems. Sensors are taped to the patient, and the computer watches for abnormal activity. When this occurs, messages are displayed on the nursing station terminal. There are even plans to monitor patients remotely after they leave the hospital.

Monitoring Patients

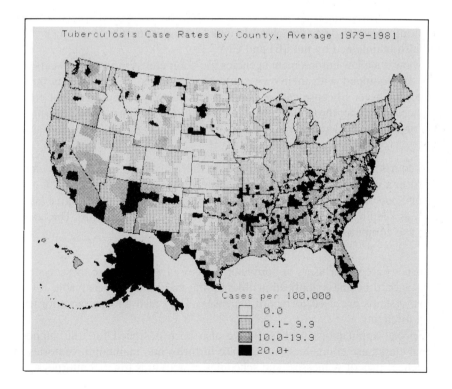

FIGURE C2.8

Health officials use computers to monitor public health (Courtesy Centers for Disease Control)

Diagnosing Illness

Doctors are using computers to help them diagnose illnesses. These computer systems accept a description of the symptoms and other data. They then list possible illnesses and suggested treatments.

These systems are certainly no match for an experienced doctor. Still, they have had some success in identifying and treating rare diseases. They can also be useful in situations where an experienced doctor is not available.

Guarding the Public's Health

Public health officials use computers to analyze data concerning new diseases and to monitor potential epidemics. The Centers for Disease Control is one organization with this responsibility. Researchers collect data for medical specialists to input into computers, thus helping them to guard the public's health.

STUDY OBJECTIVE

6. Describe eight ways in which computers are used in the health professions and identify the health professionals who use each.

LEGAL PROFESSIONALS

Computers are used by police officers, FBI agents, legal secretaries, attorneys, and judges. In law enforcement, computer systems are used to keep criminal data. The FBI maintains the National Crime Information Center (NCIC). See figure C2.9. Records of criminals, stolen property, and crimes are kept on files in this system.

Police Officers

State law enforcement agencies can query the NCIC system whenever they need information. They can also add data to the system. Other computer files are also maintained by the FBI and CIA.

Many state law enforcement agencies use computer systems. Patrol cars can now be equipped with their own computer terminals. When a car is pulled over, the driver's license can be checked immediately. The officer just enters the license number through the patrol car's terminal. Within minutes, the officer can obtain a complete driving history.

The Courts

The courts use computer systems to help the judges, secretaries, and clerks perform a variety of jobs. Case histories are kept by computer systems. Courtrooms, personnel, and cases are scheduled by computer. Administrative tasks, such as keeping track of costs, are handled by computer systems. The courts also use computers to help select jurists.

Attorneys and Related Professionals

Attorneys are major users of computer systems. Law firms use these systems for standard business applications like billing and accounts receivable. Computer systems are used to record expenses. They also allocate an attorney's time to clients.

Special applications packages have also been designed for trial support. Legal clerks use computers to keep case histories and maintain inventories of evidence, lists of witnesses, and schedules of activities for trial attorneys.

A clerk accessing data through National Crime Information Center (Courtesy FBI National Crime Information Center)

Computer applications in the legal professions

Legal Element	Application
Law Enforcement	National Crime Information Center
	Online access to drivers' licenses and other data
Courts	Case histories
	Scheduling courtrooms, personnel, and cases
	Administrative tasks
Attorneys	General business applications
	Allocation of attorney time
	Trial support
	Word processing
	Legal research

Legal secretaries frequently use word processing systems to store, retrieve, and edit legal documents. Some law firms have taken the automated office a step further. They have linked their word processing station to the central computer system. This combined system allows the firm to centrally locate several hundred standard paragraphs for wills. When a lawyer prepares a will, he or she selects the standard paragraphs that are appropriate.

If slight modifications are needed, paragraphs are copied from disk storage into the word processor and changed. The word processor passes a file of paragraph numbers and changes to the central computer system. There the data is stored along with the client's name.

Whenever a law change impacts one of these paragraphs, a program on the central system searches all the wills to determine which ones need changing. A list of clients with affected wills is sent to the word processor. The word processor then uses these names in form letters telling these people of the law change. Meanwhile, a lawyer rewrites the standard paragraph to conform to the new law. The new standard paragraph is then filed.

When responses are received from people who want their wills updated, this fact is input to the central computer system. The system sends the list of paragraph numbers to the word processor. The new wills are prepared while the central computer conveniently calculates a bill for each client. The bills are typed by the word processor and sent to the client a few days later.

Another promising legal application of computing concerns research. Legal librarians use computers to search files of legal history, as in figure C2.11. Relevant past cases and legal precedents are found much faster this way.

STUDY OBJECTIVE

7. Briefly describe ten computer applications for the legal profession and identify the professional who would use each.

FIGURE C2.11

Legal librarian using a computer for research

The main newsroom at *USA Today*
(Courtesy Gannett Company, Inc.)

Journalism has changed dramatically over the last 20 years. The image of a reporter sweeping that last page out of the typewriter while shouting for the copyboy is no longer true. Now, journalists pound on keyboards attached to CRT terminals. Their terminals link them electronically to the desk editor with the push of a button. The copyboy is gone.

Small, portable terminals and microcomputers are even letting reporters take computers into the field. By carrying a power pack along with the computer, a reporter can write and store a story on the spot. A nearby telephone allows the reporter to transfer the story back to the main office.

Both the reporters and their editors use word processing programs to write and edit their stories. These programs are sometimes referred to as **text editors** by the journalists. They work the same way as the programs used by word processors.

The factorylike atmosphere that once prevailed in the typesetting department before a newspaper went to press is also changing. The small foundries with their molten lead for typesetting are no longer needed. In some cases, copy is

JOURNALISTS

Reporters and Editors

Newspaper Production

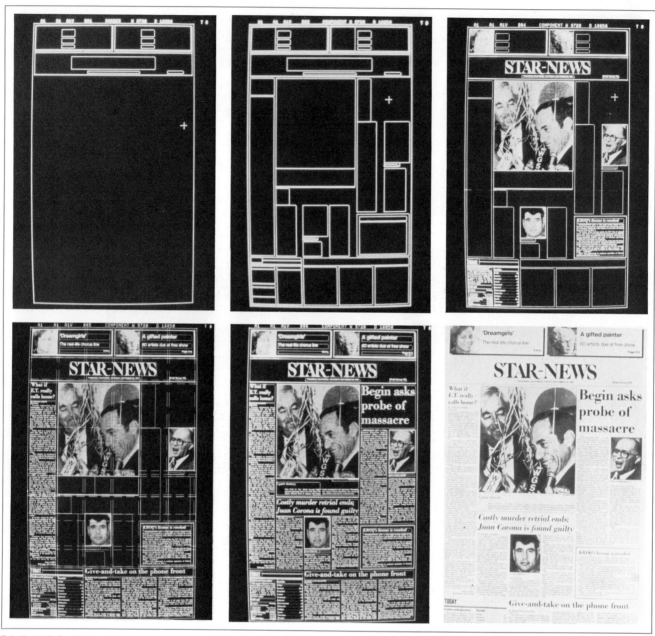

Online development of a front page
(Courtesy Knight-Ridder Newspapers, Inc.)

now photographically set by computers and the paper put together with scissors and paste.

Newspapers are now directly linked to large news-gathering services like United Press International (UPI) and the Associated Press (AP). The news services' computers constantly update their databases. As the databases are updated, the local newspapers receive instant notification on their dedicated terminals.

Stories or syndicated columns are electronically retrieved from the database when they are going to be used. These articles, along with those written by local reporters, can be put together online (as shown in figure C2.13) or cut and pasted together as mentioned earlier. The completed page is then made into a reverse-image plate and sent to the printing press.

8. Define text editor.

9. Briefly describe three ways computers are used in journalism.

ARCHITECTS

The first architectural design was probably drawn in the sand. Today, architects can call up a design on a CRT and have the computer rotate the image so it can be viewed from various angles. In addition, computers are storing contracts, scheduling work, performing calculations, and maintaining financial records for architectural firms. Figure C2.14 lists common computer applications used by architects.

FIGURE C2.14

Computer applications used by architects

Design Support
  Computer Assisted Design (CAD)
  Automated Drafting (AD)

Word Processing
  Building Specifications
  Proposals and Contracts
  Checklists and Construction Details
  Index of Drawings and Legends
  Building Codes and Zoning Laws

Project Scheduling
  Workloads
  Project Deadlines
  Agendas

Design Analysis
  Stress
  Plumbing
  Electrical
  Structural

Accounting and Financial Management
  Cost Estimates
  Feasibility Studies
  Business Applications
  Performance Evaluations

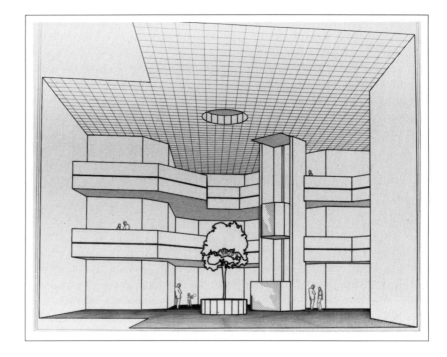

Interior view of a building printed by a plotter (Courtesy Calcomp, Inc., Anaheim, California)

Design Support

Computer-Assisted Design (CAD) systems represent one of the more spectacular uses of computers in the design and construction of buildings. Images are designed using screen displays, and plotters then draw the results on paper.

In figure C2.15, a CAD system was used to create a picture of a building and its interior spaces. The architect can then view the picture from different angles and distances. For example, the architect could view the building as if he or she were standing across the street or walking in the front door.

Another computer application for architects is **automated drafting (AD).** It is different from computer-assisted design. The AD system saves time by having the computer create detailed drawings like the one in figure C2.16. The design information can come from an extensive database, or the architect can enter the data. Digitizers are being used in some cases to convert existing drawings into a computer-readable form.

While CAD and AD have a bright future, they represent only a small part of the computer's impact on architecture.

Word Processing

Word processors have become invaluable to many professionals, including architects. Architects are using word processing to write building specifications and contracts. Job proposals are stored using the word processor. These documents can then be recalled for reference and modified upon request.

When large projects are in the making, the word processor provides an ideal means of organizing various phases of the project. Standard working-drawing checklists and construction details can be permanently stored. While the checklists and details can be changed to meet individual project needs, they improve

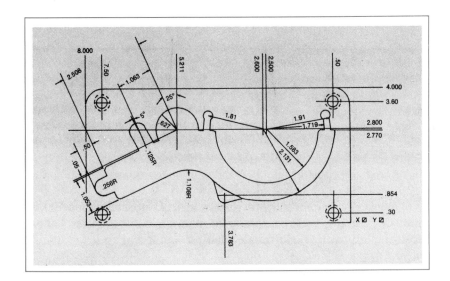

FIGURE C2.16

Drawing produced through automated drafting (Courtesy N.C. Laboratories, Inc.)

quality control by reminding the architect of small details. The architect is then free to concentrate on special design requirements.

It is very common to have hundreds of drawings and other documents related to a single project. Here again, the word processor is used to coordinate the paperwork. An index can be made for all the drawings and their legends. The index can also contain descriptive details about the drawings and identify who is working on a particular aspect of the design.

On top of all this is the need to keep up with government paperwork. Building codes, zoning laws, and other local regulations can be available on the word processor. The architect can then check proposed design specifications against these regulations.

Project Scheduling

Architectural firms working on several projects use computers to schedule workloads and project deadlines. Using the computer to help coordinate various projects helps a firm maximize resources and hopefully avoid time and cost overruns.

Computers also maintain **electronic agenda** of work assignments for each staff member. These agenda can be updated easily with new deadlines and meetings. Using the computer this way helps the staff stay on top of schedule changes as the project proceeds from one phase to another.

Design Analysis

Some people say that computers are at their best when doing calculations. Architects, in particular, make good use of this ability by making stress analyses of building designs along with other design checks. Many computer programs are now available to help solve plumbing, electrical, and structural problems.

Accounting and Financial Management

Architectural firms, like any business, use computers for business data processing. The business applications detailed in the previous chapter also apply here.

These firms have paychecks to send out, bills to pay, and accounts to keep up-to-date.

In addition, many firms are using special programs to analyze the efficiency of their offices. These programs are part of a financial management system. The idea is to take payroll data, cost estimates, and other data from business operations to evaluate the firm's performance. The output from the financial management system is then used to improve performance on other projects.

Another problem critical to the financial survival of an architectural firm is cost estimates. Most building projects are awarded to firms through a bidding process. Each firm interested in a project estimates its costs and submits a bid. The bid outlines what the firm will do and their price for doing it. The project is usually awarded to the lowest bidder.

Computers are used in a feasibility study to help estimate the final cost of a project. A feasibility study is a preliminary review of the job in which time and costs are estimated. A firm can actually lose money if its bid is too low. Therefore, computers are used to help make the most accurate estimate possible.

STUDY OBJECTIVES

10. Define CAD, AD, and electronic agenda.

11. Describe five ways architects use computers and identify applications for each of these categories.

SCIENTISTS

If there was ever a catchall job description, "scientist" is it! There are as many different kinds of scientists as there are sciences, maybe even more. But one thing biologists, chemists, nuclear physicists, astronomers, and other scientists have in common is their reliance on computers.

Scientists were on hand when the first computer was turned on. They were the original users. The first high-level programming language–FORTRAN, for FORmula TRANslator—was designed for their use.

New scientific applications usually come about as a result of **research and development (R&D)** projects. After being thoroughly tested as part of an experiment, successful applications find their way into daily use. Many man-

FIGURE C2.17

Computer applications used by scientists

- Reference Searches and Retrievals
- Experimental Models or Simulations
- Process Controls
- Data Analysis
- Word Processing

ufacturing processes were developed as part of R & D projects. Figure C2.17 outlines five ways scientists use computers.

Reference Searches and Retrieval

The first step in a research project is to explore what has already happened. An understanding of past mistakes and successes helps scientists formulate a **hypothesis.** A hypothesis is a formally stated question or idea. Scientists then set out to prove or disprove this hypothesis.

Finding material related to a research project can be a big job in itself. No one library will contain all the needed resources. Computers can be used to scan large databases for related materials. Scientists, like students, can save hundreds of hours by having the computer do the initial search.

Given a keyword, title, or author's name, the computer can identify the sources and the libraries holding them. The scientist then reviews these selections and pulls from them the needed information.

For example, scientists interested in volcanic activity in the Pacific Ocean would have to research past activity in the area. Using a computer search, they could call up historical data about the Pacific. In addition, the computer could find material related to recent volcanic activity in other areas.

Experimental Models or Simulations

Since many approaches to testing a hypothesis can be taken, computers are used to help select the best approach. As scientists formulate a particular hypothesis, they simulate it, or make a model of it, using a computer.

The computer simulation is based on programs with complex mathematical formulas. The scientist tries different inputs to see the simulated results. While the results are just computer estimates, they give the scientist an idea of what could happen.

Figure C2.18 shows a simulation of the effects of volcanic fallout. Scientists input different wind speeds and directions at the time of eruption. The computer simulation then maps out the areas affected by these factors.

If possible, the next step is to see what really happens. If the results are vastly different, then the model might be changed. There is an old saying when an experiment does not turn out as expected: "There is no such thing as a dumb rat, just dumb people"—or in this case, dumb simulations.

Process Controls

Computers are also useful in running or monitoring equipment. Some instruments are so delicate that they can only be controlled by computers. In other cases, the equipment is in far-off places like outer space or the ocean floor. In these cases, computer control is the only practical solution.

Computers are ideal monitors because they never sleep and can devote 100 percent of their attention to a project. They can monitor everything from the pulse rate of a humpback whale to the hiccups of an active volcano.

Process control systems are designed to accept different types of environmental input. A blood analyzer, a weather satellite, and a radioactivity detector can all input data to a process control system.

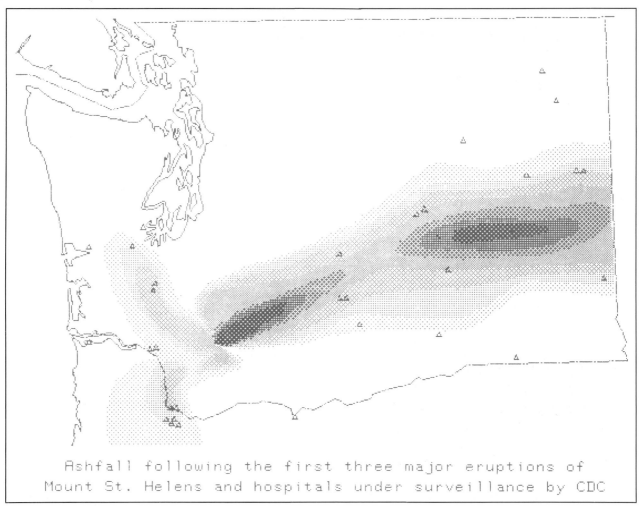

Ashfall following the first three major eruptions of
Mount St. Helens and hospitals under surveillance by CDC

FIGURE C2.18

Simulation of the effects of volcanic
fallout (Courtesy Centers for Disease
Control)

Data Analysis

Once all the data has been collected, the scientist still needs the computer's data processing ability. Complex calculations needed for current research projects would require hundreds of years to do by hand. Instead, special statistical programs—called **statistical packages**—are available so that computers can perform the standardized computations needed for analyzing data.

The data is first collected and prepared for input. Then the statistical package is loaded into the computer. Fast and accurate results are provided as the input data is processed. There are statistical packages available that also produce graphic reports.

In other cases, computer systems are online and analyze the data as it is

FIGURE C2.19

Environmental data is sensed by the seismograph and sent back to the lab (Courtesy Stephen Malone, University of Washington)

collected. Process control systems are linked to the computer performing data analysis. Sometimes one computer performs both tasks. Figure C2.19 shows scientists setting up a seismograph, an instrument that takes earthquake shock-waves as input and prints out the location and intensity of the quake.

In either case, the scientist still must interpret the reports output by the computer. One of three possible scientific conclusions can be drawn from the results. The data either supports the hypothesis, disproves it, or does not provide enough information for the scientist to decide one way or the other. In the last situation, the scientist must continue the research.

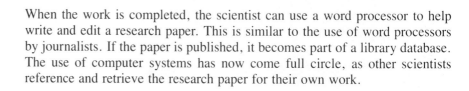

Researcher from the University of Washington using a computer to analyze data from Mount St. Helen's eruption (Courtesy Stephen Malone, University of Washington)

Word Processing

When the work is completed, the scientist can use a word processor to help write and edit a research paper. This is similar to the use of word processors by journalists. If the paper is published, it becomes part of a library database. The use of computer systems has now come full circle, as other scientists reference and retrieve the research paper for their own work.

STUDY OBJECTIVES

12. Define: R&D, hypothesis, and statistical package.

13. Identify five ways computers can be used by scientists.

14. Briefly describe how a scientist with an idea can use a computer to prove or disprove the hypothesis.

SUMMARY

Today, professionals in many fields are finding computers to be useful tools. Educators are using computers as the object of instruction and to assist in the educational process. They are also using computers behind the scenes to help manage instruction.

Many people in the health professions rely on computers to keep patient records, analyze the results of tests, control equipment, and monitor extremely ill patients. In doing these and other jobs, computer systems have reduced paperwork and allowed these professionals to get back to helping people.

Police officers, lawyers, judges, reporters, and architects are all using computers in one way or another. These applications can range from maintaining business records to scheduling court cases or designing skyscrapers.

Scientists are using computers to assist them in every phase of research and development. Computers help them research past mistakes and formulate new ideas. These ideas can then be tested with the results analyzed and output by a computer.

Here lies your challenge as tomorrow's professionals. Computer systems will no longer be new or imposing machines. They will be just another tool in your grab bag of modern technology. Your understanding of computers will take this technology to new heights. You should expect easy-to-use and practical systems. It is your responsibility to demand the most from them.

CHAPTER C3

People Using Computers on the Job for Better Lives

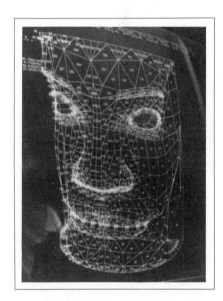

The development of microprocessors has helped put computer technology into a wide array of products. In turn, these products have enabled computers to perform an even wider range of applications. This trend will continue as people gain experience and understanding of how computers can help them do their jobs more efficiently.

Two factors will work together to make the 1980s a very interesting decade. First, and most obvious, is the incredible decrease in the cost/performance ratio of computers over the last three decades.

Second, a new generation of computer systems is being designed for users who are not computer professionals. As users gain more access to computers, they will not accept just any mish-mash as a computer system. The informed user will demand that computer-based products be flexible and easy to operate. These new systems are said to be **user friendly.**

As a result, microprocessors in the form of microcomputers and other products are now found on farms, stages, movie sets, sidelines, and on the floor of the U.S. Congress.

ARTISTS

John LaFriend's footsteps echoed through the auditorium as he walked across the stage. He was here to make a sound check on his equipment. Earlier in the

FIGURE C3.1

John LaFriend preparing for a performance

day, he and the road crew had set up the keyboard and electronics that composed his synthesizers. He actually had several that he used during a concert.

The equipment towered over him on three sides when it was all set up. He was here now to double-check everything for tonight's performance. One loose connection or pulled plug meant disaster.

After graduation from high school, John's band played the local bar circuit. With part-time jobs during the day, they were able to earn enough money to live. That was three years ago.

With the addition of a new drummer and guitar player, they were now "good" enough to be booked as a lead-in for a touring band that was in town. While the money was not going to put them on easy street, the exposure and the taste of fame had set the stage for an exciting evening.

A computer would be there to help John in the spotlight. His synthesizers were controlled by microprocessors. Input came from the keyboard and other knobs and switches on a control panel (see figure C3.2).

The microprocessor monitored all the input devices and sent signals to a music generator that processed the signals and transformed them into audio signals. The output was the music that filled the auditorium.

John's synthesizers represent an interesting blend of technologies. The microprocessor accepts and stores the input data as bit patterns—0's and 1's—just like other computers. These bit patterns are often called a **digital signal.**

On the other hand, our ears hear music as a continuous sound called an **analog signal.** An analog signal is made up of a blend of frequencies we recognize as a note from a piano or the voice of a singer.

Musicians

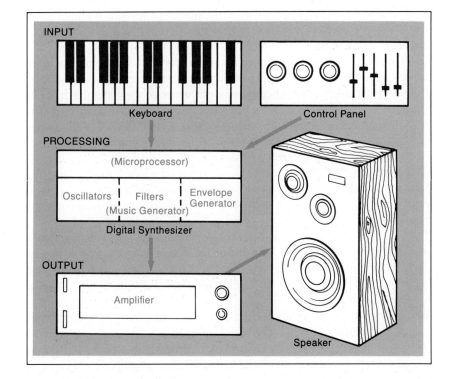

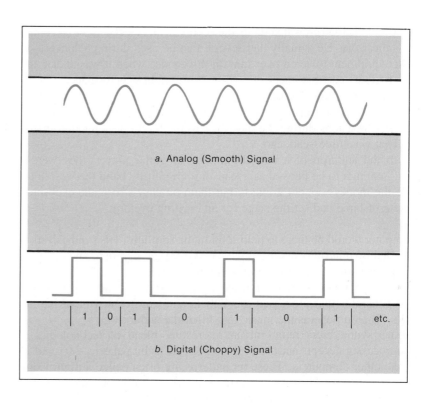

a. Analog (Smooth) Signal

| 1 | 0 | 1 | 0 | 1 | 0 | 1 | etc. |

b. Digital (Choppy) Signal

FIGURE C3.3

Analog and digital signals

The sound, or analog signal, is produced in both cases by the vibration of strings. In a piano, it is the vibration of the piano strings as a hammer strikes them. A singer's voice is produced by the vibration of vocal cords as exhaled air passes through them.

Early synthesizers did not have a translation problem, since everything was processed as an analog signal. These analog synthesizers are still popular today.

Digital synthesizers using microprocessors are much more flexible and even programmable. However, they must translate the digital signals from the microprocessor to an analog signal we hear as music. Figure C3.4 is a digital representation of the first four notes of Beethoven's Fifth Symphony.

A program for a synthesizer is a stored set of instructions representing different settings of the instrument. Once a musical sequence is programmed into the synthesizer, the musician can recall the music and have it played during a performance. The musician can then be playing another part of the arrangement at the same time.

The use of computers in music does not stop here. Very sophisticated mixing boards using microprocessors help blend the music into a consistent sound throughout the auditorium. The computer helps analyze and equalize the sound both there and in the recording studio by making sure one instrument does not drown out the others.

When musical scores are arranged for movies, computers help synchronize the sound with the picture. Computers are used a great deal in the movie industry—to help coordinate the movement of props, to help control the cameras, and even to prepare some of the visual images and special effects.

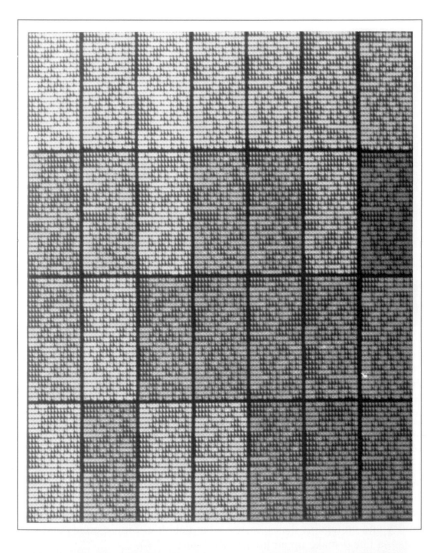

FIGURE C3.4

Digital representation of the first four notes of Beethoven's Fifth Symphony (Courtesy 3M Corporation)

FIGURE C3.5

Audio technician at a recording console (Courtesy Richmond Newspapers, Inc., an Affiliate of Media General)

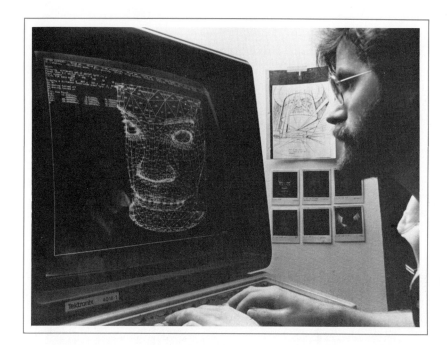

This animator is using a computer to create a character for the movie *TRON*
(Photo by Peter Angelo Simon/Phototake)

Visual Artists

Graphic artists and producers have discovered that computer systems can be used to create art as easily as they create plans and designs for engineers.

CAD systems produce a wide variety of images. Both two-dimensional and three-dimensional forms are designed using a variety of input devices. These devices range from standard keyboards to light pens and digitizers. Digitizers allow artists to input drawings directly into a computer.

The computer stores a drawing as a series of points. Each point has its own location or coordinate in the drawing, like the numbered dots in the draw-by-number drawings you did as a child. The coordinates for a drawing are stored in memory and on tape or disk like any other data file. Single points and sets of points—a line—make up an image (see figure C3.6).

Once the image is in the computer, coded instructions representing color, dimensions, and textures are added to the data file. Movement, or animation, can be created by quickly displaying slight variations of the original image.

Many advertisements in magazines and on television use images formed by computers. Background shots in movies have been enhanced using computer-constructed images. In a few cases, computer-generated graphics have created whole movie scenes.

STUDY OBJECTIVES

1. Define user friendly, digital signal, and analog signal.
2. Identify input, processing, and output components for a digital synthesizer.
3. Briefly describe a program for a synthesizer.

4. Describe two additional computer applications related to music.

5. Explain how a computer can store and animate a drawing.

FARMERS

Old McDonald now has a computer on the farm. It helps him monitor and control his land, livestock, equipment, and money. Using computers is not new to most farmers. They have had access to the computing resources at universities and government agencies for some time.

These services were batch oriented. The farmer would gather data concerning farm activities, like crop and dairy yields, and send them in for processing. The data would be processed as a batch and returned to the farmer a few days later.

The availability of powerful and inexpensive microcomputers has allowed farmers to bring computing power home. Once there, the computer lends itself to a wide variety of farm management activities.

Financial Record Keeping and Planning

Like every business person, farmers must keep accurate records of their activities. Data concerning payroll, bills, inventory, sales, and other income and expense items can be processed using computers and standard accounting software.

An electronic spreadsheet is a popular application that is quite useful for farm management. The spreadsheet allows the farmer to itemize income and expense items. Figure C3.7 shows a crop production income and expense work sheet created by an electronic spreadsheet.

The spreadsheet format provides farmers with a great deal of flexibility. When estimating costs for next year, a farmer can manipulate the figures on last year's work sheet. The computer then recalculates the work sheet figures using the new data.

Using computers, farmers can simulate the best and worst possible situations. As a result, they can make better plans and have alternatives available for the next year.

Crop Management

In the past, it has been very difficult for farmers to anticipate the best mixture of crops, fertilizers, and chemicals to use on their fields. They want to maximize the yield a particular section of land provides while minimizing costs.

Computers can help in two ways. First, a computer can maintain records for this year's crops. This enables the farmer to identify all the costs and to pinpoint the final profit or loss.

Second, a computer can keep production records over many growing seasons. This data can help the farmer determine when and what type of crops to plant on a section of land. In addition, these records tell the farmer what pesticides have been previously used on the land. The farmer can then minimize the use of these and other chemicals.

Dairy Operations and Milk Production

Dairy herds, like a crowd of people, are made up of individuals with special needs and different capabilities. Farmers must understand these individual differences so they can get the most milk from each cow.

```
       CROP PRODUCTION INCOME AND EXPENSE WORKSHEET
========================= RESULTS AT 21  =================================
NAME OF               COW        OATS       CORN      CORN     MIXED
ENTERPRISE            REPLACE                GRAIN    SILAGE    HAY
---------------------------------------------------------------------------
NUMBER OF UNITS       46.50      47.00      117.00    14.00   105.00
INCOME                2224.50
EXPENSES              636.50     63.26      111.75   117.00    74.15
LABOR HOURS             75        4           5.9     11.5     11.7
CORN RAISED                      35.3        100
CORN FED              102
HAY RAISED                                             5.3      4
HAY FED                 9.9
BUY HAY, $/TON         50.00              BUY CORN, $/BU        3.20
SELL HAY, $/TON        45.00              SELL CORN, $/BU       3.00
PROPERTY TAX          1850.71             BUY LABOR, $/HR       4.19
LAND RENT             2125.00             SELL LABOR, $/HR
INSURANCE             1884.03             UNPAID LABOR, HR      3000
INCIDENTAL LABOR
INTEREST              8000.00
   TOTAL FARM EXPENSE 13859.74

-----------------------------------------------------------------------
              OUTPUT CALCULATIONS
-----------------------------------------------------------------------


LABOR REQUIREMENTS
   LABOR REQUIRED, HR    5755.3
   LABOR HIRED, HR       2755.3
   LABOR EXCESS, HR         0
BU CORN EQUIVALENT                        TONS OF HAY EQUIVALENT
   PRODUCED             13359                PRODUCED            494.2
   FED                   4743                FED                460.35
   SOLD                  8616                SOLD                33.85
   PURCHASED                0                PURCHASED              0
-----------------------------------------------------------------------
INCOME          103439.25       .00        .00       .00       .00
TOTAL INCOME    130810.80
EXPENSES         29597.25     2973.22   13074.75   1638.00   7785.75
TOTAL EXPENSES  80473.417
NET INCOME       50337.38
-----------------------------------------------------------------------
```

FIGURE C3.7

Output from an electronic spreadsheet
(Courtesy Roger C. Brook, Michigan State
University)

Computers are being used by many dairy farmers to calculate the amount of feed needed to maximize milk production. To do this, the computer must have access to historical data about past feeding schedules and milk production. This data can then be processed to determine the correct amount of feed for each animal.

Some farmers are using process control systems for feeding. Each cow is fitted with a transistorized collar for identification when it steps into a feeding

F I G U R E   C 3 . 8

Monitoring devices in dairy barn
(Courtesy Roger C. Brook, Michigan State
University)

stall. A computer then checks a data file to determine how much the cow has already had to eat. The optimum amount of feed is part of the cow's record.

The computer then figures how much feed to give the cow and activates the feeding bin. The bin releases the desired amount of feed. No food is released if the cow has already had its quota. This system also notifies a farmer when a cow is not eating. The farmer then checks the animal to see if it is hurt or sick.

Livestock Records

Some farmers use computers to maintain livestock records. The original cost, identification, maintenance costs, newborns, losses due to death, and selling price can be a part of a computerized inventory.

When livestock is used for breeding, special records are maintained. These records contain historical data about an individual animal's parents, offspring, special characteristics, and medical history.

Some breeding cooperatives have developed databases to track selected breeds of livestock. Thoroughbred horses, beef and dairy cattle, and other livestock are being registered in various databases. Computers are then used to provide breeding characteristics and histories for registered animals. Farmers access the databases to find ideal matches when breeding livestock with special characteristics.

Commodity Market Activity

The commodity market sets prices for farm products. It works like the stock market in that prices vary from day to day as traders bid prices up and down. Farm goods are sold at a profit or loss, depending on their value on the commodity market. Therefore, if farmers can follow the market, it helps them maximize profits or minimize losses by selling at the right time.

Farmers usually follow the commodity market in the newspaper. For more detailed and up-to-date information, farmers with microcomputers can now be linked directly to commodity market information.

Computer systems used by the commodity market can be accessed by microcomputers through the telephone. After dialing the computer number, the farmer uses special equipment to connect his computer to the home telephone. He then can selectively list the latest commodity prices.

STUDY OBJECTIVE

6. Briefly describe five areas in which a farmer can use a computer.

GOVERNMENT WORKERS

The federal government has been involved with the development of automated data processing systems since the 1800s. Computers are now indispensable to many government operations. However, only the six listed in figure C3.9 will be discussed here.

The Census Bureau

Every 10 years, the Census Bureau is responsible for finding out how many people are living in the United States. This mandate has been the driving force behind many new ideas in automated data processing, the first being the use of punched cards to produce the census of 1890.

The first commercial computer—UNIVAC I—helped process the census data of 1950. This machine represented the first step in bringing computers out from the research lab and eventually onto the desk top. UNIVAC I was replaced by more sophisticated computers in the 1960s and is now in the Smithsonian Institute.

The gathering of census data has come a long way since census takers first went door to door. Census forms in 1980 were filled out with pencils and

FIGURE C3.9

Six areas of computer use by the U.S. government

1. Census Bureau
2. Internal Revenue Service
3. U.S. Postal Service
4. Department of Defense
5. National Aeronautics and Space Administration
6. U.S. Congress

mailed back to the Census Bureau. Optical scanners input data concerning more than 200 million people directly into the computers for processing. The initial results were available within a year.

Internal Revenue Service

The people working for the Internal Revenue Service (IRS) make extensive use of computers. They use the computers to check income tax returns and to store the data. When errors are found, the computer produces a letter of explanation. If you are lucky enough to get a tax refund, the computer prepares the check.

U.S. Postal Service

The U.S. Postal Service uses computers to help sort the mail. Special input devices read the zip codes from letters and sort the letters into regions. The new nine-digit zip code will enable the computer to sort mail by city block and even identify individual buildings.

Department of Defense

Some of the most sophisticated computer systems in the world are employed for our nation's defense. Computers are used as part of early-warning systems in case of attack. They are also used to track aircraft and satellites and to coordinate the activities of our military forces.

Buried deep in the mountains of Colorado are the North American Defense (NORAD) computer systems, which are responsible for coordinating the nation's defense. These computers are in communication with computers based around the world.

Every military command center, ship, and plane uses computer technology. Computers also simulate emergencies to see if military personnel can react appropriately.

FIGURE C3.10

Military personnel training on missile air defense system (Courtesy Sanders Associates)

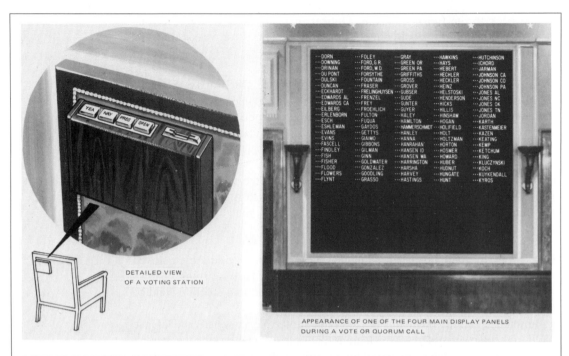

DETAILED VIEW
OF A VOTING STATION

APPEARANCE OF ONE OF THE FOUR MAIN DISPLAY PANELS
DURING A VOTE OR QUORUM CALL

APPEARANCE OF A SUMMARY DISPLAY PANEL WHILE A VOTE IS IN PROGRESS

FIGURE C3.11

Computer system used by the U.S.
Congress

Computers are used by the government for research, most notably by the National Aeronautics and Space Administration (NASA). Their computers are used to track satellites, control cameras, and perform research experiments along with other activities. Computers pilot research satellites into the depths of space and have helped land men on the moon.

National Aeronautics and Space Administration

Back on earth, computer systems are frequently used by politicians. Computerized voting systems are popular in many areas. In some systems, citizens vote by punching holes in cards to create a machine-readable source document. The votes are then counted to determine the election outcome.

U.S. Congress

Computers are also being used by legislators. The U.S. Congress uses computers to tally votes. Legislators use computer systems to determine the status of votes and the names of present or absent members.

---

7. Identify six areas of government that use computers and describe one computer application from each area.

STUDY OBJECTIVE

WEATHER FORECASTERS

John Lafriend's concert debut was the pinnacle of his career as a paid musician. After the concert, the band still struggled to make ends meet. Within a year they parted ways.

These were dark days for John. To pull himself out of it, he sat down and made a personal inventory. He listed all the things he liked to do and places he would like to visit. He also wrote down all the things he thought he was good at.

After completing the inventory, a friend suggested he talk to a military recruiter. Since his father had been in the navy, John made an appointment with the local navy recruiter. John explained to the recruiter that he was looking for skills he could use the rest of his life. He also mentioned his interest in computers and electronics.

The recruiter listened to John, explained the service's philosophy, and suggested he take their aptitude/placement test. This test would indicate occupations for which John would be eligible.

By the end of the year, John was at Chanute Air Force Base training to be an aerographer's mate—that is, a meteorologist. His responsibilities would eventually range from collecting meteorological data to preparing weather maps and forecasts. This meant working with a variety of electronic instruments and, of course, computers.

Aerographer's Mate John LaFriend

A meteorologist, or weather forecaster, oversees the collection of data about air pressure, temperature, humidity, wind speed, and wind direction. Visual observations, radar sightings, ground-based instruments, instruments suspended from weather balloons, and satellites are all used to collect this data.

Aerographer's mate, John LaFriend, briefing pilots

As the data is collected, it is input into a nearby computer. This computer is part of a network of computer systems representing hundreds of observation stations.

The network feeds all the weather data into a central computer at the Air Force Global Weather Center in Omaha, Nebraska. This computer system

National Weather Service computer network (Courtesy National Weather Service)

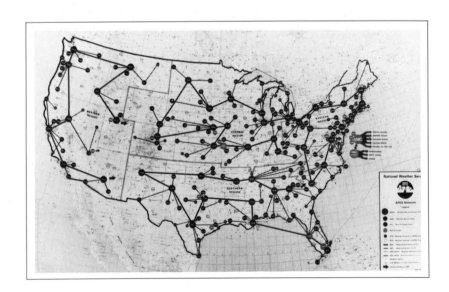

makes millions of calculations in simulating potential weather conditions. The resulting output is used to create weather maps and long-range weather forecasts.

These forecasts are used to brief pilots, ships' captains, and others on future weather conditions. In addition, the meteorologists are responsible for issuing weather warnings when severe weather is predicted.

Your local and national weather forecasts are provided by the National Weather Service. Although this network of civilian weather forecasters work independently of their military counterparts, their jobs are very much the same. They make periodic observations of local weather conditions and use the computer network shown in figure C3.13 to input the data into a central computer system in Washington, D.C. This system processes the latest observations from around the country. The output is then compiled into a local forecast.

National Weather Service

8. Describe the responsibilities of a meteorologist.
9. Explain how a computer is used to prepare a local weather forecast.

STUDY OBJECTIVES

Traveling by air today would be impossible without the help of computers. They help forecast the weather along a flight path, watch air traffic, and help the pilot fly the aircraft.

PILOTS, NAVIGATORS, AND AIR TRAFFIC CONTROLLERS

FIGURE C3.14

Air traffic controller's CRT (Courtesy Sanders Associates)

Air Traffic Control

Located at most major airports, air traffic controllers are responsible for monitoring airplanes as they approach and depart the airport. With the help of computers, each airplane in an area is identified and watched.

As radar picks up an approaching airplane, the air traffic controller makes radio contact with the pilot. The airplane's identification number, course, speed, and altitude are input into the airport computer. The controller's CRT then displays the airplane's location, along with the location of other traffic in the area. The display is constantly changing as airplanes land and take off.

The computer system is also programmed to watch for possible mid-air collisions. When the possibility arises, a warning is displayed on the CRT. The air traffic controller then notifies the pilots of the appropriate corrective action.

Computers in the Sky

On-board computers help pilots and navigators fly the airplane. Navigational computers with the latest wind speed and direction-use input data from ground stations to locate their position and calculate the best flight path. Private pilots responsible for both flying and navigation find navigational computers especially useful.

Pilots flying larger airplanes usually leave the navigation to their copilots or flight engineers. They can then concentrate on flying. Computers come to their aid in the form of automatic pilots—called **autopilots.** Autopilots can maintain an airplane's altitude, speed, and course while in flight.

FIGURE C3.15

Cockpit of a Boeing 767 airliner (Courtesy The Boeing Company)

COMPUTER GRAPHICS

An Art, A Science, A Tool

A picture is worth a thousand words, but why? Some experts believe that there are fundamental differences between the way the human brain processes words and the way it processes pictures. Words are processed one at a time. Visual images, on the other hand, seem to be processed in parallel. Many separate brain circuits process different parts of the visual image simultaneously. Consequently, humans are able to assimilate more data graphically than they can by reading words or tables of data.

BUSINESS GRAPHICS

Business data can be complex. A table of monthly sales data for six different salespeople may be hard to interpret. When this data is converted to a graphical format, however, relationships among salesperson performance are easily seen.

Because of the advantages of graphics, businesses have used them for years. Unfortunately, until recently, graphics were both slow and expensive to produce. A human artist was often required to work for hours to produce one graph. With the advent of the computer, and especially the microcomputer, that situation has changed. Today, multicolor pie charts, bar graphs, and line plots can be displayed on a computer screen in a matter of seconds. Furthermore, little operator training is required.

Business graphics can be produced in a variety of forms. They can be displayed on a CRT or on a special graphics terminal. Simple graphics can be printed on paper using a dot-matrix printer; more complex graphics must be printed with a plotter. Because such graphic output is in electronic form, it can

An extensive display of graphics hardware by Tektronix.

be sent over communications lines and displayed in locations far removed from one another. Graphics can also be recorded on 35-millimeter film for slide presentations.

Common business graphs, such as bar graphs and pie charts, are quickly produced with business graphics hardware and software.

3-D graphics can be used to provide an interesting presentation of a business graph or chart.

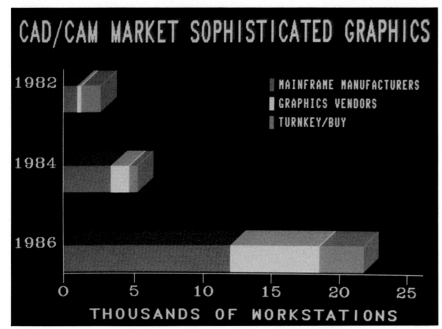

This colorful bar graph projects growth for engineering design graphics.

Graphics used in process control applications visually inform the operator of any changes in the process.

ENGINEERING GRAPHICS

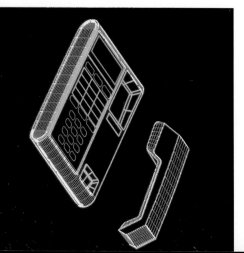

Computer-assisted design (CAD) and computer-assisted manufacturing (CAM) were two of the earliest applications of computer graphics. CAD technology is used by engineers to design products, develop plans for architectural projects, and define the flow and operation of manufacturing processes, as well as for other applications. Once a design has been drawn, the computer can enlarge it, reduce it, or rotate it to be viewed from a new angle. Details of manufacturing techniques, such as the length, location, and order of cuts, can be shown on the drawing. Such cutting sequences can be output to numerically controlled machines that cut the material according to the design specifications.

For even greater utility, drawings can be combined. Engineers can determine if two parts will fit together, and composite designs can be developed. In this way, the work of several engineers can be combined into one drawing.

Airplane design and manufacturing frequently involve CAD/CAM, or, to use a new term, computer-assisted engineering (CAE). In the design of an airplane, the surface shape is critical. Engineers make line drawings that reveal

An engineer uses CAD/CAM graphics to transform a set of specifications into a graphic model of a familiar telephone.

surface shape. More detail can be added to the drawing as the design progresses. The computer can show the entire airplane or only a particular portion, such as the left wing.

CAD/CAM has enabled engineers to design this Boeing 767.

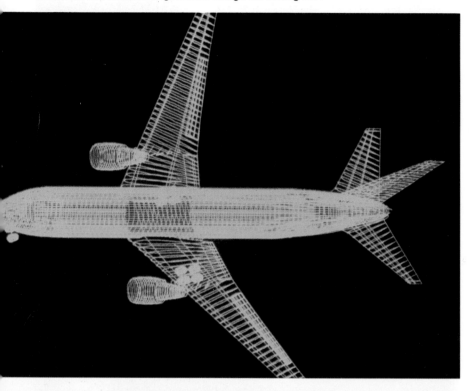

Space flight vehicles were early subjects of sophisticated design graphics.

In the future this model of the airplane will be done with a hologram.

Electronic circuits are frequently designed using CAE. Symbols for common electrical components, such as resistors, transistors, and the like, are moved about on the graphics screen and connected to form a circuit.

Solid object modeling displays objects in three dimensions. Shading and highlighting can be added to the object to create a realistic picture.

Engineers at General Motors have used graphics for auto design for years.

Graphics allow the designer to view the object from a variety of angles.

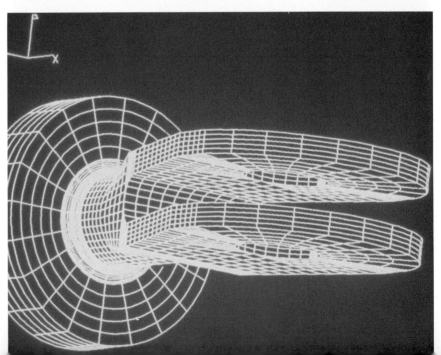

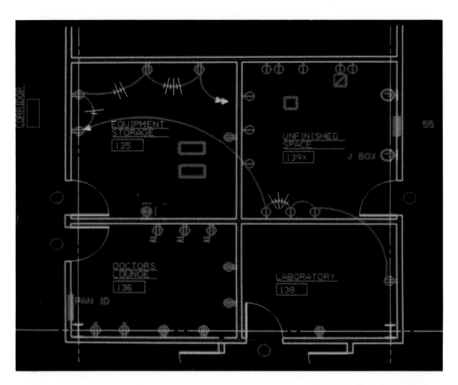

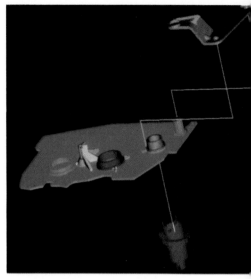

Modeling of solid objects provides a 3-D image of these mechanical parts.

An architect's building design.

The light pen is a common input device when graphics are used for electronic testing.

Graphics are produced on a screen by illuminating spots, called *pixels* (picture elements). For a black and white display, the pixel is either illuminated or not. For color displays, pixels contain cells of blue, green, and red. To produce a color, one or more of these cells is illuminated.

Characters, such as letters of the alphabet, are produced by illuminating groups of pixels, a process similar to that used in a dot-matrix printer. Illuminating pixels in a circular pattern, for example, produces a zero.

Suppose a screen consists of 80 rows and 100 columns of pixels. Any particular pixel can be identified by its row and column number. Thus, pixel (20,30) is the pixel in row 20, column 30. To draw a shape, we need only specify which pixels are to be illuminated.

A screen having only 60 rows and 80 columns of pixels would generate low-quality images. A standard TV screen has 512 pixels horizontally and 256 pixels vertically. A professional-quality graphics screen would have more. The Tektronix 4054, for example, has 3125 rows and 4096 columns of pixels. The greater the number of rows and columns, the higher the *resolution* of the image. To obtain high resolution, a special screen is required, and, because there is more data to store, larger main memories and magnetic storage are needed.

There are several ways of generating computer graphics. At the lowest level, commands to graphics programs are embedded in application programs. In BASIC on the Apple computer, for example, the sequence of commands shown at the left will cause a square to be drawn.

The first command draws a horizontal line from column 30 to column 50 at row 20. The second command draws a horizontal line from column 30 to column 50 at row 40. The third command draws a vertical line from row 20 to row 40 at column 30, and the last command draws a vertical line from row 20 to row 40 at column 50. Other systems have similar commands.

A second way of drawing graphics is to move a pen from one place to another. Commands are available to lower, raise, and to move the pen about. A line is drawn whenever the pen is moved while it is in the down position.

```
10   HLIN 30, 50 AT 20
20   HLIN 30, 50 AT 40
30   VLIN 20, 40 AT 30
40   VLIN 20, 40 AT 50
```

Drawing a Square Using Apple BASIC
Graphics Commands

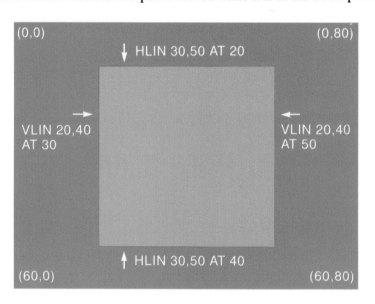

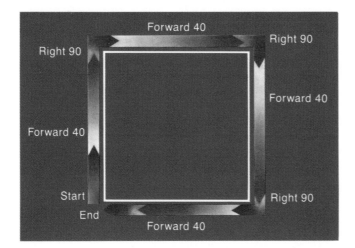

The programming language LOGO operates in this manner. The LOGO pen, however, is carried by a (simulated) turtle. The turtle can rotate and move forward and back. A line is drawn whenever the turtle moves with its pen down. The LOGO commands shown at the right will draw a square.

The first command tells the turtle to lower its pen. Then the FORWARD 40 command instructs the turtle to move forward forty units or steps. The RIGHT 90 command instructs the turtle to turn 90 degrees to the right. Commands are repeated to draw the square.

The commands embedded in Apple BASIC and the LOGO commands are both procedural. The user instructs the computer to take specific actions to produce the graph.

Some graphics packages are nonprocedural. For these, the user simply states what graphic design is desired and provides necessary data. Specific commands for generating the graphic are then issued by the graphics program. The following is typical of the interaction needed to generate a pie chart. Small letters are printed by the program; capital letters are provided by the user.

```
PENDOWN
FORWARD 40
RIGHT 90
FORWARD 40
RIGHT 90
FORWARD 40
RIGHT 90
FORWARD 40
```

```
graphic desired: PIE
title: SALES BY SALESPERSON
number of data points: 4
data and label: 270, FRED
data and label: 817, JANE
data and label: 775, DON
data and label: 439, MARY
```

With this input, the graphics program will produce a pie chart showing percentages of sales. Each piece of the pie will be labeled with the name of the appropriate salesperson.

Graphics packages like this are available to produce bar charts and XY plots as well as to compute and plot data trends and other similar graphs. The computer graphics spectrum is broad and extends from simple graphs like bar charts, to intricate designs produced according to mathematical equations, to the sophisticated graphics involved in computer animation.

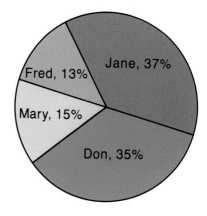

Pie Chart Produced Using Nonprocedural Graphics Program

SCIENCE AND GRAPHICS

Computer graphics are used in many scientific disciplines. For example, photos from space are produced using *image processing* techniques. Cameras sense light intensity or colors and record the sensations as digital data. This data is transmitted to earth, where it is interpreted by programs and transformed into a visual image. In some cases, images are improved by processing; programs analyze the digital data statistically and make lines more definite or add (or subtract) shadows. Image processing techniques can produce graphics from photographs and TV screens as well.

Imaging by satellite.

This color mosaic uses 42 Landsat images to depict the entire state of California.

This image was captured by NASA's Deep Space Program.

Scientific disciplines produce large amounts of data. Imagine the tables of data needed to describe the location of clouds over the United States! Yet, a map with clouds drawn over it is easily understood. Complicated results of scientific studies or experiments can also be shown graphically.

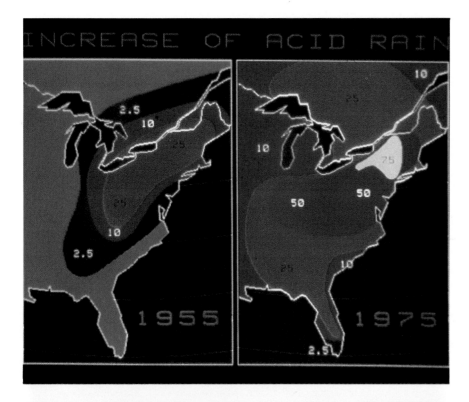

This graph presents a tremendous amount of data, yet it is quickly understood.

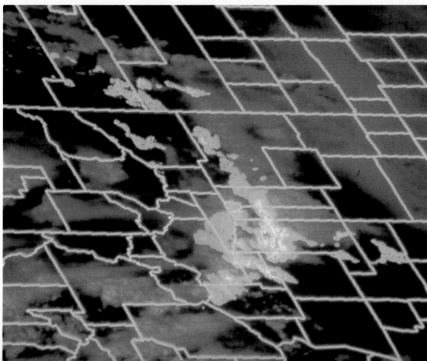

Scientists can use weather graphics displays for both study and explanation.

Astronomers, physicists, and chemists use graphics techniques to combine data and build models of the phenomena they study. In astronomy, for example, a graphical model of a constellation could be constructed from thousands of recorded observations.

In medicine, image processing is used to view the functioning of internal organs. These same techniques are used in industry to inspect objects that cannot be seen directly. Movement, growth, and change can be studied using graphical simulation. For example, in botany the growth of a plant can be simulated by producing images of the various stages in plant development. Simulation is used in other sciences as well.

Graphics can aid in visualizing and understanding a critical process within the body.

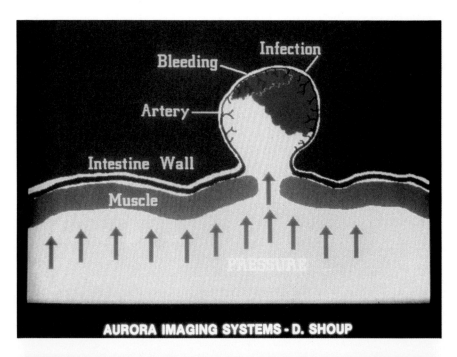

A CAT-Scanner (for computer-actualized tomography) scans the body and transmits a map of dots to provide color images of internal organs.

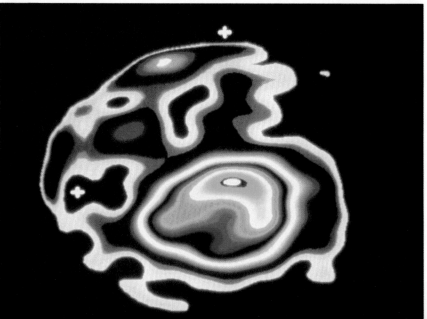

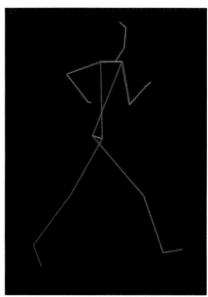

Medical researchers at the Olympic Training Center in Colorado use a digitizer to input data necessary to synthesize motion. Millions of bits are processed to produce stick figures that can then be used to analyze a runner's form and performance.

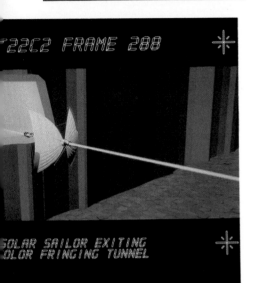

In the movie *Tron*, new developments in computer graphics were applied to animation in a process called *computer-generated imagery*.

Animation generated by computers is used for both video games and cartoon features.

Many scenes in recent science fiction movies, like *Tron* and *Return of the Jedi*, have been produced using computer graphics and a process called *animation*. Using this process, a mathematical description of one or more objects is stored in the computer. Then, computer programs move the object from one location and orientation to another location and orientation. The movement is recorded on film.

Animation requires that equations regarding object shape, object movement, location and movement of light source, location and movement of camera, and other parameters be input to the computer program. Adjusting the shape, colors, and shadows of an object as the object, the camera, and the light source move is exceedingly complex. In fact, in *Tron*, over two hours of processing were required on a VAX computer to generate a 52-second scene.

Computer graphics are used in other forms of entertainment as well. Much of the excitement of video games, for example, is due to their high-quality graphics.

Computerized frame creation for animation.

In addition to its applications in the entertainment field, computer graphics has become an art medium in itself. Abstract and geometric designs can be constructed by plotting curves according to mathematical equations. Computer programs can even produce original designs. Random numbers can be input into equations that specify points to be drawn. Each time the program is run, a different graph is generated. Authors of the program have no idea what designs will result.

With some graphics systems, pictures can be painted by moving a cursor around the screen. The artist selects a color and then paints the screen with the cursor, just as a canvas would be painted with a paintbrush.

Computer art has been developed to the point that it is virtually impossible to distinguish it from photographs and paintings.

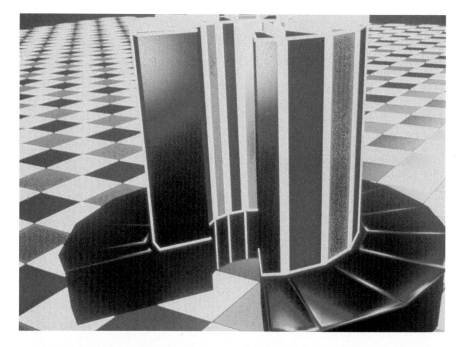

The CRAY-1 is a mainframe super computer built by Cray Research; this is a computer art rendering of the CRAY-1.

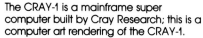

The CRAY-1's self-portrait?

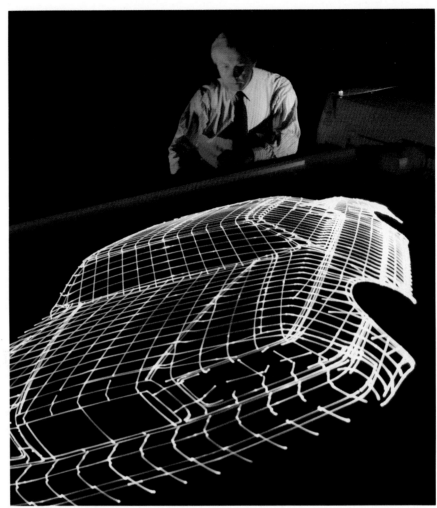

Research in 3-D graphics should make images in the future even more exciting.

Will the engineers use holograms in CAD/CAM applications in the future?

Some military aircraft have computers that can keep a plane just a few feet off the ground over even the most rugged terrain while flying several times the speed of sound! A few research planes and military cruise missiles can even fly without a crew. They are controlled from the ground and rely on automatic pilots and navigational computers.

While an autopilot is an important use of computer technology, it will never replace an airline pilot. As flight-oriented computers become more sophisticated, autopilots will take on additional responsibility. However, there will always be someone there to take over in an emergency. It must be stressed that computers are used to assist the air traffic controller, navigator, and pilot, not replace them.

10. Briefly describe how air traffic controllers, navigators, and pilots use computers.

11. Define autopilot.

STUDY OBJECTIVES

Many sports arenas are using computer-controlled scoreboards to inform and entertain the fans. You will also find computers being used behind the scenes to coordinate events, train athletes, and monitor their performance.

Sports commentators need to have access to an awesome array of statistics kept about an individual athlete or sporting event. They use this information to keep their audiences informed about players' lifetime averages or averages from the

COACHES AND ATHLETES

Analyzing Individual and Team Performances

FIGURE C3.16

Computerized scoreboard (Courtesy Intel Corporation)

- Store Team Statistics
- Store Individual Statistics
- Analyze Individual or Team Performance
- Analyze Body Movements and Form
- Time Events
- Score Events
- Coordination of Events

week before. The same source provides information about this year's team and compares it with the championship team from four years ago. As you might expect, these commentators are using computers to cross-reference and calculate these facts and figures.

Coaches are using computers in the same way. By knowing what an individual has done in the past, a coach is in a better position to anticipate what he or she can do today. There are even computer services that compile data about high school and college athletes to sell to professional clubs.

Many professional sports teams use computers in analyzing potential draft choices. Once a player is drafted, they use the computer to analyze tests and to store training statistics.

Computers can also be used to analyze opponents' past performances and provide data that would help identify their potential weaknesses. The coaching staff uses this data to anticipate future actions.

Computers are even being used to analyze how athletes move. Their body movements are input into the computer through specialized sensors or by digitizing films of the athlete in action. The body movements can then be graphically reproduced. These movements are also compared with computer models.

Sometimes the computer can spot subtle variations in an athlete's form that could hurt the athlete's performance. Computers represent another training tool that coaches can use to get the most out of an individual.

Timing, Control, and Record Keeping for Sporting Events

The Olympic swimmer making her final turn and the marathon runner on his final kick to the finish line will both be timed by a computer. The swimmer's goal is to touch the timing device suspended in the water at the end of the pool. This input device allows the computer to immediately calculate the time to the nearest thousandth of a second. It then flashes the time to the swimmer, judges, and crowd.

As the marathon runner crosses the finish line, he is given a number and the computer is notified that another runner has completed the race. After everyone has finished, the runners match their numbers to the posted computer times to determine their final standing and time.

Most Olympic and national sporting events are now timed using computers. Computers provide an accurate means of recording and storing times for many

FIGURE C3.18

Computerized scoring machine in a
bowling center (Courtesy Brunswick Corporation)

athletes competing in a variety of events. Automobile and horse races are also
timed using computers.

Other sports activities use computers to keep track of scores. For example,
your local bowling center might use an automatic pin scorer. The pin scorer is
really a computer linked to the pin-setting mechanism. As the mechanism resets
the pins for the next roll, it inputs to the computer the number of pins knocked
down. The computer uses a program with the scoring rules to figure the score.

If you are in a bowling league, the computer can also figure your handicap,
record each team's pin totals over the weeks of play, and print team standings.

The ability of computer systems to store data is a hidden advantage to using
them in sports. The coordination of large sporting events, like the Olympics,
would be an enormous task without the assistance of computers.

Computers can coordinate starting times and schedule referees and judges
at different events. They can make sure two events do not overlap one another.
Scores and times can be immediately figured and posted. This data can then
be sent across the Olympic compound or across the world. In addition, computers can keep medical records on all visiting team members and assign sleeping accommodations.

---

12. Identify and describe seven ways coaches and athletes use computers. STUDY OBJECTIVE

FIGURE C3.19

Pete Clark working on an industrial robot

BLUE-COLLAR WORKERS

The arm smoothly swung over to the conveyer belt. The mechanical hand flexed and firmly grasped a set of valves. It then moved toward another belt. Midway through this graceful motion, it suddenly jerked and stopped.

"Well, Mike, you were certainly right about this one," said robotics engineer Peter Clark. "It looks like a hydraulics problem to me. Take a half-inch wrench over to the third joint and check that line."

Pete Keeps in Step with New Technology

Pete had been working for the right company, at the right time, with the right skills to get ahead. First he had proved himself while working as a service technician. Then he had decided to use the company's educational benefits to go back to school. After management decided to make industrial robots, Pete's job record and the fact that he was back in school made him a natural choice to be part of the first service team.

His job as a robotics engineer had been fast paced and exciting from the beginning. Many companies were interested in increasing their factory productivity by using industrial robots.

Pete still spent a lot of time on the road. He helped with initial installations and was sometimes called back when the other engineers had problems.

Pete had read about people-like robots as a kid. However, the robots Pete installed didn't look like people at all. These industrial robots are basically metal boxes with an attached mechanical arm.

Industrial Automation

Robots represent just one aspect of a new wave of industrial automation that will be the focus of a lot of attention. Robots represent both the good and the bad impact computers are having on the workplace. In their favor are the positive effects robots can have on quality and productivity. Unfortunately, they will also displace people from jobs.

There are factories in some parts of the world that are completely automated. The engineers and programmers don't have to be there. Only a few service technicians are around to repair equipment when it breaks down.

If we could take a quick look at the future, we would probably see robots and other forms of automation used quite extensively in industry. The robots of today are partially a product of our need to put machines where we could not go. Industrial robots like the one in figure C3.20 were originally placed in working conditions unfit for people. Later, they automated dull and boring jobs that no one wanted.

Now, many manufacturing applications are being automated. Machines are tireless, noncomplaining workers. Those that are programmable have a great deal of flexibility and can be used for many jobs.

The advent of automated factories will allow for a greater variety of products. It should keep costs down while improving quality. On the other hand, people preparing themselves for tomorrow's work force must realize that good-paying manual labor jobs will be harder to find.

The role people play in manufacturing is drastically changing. Fewer jobs will require people to haul and assemble parts. These jobs will be done by industrial robots. Instead, workers like Pete Clark will be trained to install, program, and repair these machines.

FIGURE C3.20

Industrial robot (Courtesy Computervision)

STUDY OBJECTIVES

13. Briefly describe three advantages and one disadvantage to expanded applications of robots and other forms of automation.
14. Identify three jobs that people will have in an automated factory.

SUMMARY

New, inexpensive computer systems that are designed to be easy to operate have been applied to a variety of fields. Musicians and other artists are using computers to explore and expand the media in which they work.

Farmers are using computers to help control their valuable resources and to produce food at a lower cost. Government workers in the Census Bureau, Internal Revenue Service, and Postal Service use computers to improve services. Military personnel and government researchers employ computers to extend their senses and then help them analyze what they have found.

Computers are helping people forecast the weather, fly airplanes, and monitor the airways. They are also used to help train athletes, to time and score events, and to analyze team or individual performances. Workers are finding that computers are replacing some jobs and creating others.

The ability of people to apply computer technology to such a wide variety of activities indicates the tremendous potential this tool has in our society. These applications will expand as our understanding of this powerful resource expands through experience.

UNIT D

Bringing People and Computers Together

At one time computer systems were affordable only to big business and government. Owning a computer required lots of money and computer professionals to oversee it. This is no longer the case. The first part of Unit D examines how a family might approach buying a computer for their personal use. You see how to evaluate software and compare hardware. Procedures for setting up the system for day-to-day operations and for special problems are also covered. In addition, the qualifications and skills necessary to sell computers are examined.

The development of two computer systems is the focus of the second part of the unit. To start, Harold Johnson develops a record-keeping system for his paper route. The mistakes and successes of a beginner are analyzed. The other project starts several years later and involves Harold Johnson as a computer professional, working on a systems development project for an automotive company. The job of a systems analyst is highlighted as you follow the steps professionals use when developing new computer systems.

Advanced computer systems is the final topic in Unit D. The components of teleprocessing, distributed, and database systems are put together. You explore the reasons for developing computer systems that communicate with remote components or other computers. In addition, the advantages and disadvantages to using sophisticated communication and data management programs are outlined.

CHAPTER D1

Buying a Computer

The appearance of inexpensive microcomputers has fueled people's desire to buy a computer. Many of these machines are now affordable to the average person.

As with any important decision, buying a computer requires time: time to analyze the reasons for buying, time to explore different alternatives, and time to check with others who will be affected by the final results.

If a computer is going to be used properly, informed users must first identify why it is needed. Then they must make sure the other components are ready after the hardware is purchased. Computer programs must be available. Procedures for collecting data must be established. In addition, people must be trained to operate the equipment.

The steps that Harold Johnson's family went through to purchase a home computer are a case in point. They spent several weeks evaluating their needs, along with equipment and programs.

It all started a few weeks before Harold's birthday, when his father asked what he would do with a home computer. After giving it some thought, Harold described several ideas. He also let his father see the list of personal applications shown in figure D1.1. Harold and the other students in Mrs. Dingman's class had developed the list as part of a class project.

F I G U R E D 1 . 1

Applications for home computers

Money Management
Household Budget
Investment Portfolio

Record Keeping and Correspondence
Address and Phone Number List
Calendar of Events
Home Inventory for Insurance
Recipes and Menus
Social Correspondence

Hobbies
Games
Routing for Model Railroads
Coin and Stamp Collection
Inventories
Film Processing Data
Team Scoring and Averages

Education
Computer Assisted Instruction
Programming
Typing/Word Processing
Other Homework

Home Control
Heat
Lights
Security
Appliances

Access to Outside Data
Newspapers
UPI and AP Databases
Stock Market
Reservations for Travel
Electronic Mail
Catalog Shopping

The next evening, the family discussed getting their own microcomputer. Mr. Johnson wanted to approach buying their home computer the same way he had approached buying a computer for work.

Mr. Johnson was chief biochemist at a plastics company, and he felt that his employees were spending too much time "number crunching" and record keeping. Harold's interest in microcomputers had made his father aware that small computers could perform many of the calculations his employees were doing by hand.

DEFINITION OF SYSTEM REQUIREMENTS

Mr. Johnson approached the director of data processing about getting a microcomputer to aid the laboratory work. The director was very supportive, and a few days later a systems analyst stopped by to discuss the idea.

Developing a Needs Analysis for Work

The systems analyst suggested that Mr. Johnson and his employees develop a **needs analysis.** A needs analysis is an itemized list of jobs for which users need help. In this case, it was a list of potential computer applications for the biochemists. A need was described as the difference between what is currently being done and what should be done. A needs analysis would help determine the type of computer system that would be most useful.

The needs analysis was the first of four steps used by the systems analyst in the systems development process. The four steps are:

1. To define requirements
2. To evaluate the alternatives
3. To design the computer system components
4. To implement the computer system

After several months of work, all four steps were completed. The scientists were using their new microcomputer for a wide variety of projects. Mr. Johnson was also very impressed with the four-step process for designing a computer system. He wanted to follow the same steps in developing a home system.

Developing a Needs Analysis for Home

During the next few weeks, Harold's family put together a needs analysis. They jokingly called it a wish list. Each member of the family identified different ways they would use a home computer. The Johnsons' needs analysis is given in figure D1.2.

The needs analysis helped the Johnsons decide on some minimum requirements for the computer system. By knowing what they wanted the computer to do, they were ready to evaluate different software and hardware.

STUDY OBJECTIVES

1. List six areas of use for a home computer and give an example of each.
2. Describe a needs analysis and how it is used in systems development.
3. Identify the four steps in the systems development process.

Mr. Johnson
  Investment Portfolio (market analysis package)
  Home Inventory for Insurance (electronic spreadsheet)
  Reports for Work (word processing)

Mrs. Johnson
  Family Budget (electronic spreadsheet)
  Christmas Letter and Others (word processing)
  Mailing List of Family and Friends
  List of Important Dates

Harold
  Computer Programming for Mrs. Dingman's and other classes (BASIC)
  Physics Homework
  Record Keeping for Newspaper Route
  Games

Sarah
  Word Processor for Composition and Typing Class
  Games
  Record Keeping for Softball Team

F I G U R E   D 1 . 2

The Johnsons' wish list (needs analysis)

EVALUATION OF ALTERNATIVES

The next step was to identify three or four practical alternatives. To do this, Harold brought home several computer magazines from the library. Everyone in the family read different articles about computers and applications packages to get an idea of what was available. They also talked to friends with computers and went comparison shopping at local computer stores.

Software Considerations

The selection of software can be a tricky affair. If the software is already written, then the user should take the time to evaluate it thoroughly. It is best to evaluate the software first—before deciding on the hardware.

A specialized program for home or office use is not easy to find. A user should still try to work with such a program before making any purchase decisions. The old adage "Buyer Beware!" is especially true when you are buying software.

There can be problems in evaluating mail-order software. Software houses are reluctant to send users a preview copy, since programs are easily copied. The software houses are afraid people will copy the program and then send the original back. Their mistrust is well founded.

A wide variety of software for personal and business applications can be found in local stores. The Johnsons decided to look there for off-the-shelf applications packages.

```
             Muskegon Community College
                      MAIN MENU

E - Enter the EDITOR (create a new or update an old program/file)
D - Delete a program/file
L - List the diskette directory
A - Alter (rename) program/file

*** Text in buffer will be lost when the commands below are executed

R - Run (compile and execute) a program on the host system
P - Print program/file on the lab printer
C - Compile a program on the host system
B - BASIC (enter the BASIC interpreter)
K - Compile a program (local languages only)
X - Execute a compiled program (local compiles only)
Q - Quit (log off the host system)

Press the letter of the function to be executed? ▮
```

FIGURE D1.3

Program menu on a CRT

Even computer programmers look for applications packages when possible. If a program already exists, it would be foolish to spend a lot of time writing another one.

There are nine questions users should ask themselves when evaluating an applications package.

Is the program easy to use? While most programs work correctly, some can be difficult to use because the instructions on the screen are unclear or incomplete. This may cause the user to make mistakes. It is also very frustrating to work with a program and not know what to do next.

Question 1

Many programs list all the available options on the screen. This list of options is called a **menu.** Usually, there is a number or letter associated with each option, as shown in figure D1.3. All the user has to do is enter the option.

Does the software come with manuals and other forms of easy-to-read documentation? Even carefully thought-out programs need some type of written support, such as a user's guide and operating instructions. The care with which documentation is written provides one of the best ways of evaluating an applications package. Good programs usually have good documentation, while poorly written programs do not.

Question 2

Some software houses will provide a special telephone number—a **hot line**—users can call when they need help. While access to a hot line does not guarantee the quality of a product, it is sometimes a good indicator.

Does the software work the way the user wants it to, or will changes be necessary? One reason for buying software is to avoid the extra time and expense

Question 3

of writing it. Programs that must be altered need someone with a knowledge of programming to do the work. Sometimes programs are protected to prevent people from altering them.

This is not to say that buying a program with the intent of changing it is wrong or undesirable. Buying an applications package and then altering it can be quicker than developing it from scratch. But this alternative is usually chosen by people with a good understanding of programming. The Johnsons are not in a position to buy a program that needs to be modified before they can use it.

Question 4

Is the program upgradable? Users should find out if the software house is responsible for notifying them of changes and new versions. While the user may have to pay for newer versions or **releases,** such updating suggests that the software house is committed to supporting its product.

Applications packages with several releases are usually numbered. For example, there are several releases of the Wordstar word processing program. The first release was called Wordstar 1.0. Software houses increment the first number as new versions are made. The second number indicates the number of minor revisions. Therefore, Wordstar 2.2 is the second version with two changes.

Question 5

How flexible is the program and can it be used for more than one job? To get the most for your money, it is often beneficial to buy an applications package that can be used for a variety of needs. Word processing packages are a good example. This software can be used to write a term paper, the family's Christmas letter, or a report for work.

Question 6

Can data stored by other programs be accessed by the software, and vice versa? Integrated applications packages from one software house can use the same data files. For example, the VisiCorp software house has several products that can access common data files. Data first processed by their VisiCalc program can be stored and then accessed by their VisiPlot program.

This feature is desirable because the user needs to enter the data only once. With the data safely stored on disk, the user can create many different calculations and reports using the appropriate software. On the other hand, if the user wants to process the data using independent software, the data may have to be entered again.

Question 7

Which computers does the software work on? The answer to this question will directly affect the steps taken in evaluating hardware. Most informed users evaluate the software first. Then they evaluate the hardware that runs the software they selected.

Question 8

Does the software require special equipment? Some applications packages are designed to work with specialized hardware. For example, there are many game programs that are designed to accept input from joysticks. Therefore, microcomputers using this software must be able to be used with joysticks.

How much does the software cost? While applications packages for microcomputers cost far less than those for bigger computers, they can still cost hundreds of dollars. When budgeting to buy a microcomputer, the potential user should budget as much money for software as for hardware.

Question 9

"You get what you pay for" usually applies when you are buying software. Well-written and well-documented programs take hundreds of hours to perfect and usually cost more.

The Johnsons went to several stores to look at three types of applications packages: games, word processsing, and electronic spreadsheets. The electronic spreadsheet was to help Harold's mother with the household budget and his father's home inventory.

After taking the time to evaluate software, the Johnsons had a pretty good idea of the kind of hardware they needed. Many of the applications packages had minimum requirements for the hardware.

Hardware Considerations

The Johnsons made a list (see figure D1.5) of hardware specifications they wanted to compare. As they talked to salespeople and read articles about different brands of computers, they made the following comparisons.

Processing hardware is often classified according to the number of bits that make up a single instruction. Generally, the more bits in an instruction, the more powerful the processing hardware. Microcomputers have either 8-, 16-, or 32-bit instructions.

Comparison 1: Microprocessors

The difference in power between an 8-bit microprocessor and a 16-bit micro-

Manufacturer			
Model			
Cost			
Microprocessor			
• Instruction Size			
Memory			
• RAM			
• Maximum RAM			
• ROM			
Operating System			
• ROM or Booted			
Programming Languages			
• Compiler			
• Interpreter			
Screen Display (rows × columns)			
• Color			
• Graphics			
a. high resolution			
b. low resolution			
Keyboard (membrane or standard)			
• Cursor Control			
• Function Keys			
• Numeric Keypad			
• Detachable			
Input/Output Ports			
• Serial Ports			
• Parallel Ports			
Storage Devices			
• Tape Drive Cost			
• Floppy Disk Drive Cost			
• Floppy Disk Storage Capacity			
• Hard Disk Drive Cost			
• Hard Disk Storage Capacity			
Special Equipment			
• Modem			
• Joystick			
• Voice Synthesizer			
• Music Synthesizer			
Compatible with Model			
Manufacturer			
Service Contract			
• Cost			
• Period of Time			
• Location of Service Center			

FIGURE D1.5

Computer comparison checklist

processor can be shown through an analogy using telephone numbers. A 7-digit number—XXX-XXXX—has the power to connect you to all the telephones in a given area code. A 10-digit number—(XXX) XXX-XXXX—that includes an area code has the capability to connect you to any telephone in North America. The larger number of digits gives you more range. In the same way, the larger instruction size gives the computer more power per instruction.

Two types of memory units are used in a microcomputer. **Random access memory (RAM)** is used to store programs and data temporarily. When discussing the storage capacity of memory, people usually refer to RAM.

There are three ways to compare hardware regarding RAM capacity:

1. The amount of RAM that initially comes with the machine
2. Whether memory can be added at a later time
3. The maximum amount of memory the machine will support

The amount of RAM is critical because it determines the program size and volume of data that can be used by the computer. If there is only 3K of RAM available, the user cannot load a 16K program. Even a 3K program will leave no room for the storage of data.

For this reason, people need to know if the computer has enough RAM memory to "get them by." Some computers really don't have enough memory. Therefore, the additional expense of more memory must be figured into the original purchase price.

As the user learns to work with the computer, the demand for RAM memory space increases. The user should know if memory can be added to the machine at a later time. In addition, it is often important to know in what amounts it can be added. Most machines with expandable memories will allow users to add to the memory in lots of 8K, 16K, or 32K. Computers are said to be upgradable if memory or other features can be added at a later time.

Software evaluations also provide users with an idea of their future memory requirements. If they want to use an applications package that requires 128K of memory, it is good to know that the computer will support it.

For example, the Johnsons eventually want to use a word processing program that requires 64K of memory. They do not need to buy a computer with that much memory right now. However, the computer that they purchase should be upgradable to over 64K in the future.

Another type of memory called **read only memory (ROM)** is also used in a computer. The contents of ROM cannot be changed. Programs like the operating system and interpreters are stored in ROM when the computer is put together. These programs are used by the microprocessor, but the contents—like a reference book—are never changed.

Applications programs must be compatible with the machine's operating system. Unfortunately, no standard currently exists for microcomputer operating systems. Microcomputers use a wide variety of operating systems developed by either the manufacturer or an independent software house.

Computers with the manufacturer's operating system use applications packages designed for that system. For example, Apple computers come with the

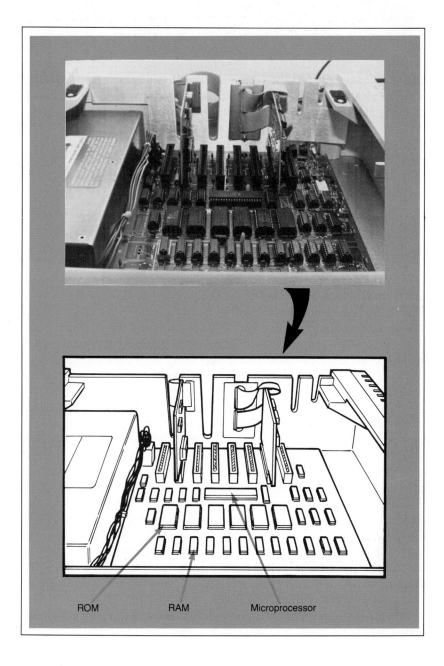

Microcomputer circuit board

Applesoft operating system. Only Applesoft-compatible programs will work with this operating system.

Independent operating systems have the potential of running on a variety of computers. There is usually a greater choice of applications packages designed for such systems. Two popular operating systems are the Control Program/ Microcomputer (CP/M) system and the Disk-Operating System (DOS). An Apple computer using the CP/M operating system can run programs designed to be used with CP/M.

The operating system can be built into the computer by placing it in ROM. When the operating system is put in ROM, it is ready to go when the computer is turned on. Usually, the more ROM a computer contains, the more powerful the operating system.

In other cases, the operating system is stored on disk and read into RAM after the computer is turned on. Loading the operating system into memory is called **booting** the system.

The most popular operating systems offer both compilers and interpreters to translate high-level programming languages into machine language. Users interested in designing and writing their own programs should check to see what languages are offered with the computer. Each operating system usually supports several processing programs that translate high-level programming languages.

Comparison 4: Programming Languages

While the standard screen display has room for 24 rows of 80 characters, there are many variations from which to choose. In addition, several computers offer special graphic capabilities and the use of color.

Comparison 5: Screen Displays

Microcomputers especially have a wide variety of screen displays. Some people use a television set for displaying output. Most users find it desirable to have as many characters as possible on a single line. Word processors and electronic spread sheets that display reports or many columns of numbers often need a lot of room on each line.

Color and special graphic capabilities can cost more. However, they are desirable on computer systems that are intended to be used for games or fancy displays. Screen displays using color and graphics are far more interesting than

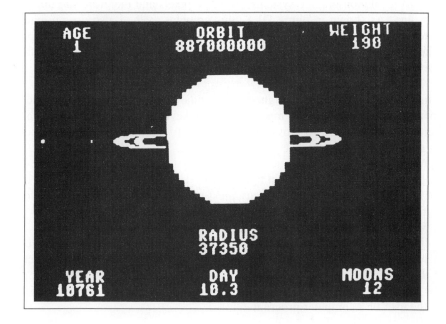

FIGURE D1.7

Low-resolution graphic (Courtesy Commodore Computer Systems)

FIGURE D1.8

High-resolution graphic

a screen full of numbers and letters. For this reason, many people feel that the extra cost is worth it.

Graphic displays are often broken down into two types: **low resolution** and **high resolution.** The difference is in the number of picture elements—pixels— used to form the graphic display. Low-resolution graphic systems usually use the same number of pixels for graphic displays and standard characters.

High-resolution graphic systems use more pixels and therefore can draw a finer line. As shown in figure D1.8, this graphics method also does a much better job of drawing curves, since more pixels are used to define the shape. When color graphics is possible, software capabilities sometimes limit the colors available with high-resolution graphics.

Comparison 6: Keyboards

While most keyboards are designed like standard typewriter keyboards, additional features vary between machines. Some keyboards are detachable. This feature allows the user to move the keyboard into the most desirable position for data entry.

A few computers have touch-sensitive—sometimes called **membrane**— keyboards like the one shown in figure D1.9. The keys on these keyboards do not move when pressed. Instead, any pressure on the flat surface is registered by the keyboard, and the appropriate character is sent to the computer.

Most keyboards have responsive keys that move when they are pressed. In addition to the standard set of keys for letters, numbers, and special characters, there are other keys. Some of these keys allow the user to control the movement of the cursor on the screen. Others have special uses during programming. A few keyboards even have numbered function keys whose use can be defined by the user or a computer program.

FIGURE D1.9

Touch-sensitive keyboard

FIGURE D1.10

Standard keyboard with function keys and numeric keypad

In some cases, a smaller numeric keypad is set to the right of the regular keyboard. The numeric keypad contains the digits 0 to 9, a decimal point, a comma, and other mathematical characters. It is usually laid out just like a calculator's keypad (see figure D1.10).

Comparison 7: Input/Output Ports

Computers are equipped with plugs, or ports, so that they can be connected to other devices. These ports are frequently referred to as input/output or **I/O ports,** since they can attach to either input or output devices.

The I/O ports are usually on the back of the computer. As you would expect, the number of devices you can attach to the computer depends on the number of I/O ports.

Generally, the I/O ports are either **serial** or **parallel.** Data is sent between the computer and the attached device one bit at a time with a serial I/O port, as shown in figure D1.11. With a parallel I/O port, the bit pattern for a single character is sent at the same time, as shown in the same figure.

Different peripheral devices will have different I/O port requirements. The advantage to using a parallel I/O port is that it is faster. However, the equipment must be relatively close to the computer. While serial I/O ports do not provide as high a transmission speed, peripheral devices can be much further away.

Printers, tape drives, disk drives, and even additional memory are attached to the computer through the I/O ports. When the appropriate port is not avail-

Serial and parallel ports

Comparison 8: Storage Devices

able, a different port can be used if an **interface** is available. An interface will convert one type of signal to another. Let's say a serial port is not available to connect a serial printer. An alternative is to use a serial-to-parallel interface connecting the printer to a parallel port (see figure D1.11).

Most computer users are faced with the decision of using either tapes or disks for permanent storage. The decision usually boils down to a dollars-and-cents issue.

Tape drives provide an inexpensive means of storing programs and data files. However, access time is relatively slow. In addition, tapes allow only sequential access to data and programs.

When faster access speeds and direct access are desirable, storing data on disk is the only way to go. While this alternative is more expensive, most people do not regret the decision.

One way to evaluate disk drives is to determine the number of characters stored on disk for each dollar you spend. This is called a **storage/cost ratio.** To calculate the storage/cost ratio, find out how many characters can be accessed from the disk when it is in the disk drive. If a floppy disk must be turned over to access data on the other side, count only the amount of data stored on one side. Divide this number by the cost of the disk drive.

This method will work when comparing either floppy disk drives or hard disk drives. Although comparisons are made between a hard disk drive and a floppy disk drive, remember that hard disk drives provide faster access time. In addition, they are more dependable over many years of service.

As mentioned earlier, some applications packages need special input or output devices. Usually, this equipment is not part of the original purchase. Most users wait to buy special hardware until they have bought the corresponding software.

Comparison 9: Special Equipment

Acoustic couplers, printers, joysticks, and voice and music synthesizers are hardware devices that attach to computers. The **acoustic coupler** uses a telephone headset to connect a computer to a telephone. An acoustic coupler provides a way to transfer programs or data between remote computers using the telephone.

Minicomputer and mainframe systems almost always include a printer when initially purchased. However, a printer can cost as much as a microcomputer. Many users with smaller systems therefore delay the purchase of a printer. Their ability to get by without one depends on the applications programs they use.

When the computer is used for word processing, a letter-quality printer that can handle single sheets of paper is helpful. Otherwise, most users find a dot-matrix printer sufficient and more affordable.

When the computer is primarily used for entertainment, especially games, joysticks and synthesizers can enliven the action. Many game programs are written so that the users control the action by using the joystick.

A few computers come with a music synthesizer. In other cases, voice or music synthesizers are available options. Game programs, in particular, use sound output. The charm and intensity of many games are a product of the sound generated by a synthesizer.

Compatibility refers to the ability of some computers to use the programs or hardware of another computer. In some cases, computers manufactured by the same company are compatible. Tape drives, disk drives, and other hardware can be compatible too.

Comparison 10: Compatibility

This feature is especially important when users outgrow their computer. By that time, they will have a lot of time and money invested in software and additional hardware. It is desirable to find a more powerful computer that is compatible with the older system. This allows the user to expand the system capacity without losing the use of software and hardware already owned.

The repair and maintenance of a computer system can be a very frustrating experience for any user. To minimize the problems, manufacturers and computer stores offer service contracts at an additional cost.

Comparison 11: Service

The type of repair service the user receives depends on the service contract. Users who are willing to bring their computers to a service center can obtain inexpensive service contracts. Some service contracts will contain an on-site repair provision. This means that a service technician like Peter Clark will come to the computer center to repair the equipment.

Without a service contract, the user must pay for necessary repairs as they occur. With smaller computers, they must bring the computer to a service center, where they are charged for the cost of the repair. Some microcomputers must be shipped to an out-of-state repair center. People with larger systems

HILTON-FROST
BUSINESS EQUIPMENT. INC.
162 APPLE AVENUE
MUSKEGON. MI. 49442

FULL COVERAGE MAINTENANCE AGREEMENT

The Hilton-Frost Company agrees to perform preventive maintenance service and furnish necessary replacement parts on the equipment listed by model and serial number and for the prepaid fees shown subject to the following:

1. The equipment will be cleaned, lubricated and adjusted periodically, at the Periodic Maintenance Frequency shown. Any necessary suggestions to the operator will also be furnished at the time service is performed.

2. Service under this agreement includes replacement of all standard parts to maintain equipment in good condition and labor necessary to make such replacement of parts, technical adjustments, cleaning and lubricating.

3. This Agreement does not include furnishing or replacement of expendable operating supplies including Diazo Lamps and Glass Cylinders. Installation of supply items will be performed without charge if the Service Representative is present for regular service reasons. A regular service charge will be made if a special call is requested only for the purpose of installing supply items.

4. Labor, parts and expense necessary to repair damage caused by accident, misuse, fire, water or to alter or rebuild equipment are not covered by this agreement. When such service is required, an estimate of charges will be submitted for approval before work is started. This Agreement does not provide for labor necessary to install additional conversions or accessories after initial machine installation.

5. This Agreement covers, in addition to regularly scheduled maintenance calls, emergency repair requested by the user and found to be necessary by the Service Representative to keep equipment in operating condition.

6. This Agreement covers labor for replacement but does not include the cost of motors replaced due to changes in power line specifications.

7. It is understood that the equipment covered by this Agreement is in good condition on the date this Agreement becomes effective. Machines which require repair or overhaul will not be accepted for maintenance service. In such event, necessary repairs, if requested, will be made at current established rates and shall be in addition to maintenance rates. Maintenance service will be rendered on all machine models that are not more than ten (10) years old. Machines over (10) years old will be placed under maintenance at the option of the contractor.

8. All service under this Agreement will be performed on the customer's premises during regular business hours of Hilton-Frost's service office. Emergency Service Calls required by Customer to be performed outside of Hilton-Frost's normal business hours will be billed at the then current Hilton-Frost hourly rates for overtime labor. Machines used for multiple shift operation are subject to an extra charge.

9. This Agreement shall become effective on the date accepted by Hilton-Frost or if equipment is in warranty at the expiration of the equipment warranty period and shall remain in effect until cancelled by either party on 30 days advance written notice, provided that after the end of any prepaid period, the continuance of this Agreement shall be at Hilton-Frost's then current rates. Such cancellation may be effected as to the entire Agreement or as to any one or more of the machines covered hereby. Upon such cancellation prior to the end of any prepaid period, Customer will be refunded the pro-rata amount applicable to the remainder of such period.

10. Unless otherwise indicated herein, additional equipment purchased from Hilton-Frost Bus. Equip., Inc., will be automatically covered by this agreement at applicable then current rates, upon expiration of the warranty period. The first invoice for preventive maintenance service for such machine under this Agreement will serve as confirmation that the machine is so included.

11. Fees plus applicable taxes payable annually in advance. Terms net on receipt of invoice.

Sold To:

Customer's Name_____

Address_____

City, State, Zip _____

By _____

By _____ Date _____ Title _____

Title_____

(Date Signed by Customer)

Model and Serial Numbers	Periodic Maintenance Frequency	Annual Fees	Effective Date

Special Billing Instructions:

Total Annual Fee _____

THANK YOU THIS IS NOT AN INVOICE
BILLING WILL BE ISSUED LATER

FIGURE D1.12

A typical service contract for computer equipment (Courtesy Hilton-Frost Business Equipment, Inc.)

pay the repair person for mileage and driving time in addition to the repair costs.

After looking at many different computers, the Johnsons finally completed their checklist. It was now time to select a computer system based on their needs analysis, software priorities, and hardware evaluation.

The Next Step

4. Define menu, hotline, RAM, ROM, booting, interface, and acoustic coupler.
5. Identify three sources of information about computers and applications packages.
6. Identify nine questions that need to be asked when you are evaluating applications packages.
7. Briefly explain how instruction size relates to the power of a microprocessor.
8. List three ways that RAM capacity is important in the comparison of computers.
9. Identify two ways that an operating system can be accessed by a computer.
10. Describe the difference between low-resolution and high-resolution graphics.
11. Describe how data is transferred with serial and parallel ports.
12. Be able to use the storage/cost ratio to compare disk drives.
13. List 11 areas of comparison in the evaluation of hardware.

SELECTING A COMPUTER SYSTEM

Like most users, the Johnsons quickly realized that the hardware and software were going to cost more than they had expected. They had to decide what they wanted of the system right now. Then they could select hardware and programs to purchase. The needs analysis was especially useful, since it allowed them to make decisions based on future needs as well as immediate ones.

People-Related Decisions

Harold's parents decided that the family's needs fell into two groups. The first group could use inexpensive hardware and applications packages. This group essentially met the children's needs. They could run games and Harold could program the computer to do his homework and other things.

The second group would require more expensive software and hardware. This group included most of the items Mr. and Mrs. Johnson wanted.

Harold's parents were caught in a bind. They could purchase an inexpensive computer to start. The whole family could learn to use the computer by playing games. If they found that everyone enjoyed using the computer, it would be easier to justify more expensive hardware.

On the other hand, both Mr. Johnson and Harold had experience working with computers. They did not have to learn how to use the computer. Mr. Johnson, in particular, knew that he could use a computer at home. Therefore, they decided to buy a computer system that matched their experience. This meant spending more money than they had initially planned.

Many organizations acquiring a new computer system face the same decisions as the Johnsons. When inexperienced users are involved, organizations try to select the most important and, if possible, least inexpensive and easy-to-use applications first.

Software Decisions

The Johnsons spent a good deal of time evaluating applications packages. Eventually, they were going to purchase three types of software for the computer: a word processing program, an electronic spreadsheet, and game programs.

Since the word processssing program really needed a printer to be useful, they decided to wait and buy both at the same time. Which electronic spreadsheet to buy was an easy decision. Mr. Johnson wanted to purchase the same software he used at work.

The games were fun to evaluate and everyone knew what they liked and didn't like. In other words, programs can be easy to evaluate if the user knows what he or she needs.

Hardware Decisions

The Johnsons now had to decide on the brand and model of computer they wanted. Their hardware checklist provided the data to help them decide on the best choice. The software requirements for memory and permanent storage also provided minimum requirements for the hardware.

FIGURE D1.13

The Johnsons comparison shopping for a microcomputer

The Johnsons were looking for a microcomputer with a responsive keyboard and 64K RAM. It was understood that the screen would display 24 rows with 80 characters in each row. In addition, they wanted two floppy disk drives for permanent storage and backup. On top of all this, another I/O port had to be available to attach a printer when they decided to buy one.

Harold wanted to be sure that the computer was programmable in BASIC. He also asked that they look for machines that had color, graphics, some type of sound synthesizer, and joysticks. These options were particularly useful for games.

Finally, they decided against a service contract for repairing the computer as long as it could be locally serviced. No one was very thrilled about shipping the computer out of state for service.

The hardware the Johnsons finally selected was based on their needs and opinions. Other families or organizations with different needs and opinions might make another choice.

STUDY OBJECTIVE

14. Describe how the Johnsons used experience to help them decide on the type of computer system to buy.

INSTALLING THE COMPUTER SYSTEM

The Johnsons purchased their first computer on Harold's birthday. They went into the computer store, found the salesperson they had talked to before, and bought the computer, disk drive, joysticks, and electronic spreadsheet. The salesperson gave them their first game program.

Grandfather's oak desk had been cleared in the basement for the computer system. Their old color television would be the CRT. After getting the computer home, they carefully unpacked everything and put it on the desk.

Setting Up the System

Inside the box with the computer was a user's manual. The first section in the user's manual explained where and how to set up the computer.

Most micros and minis do not require air conditioning or a special environment. However, some care should be used when setting up the equipment. Computers will provide users with steady, reliable service if they are placed in cool, dry work areas that are relatively free of dirt and static electricity.

Static electricity can be the source of many problems. It is even possible to damage the computer's internal circuitry just by walking across a new carpet and accidentally "zapping" the computer. It is best to set up the computer in an area without carpeting.

Another problem with electricity relates to power fluctuations. It is possible to lose a program in memory or to have the computer's circuitry damaged by a power surge. To avoid this problem, there are products on the market that protect computers from power surges. Some of these products are designed to protect microcomputers. They plug into a wall socket, and the computer, in turn, plugs into the device. While these products are relatively expensive, they can prevent a costly repair bill or the frustration of having to retype a lost program.

AC power surge protector (Courtesy Electronic Protection Devices, Inc.)

It is usually a good idea to set aside space on both sides of the computer as a work area. This allows those working with the machine to spread out their work sheets and notes when programming or entering data.

In addition, most businesses recommend that the home row of the keyboard—the row with the letters A, S, D and J, K, L—be about 28 inches from the floor for adults. This is lower than most desks, which are normally 31 inches high. Because of this, Mr. Johnson added an adjustable shelf to the desk so that everyone could move the keyboard to a comfortable height.

Another consideration when setting up a computer system is the storage of tapes and disks. Large computer centers place storage media in a fireproof library. For home use, a designated shelf or filing cabinet is fine for storing tapes and disks. In addition, users might want to place important backup copies in another area or even a safety deposit box at the bank.

Having a designated place to store everything is especially important when several people will be using the system. It prevents things from being misplaced and helps everyone keep the work area ready for the next person.

Procedures for Day-to-Day Operation

Each computer has its own start-up procedures. These procedures (like those in figure D1.15) can be found in the user's manual. They are often copied onto a separate piece of paper and posted near the computer until everyone is familiar with them.

Since computers have very few moving parts, they are extremely reliable and require very little maintenance. Problems are a little more frequent with peripheral devices like tape drives, disk drives, and printers, which have moving parts.

Many problems can be avoided, or at least minimized, if users regularly follow a few simple preventive maintenance procedures. The list of preventive maintenance procedures in figure D1.16 should be checked against the user's

1. Turn on computer using switch on back left
2. Turn on CRT using button on right front side
3. Check screen to verify if memory is OK
   If not turn off computer and CRT and call dealer
4. Insert disk with operating system into disk drive A and press RETURN key*
5. Computer is now ready for use

*This step boots the operating system into RAM.

Computer:	Blow accumulated dust off circuit boards
Tape Drive:	Align read/write heads
	Clean read/write heads
	Demagnetize read/write heads
Disk Drive:	Clean read/write heads
Printer:	Blow accumulated dust off circuit boards
	Keep inside clean of paper shavings
	Clean print head
	Change ribbon on impact printers

manual for each piece of equipment. The user's manual will describe acceptable maintenance procedures in detail.

Kits are available to clean the read/write heads of tape and disk drives. Special cassette tapes that demagnetize tape drive read/write heads can also be purchased. The secret to preventive maintenance procedures rests on using them. It's like flossing one's teeth. If a person gets in the habit of always doing it, a lot of problems will be eliminated. If it is done once in a while, some problems will be minimized, but others will pop up. If it is never done, time and disaster will eventually catch up.

Often, there are early-warning signals. For instance, a user might have to try several times before loading a program into memory. Eventually, the user may not be able to load any program, no matter how many attempts are made. In this case, the user should clean the read/write heads on the drive. If the problem can be spotted ahead of time, it can be corrected before more serious problems occur.

However, if the computer is used by a group of people, the early-warning signs may go unnoticed until it is too late. Therefore, when several people use a computer system, they often keep an **error log.** One page from an error log is shown in figure D1.17. The error log is used to document any problem users

	LAB IDENTIFICATION _____
	SERIAL # _____
	PAGE _____

ERROR LOG

DESCRIPTION OF EQUIPMENT _____

MANUFACTURER _____

SERVICE LOCATION'S ADDRESS _____

SERVICE LOCATION'S TELEPHONE # ( ) _____ WARRANTY DATES start _____ end _____

Date & Time	Symptom and Explanation	Noted By	Corrective Action	If Equipment Leaves	
				Date out	Date in

FIGURE D1.17

Log to keep track of equipment problems

have when operating the equipment. Recurring problems can then be identified and fixed.

The error log is also a convenient place to record the manufacturer's and computer store's address and telephone number in case of an emergency. In addition, it can contain the name and telephone number of the person responsible for repairing the equipment.

Finally, users should have an end-of-the-day routine. This will include making a backup copy of any important data or programs used during the day. All equipment should be turned off and time should be taken to store tapes, disks, and manuals in the appropriate spot.

We would be fooling ourselves if we didn't prepare for problems. So every user should be familiar with troubleshooting procedures.

Each component of the computer system is a potential source of problems. People can forget to plug in the computer or they can load the wrong program. Bad data can cause a program to work incorrectly. Hardware can malfunction, or a program can have a bug. Finally, procedures could be wrong or followed in the wrong order.

The first rule in handling problems is to stay calm. The second rule is to avoid jumping to any fast conclusions. There is nothing more embarrassing than taking a computer in for repair only to have the service technician find a blown fuse.

The key to handling problems is to prepare for them by having procedures ready when possible. Figure D1.18 is an example of a troubleshooting checklist from a user's manual. These checklists usually describe different problems and ways to solve them.

If the troubleshooting checklist doesn't help the user solve the problem, then the user will have to rely on outside resources. A hot line is sometimes available when problems occur with hardware or an applications package. The user can use the hot line to contact a knowledgeable representative from the software house or manufacturer.

To make the best use of this telephone service, the user should assemble a list of questions to ask before calling. In addition, any related manuals and the computer should be ready so that the user can try suggestions.

When the software or equipment is purchased locally, the salespeople can be contacted for assistance. They might be able to help solve the problem or direct the user to someone who can. If the hardware is under warranty or a service contract, it is just a matter of notifying the service department.

Problems will occur, but by following a set of troubleshooting procedures, the time and cost can be minimized. Preventive maintenance procedures will hopefully reduce hardware problems.

---

15. List four environmental and three physical considerations in setting up a computer system.

16. List nine common maintenance procedures.

17. Briefly describe the purpose of an error log.

18. List two rules for handling computer problems and describe three resources available to users when problems occur.

19. Identify where users can find start-up, preventive maintenance, and troubleshooting procedures.

There are individuals who make their living selling computers and related hardware and programs. These people work out of retail stores or local sales offices of computer manufacturers.

Problem	Probable Cause	Remedy
SYSTEM MEMORY TEST FAILS		Contact your dealer
RESET INDICATOR LIGHT NOT LIT	Power cord not plugged in	Plug in cord
	Wall outlet not live	Check outlet and circuit breaker
	Indicator light burned out	Contact dealer
	Internal connection loose	Contact dealer
DISK DRIVE INDICATOR LIGHT DOES NOT BLINK	System was not reset	Press RESET
	Indicator light burned out	Contact dealer
	Internal connection loose	Contact dealer
DRIVE TRIES TO LOAD, SEEK, BUT TERMINAL SCREEN IS BLANK	Floppy diskette inserted incorrectly	Insert SYSTEM DISKETTE with label facing up and away from slot
	Incorrect diskette inserted	Insert SYSTEM DISKETTE
	Cables and plugs incorrectly connected	Refer to Section 3.3
	Terminal is off	Turn it on
SYSTEM LOADS WITH GARBLED MESSAGE	Terminal not configured correctly	Refer to Section 5.2
	Baud rate or word setting incorrect	Refer to Appendix D
	SYSTEM DISKETTE is ruined	Make or use another SYSTEM DISKETTE

Troubleshooting checklist from Morrow MicroDecision manual (Courtesy Morrow Design, Inc.)

MICROS

Selecting Your Own Computer

Confusion. So many choices. How can you decide among all of the alternatives? The **systems development process** will help you, just as it has helped other users make better decisions when buying larger computer systems.

Which microcomputer should I buy?

How important is the vendor's name?

Should I buy color capability?

What printer do I need?

What if I want graphics?

What do I need a diskette for?

Should I do word processing?

What should I do when I get the computer home?

What programs do I need?

Where should I buy the computer?

Do I need to be a programmer?

How much should I pay?

What's an electronic spreadsheet? What can I do with one?

SOME FIRST-TIME USER QUESTIONS

A familiar retail computer store—the starting point for most personal microcomputer users.

People buy microcomputers for many reasons. Some want to manage personal records, some want to forecast stock prices, some want to educate their children, some want to manage farm records, and on and on. Experience has shown that, regardless of the eventual application, there is a common process for

developing the system. This process has four basic stages: *defining requirements*, *evaluating alternatives*, *designing components*, and *implementing the system*. This photo essay reviews the process and shows how it applies to the development of a word processing system.

Jennifer Anderson thinks a word processing system may help her in her schoolwork. First, she should determine her **requirements**.

Once Jennifer knows what she needs, she should **evaluate alternatives**, starting with software.

To use her new system effectively, she must **design** procedures. She takes a class to learn what procedures are necessary.

Implementation—Jennifer is able to use the system to improve her schoolwork and even to simplify her life.

DEFINING REQUIREMENTS

The needs the system must meet are determined during requirements definition. All five components of the system need to be considered: hardware, programs, data, procedures, and people. For example, the *hardware* may need to weigh less than 50 pounds, or *programs* may be needed that will print a special report. There may also be requirements for *data*, such as that the system have sufficient storage for a month's worth of orders. An example of a requirement involving *procedures* is the need to process every order within 24 hours. A requirement involving *people* might be that the use of the system be within the abilities of the personnel currently in the organization.

Defining requirements is important regardless of the application. For example, if the system is to keep records of farm production, how will it be used? What specifically is needed? If the system is to be used for education, for what level of education is it intended? For how many children? Is color necessary? If the system is to be used to manage business records, which records? General ledger? Inventory? Fixed assets? Cash flow? Within each of these categories there are many questions to answer.

Word Processing for Jennifer Anderson   Jennifer Anderson is a college student majoring in English literature. Jennifer writes many papers for her classes, and she thinks a word processing system would be useful to her.

This farmer wants to keep records of differences in cattle growth for different types of feed.

These children can learn arithmetic and other subjects using computer-assisted instruction (CAI) on a microcomputer.

Someone here needs help in managing
business records.

Jennifer obviously has requirements for
word processing.

Jennifer talked with her parents about it, and they said they would provide up
to $1000 to buy one.

Jennifer's friend Terry Carlson majors in computer information systems.
Jennifer asked Terry to help her find a system, and he agreed. "First," Terry
said, "make a list of the features you want."

Jennifer thought about it and produced the following list of characteristics:

1. It should be easy to use.

2. The display screen should be easy to read.

3. It should be able to produce papers up to 50 pages long.

4. It should generate dark, legible print.

5. It should cost less than $2500.

When Jennifer showed this list to Terry, he asked her if she wanted to do
anything besides word processing. Did she want to program the computer?
(No, not really.) Did she need graphics capability? (Not if it costs extra.) Did
she want an electronic spreadsheet? (Didn't know what that is. Maybe.) Did
she want to do any business processing, such as accounting or budgeting? (Not
really.) With this list of answers, Terry said, "Let's go see what's available.
We'll visit several stores, but, remember, don't buy the first thing you see."

During evaluation, alternatives are identified and one of the alternatives is selected. In most cases, alternatives for hardware and programs are considered. Sometimes, too, there can be alternative data organizations, procedures, or types of personnel who will use the system. All feasible alternatives should be considered and evaluated.

Programs can be acquired in three ways. These ways are similar to the ways that clothes can be purchased. First, programs can be acquired off-the-shelf. The user visits computer stores and tries various packages. If one is found that meets the need, it is purchased. As with off-the-shelf clothes, off-the-shelf programs can be used the same day they are purchased.

A second way of acquiring programs is to buy a package and alter it. This method is similar to buying a suit or dress and having it altered. As with clothes, program alteration takes time and involves some risk. After the alteration, the program may still not fit the need.

The third way of acquiring programs is to have them custom designed and constructed, just as one might buy tailored clothes. This alternative takes the most time and involves considerable risk. The programs may be more expensive than anticipated, and they may not meet the need. Further, custom programs usually have errors, because it is nearly impossible to produce error-free programs. Still, for very unique applications, custom development may be the only way that suitable programs can be acquired.

Off-the-shelf clothes are least expensive and can be worn the same day they are purchased.

Alteration of clothes takes time but produces a better fit.

Programs can also be bought and altered.

. . . and off-the-shelf software can also be used the same day.

Custom-tailored clothes may fit, but they certainly cost more.

Professional software development teams can produce custom-designed programs.

Computer magazines provide sources of software alternatives.

Some software alternatives—note the combining, or "bundling," of training materials with software.

Most often, off-the-shelf programs are used in microcomputer systems. For tasks like word processing, electronic spreadsheets, database management, and business graphics, there are dozens of alternative programs available off-the-shelf.

When alternatives are being evaluated, the best strategy is to start with the most limiting component. For micros, there is more hardware available than there are suitable programs. Therefore, program alternatives should be considered before hardware alternatives. Once suitable programs are found, then hardware to run those programs can be located.

For micros, the evaluation of alternatives usually comes down to identifying the cheapest alternative that meets requirements. Sometimes intangibles, such as vendor reputation or proximity of service, are also considered.

Jennifer Anderson's Evaluation During their visits to stores, Jennifer tried six or eight different systems. Terry told Jennifer to bring one of her papers with her and to plan on typing part of it using each system. Jennifer was glad she did this. She was surprised to find wide differences in capability. Apparently, the vendors meant many different things by the term *word processing*.

Terry explained to Jennifer that she needed to buy both hardware and programs. She should look for word processing programs that she liked first. Once she found a suitable word processing package, she could select hardware.

Jennifer followed Terry's advice and tried several word processing programs. She found the following packages acceptable: WORDSTAR, WORD/80, and SELECT.

Next, she looked for microcomputers that could run those packages. Terry explained that she would need the microcomputer, a floppy disk drive, a monitor (which is like a TV screen), a keyboard, a printer, and cables. Jennifer found that hardware was packaged differently. For some micros, the disk was included with the CPU; for others, it was separate. For some systems, the keyboard and monitor were one unit; for others, they were sold separately.

There was a wide choice in printers. Although Jennifer liked the full-character daisy wheel printers the best, she thought that a dot-matrix printer would provide acceptable quality. Generally, dot-matrix printers were cheaper, and she was told that they could also produce simple graphics if she ever wanted them.

The systems Jennifer tried are summarized in the chart on the next page. The cheapest systems were not adequate for her needs. The Commodore 64 would not allow 80 columns to be displayed on a screen. Jennifer found this unacceptable. Further, the monitor screen of the Osborne was too small. Jennifer had difficulty reading it.

Jennifer liked the remaining three systems. Although she thought WORD-STAR, WORD/80, and SELECT were acceptable packages, she liked WORD/80 and SELECT the best.

Cost was a problem for Jennifer. She had $1500 of her own to spend, and her parents had agreed to provide another $1000. That left her $800 short for the cheapest of the systems that she liked. She talked with Terry about this problem. He said that unless she could find the money to buy the system she wanted, she should wait.

Hardware	Program	Cost	Comments
Commodore 64		$1200	No 80-character screen
Osborne	WORDSTAR	$2000	Screen too small
Hewlett-Packard 86B	WORDSTAR WORD/80	$3475	Electronic spreadsheet and file manager included Large library of other programs
Digital Equipment	WORDSTAR SELECT	$4365	Color capability "soon" Excellent TEACH module in SELECT
IBM Personal Computer	WORDSTAR SELECT	$5150	Very large library of programs Color included in this price

Some typical micro hardware alternatives.

"If you buy a system you don't like," he said, "you won't use it. It would be a waste of money. Don't buy anything right now. Prices will probably come down, and you may be able to afford a system you do like in a year or two."

Jennifer didn't want to wait. She went back to the computer store manager and explained her dilemma. The manager agreed to reduce the price by another $250, but that was the rock-bottom price.

"Can I earn the difference?" Jennifer asked.

Eventually, Jennifer and the store manager made a deal. Jennifer could buy the system she wanted for $2500 plus 60 hours of labor. As it turned out, Jennifer was a good speaker and made many presentations to fellow liberal arts students on the benefits of word processing.

Jennifer met again with Terry. She told Terry that she wanted to buy one of the $3000 systems and that she liked WORD/80 better than WORDSTAR. What did he think about her buying the HP 86B with WORD/80? Terry said that sounded like a good decision. He told her that Hewlett-Packard had a very high reputation for quality, and, furthermore, if a problem did occur, Jennifer could have the system repaired at a nearby Hewlett-Packard facility. Terry also told Jennifer that, even though she didn't think she would use the computer for other applications, she might change her mind. In that case, the large library of programs available for the HP 86B would be an advantage.

Jennifer bought the system.

Hardware with software alternatives.

This Hewlett-Packard 86B, which is also popular with professionals for their word processing needs, was selected by Jennifer.

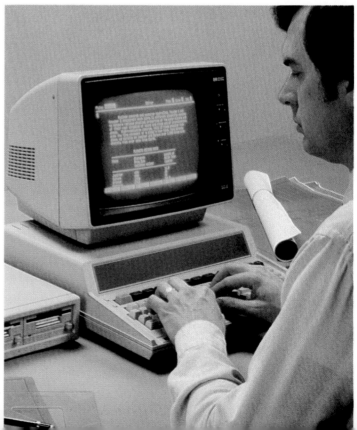

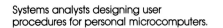
Systems analysts designing user
procedures for personal microcomputers.

The design stage is often short for micro-based systems—especially if off-the-shelf programs will be used. Usually all of the specifications for hardware are known, and there is little design to be done for programs and data. Procedures, however, often require design work. For example, there need to be procedures to start the system, procedures to backup data, and procedures to restore lost data when necessary. Considering the personnel component, job descriptions may need to be developed, and quite often training programs are designed.

Design for Jennifer   Because Jennifer bought her word processing program off the shelf, only limited design work needed to be done. Of the five components of a system, Jennifer only needed to design *procedures*. She did not need to design *programs*, *data formats*, or *hardware specifications*. This work had been done by the vendor of the programs.

Further, because Jennifer was the only user of the system, she didn't need to develop job descriptions, organizational structures, or training programs. These tasks would be necessary for a larger, commercial system.

Jennifer enrolled in a class that was included in the price of the micro (eventually, Jennifer taught this class). In the class she learned the importance of backup. As the instructor said, "Be certain that, if you make a mistake, you don't lose an important document, or, even worse, lose your copy of WORD/80 or other programs."

Working with Terry, Jennifer designed procedures to keep backup copies of all her programs, as well as important documents.

"That way, if there's a fire, or if someone steals your computer and your disks, you won't have lost everything. By the way, Jennifer, be certain that your insurance covers your computer. Lock it up, and don't brag about it to your friends."

DESIGNING THE SYSTEM

IMPLEMENTATION

The three major tasks of implementation are construction, test, and installation. During construction, hardware is received and assembled, programs are written and unit tested, data is assembled and converted to computer-sensible form, procedures are documented, and people are trained. During test, the system is used, and results are checked for validity. Finally, the system is installed and its productive life begins.

For a single-user microcomputer system with off-the-shelf programs, these tasks are simple and straightforward. They are much more complex for systems involving multiple users and custom programming or program alteration.

Jennifer Anderson's Implementation   Jennifer picked up her microcomputer from the computer store. She read the system's documentation and then assembled the components by following the manufacturer's instructions. The system was running within 90 minutes.

Next, Jennifer read the documentation about WORD/80. She found features in that product that she had not noticed during the trials at the computer stores. "Glad I read the documentation," she thought. Before Jennifer used the word processing package, she made backup copies, according to her procedures.

Next, to test the system, Jennifer typed part of one of her old papers. She had no difficulty generating the document and storing it. Unfortunately, however, she couldn't get the printer to work. For some reason, nothing happened when she tried to print her paper. She read the documentation about WORD/80 but didn't learn anything. Next, she reread the section about connecting the printer to the microcomputer. She noticed that the connector on her cable did not look like the connector in the picture in the instructions. She called the computer store, gave them the cable number, and found out that she had received the wrong cable. Jennifer went back to the store, obtained the correct cable, and installed it. This time, she had no difficulty printing her paper.

Micros in offices can assist with record keeping and perform word processing.

New music synthesizers play musical compositions that have been written, programmed, and stored on a micro.

Computer camps have become a popular method of introducing kids to microcomputers.

Micros are used at home by writers for personal word processing.

An effective computer system makes life easier, whether for bicycle sales, auto repair, architectural drawing, or other activities. It reduces menial labor, increases information, and helps people do more with less effort. The wrong computer system makes life harder. People will ignore or work around an ineffective computer system. After a while, the microcomputer will be gathering dust in a corner—the 1980s version of the hula hoop.

The key to developing an effective system is to follow the four-stage process. First, determine what the system is to do. Then, evaluate alternatives, with as much hands-on experience as possible. Next, design procedures and other components as necessary. Finally, assemble, test, and use the system. This process works whether the microcomputer system will be used by kids for education, by families managing the farm, by business people managing a business, or by students writing term papers. Try it.

Keeping an inventory of parts is not a difficult task for a small business with a micro system.

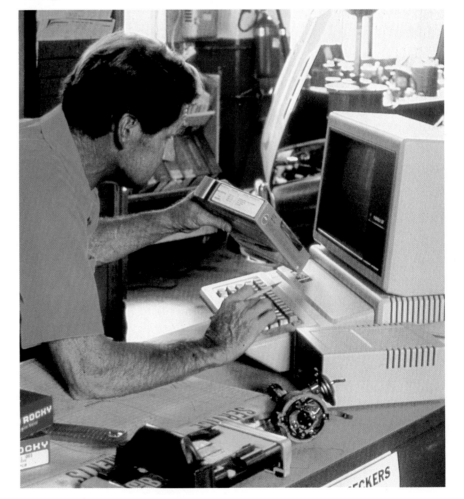

Microcomputers are being used more and more by small retail businesses.

A Nebraska farm family monitors and controls the diet of its dairy cows with a home micro system.

Professional engineers and architects may have graphics requirements for their micros.

TIPS ON BUYING A PERSONAL COMPUTER

COMPUTER SHOPPING CHECKLIST—TIPS ON BUYING A PERSONAL COMPUTER

Below is a summary of what you need to know when you shop for a personal home computer:

- Have a good idea of what computer applications you want: word processing, data management, entertainment, education, budgeting, and so forth.
- Know the functions of the basic computer hardware.
- Check with friends or colleagues who have recently purchased a computer for information and recommendations.
- Shop several different stores, different models, and different manufacturers. Call the Better Business Bureau for a reliability report on a specific company.
- Be sure to test the demonstration model and programs the retailer has available. Are the instructions easy to use and understand?
- Get firm prices on the computer equipment and software. Ask about the costs of expansion. Are both hardware and software readily available?
- Get the terms of the warranty and service arrangements.
- Ask about computer training and clubs.
- Check the refunds and exchange policy before buying.
- If the computer will be used in a home office or professional arrangement, find out if its use will be tax-deductible.

SOURCE: Better Business Bureau, *Tips on Buying a Home Computer,* 1983.

QUESTIONS

1. Describe the four stages of systems development.
2. Why did Terry caution Jennifer not to buy the first system she saw?
3. Does Jennifer's list of desired features seem complete? What other factors might you consider when buying a word processing system?
4. Do you think it was important for Jennifer to take one of her papers and actually use potential systems? Why? What should Jennifer have done if one of the salespeople would not let her try the system?
5. If Terry's expertise had not been available to Jennifer, where else could she have obtained advice and assistance for buying the microcomputer?
6. Name and describe the three ways that computer programs can be acquired.
7. Why does it make more sense to search for acceptable programs before searching for hardware?
8. Do you see why it was important for Jennifer to test her system? What would have occurred if Jennifer had waited until the night before her next paper was due to use her system? What might have happened if Jennifer had waited a month or two before complaining to the computer store about the incorrect cable?

BRIAN WEEK
Retail Sales Clerk

DENISE BUECHELER
Retail Sales Clerk

work, so I have to be service-oriented in my job. I view myself more as an "applications consultant" than a salesperson. Most of the knowledge you need to have about computers can be picked up as you try out each computer you sell. If I have a weakness it's that I don't know enough about business and accounting.

Being just out of high school can sometimes be a problem. But with microcomputers, older people often realize that younger people may have more experience and knowledge than they do.

RESPONSIBILITIES
We wait on retail customers who come into the store. *Computerland* stores are independently owned franchises, and all have different salary- and sales-commission plans.

BACKGROUND—BRIAN
I really didn't have any computer background. I played around with an Apple at school. I worked in a couple of restaurants and sold automotive components for six months. In school I did well in both math and English.

BACKGROUND—DENISE
In college, I majored in psychology and was planning to work with emotionally disturbed children. Then I decided to minor in business and that made me change my mind and try sales. I was a B student in high school, and my aptitude tests in college always indicated that I should work with numbers instead of people.

SKILLS REQUIRED—BRIAN
People buy microcomputers without knowing how they are going to

SKILLS REQUIRED—DENISE
As with most sales jobs, to be successful you need to be energetic and a little aggressive. In retail stores, youth is not as much a problem as it would be calling on customers. When I was looking for a job, one of the first computer stores I went into had a teenager as their technical service manager. My first job after college was in pharmaceutical sales. The pace is much faster here selling computers.

FIGURE D1.19

Computer store

Salespeople working out of sales offices usually cover a given geographic area or sales territory. They are then responsible for all the customers in that territory and for finding new customers. Salespeople working in retail stores are responsible for greeting customers who walk into the store and helping them find what they need. Manufacturers often hold training seminars to familiarize salespeople with the products they sell.

Educational requirements vary from one organization to the next. Some will require a college education. Other companies will hire individuals based on prior work experience or the way they present themselves during an interview.

A salesperson's success is based on how he or she looks and interacts with people. Those responsible for a sales territory usually travel a lot and should enjoy it. To be successful in sales, one must also know how to qualify a customer's needs, then follow up with a professional presentation and proposal.

Computer salespeople are usually paid on commission. Commissions are based on a percentage of the total sale. Therefore, a salesperson's salary is only limited by the energy he or she puts into the job.

STUDY OBJECTIVE

20. Identify the responsibilities of a salesperson and describe what his or her success depends on.

The decision to purchase a computer should not be made hastily. It is recommended that four steps be used when buying a new computer system. The first step in this systems development process is to identify how the computer is to be used. The exploration of potential uses is referred to as a needs analysis.

The next step is to evaluate alternatives. Both programs and hardware need to be evaluated. Programs are usually evaluated first. At this time, a series of questions needs to be asked to find out what software is of use to the user. Hardware options are then evaluated. Usually, a checklist is made to help in the evaluation process. Once the checklist is complete, hardware can be compared.

The third step in the systems development process is to design the computer system. At this time, the programs and hardware are selected based on the needs and experience of the user.

In the final step, the hardware and programs are purchased and set up. User's manuals that come with the programs and hardware provide a wealth of information. These manuals outline start-up, preventive maintenance, and even troubleshooting procedures the user needs to follow.

CHAPTER D2

Developing New Systems

A computer system's great appeal is its ability to perform many different tasks. For example, we can change a computer from an accounting machine into a market research tool by loading a different program. Other computers can do both jobs at the same time.

Computer applications are limited only by our imagination. The more we know about computers, the better prepared we are to create new uses. As a result, there will continue to be a demand for new applications programs. Some people feel that the next growth industry will be software design.

For the average user, a computer system's critical component is software. This is the component that transforms general-purpose hardware into a specialized tool. However, users are sometimes forced into using computer programs that do not meet their needs. In other cases, the applications packages they need do not exist.

In the previous chapter, we discussed the four steps in buying a computer system. The focus was primarily on hardware and applications packages. However, hardware may not be purchased every time a new system is developed. Often, new systems are developed around existing hardware. Therefore, you will find differences in the way systems are developed. In particular, the activities performed at each step depend on how the programs are acquired.

Let's examine three typical ways of acquiring computer programs. We can then explore how the systems development process changes.

ACQUIRING PROGRAMS

Once we have identified our needs, we can obtain computer programs in three different ways. These methods are similar to the methods used to purchase clothing.

Off-the-Shelf Programs

When we buy clothing off-the-shelf, we go to the store, try something on, and buy it if

- It fits
- We like it
- We think it's worth the price
- We can afford it

We can wear those clothes the same day. There is little risk in this approach, but a perfect fit is not guaranteed. We may not be able to find what we want, especially if our needs are unique. For example, someone six feet tall and weighing 87 pounds who wants a pure silk shirt with a hissing rattlesnake on the back may not find what he wants (figure D2.1).

Similar comments apply to applications packages. We can go to computer or software stores and try a program. We can buy it if

- It fits the need
- We like it
- We think it's worth the price
- We can afford it

FIGURE D2.1

Unique requirements

We can use the program the same day. There is little risk, but we may not get a perfect fit or find what we want.

The analogy breaks down in one way. Usually, only one person wears an item of clothing, but many people use a computer program. It would be as if we had to buy a single shirt for many people. There would have to be compromises. Some users would have to accept characteristics they did not want, and others would have to forgo features they did want.

Program Alterations

A second way of buying clothes is to find something that almost fits and have it altered. With this method, we are more likely to get a better fit, but there is more risk and time involved. We will have to buy the clothing before the alterations; after the alterations, the clothing still may not fit. Also, it may take a week or two for the alterations to be done.

A similar approach can be taken with programs. We find programs that almost fit the need and then have them altered. As with clothing, we can have someone else make the alterations or we can alter the programs ourselves—if we have the necessary skills. The alterations may or may not be successful. In

Custom-Tailored Programs

addition, the alterations will take time, which is often measured in months, not days.

A third way of obtaining clothing is to have them designed and tailored to our needs. We go to a designer or tailor who makes the garment just for us. If the designer/tailor is good, we are likely to get what we want. This may be the only way we can obtain the pure silk shirt.

There is considerable risk in this approach. The designer may run over time and budget. The designer may not understand our needs. Our needs may change while the garment is being made. The designer may make what he or she wants instead of what we need. In some cases, the designer may persuade us to use the latest fabric or fashion when a conservative cotton garment would do.

On top of all this, creating the garment will take a considerable amount of time. It will take time just discussing the idea and going for fittings.

Programs can also be custom-tailored. The user meets with computer professionals and describes what is wanted. The computer professionals may be in-house employees, they may be on a special contract, or they may work for a software house. People with computers at home can take the time to learn to program in order to write their own software.

All the risks in buying custom clothing also exist for building custom programs. The cost of programming may exceed time and budget demands. The designers and programmers may never understand the need. The computer people may be anxious to force users into the latest technology—whether it is required or not. And people trying to write their own programs may not have the necessary skills or time to complete the project.

On the other hand, custom-programming may be the only way to get what is needed. We cannot buy programs that do not exist. If the need is great enough, custom-programming can be worth the time and expense. It depends on how important the programs are to the users. Sources of programs are summarized in figure D2.2.

STUDY OBJECTIVES

1. Briefly explain why programs may be considered the most critical component of a computer system.

2. Identify three ways of acquiring new programs and describe the advantage and disadvantage of each.

Off-the-Shelf
Buy and use programs as they are
Alteration
Buy programs and alter them (or have them altered)
Custom Design
Design and write programs to order

To review, the systems development process consists of four steps:

1. Define the system requirements.
2. Evaluate the alternatives.
3. Design the computer system components.
4. Implement the computer system.

Unfortunately, every professional has been tempted to bypass some of the steps in this process. Many have horror stories about "quick and dirty" systems development projects. A quick and dirty system is one that is developed without going through each step in the development process. In the long run, these systems can take longer to get working because critical features are left out. Later, they are harder to modify.

The difference between systems developed by inexperienced analysts versus professionals is often related to the systems development process. Systems developed by inexperienced analysts have many similarities to quick and dirty systems. The analysts skip over development steps. As a result, these systems usually take more time than expected to develop, are hard to modify, and often have errors.

3. Identify three potential problems that result from quick and dirty systems development projects.

STUDY OBJECTIVE

HOMEGROWN SYSTEMS

Harold Johnson unlocked the ground floor door and entered the apartment building just as he did every afternoon. He and his sister Sarah made their way around the building, dropping newspapers at selected doors. Harold covered the ground floor while Sarah delivered to the upper floors.

Stopping at apartment 1-D, he rang the door bell and waited for a response that never came. He left a handwritten bill with the paper and finished his rounds. This same process was repeated in every building.

Harold had one of the best paper routes in the area, since his route consisted primarily of apartment buildings. Each building had several customers. This meant that he and Sarah could make their rounds much faster than carriers who went from house to house. It was especially nice on rainy days, when he could get inside to deliver the papers.

However, collecting was sometimes difficult. Several customers were hard to catch, since they worked odd hours. As a result, many weeks went by before he could collect from them. In a few cases, he had to make special trips to the apartments to make collections.

Out of desperation, Harold had tried to include bills with a few customers' papers. This had been very successful, but writing each bill by hand was time-consuming.

Harold's experiment with billing customers occurred just as his family started to think about buying a home computer. So he included record keeping for his

FIGURE D2.3

Harold and Sarah Johnson delivering
papers

paper route as part of the needs analysis. His idea was to design a computerized record-keeping system that printed bills.

By the time his family purchased their computer, Mrs. Dingman had taught Harold a lot about computer programming. Given a programming assignment, he could write an efficient and easy-to-use BASIC program. But it wasn't until he developed the customer record-keeping system that he realized the difference between computer programming and systems design.

The Need

The first step in the development of a new system is to define the need. A systems analyst can then help the user determine if a computer will provide the best solution. There are some cases where the solution is not a new computer system. Instead, the solution may be the better management of data, procedures, or people.

If a computer system provides a possible solution, then the analyst performs

COLLECTION LIST

CUSTOMER	AMOUNT DUE	NUMBER OF WEEKS
Name 1 Address 1	$9.99	9
Name 2 Address 2	$0.99	9
Name 3 Address 3	$9.99	9
Name X Address X	$9.99	9

FIGURE D2.4

The original design for Harold's collection list

a **feasibility study.** The feasibility study determines if the system will be practical from a technical and financial viewpoint. In some instances, the technology may not be available to solve the problem. In other situations, it may be too expensive.

Harold needed a billing system for his paper route. There were several good reasons for starting this project. First, the record keeping was boring and time-consuming. Second, he wanted the computer to calculate his weekly collection list, shown in figure D2.4. Third, the computer could print bills like those in figure D2.5. Harold wanted the computer system to print a bill for every customer owing money. However, this project required a printer.

Since his family now owned a home computer, Harold's idea was technically feasible. The financial feasibility rested on his father's help in buying a printer.

The first alternative is usually to find an off-the-shelf program that meets everyone's needs. If it can't be found, the second alternative is to alter an existing program. When all else fails, time and effort are taken to custom-design the program.

The Alternatives

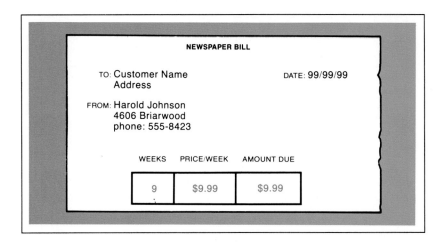

Time is also necessary to thoroughly evaluate hardware. In Harold's case, a printer was critical to the project's success. Luckily, his parents offered to help buy the printer, since they eventually needed one for word processing. Harold and his father defined their need and then evaluated several dot-matrix printers in their price range.

While we should not expect to find a wealth of applications software to meet Harold's needs, there are still reasons for looking. One reason is to help with designing the software. Since the next step is to design the system, even unusable systems could provide useful ideas.

Another reason is that we don't know what is available until we look. If another carrier had a home computer, then there is certainly a chance that he or she developed a customer record-keeping system. We already know that it is easier and less risky to alter a related program than to design one from scratch.

Harold's first mistake was to ignore other alternatives. He was bound and determined to custom-design this system. He didn't even bother to explore other solutions.

The Design

In the design step, decisions are made concerning the following items:

- Training people
- Organizing data
- Structuring programs
- Purchasing hardware
- Creating procedures for maintaining the system

The design of any system should be from the top down. The systems analyst refines the project down into a workable set of programmable units or **modules.** This process is called **top-down design.** It allows the systems analyst to break a complex project into easier-to-understand sections or modules.

Top-down design lends itself to the **modular development** of computer programs. A program is developed as a set of interrelated modules. This allows

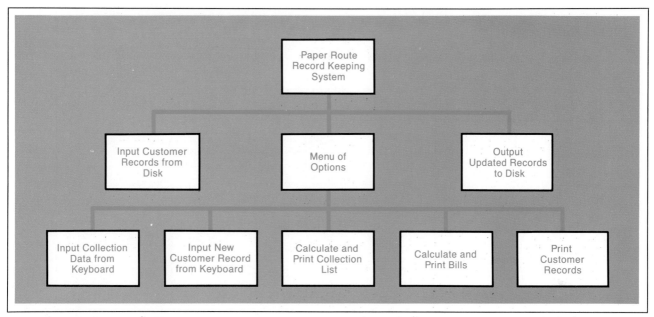

FIGURE D2.6

First hierarchy chart

each module to be independently tested. In addition, problems are easier to locate. For example, if there is an error in the bill, then only the module that calculates and prints the bill needs examination.

Modular development also allows the programmer to concentrate on one part of the programming project at a time. Another advantage is that it allows several people to work together as a programming team. In this situation, each team member can work on a different module.

Harold had assumed the role of both systems analyst and programmer. His initial program design called for three main modules with a menu that selected one of five remaining modules. The program structure is shown by the **hierarchy chart** in figure D2.6. The hierarchy chart—or **structure chart**—helped Harold organize the program into modules. It showed all the modules in the program and their relationship to one another.

This hierarchy chart will later highlight Harold's mistakes in the design step. While he knew how to design a computer program, he had never designed a complete computer system. Therefore, he skipped over the design of several system components.

All five components of a computer system must be considered in the design step. However, Harold only addressed two: hardware and programs. He needed a printer, so he and his father agreed on one. Mrs. Dingman had made him aware of flowcharting and pseudocoding as program design techniques. So he pseudocoded the program before writing it.

As shown in figure D2.7, the data and procedure components needed attention as well. By skipping the design step for these components, Harold was

SYSTEM COMPONENT DEVELOPMENT STEP	HARDWARE	PROGRAMS	DATA	PROCEDURES	PEOPLE
NEEDS ANALYSIS	Paper route record keeping, calculation of amounts due each week, print collection list and bills. Check technical and cost feasibilities				
EVALUATE ALTERNATIVES	Look at and price printers	Look for applications packages to use and compare against needs. If necessary, compare cost of alterations against cost of custom design.			
DESIGN	Decide on a printer and order it	Top down design, Pseudocode program if applications package not found	Determine contents of customer record	Develop backup, updating, and end of year procedures	*For Harold's and His Customer's Use*
IMPLEMENT	Buy printer and install it	Write program and test it	Create customer file and check contents for accuracy	Label and format disks. Get notebook for collection lists. Arrange a place to store disk	

FIGURE D2.7

Summary of development steps for Harold's record-keeping system forced to make major changes to his program after large portions had been completed.

The Implementation

In the final stage of the systems development process, all five components are brought together, installed, and tested.

Each of the system's five components must be considered. When necessary, new personnel are hired. Test data is developed. If new hardware has been purchased, it is set up and readied for operation. Programs are purchased or written. Procedures are documented and tested by operations personnel and users.

A system test will determine whether the system is ready or not. During this test, critical users and operations personnel follow defined procedures. An evaluation is made to determine if the system is ready. If it is, installation proceeds. Otherwise, the system is corrected and retested.

Installing a New System

One of four methods is used when installing a new computer system. The first one is the **plunge.** The new system is started and the old system stopped. This method is very dangerous. If the new system has a problem, there is nothing to fall back on. For this reason, the plunge method should rarely be used.

A second method is to run the new system in **parallel** with the old system. If any problems develop, the old system is still available. However, this approach is expensive because two systems must be supported. Many organizations view this expense as a form of insurance.

When following the **pilot** method, the new system is used by a limited number of users at the start. For example, Harold might use his system for only one apartment building at the beginning. Once the system was found to be working correctly, it could be used for the whole paper route. The pilot method limits problems if the new system is not working correctly.

Finally, installing a system **piecemeal** means implementing it in parts. In Harold's case, he could install the system for record-keeping purposes first. After this part of the system was found to be working correctly, he could add the billing portion.

Harold Runs into Problems

For Harold, everything had gone smoothly until the implementation step. The first sign of trouble came when he and his father tried to set up the new printer. It just sat there printing an odd assortment of characters.

They finally found they had the wrong cables. With the correct cables the printer worked fine. Harold's other problems were related to his program design.

The hierarchy chart in figure D2.8 is for Harold's finished program. Comparing it with the first hierarchy chart in figure D2.6, you will see that there are two additional modules.

Harold was testing the program when he realized that there was no provision for deleting a customer record. In thinking about how to get the program up and running, he had forgotten about daily procedures. He had included a module to add customers because it was needed to start the system. However, he had forgotten a deletion module because it wasn't needed until after the system was in operation.

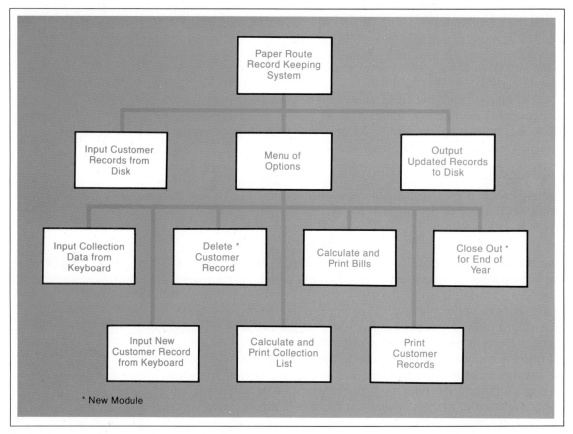

FIGURE D2.8

Final hierarchy chart

Harold's other oversight was not as easy to fix. The system was based on weekly (1 to 52) collections each year. For example, let's say he needed a collection list for week 21. If a customer's record indicated he had paid through week 19, then the computer multiplied 2—21 minus 19—times the weekly rate.

All the customer data had been entered before Harold realized that there was no way to close out one year and start another. To fix this problem, he had to add another module to the program. On top of that, he had to add a new field to each customer record.

After correcting these problems, Harold ran the computer system parallel with his manual record-keeping system for several weeks. He improved on the layout of the collection list (figure D2.9) and bills (figure D2.10) during this time. In addition, he checked the computer's calculations against his own. It soon became apparent that the system was working as he wished.

Evaluating the New System

The new system did everything Harold wanted it to do. But Harold realized that record keeping was no faster with the computer system, since he still had to spend time entering data. Still, having the computer print the collection list

CUSTOMER	DUE	WEEKS	SERVICE	LAST PAYMENT
Wing, Frank 13 Lamplight Lane/Apt 1-B	$4.00	2	Both	5/11/8-
Cobb, Max 13 Lamplight Lane/Apt 2-C	$1.60	1	Daily	5/18/8-
Taylor, Mike 13 Lamplight Lane/Apt 3-C	$2.00	1	Both	5/18/8-
Reid, Mickey 15 Lamplight Lane/Apt 4-A	$1.50	3	Sunday	5/4/8-
Belson, Al 15 Lamplight Lane/Apt 2-D	$0.50	1	Sunday	5/18/8-
Madison, Lee 17 Lamplight Lane/Apt 1-B	$2.00	1	Both	5/18/8-
Ford, Jake 17 Lamplight Lane/Apt 3-B	$8.00	4	Both	4/27/8-
Carson, Gail 17 Lamplight Lane/Apt 4-B	$4.00	2	Both	5/11/8-
Smith, Barbara 17 Lamplight Lane/Apt 3-D	$1.60	1	Daily	5/18/8-
Perkins, Bruce 51 Hidden Valley Dr./Apt 5	$6.00	3	Both	5/4/8-
Ashley, William 51 Hidden Valley Dr./Apt 7	$1.00	2	Sunday	5/11/8-
Fuller, Ron 33 Vista Ave/Apt 2-A	$2.00	1	Both	5/18/8-
Young, James 33 Vista Ave/Apt 4-A	$4.00	2	Both	5/11/8-
Hogan, Gordon 33 Vista Ave/Apt 3-C	$0.50	1	Sunday	5/18/8-
Jones, John 10 Mountain View Rd/Apt E	$4.80	3	Daily	5/4/8-
Hall, Bill 10 Mountain View Rd/Apt C	$4.00	2	Both	5/11/8-
Clark, Marty 18 Mountain View Dr/Apt I	$4.00	2	Both	5/11/8-

```
CURRENT RATES: Daily Paper—$1.60 per week
               Sunday Paper—$0.50 per week
               Both Papers—$2.00 per week
```

FIGURE D2.9

Final collection list output from Harold's program

NEWSPAPER BILL

TO: The Ford Residence   DATE: 5/25/8—
    917 Lamplight Lane/Apt 3-B

FROM: Harold Johnson
      4606 Briarwood
      phone: 555-8423

WEEKS	SERVICE	PRICE/WEEK	AMOUNT DUE
4	Daily and Sunday Delivery	$2.00	$8.00

Last payment received on 4/27/8—

NEWSPAPER BILL

TO: The Larson Residence   DATE: 5/25/8—
    917 Lamplight Lane/Apt 4-B

FROM: Harold Johnson
      4606 Briarwood
      phone: 555-8423

WEEKS	SERVICE	PRICE/WEEK	AMOUNT DUE
2	Daily and Sunday Delivery	$2.00	$4.00

Last payment received on 5/11/8—

FIGURE D2.10

Final bills from Harold's program

probably did eliminate a few errors. And the time and effort in developing the system were completely justified by the billing module. His collection rate dramatically increased with the use of the computer-printed bills.

Harold eventually went to a monthly billing system. He billed customers at the beginning of the month, and they mailed him the money. This eliminated the time and problems previously associated with weekly collections.

Lessons from Harold's First Systems Development Project

The first and most valuable lesson a person can learn when developing a system concerns time. The more time spent on the first three development steps, the fewer problems there will be in the last. Unfortunately, many people want to jump to the implementation step. Their quick and dirty systems usually create more problems and result in more wasted time and headaches than they bargained for.

A second lesson to be learned concerns viewpoint. In developing a new system, try to view the finished system in all its potential uses. Harold should have taken the time to think about using his system on a day-to-day basis and at year's end. He would have realized that he needed more program modules and additional fields in the customer record.

STUDY OBJECTIVES

4. Describe two services that a systems analyst provides users during the first step in the systems development process.

5. Identify two reasons for exploring limited alternatives.

6. List four advantages of the modular development of computer programs.

7. Define top-down design, modular development, and hierarchy chart.

8. Briefly describe what happens in each step of the systems development process.

9. Identify and describe four methods for installing a new computer system.

10. Identify two lessons that can be learned from Harold's first systems development project.

PROFESSIONALLY DEVELOPED SYSTEMS

Six years later, Harold scanned the employee telephone directory looking for the engineering department's extension. Finding it, he dialed 7-0389 and asked for Cal McCarty.

"Cal, Harold Johnson from data processing. Do you have time to go over the report and screen formats for the PERT project?"

PERT stands for Program Evaluation and Review Technique. A PERT system allowed the management at Miracle Motors to identify the steps or events in a project. The data identified the material and people required for each event and the time it took to complete it. In addition, each event was identified with those events that had to precede it and those events that had to follow it.

Originally, PERT systems were required for all projects funded by the government. Since Miracle Motors was a large defense contractor, it had started to use PERT systems for government work. These early systems were often developed by outsiders and based on guesswork. The timing and control engineers replaced the guesswork with real data and created a very effective management information system.

The engineers now needed to computerize a PERT system for a new line of minivans. This project required far too many reports and diagrams to be done by hand. Three engineers were relieved of some responsibilities so that they could explore the idea in more detail. Cal McCarty was to coordinate the three-person project committee.

Cal contacted the director of data processing to explain the need and to ask for assistance. A systems analyst was sent over to talk to the project committee. Of course, the systems analyst suggested that they prepare a needs analysis.

The Need

Neither the project committee nor the analyst knew whether off-the-shelf programs were available to solve the engineers' problem. They decided to write a set of detailed specifications that would enable them to design a custom program. If off-the-shelf programs were not available, then the needs analysis could be used for other alternatives.

Define Specifications

The project committee spent a week working with the systems analyst in developing a detailed set of specifications. They talked to other engineers to gain insight into other department needs. At the end of this period, they wrote a report documenting their findings. It defined three major points:

1. There was a need to keep accurate records of event descriptions, materials, personnel, and related data for designing a new vehicle. The data had to be organized in several ways. For example, some reports were arranged by date while others were organized by department. There was no problem with entering the data in batches as long as reports were available on request.

2. The system had to run on the engineering department's minicomputer. However, the data had to be available to users with access to the company's mainframe.

3. Reports generated by the system had to be in both report and graphic formats. If possible, the project engineers preferred to have the graphic output printed on a plotter.

Feasibility Study

After the specifications were defined and documented, the systems analyst helped the project team consider the feasibility of the project.

PERT systems had been developed and some software already existed. The systems analyst was confident that the system was feasible from a technical viewpoint.

The cost feasibility depended on how the programs were acquired and whether the system could use the plotter attached to the mainframe.

A third consideration was schedule feasibility. The schedule feasibility was an estimate of the amount of time it would take to finish the project. It depended on the way the software was acquired. The systems analyst suggested taking a conservative approach. If the project was feasible when custom-designed, it would be feasible if they could find programs to use or adapt.

After two days of planning and discussion, the committee estimated that the project would take 12 months to custom-design.

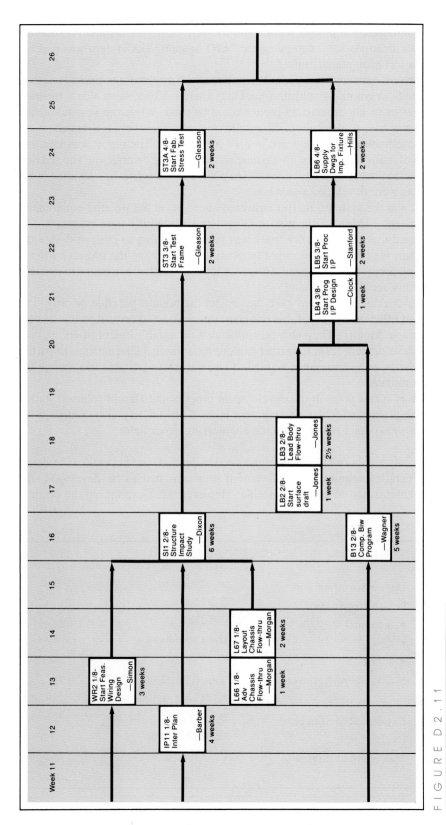

F I G U R E D 2 . 1 1

Portion of a manual PERT chart

To summarize, the project team, with the help of a systems analyst, defined the specifications for a computerized PERT system. The system was feasible from a technical standpoint.

The cost appeared to be feasible, especially if applications packages—off-the-shelf programs—could be found and altered. Costs were also a function of whether or not an existing plotter could be used. While the schedule feasibility was hard to determine, 12 months was conservatively estimated.

These findings were outlined in a 10-page report. The report was sent to a group of managers making up an independent steering committee. The steering committee met every two weeks. They were responsible for deciding what projects were developed and when.

Cal and the systems analyst answered questions at the steering committee's next meeting. Most of the questions centered around the time estimates. Cal explained that the feasibility study was based on having to custom-design the program. He added that it might be possible to complete the project earlier if working programs were found. However, the estimate had to assume that usable programs could not be found.

The steering committee gave the project the highest possible priority. The fast and efficient design of this minivan was considered critical to the success of Miracle Motors. They also recommended the establishment of an applications development team to further explore the technical alternatives. In particular, the steering committee wanted to know if it was possible to improve the time estimates.

It was at this point in the development process that Harold Johnson started as a programmer for the development team. Cal McCarty also continued his role as the contact person from the engineering department.

The Alternatives

According to figure D2.12, after the need is defined, the next task is to determine detailed requirements. If custom programs had to be developed, the requirements had to be very specific. However, after examining the original

FIGURE D2.12

Steps in an in-house systems development project

Step 1: Needs Analysis	Step 3: Select Components of System
A. Define Specifications	A. Program
B. Feasibility Study	B. Hardware
• technical	C. Data
• cost	D. Procedures
• schedule	E. People
C. Management Approval	Step 4: Implementation of System
Step 2: Evaluation of Alternatives	A. Construction
A. Detailed Requirements	B. Testing
B. Evaluation	C. Installation
C. Management Review	D. Evaluation

1. Maintain records of every event code, description, department, department manager, time allotment, due dates, and event codes for events that precede and follow.
2. Add new events on a daily basis.
3. Modify records as required.
4. Figure time needed to complete project based on time allotments for activities still to be completed.
5. Provide reports and PERT chart by due date or department.

needs definition, the development team hoped that off-the-shelf programs could be altered to meet the need.

Detailed Requirements

The team decided to determine the functions and features they would need for the PERT system. They did not attempt to identify details such as screen formats, report layouts, and the like. However, the senior programmer reminded them that if a suitable program was not found, this work would need to be done later.

A sample of the functions and features for the PERT system is shown in figure D2.13. These statements describe the general nature of the work. They do not provide the details necessary to make alterations or develop custom programs.

When the requirements were finished, the applications development team met with Miracle Motors' management and key users. Management wanted the users to attend the meeting so that essential functions or features would not be omitted. Everyone agreed that the requirements were basically complete.

Evaluation

Of the five components in a computer system, the team investigated programs first. The development team began calling companies that had similar needs and hardware. They eventually found two PERT applications packages.

Unfortunately, the applications packages were not developed for the automotive industry. NMI PERT, the more expensive of the two, had been developed by an aircraft manufacturer. The other, Fast PERT, was used by a small manufacturing firm. Figure D2.14 shows a comparison of costs.

| | Development | |
Alternatives	Cost	Time
Fast PERT	$30,000	6 months
NMI PERT	$45,000	2 months
Custom Design	$90,000	12 months

NMI PERT offered an impressive set of menu options. It could produce graphic output and more reports than the engineering department needed. The system had been designed to use a plotter similar to the one attached to Miracle Motors' mainframe. However, special programs would have to be written to allow the data to be transferred to the mainframe.

Fast PERT was also developed for the engineering department's minicomputer. As with the other package, special programs were needed to transfer data to the mainframe. In addition, Fast PERT did not produce any graphic output and was missing two reports the department needed.

The other four components of the system easily fell into place. Since the department already had a minicomputer, operating procedures and trained personnel were already available. It also appeared that the plotter attached to the mainframe could be used with both programs. Therefore, no new hardware needed to be purchased. The data requirements were nearly the same for both applications packages. Consequently, the team decided to present both program alternatives to management.

The development team performed an informal **cost/benefit analysis.** A cost/benefit analysis compares all the known costs for developing a system against the value of the known benefits. The engineers had already developed estimates of the time and money spent to maintain a manual PERT system. These estimates were used to compare the cost of the two systems.

In addition, there were intangible benefits such as timely information, useful reports, graphic formats, and flexibility. The team just listed these benefits and decided not to attempt placing dollar values on them.

The team presented the steering committee with the time and cost estimates of the alternatives, an estimate of the value of computerizing the PERT system, and a summary of intangible benefits.

The results of the time and cost study are presented in figure D2.14. The annual operation costs were the same for all three alternatives. The engineering department had estimated that over $60,000 could be saved in one year alone from reduced labor. This figure did not include the benefit of more accurate materials management, although some cost savings would occur.

It appeared that one of the two program alteration options would be more desirable. Like many decisions, this one came down to cost versus time.

Management Review

The team documented their findings and presented the results to the steering committee. The committee was pleased with the quality and direction of the work. During the meeting, costs were discussed.

The managers also wanted to know about risks and schedules. The team stated that alternative 2 would have the lowest risk because it involved less development. Considering schedule, alternative 2 would be quickest.

The steering committee had no trouble deciding how to proceed. Given the lower risk and quicker schedule, alternative 2 was chosen even though it was more expensive than alternative 1. The third alternative was never seriously considered. As one manager remarked, the $15,000 difference between alternatives 1 and 2 was insignificant considering the savings obtained by having the system four months earlier.

Harold working with a user

The development team needed to negotiate the rights to use and alter NMI PERT. Attorneys for both Miracle Motors and the aircraft manufacturer met, negotiated acceptable terms, and signed a contract.

The NMI PERT package met all the user's requirements except that it could not transfer data to the mainframe. This feature was added in order to use the plotter and to pass data to managers with access to the mainframe. The lead programmer assumed the responsibility for designing this alteration.

Up until the design step, Harold had been working behind the scenes. He had helped research the alternatives and had participated in the discussions concerning cost and schedules. The design of alterations to reports and input formats were Harold's responsibility. He worked closely with the systems analyst and Cal McCarty in finalizing these requirements with the users.

Since no new hardware was to be purchased, the team did not have to worry about ordering equipment. However, the lead programmer had to research ways of transferring data to the mainframe. In addition, similar research had to be done on using the attached plotter.

The Design

Program Alterations

Hardware

323

Harold and the others had two major design tasks to complete for the data component. First, they needed to determine the specific formats the users wanted for screens and reports.

A **print chart** like the one in figure D2.16 was used for the design of reports. The **screen layout form** in figure D2.16 served the same function with screen formats. These documents were then shown to the users for their approval. Usually, a user was asked to initial the print chart or screen layout form if it met with his or her approval. By doing this, the application teams documented that the users had seen the original design.

The second task was to determine what data was needed in establishing the initial files. For example, the PERT system required an activity code, description, department number, and other data fields. At this point, Harold needed to know exactly what those fields would be.

Harold reviewed the project specifications and discussed the needs further with the systems analyst and users. He also reviewed the documentation that came with NMI PERT. Figure D2.17 shows the **record layout form** that Harold used to design the storage format.

At the same time, the engineers needed to identify the managers in charge of each event put into the PERT system. They then had to design procedures for obtaining this data (see figure D2.18). Once the new PERT system had been installed, the data would be entered to construct the initial file.

No new employees were needed in the operation of the PERT system. The final design task was then to develop procedures for the computer operator and data entry operators/users already employed by Miracle Motors. Procedures were needed for both daily operations and error recovery.

The NMI PERT package included operations and user documentation. The development team reviewed this documentation and modified it to conform to Miracle Motors' operational practices.

In addition, several engineers mentioned that the documentation was unclear. In response to this, the systems analyst wrote supplements that were clearer. Once procedures had been designed and documented, the team moved to implementation.

The Implementation

The original NMI PERT was delivered, and the development team went about the task of making the necessary alterations. Harold used print charts and screen layout forms for tailoring screen and report formats that would meet the users' needs.

Even before all the report formats were complete, the initial data files were built. The users followed the procedures developed during the design step to build the files. Edit reports were closely examined to ensure that only correct data was stored. The senior programmer continually reminded the team that the first uses of the system had to be successful to obtain the users' confidence.

Each of the five components was tested individually, and then they were tested together. The hardware and new communications modules were tested by the lead programmer. A few adjustments were necessary to get the plotter running.

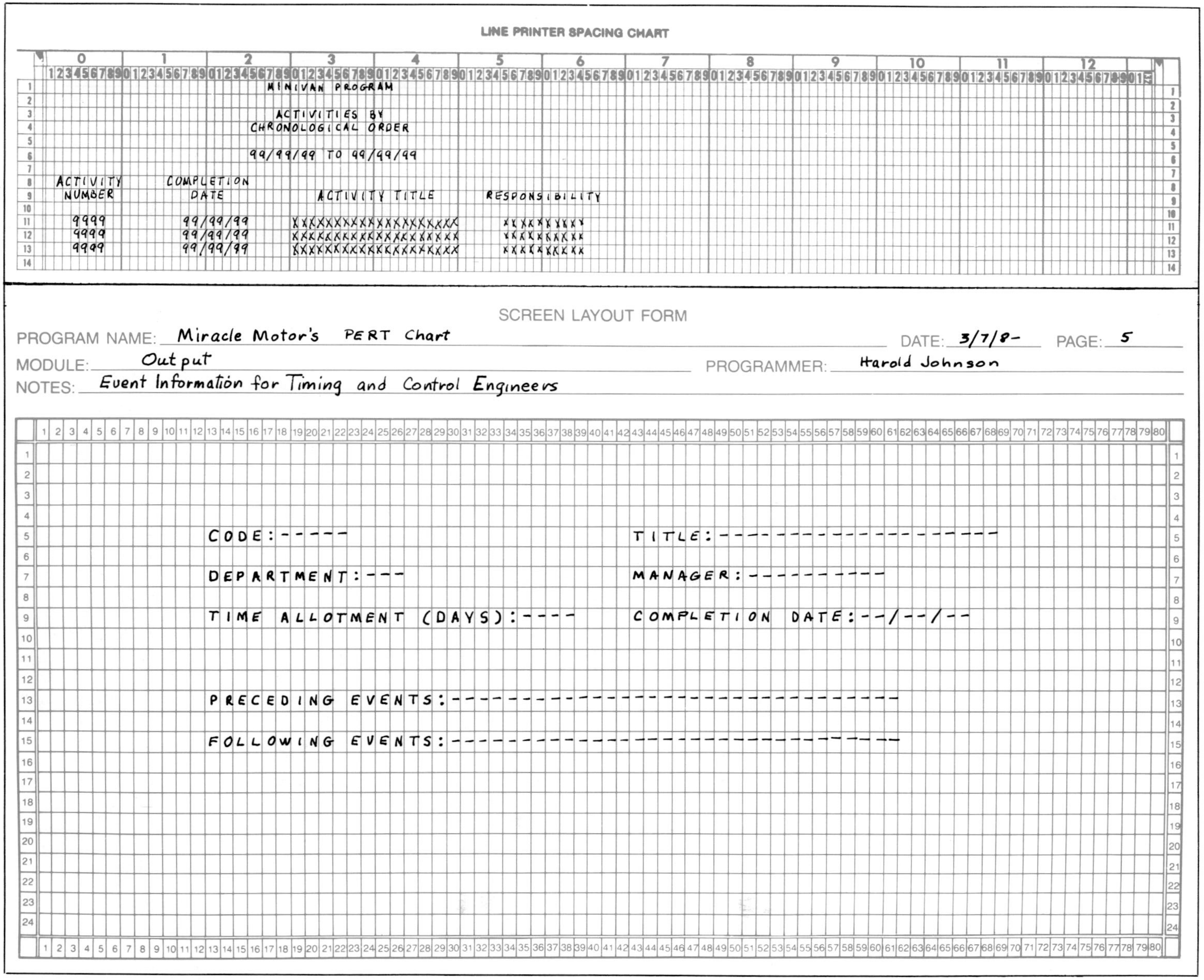
LINE PRINTER SPACING CHART
MINIVAN PROGRAM
ACTIVITIES BY
CHRONOLOGICAL ORDER
99/99/99 TO 99/99/99
ACTIVITY NUMBER
COMPLETION DATE
ACTIVITY TITLE
RESPONSIBILITY
9999 99/99/99 XXXXXXXXXXXXXXXXXXXX XXXXXXXXXX
9999 99/99/99 XXXXXXXXXXXXXXXXXXXX XXXXXXXXXX
9999 99/99/99 XXXXXXXXXXXXXXXXXXXX XXXXXXXXXX
SCREEN LAYOUT FORM
PROGRAM NAME: Miracle Motor's PERT Chart
DATE: 3/7/8-
PAGE: 5
MODULE: Output
PROGRAMMER: Harold Johnson
NOTES: Event Information for Timing and Control Engineers
CODE:-----
TITLE:------------------
DEPARTMENT:---
MANAGER:----------
TIME ALLOTMENT (DAYS):----
COMPLETION DATE:--/--/--
PRECEDING EVENTS:------------------------------
FOLLOWING EVENTS:------------------------------

FIGURE D2.16

Layout forms for printed and screen reports

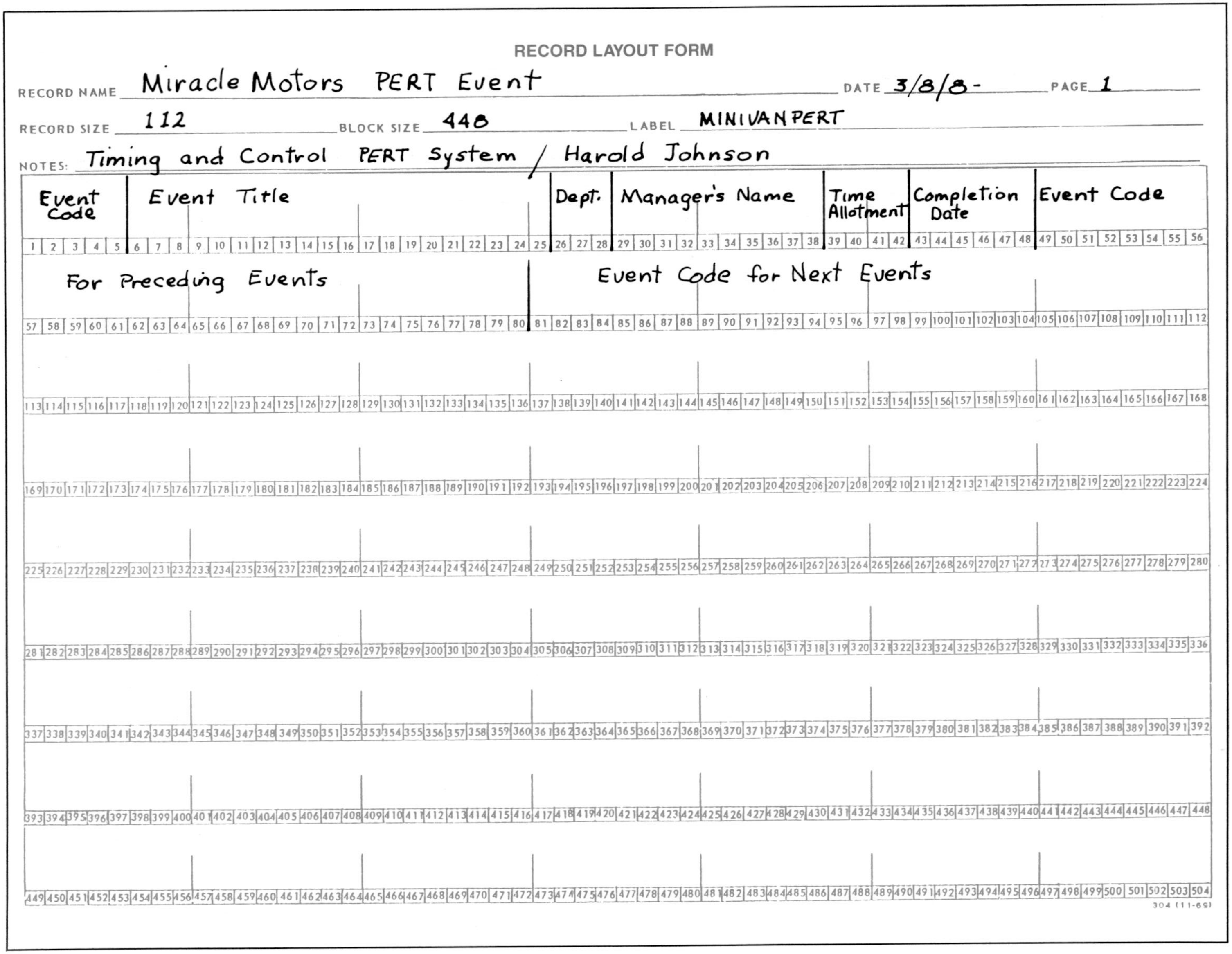

RECORD LAYOUT FORM

RECORD NAME __Miracle Motors PERT Event__ DATE __3/8/8-__ PAGE __1__

RECORD SIZE __112__ BLOCK SIZE __440__ LABEL __MINIVAN PERT__

NOTES: __Timing and Control PERT System / Harold Johnson__

Event Code	Event Title	Dept.	Manager's Name	Time Allotment	Completion Date	Event Code

For Preceding Events

Event Code for Next Events

304 (11-65)

FIGURE D2.17

Record layout form that Harold used to design the storage format

MIRACLE MOTORS INC.
Intercompany Correspondence

DATE: March 6, 198–

TO: Department Managers

FROM: Gordon M. Gasiorek, Director Timing and
      Control

SUBJECT: MINIVAN PERT SYSTEM

We have been asked to support Program Management in the development of a PERT system for the
minivan program. Your department is responsible
for activity that must be performed to support
this program. Timing and Control requests your
cooperation in answering the following questions:

• Identify and define the activities that must be
  accomplished by your department.

• Forecast the length of time required to accomplish each activity.

• Identify the departments that <u>you depend on</u> to
  accomplish your activity.

• Identify the departments that are recipients of
  the results of your activity.

This information should be available for pick–up
and review with Timing and Control personnel by
March 16, 198–. Any questions you have will be
answered by Cal McCarty on 7–0307.

GMG/eah

cc Cal McCarty   Joe Kinzer
   Mike Landsford   Harold Johnson
   Pat Allan

FIGURE D2.18

Correspondence about data collection
procedures

Harold tested the main program modules of the PERT system using data he had created for this purpose. He found that two reports were not formatted correctly. The formats were easily corrected the next day.

The team tested data by examining printouts of the initial files. This was a time-consuming task. Data that had been identified as incorrect during construction was examined again to make sure it had been changed.

Procedures were reviewed with the users and operations personnel. Since they had been involved with the development of the system from the start, the team felt that everyone was well prepared.

After each component was tested separately, an integrated test was conducted using sample data. The programs were loaded into the computer, data input, sample reports produced, and so forth. Several problems were identified that resulted in adjustments to the procedures.

Installation

The applications development team decided to use the pilot implementation method. The designs for the new minivan had just come from the drafting department and were being delivered to the modeling department. The engineering department had identified the jobs and time required to make prototype models of the minivan. This data was to provide the first real test of the new PERT system.

The system was installed and put to use. Reports and graphic output generated by the system were compared with data kept manually. No significant errors were found. At the end of the month, the team recommended to management that all the production data for the minivan be entered into the system.

The computerized PERT system was up and running within two months after the steering committee had approved the chosen alternative. Since this was just on schedule, management was very pleased.

Evaluation

After several weeks, the development team sat down to discuss the results with the original project committee. The evaluation was intended to help solve any current problems and to improve future systems development projects. They discussed each other's roles in the development process and ways to improve communications. A few suggested changes, and ways to implement those suggestions were discussed.

The systems analyst also sent a summary report, shown in figure D2.20, to the steering committee and director of data processing. The development team members were then dispersed to other projects. Further changes to the PERT system would be handled by maintenance programmers.

STUDY OBJECTIVES

11. Identify and describe three types of feasibility studies.

12. Briefly describe a reason for having users meet with management and systems development personnel to review detailed requirements.

13. Describe a cost/benefit analysis.

14. Identify the uses of a print chart and screen and record layout forms.

15. List two purposes for a final project evaluation.

16. Identify and describe each step in an in-house systems development project.

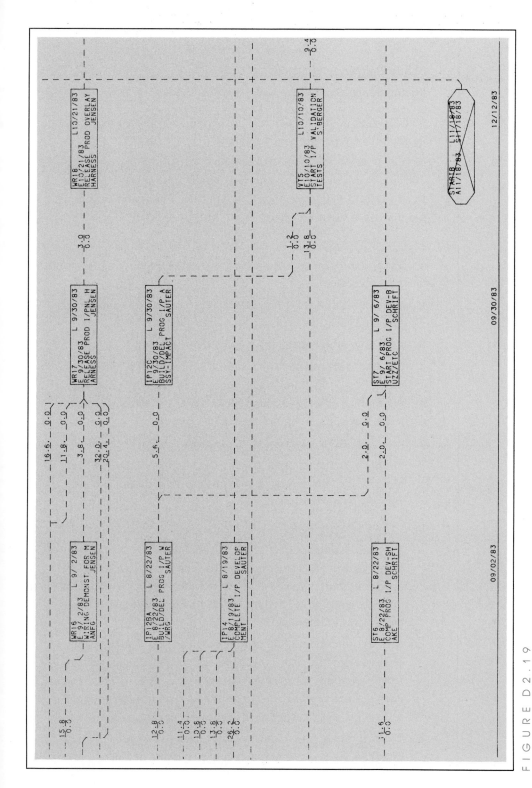

F I G U R E D 2 . 1 9

Part of a PERT chart printed by the plotter

329

```
                  MINIVAN PERT PROJECT

Start February 4, 198—

Operational April 1, 198—

Total Development Time—8 Weeks
```

<u>Reason for System Development:</u>

Request from Program Management for help in getting the minivan design and development back into a time frame that would support both the Program Van and Launch and keep it that way.

<u>Technique used:</u>

1. Determine what activities still had to be accomplished.

2. Sequence these activities in order of required completion.

3. Affix accountability for each activity.

4. Obtain agreement from each accountable partici- pant that he/she will complete activities for which he/she is accountable in a time span that will support Program Van and Launch.

5. Use the PERT system to document 1, 2, 3 and 4.

6. Supply Program Management with the information needed to keep the minivan on schedule for the rest of the program.

<u>Results:</u>

1. Program Management, from Chief down, has reviewed the system and the documents that can be used to monitor and control the remainder of the minivan design and development and have agreed that we have fulfilled their request.

2. Timing and Control has benefited in that it has experience in the development of a computerized PERT system. They have developed a log of dos and don'ts that will be organized into a procedure prior to starting further development projects.

3. This system can now be modified for use by all Program Managers for future programs.

Summary of minivan PERT project

MARIA ELENA
Programmer/Analyst

RESPONSIBILITIES

I am working with a team of five people. We're designing a new payroll system for the entire corporation. Right now, I'm working on designing the screens for the users. The users are actually five different departments within Hewlett-Packard: personnel, payroll, retirement planning, tax and benefits, and company records.

First, we are building an experimental model, called a prototype, for users to review and try. Eventually we will distribute software to fifty different locations, each with their own terminals and configurations.

MY BACKGROUND

In high school I was a C-B student. I liked secretarial and math courses the best, although the highest math course I took was algebra.

After high school I got a job at Sylvania Electric as a clerk typist. When they found that I had taken a keypunch class in an evening adult-ed course, they pulled me into the keypunching department. During the next four years I worked as a keypunch operator. However, at the same time I took an introductory data processing course at the local community college, and a COBOL programming course offered to Sylvania employees during the evenings. Then I got a job as a maintenance programmer.

SKILLS REQUIRED

When I was a junior programmer, 80 percent of my time was spent on coding. The other 20 percent was spent in meetings doing what they call "structured walkthroughs." Now that I am a programmer/analyst, I only spend 20 percent of my time coding. I really enjoy coding and miss doing more. I need a communications or speech class to help me. Now, I spend a lot of time with the users, as well as meeting with my design team.

MY FUTURE?

Computer careers are good opportunities for women. Women that have taken secretarial training have an easier transition into computers through word processing if they are willing to work hard and upgrade their skills. Math is no longer as important, since there are so many tools such as software and calculators available to help you. And programming in a language like COBOL is almost like English anyway. My goal right now is just to finish this payroll-project with my design team, which will take over two years! I like computers. I like making machines work for me.

CAREERS AS A SYSTEMS ANALYST

The future is very bright for individuals with the skills to be systems analysts. These people are the cornerstone to any systems development project. Communications skills and an understanding of the user's need are important when analysts are called on to help develop a computer system.

A systems analyst must also be knowledgeable about each component of a computer system. This knowledge is used in performing feasibility studies, defining specifications, writing proposals, and designing final requirements. Systems analysts are involved with every step of the systems development process except for writing or altering computer programs.

To become a systems analyst in today's job market requires a four-year college degree and experience. Course work at college will cover a wide range of educational areas. Students can expect to take classes in English, writing, business, and management, as well as computer-related course work.

The systems analyst's ability to speak and write clearly is critical to his or her success. An analyst will be called on to educate and question users about their computer-related needs. Later, these needs must be communicated to programmers.

Eventually, the analyst presents the development project to management in the form of a proposal. This often requires the analyst to get up in front of a group of people and make a formal presentation.

On some systems development projects, a programmer might take on the responsibilities of a systems analyst. This position would then be referred to as a programmer/analyst. This person would be responsible for each step in the systems development process.

Computer programmers often reach a point in their career where they are asked to become systems analysts. At this time, the programmer must evaluate what he or she wants from a job. Those who want a more people-oriented position choose to become systems analysts.

STUDY OBJECTIVES

17. Identify the minimum educational requirements for people seeking a job as a systems analyst.

18. List three skills a systems analyst must have to be successful.

SUMMARY

As users become more experienced with computers, there will be a growing demand for the development of new computer systems. However, systems development does not always mean that new hardware must be purchased.

New programs are often acquired for existing hardware. Programs can be acquired in three ways: off-the-shelf, altered off-the-shelf, or custom-designed.

Off-the-shelf programs or applications packages provide the quickest and least risky means of obtaining programs. However, the program may not meet all the user's needs. In other cases, compromises will be required when several people use the same program.

Altering off-the-shelf programs provides a means of acquiring programs that meet a specific need. However, this alternative involves more risks and needs more time with no guarantee of having the needs met.

Custom-designing programs is the only option available when off-the-shelf programs cannot be found. This alternative is the most costly in terms of time and money. There are also more chances for error in design or implementation.

Variations of the systems development process are used with all newly acquired programs. Skipping steps usually leads to mistakes and time-consuming last-minute changes. Time should be spent to thoroughly review all potential uses of the system.

Professionally developed programs are often the work of an applications development team. A systems analyst acts as the contact person between the development team and the users. The analyst helps the user make a needs analysis.

Later, the analyst works with the users to define specifications. With management's approval, the development team evaluates alternatives and decides on a final system design. The programmers are then responsible for writing or altering the computer programs and manuals.

CHAPTER D3

Advanced Computer Systems

The fundamental computer systems we have discussed are the basis from which more advanced systems grow. In this chapter, we will consider three types of advanced computer systems.

First we will examine teleprocessing systems. The prefix "tele" means distance. Within these systems, the processing is done some distance from the user at a central location using one computer.

Next, distributed computer systems will be explored. These systems are similar to teleprocessing systems, except that processing is not centralized in one location. Instead, data storage and processing are distributed among several computers.

We will devote the last part of the chapter to a discussion of database management systems. These systems allow data items to be identified by their relationship to one another. This type of organization results in easier access to data and less duplication.

TELEPROCESSING SYSTEMS

Simply stated, **teleprocessing** is data processing at a distance. The word is derived from a combination of the terms telecommunications and data processing. By now you know what data processing is, so only telecommunications needs to be defined.

Telecommunications is long distance communications, using a signal like those used in radios and televisions. The subject of telecommunications is a broad one that includes the transmission of voice, messages such as telegrams, facsimile (pictures), and data. The last is called data telecommunications or **data communications.** It is concerned with moving data between terminals and computer or even from computer to computer.

FIGURE D3.1

Teleprocessing system: linking many cities to one computer

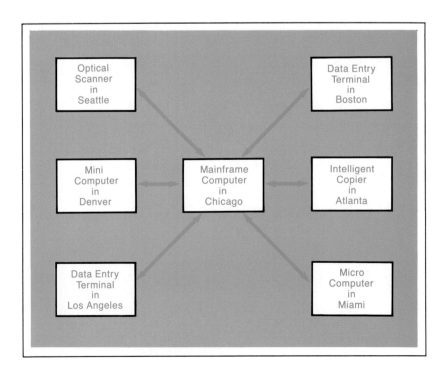

336

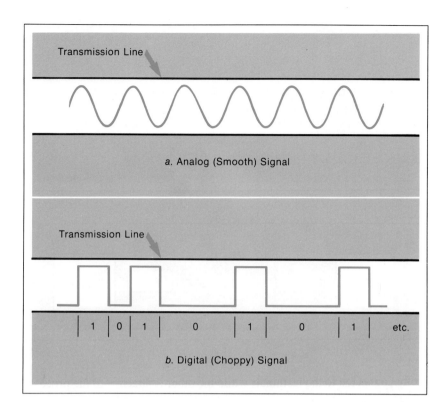

a. Analog (Smooth) Signal

| 1 | 0 | 1 | 0 | 1 | 0 | 1 | etc.

b. Digital (Choppy) Signal

FIGURE D3.2

Modes of communication lines

Components of a Teleprocessing System

Hardware and Programs

A **teleprocessing system** is a computer system in which one or more of the five components are physically remote from the main computer. The components in figure D3.1 are connected together by telecommunications equipment.

There has always been a need to transfer data from one point to another. Data has been carried through telegraph lines as Morse code signals. It has also traveled across the country through telephone lines. Currently, most telephone lines handle analog signals. The human voice, like music, is an analog signal.

There are two methods available for transferring data between computer components. One way is to use digital lines designed to carry bit patterns—a digital signal. The other way is to use standard telephone lines by changing the bit patterns into an analog signal (see figure D3.2).

If digital lines are used, then arrangements must be made to access these communication lines. On the other hand, standard telephone lines are available almost everywhere. But sending a digital signal on an analog line is not easy either. Special equipment must be used to transform the bit patterns into an analog signal.

The transformation of bit patterns into an analog signal is called modulation and demodulation. To connect a terminal to a distant computer, a **modem**—MOdulator/DEModulator—is used. The modem transforms the bit patterns from the terminal into an analog signal that can be sent along standard communication lines (see figure D3.3).

At the other end, another modem receives the analog signal and converts it back to the original digital signal. As shown in figure D3.4, one modem is

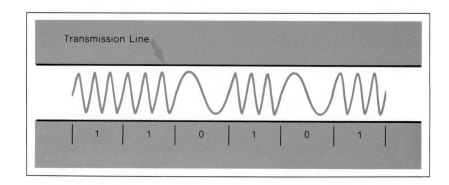

FIGURE D3.3

Analog signal representing 110101

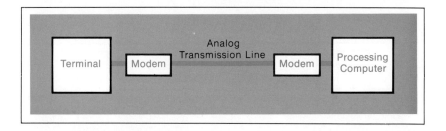

FIGURE D3.4

Use of modems on an analog
transmission line

directly connected to the terminal, while the other is attached to the processing hardware.

Some modems are designed to use a regular telephone receiver. These special modems are called acoustic couplers. They have two cups in which the earpiece and mouthpiece of the receiver are placed.

To support teleprocessing the central computer must be directed by special systems software called a **communications control program.** The communications control program handles the transfer of data to and from the remote terminals.

As data is delivered to the processing computer, it is passed to the communications control program. This program determines whether the data needs immediate attention or can be stored for processing later. If the data needs immediate attention, the communications control program passes the data to the appropriate applications program.

Depending on the complexity of the teleprocessing system, the processing hardware can come in several configurations. In the most direct configuration, the central computer is responsible for handling the remote terminals. It accepts all the data from incoming communication lines. The communications control program checks errors, corrects them if possible, and keeps track of each remote terminal.

In more complex teleprocessing systems, a **front-end processor** is used to free the central computer from communication tasks. The front-end processor is a computer dedicated to handle communications to and from the central computer. This is much like an administrative assistant who handles calls for a business executive. The front-end processor resides close to the central computer and accepts input from terminals.

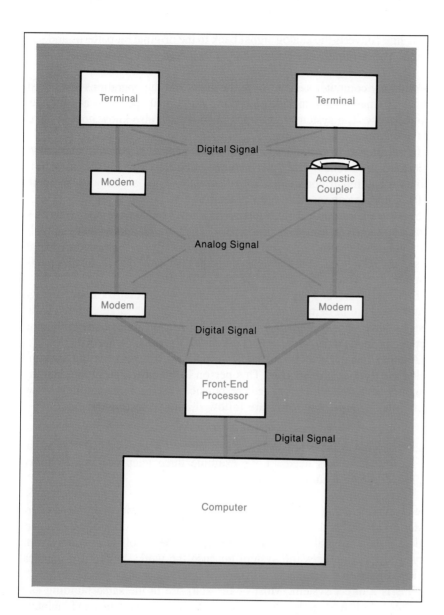

FIGURE D3.5

Teleprocessing system with front-end processor

When acoustic couplers or modems are used, the front-end processor is responsible for answering the phone. It also checks for transmission errors, makes corrections, and monitors each terminal. It then sends the data to the central computer for processing.

Figure D3.5 shows a diagram of a teleprocessing system that uses a front-end processor. When the processing is complete, the computer sends the output data back to the front-end processor. The front-end processor determines which terminal receives the output and sends the data to a modem. The modem transforms the digital data into an analog signal.

The data is sent through standard communication lines. A modem at the end of the line converts the analog signal back to the original bit patterns and passes them to the terminal. The output data is then ready for the user.

As with any computer system, both the users and the operations staff must be trained. Training should include procedures for normal operations and for backup and recovery. The systems development staff must also know how to develop and maintain online programs.

In addition to the standard training and personnel requirements, several specialists are needed. **Hardware communications specialists** know how to maintain and repair communications hardware. They are important members of the communications development team.

Software communications specialists know how to develop and write systems programs for front-end processors. They are also knowledgeable about communications control programs. The level of expertise needed to maintain these programs is much the same as the expertise needed to maintain operating systems.

Both hardware and software communications specialists command good salaries and are in demand. Only organizations having large communications systems have such specialists on staff. Other organizations contact the manufacturer or independent consultants when this expertise is needed.

Another person who is especially important to teleprocessing systems is called the **data administrator.** This person is the custodian of the data in the teleprocessing system. He or she is responsible for resolving conflicts between users, making sure procedures are followed, and protecting the data.

Three Examples of Teleprocessing Systems

Teleprocessing systems are designed in a variety of ways. The design is based on the organization's needs. Let's examine three teleprocessing systems to explore common features and differences.

The Hospital

The hospital that Sue McKnight works in is the simplest form of teleprocessing system. The staff and data entry operators use CRTs to process the direct access patient files. Terminals are located throughout the hospital. Therefore, this is considered a teleprocessing system because the work stations are physically removed from the computer.

This is a direct system. Most of the staff are in the same building as the computer. As is frequently the case, all the hardware is supplied and maintained by the same manufacturer. This eliminates compatibility problems.

The Bank

Figure D3.6 shows the teleprocessing configuration for the bank in which Martha Baker works. This medium-sized bank has three branches and operates a credit card authorization center. In addition to teller terminals, there are automatic teller machines and a **remote job entry (RJE)** station. The RJE station has a scanner, printer, and CRT for the operator to use. This equipment is used to submit batch jobs from the remote processing center.

The bank's teleprocessing system is considerably more complex than that of the hospital. The communication lines are much longer and involve the telephone company. The hardware is supplied by several manufacturers. Get-

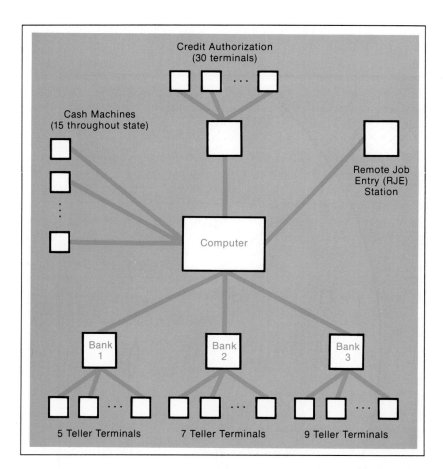

Credit Authorization
(30 terminals)

Cash Machines
(15 throughout state)

Remote Job
Entry (RJE)
Station

Computer

Bank 1

Bank 2

Bank 3

5 Teller Terminals   7 Teller Terminals   9 Teller Terminals

FIGURE D3.6

Teleprocessing system for Midstate Bank

ting the hardware to work together is not easy. When one manufacturer blames the problem on another, maintenance and troubleshooting are difficult.

In addition, the operating system was designed for general-purpose applications. For the bank's special needs, communication and operating systems specialists are necessary. They develop, install, and maintain the hardware and programs.

A third teleprocessing configuration is depicted in figure D3.7. Clearly, this is the most complex of the three examples. John LaFriend and other weather observers from around the world communicate with the central computer at the Air Force Global Weather Center in Omaha, Nebraska.

Not only are different pieces of equipment used, but the service also involves multiple communications media. Telephone, microwave, satellite, and other types of communications equipment are used. All of it must work together in spite of different speeds, conventions, and manufacturers.

Since this is a large and complex configuration, many computers are involved. Front-end processors are used to handle communication resources and traffic,

Naval Weather Service

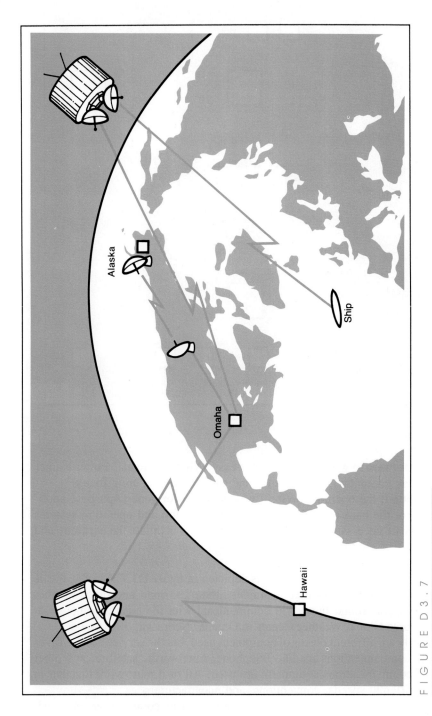

FIGURE D3.7

Part of the teleprocessing system used by the Navy weather service

FIGURE D3.8

Remote job entry (RJE) station (Courtesy Northern Communications Corporation)

freeing the computer to process data. To build this system and maintain all the equipment requires a large staff of communications specialists.

Teleprocessing applications can be divided into two broad categories: offline and online. For offline applications, the data is transmitted from a remote location to the central computer and stored. When the transfer of data is complete, the computer processes it and then returns the output to the remote location.

Teleprocessing Applications

Batch data transmission is often a good example of offline processing. Data is input via RJE equipment like that in figure D3.8. The data is stored on disk. At a predetermined time, the data is sent to the central computer. The batch of data is then processed by an applications program running on the central computer. The results are returned to the RJE station and printed.

Offline Systems

For online teleprocessing applications, the remote terminal is directly connected to the processing computer. Data is usually not sent in batches. Instead, a single record or message is sent, it is acted on by the processing computer, and the results are returned. Then another message is sent and the process is repeated.

A **query system** is an online applications. The user sends a request for information, like "How many seats are available on Flight 102?" The processing computer determines the answer and returns it to the terminal. Questions are acted on one at a time, not in batches.

Online Systems

Rationale for Teleprocessing Systems

Online program development is another application. Programmers write programs at terminals by sending one statement at a time to the processing computer. The computer either translates the code or stores it for later translation. Unlike RJE, the program is not sent as a batch, but one line at a time.

Organizations develop teleprocessing systems for two major reasons. The first reason is that such systems are geographically dispersed. The data originates, is processed, and is used at different places. In the bank example, customers do business at a local bank branch. However, the data is processed at a central facility. Reports like the bank's financial statement then go to the bank's headquarters at still another location.

A second reason organizations develop teleprocessing systems is that such systems are economical. Rather than having separate data processing facilities for every branch, an organization establishes a central facility. The local branches are then connected by telecommunications link to the central computer. This system allows the organization to gain **economics of scale.** Economics of scale means that there is a cost reduction by having one large system instead of several smaller ones.

Unfortunately, economics of scale has a limit. At first, the average cost decreases as the size of the system increases. Figure D3.9 shows the average cost of data processing as it relates to the size of the system. As you can see, there is a point where the computer system becomes hard to manage and the average cost starts to go up.

When a single computer system becomes too large to manage, another will be acquired and some applications transferred to it. The result is one large teleprocessing network with applications being processed by two separate computer systems. This is called **distributed data processing.**

To review, there are three major configurations of data processing systems.

FIGURE D3.9

Average cost of data processing versus size

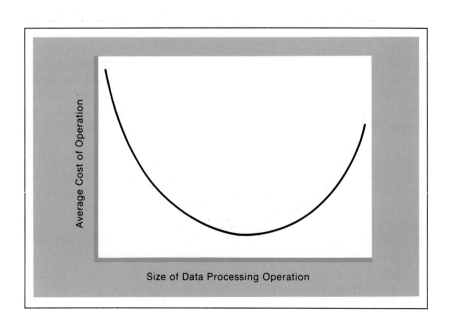

In the first part of the text, we limited our discussion to centralized processing systems. These systems use a single central computer for processing. All five components are located near the computer.

In the second major configuration, the components of the computer system are geographically separated. They are united into a system by telecommunications equipment. Processing of data is still done on a single computer. Systems of this type are called teleprocessing systems.

Finally, in the third configuration, the system components are geographically separated and applications are processed on more than one computer. Systems of this type are referred to as distributed data processing systems. Let's examine distributed data processing systems in more detail.

STUDY OBJECTIVES

1. Define telecommunications, teleprocessing system, data communications, RJE, and economics of scale.

2. Describe the functions of a communications control program and front-end processor.

3. Briefly describe how digital data is transferred from a terminal to a computer and back through the use of a modem.

4. Identify three types of procedures that teleprocessing users and operations personnel must be trained to handle.

5. Briefly describe the responsibilities of a hardware communications specialist and software communications specialist.

6. Describe two categories of teleprocessing applications.

7. Identify two reasons for developing teleprocessing systems.

8. Briefly describe the three major configurations of data processing systems.

DISTRIBUTED DATA PROCESSING SYSTEMS

The unique characteristic of a distributed data processing system is not that the users or terminals are distributed. It is not that there is more than one computer in use. The fact that more than one computer handles the applications programs makes this system unique.

An **applications node** is a computer system within a distributed network that does applications processing. Each applications node has a computer, programs, data files, procedures, and users—all the components of a computer system.

Distributed processing allows the applications processing to be done in the place that is best for the user, not where the central computer happens to be. Miracle Motors uses a distributed data processing system. Figure D3.10 depicts the central computer and the applications node for the engineering department. For the most part, the engineers have control over their own data and the use of the minicomputer. However, data is transferred to the central computer for use of the attached plotter. Reports are also sent to the central computer for distribution to management.

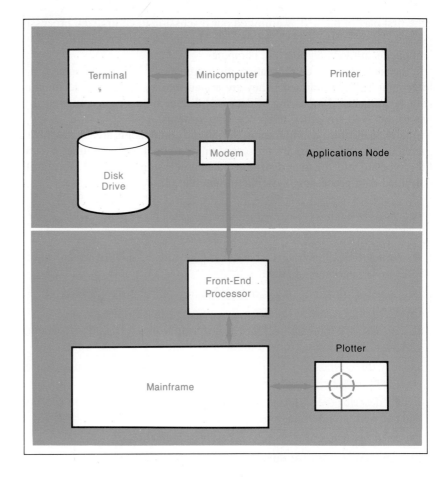

FIGURE D3.10

Applications node for the engineering
department

Components of a Distributed System

Hardware

As we might expect, there are many variations to distributed data processing systems. They can range from a minicomputer with a few applications nodes using microcomputers to a worldwide network of large mainframe computers.

The major hardware components of a distributed processing system are computers and communication lines. The computers at each applications node can be micros, minis, or mainframes. These computers are employed for both applications processing and communications control.

Sometimes a single computer handles both functions. At other times, one computer is dedicated to applications processing and another, such as a front-end processor, to communications control.

There are three basic types of computer networks: **star, ring,** and **hybrid.** Figure D3.11 shows a star organization. A central computer is connected to other computers in the network by communication lines. In a star network, the central computer usually controls the flow of data to and from the applications nodes.

A ring network is illustrated in figure D3.12. Each computer is connected

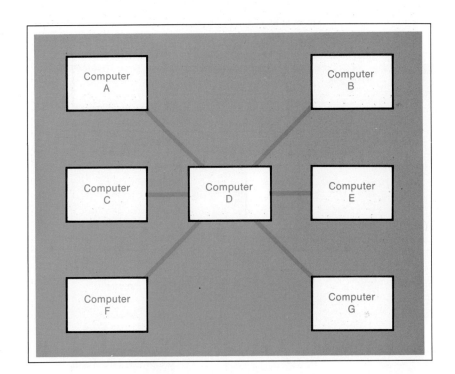

FIGURE D3.11

Star network

FIGURE D3.12

Ring network

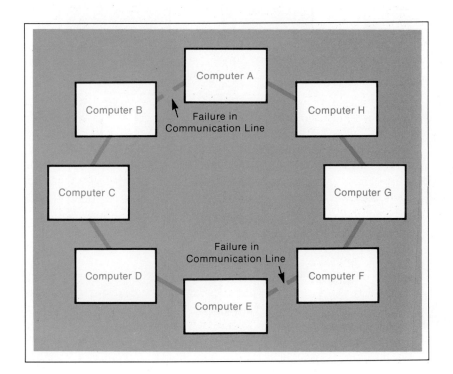

347

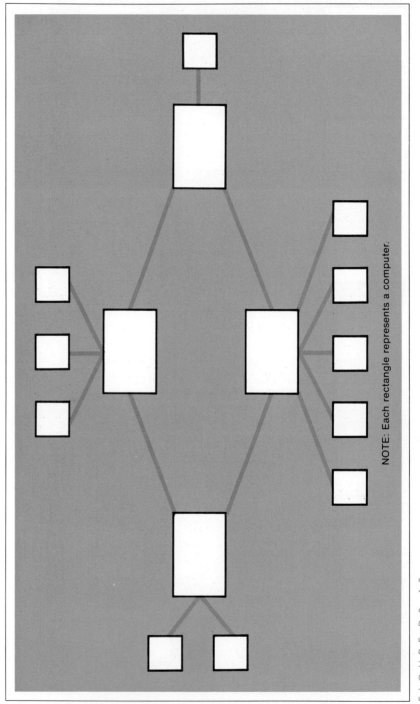

NOTE: Each rectangle represents a computer.

FIGURE D3.13

Hybrid network

to some or all of its neighbors. In most ring organizations, no computer has central control over the others. Each computer operates independently.

In figure D3.12, none of the computers are directly connected to all the other computers. This is acceptable. Probably, computer A seldom needs to communicate with computer C. When it does, it can send its message to computer B. Computer B can then forward the message to C. So each computer needs a program to forward messages to a neighbor, but does not need a direct connection to each computer.

The third type of distributed hardware organization is called a hybrid. This is a combination of a ring structure and a star structure. As shown in figure D3.13, the hybrid consists of a ring of computers, each of which is the center of a star. The hybrid organization is used with large computer networks.

Each node in a distributed system must have an operating system, a communications control program, and applications programs. Each type of program has special tasks, as shown in figure D3.14.

The operating system must be able to access files from computers at different locations. To do this, the operating system from the first computer generates a message to the other computer to obtain the data. The first computer may also receive a transaction that must be processed by yet another computer. In other words, a transaction is passed from one computer to another.

The communications control program has additional duties in a distributed network. It must be able to receive messages from any computer connected to its node, translate them, and send them to the correct applications program. In addition, the communications control program must be able to transfer requests from local applications programs to other computers in the system. These requests could be for data kept on the other applications node.

Applications programs must be written to minimize their dependence on the local computer system. It would be impractical to rewrite the program every time it is moved from one node to another. Systems developers go to great pains to make these applications programs independent of their environment.

System/Program	Function
Operating System or DBMS	Locate input/output files on another computer Generate messages for remote input/output
Communications Control Program	Receive messages from other nodes Send messages to other nodes Translate computer codes
Applications Programs	Issue location-independent requests for input/output

An applications program is designed to access a file without knowing where the file is located. Similarly, the program may process data from a user without knowing whether the user is connected to the local computer or another computer on the network.

This independence actually makes the job of the applications programmers easier. They do not have to learn the details of every computer system in the network. Instead, the programmers learn a generalized way of performing input and output. The burden is on the operating system and communications control program to execute these generalized instructions.

The programmers can then develop and test software on a single system. When the programs are ready for installation, they are transferred to the applications node. This process is called **downline loading.** Not only does downline loading save money, it also saves time because the programmers do not physically move from system to system.

Data

In a distributed system, data can be broken into two broad categories: **local** and **global.** Local data is needed only at one applications node. Local data is processed solely by the applications programs that run on the local computer. Nodes never request data that is local on a different node.

Global data is needed by programs that run on at least two computers in the distributed system. The percentage of local versus global data varies within organizations.

As to the question of where to locate the data, one basic principle is that local data stays local. It almost never makes sense to move local data from the node on which it is used. The communication cost is too high.

Unfortunately, it is not so easy to decide where to put global data. One option is to centralize the data at one location. The other option is to scatter the data across several locations.

One advantage to centralizing data is simplicity. Every node knows where the data is located. The biggest disadvantage of this option is that accessing the global data kept on a single system can create a performance bottleneck. A "traffic jam" could easily occur if several nodes needed global data at the same time.

A second disadvantage to keeping global data on one system concerns reliability. If the system with the global data fails, then none of the nodes will have access to the data.

Scattering global data eliminates the performance bottleneck and reliability problems. Unfortunately, it is much harder to update scattered data than it is to update centralized data. A **data directory** is used to locate scattered data. The data directory identifies the system that holds different pieces of the scattered global data. A directory is available at each applications node. It is used by the operating system whenever scattered global data is needed.

Some major problems can arise when global data is scattered. First, special care must be taken to identify where and when data is used. Otherwise, it may be impossible to recover the data if a system failure occurs. Second, care must be taken when updating this data. Only one user at a time should be able to access and change the data.

Why Personnel Are Not Distributed	Ways to Avoid Distribution
Too expensive	Training users to run systems
Hard to obtain and train	Designing systems for ease of use
Difficult to support and control	Training key personnel
	Loading downline
	Providing temporary data processing personnel
	Centralizing development

FIGURE D3.15

Distributing considerations for data processing personnel

Personnel

It is sometimes easier to distribute hardware, programs, and data than to distribute personnel because the nonhuman factors are less expensive. As electronic technology becomes cheaper, inflation and other factors are making personnel more costly.

In particular, systems development personnel are difficult to distribute. Good programmers, systems analysts, and communications specialists are hard to find and need to work together. Therefore, these people are not distributed with hardware, programs, and data. Instead, they are often consolidated at one location.

Distributed systems are usually designed at one location and operated by users at other locations. These people are already trained in their jobs and have the support of the organization.

However, a user cannot be expected to perform the same tasks as a well-trained computer professional. This fact is considered in the design of distributed systems. The programs are written to be easily used. Operations procedures must be simple, well documented, and as self-explanatory as possible.

To reduce the burden of training, some organizations have chosen to have two or three users at each node designated as key personnel. These people are given special training. They are called upon when equipment fails, when the user is having problems, or when backups must be performed.

There are some tasks that are too difficult for the key personnel to perform, such as installing new equipment or programs. These tasks can be performed by computer professionals who visit the distributed location. In other situations, downline loading of programs allows the computer professionals to install programs without physically being at the location.

Procedures

The procedures needed to operate a distributed system are basically the same as those needed for other data processing systems. Because the computer may be operated by inexperienced personnel, the procedures must be well documented and easy to understand. Users will need procedures on how to run the computer, including backup, recovery, and other special tasks.

Distributed computers are intended to communicate with one another. Therefore, procedures must be available explaining how to make such connections and what to do if the connections do not work. Users or operators must know what their responsibilities to other computers are when their computer fails. They must also know what to do when another computer in the network fails.

Procedures and standards for program development are also important in distributed systems. Generalized procedures for handling input, output, and other program functions must be followed.

Characteristics of Distributed Systems

There are several advantages of distributed data processing systems. First, they can be less expensive. It is often cheaper to use microcomputers and minicomputers to perform certain tasks rather than a larger mainframe. This can also reduce data communications costs because the data is processed close to the source.

Other Advantages

Distributed systems give the users greater control over the processing of their data. Often, users operate the computer themselves. They can determine the quality and the scheduling of services they receive.

Another potential advantage is that distributed systems can be useful when the systems development staff is behind in development schedules. Applications packages running on smaller systems may be available that accomplish the user's need.

Finally, distributed systems can be tailored to a company's organizational structure. For example, the engineering department at Miracle Motors works independently of the accounting department. Very little of the data needs to be shared between these two departments. Thus, the applications node is designed to allow the engineers control over their own data and computer resources. Another company with a different organizational structure might design the system in another way.

The advantages of distributed data processing systems are summarized in figure D3.16.

Disadvantages

There are also several disadvantages of distributed processing systems. First, they are complex to set up. Communication facilities must be obtained to connect the computers to one another.

Furthermore, programs must interact with one another. Close coordination is required throughout the distributed system to ensure that all the data is

FIGURE D3.16

Advantages and disadvantages of distributed processsing systems

Advantages	Disadvantages
Can be less expensive	More complex to build
Greater control to users	Close coordination required for
Quicker development if off-the-shelf	data compatibility
programs can be used	Greater need for standards and documentation
Tailored to organizational structure	Problems of multivendors

compatible. For example, confusion could result in the reporting of sales data. One division could report sales data from the previous month, while another division reported sales data from the current month.

A third disadvantage is that distributed systems often run without the guidance of data processing professionals. This practice is risky unless the users are well trained. Users should have access to complete, well-written documentation of all necessary procedures.

Finally, distributed systems are often a mixture of equipment. The computers, communication lines, and programs may be supplied by a variety of manufacturers. It may be difficult to make the equipment operate together. Figure D3.16 summarizes the disadvantages of distributed data processing systems.

STUDY OBJECTIVES

9. Define applications node, downline loading, and data directory.
10. Describe three types of distributed networks.
11. Identify the functions of an operating system, a communications control program, and an applications program in a distributed network.
12. List two categories of distributed data and describe how each is handled.
13. Briefly explain why computer professionals are not distributed and explain how training and problems are handled.
14. Identify procedures that help inexperienced personnel use distributed processing systems.
15. Describe four advantages and four disadvantages of distributed data processing systems.

DATABASE SYSTEMS

"Look at this, John," said Tricia Lucero. "We get three separate mailings from Midstate bank. One is for our checking account, another is for our savings, and the third is for the car loan. It's confusing. Every week we get another piece of paper from them. Why don't they put it on one statement? It would sure save on their mailing costs and be less confusing for me."

"Fred, FRED, FRED! Where is that data I wanted on the Parks loan application? I asked for it a week ago. We need to take some action on this request. Get it for me!"

"I'm sorry, Ms. Baker, I can't find it in all these computer printouts. I asked data processing to give me the data last week. They said it would take a month to write the program. I told them you had to have it right away. The next morning these three boxes of computer printouts were on my desk. I guess the data's in here somewhere."

These people are all expressing frustration with the information system used at the bank. Martha Baker, in particular, was frustrated as she tried to perform her job as one of the bank's loan officers.

She had made a very important career decision more than 10 years ago when she chose to change jobs. While she had liked her work in accounting, she

FIGURE D3.17

Loan officer Baker inquires about the Parks' account

always regretted not having more contact with the customers. Her decision to switch to the finance department had not been easy. However, she had liked the credit analyst job to which she had been transferred.

Credit analysts decide who is to receive loans from the bank. They review the customer's needs, sources of income, and other financial obligations before making a recommendation. This job had provided Martha with the customer contact she wanted. Her accounting background also came in very handy as she analyzed various reports.

Martha's hard work and positive interaction with the bank's customers had paid off. Throughout the years, she received periodic raises and more responsibilities. Becoming an officer of the bank was everything she had hoped for when she made the career change so many years ago.

As we might have expected, computers were very much a part of Martha's career path. Usually, they had provided helpful information and made her job easier. Right now they were having the opposite effect.

File Processing Systems

Figure D3.18 shows three customer-oriented batch systems used at the bank. These systems independently handle the records for checking, savings, and loan accounts.

In figure D3.18a, a system flowchart for processing checking accounts is shown. Every evening, deposit slips and canceled checks are prepared for input into the check processing program. Along with the checking account file, the

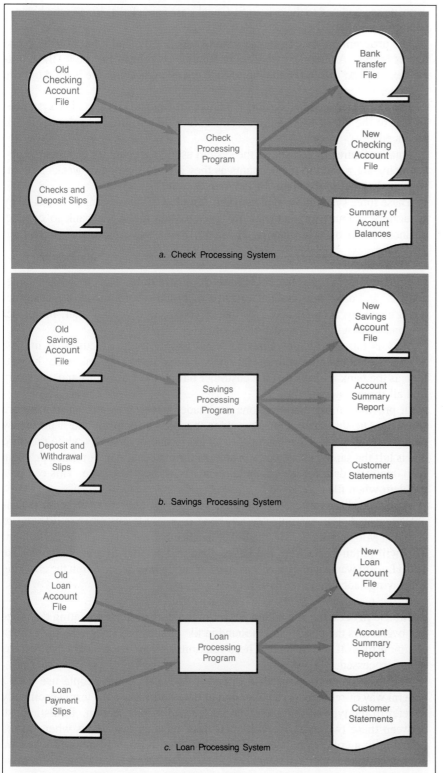

a. Check Processing System

b. Savings Processing System

c. Loan Processing System

File processing systems

deposits are updated to the accounts. Checks are canceled as long as the balance is large enough.

The program produces a new checking account file and a file of bank transfers as output. A summary of account balances is printed for use by the tellers the next day. At the end of the month, the checking account file is used to print customer statements.

The customer savings system is shown in figure D3.18b. This system is similar to the check processing system except that no file of bank transfers is produced.

Finally, figure D3.18c shows the system used to account for customer loans. Payments are posted to the accounts as they arrive. Every two weeks a report is printed showing the status of the loan accounts.

These three systems are typical batch-oriented file processing systems. They accurately account for financial transactions that allow the bank to conduct business in an orderly manner. However, as we have seen, they have their disadvantages.

Problems with File Processing Systems

File processing systems like these have **duplicate data.** The customer's name, address, and other personal data may be recorded several times. If a customer has a checking account and a savings account along with a loan, his or her personal data will be recorded three times.

Why is this a problem? Consider what happens when a customer moves. All the files containing address data must be updated. This task is not hard as long as the bank realizes that the customer has all three accounts and can easily find all three account numbers.

In practice, most modifications are made successfully and customers are satisfied. On some occasions, however, people can slip up and a necessary change is not made. Changes may be made in one or two files while the third one is left the same. This creates problems for the customer. A related problem with duplicate data for the computer center is wasted file space. This can be a problem when files are large.

A second disadvantage of file processing systems is that common data is not integrated. For example, data related to a single customer is difficult to obtain at Midstate Bank. Martha Baker needs information about the Parks loan. This will require data from the Parks' loan and savings accounts. People like Tricia Lucero want an integrated statement detailing transactions from the checking and savings accounts.

Components of a Database System

Database processing is a technique for organizing and manipulating data files that overcomes the disadvantages found in file processing. Relationships between common records are defined. These relationships are then used when data is being processed.

The term database is used in different contexts. Some people use it as a general way of referring to a collection of data. Others use the term specifically to refer to the type of integrated data discussed in this section. To distinguish between these two uses, we will spell **data base** as two words when we are referring to a collection of data. One word, **database,** will be used when we are referring to integrated data.

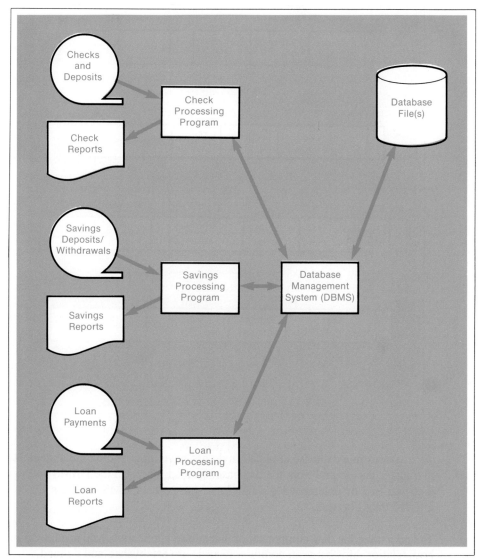

FIGURE D3.19

Bank processing using database technology

Midstate Bank is a candidate for combining the checking, savings, and loan records into a single integrated database. With the relationships between a customer's data defined, personal data needs to appear only once. It would also be possible to access data for both savings and checking accounts in order to print one monthly statement.

Figure D3.19 shows how programs relate to the database. Compare this diagram with figure D3.18. In figure D3.18, the programs perform input and output operations directly. In figure D3.19, the programs use a special systems program called a **database management system (DBMS)** to do the input/output.

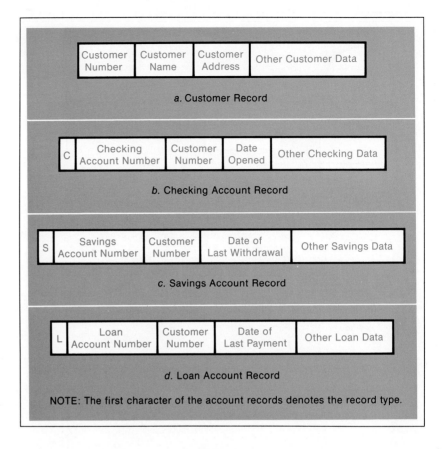

Four record types in the bank database

Programs in a database application do not have input and output statements to transfer data to and from the database. Instead, they call the DBMS and ask it to retrieve or enter needed data. In a sense, the DBMS operates like an internal data librarian.

Data

To understand the data component of a database application, you need to know how relationships between common records are established and defined.

We have defined a field as a collection of characters, a record as a collection of fields, and a file as a collection of records. We have also said that a database is a collection of integrated files. Another way of saying this is that a database is a collection of files and record relationships.

The words "and record relationships" are important. If a database were only a group of files, the files would not be integrated. For example, the records in the checking account file would not directly correspond to any records in the loan file.

Consider the processing needs of Midstate bank. Figure D3.20 shows four types of records. The first contains data about the customer. The second record is the checking account record. It has an account number, account type, balance, and other data. The remaining two records have data about savings accounts and loans.

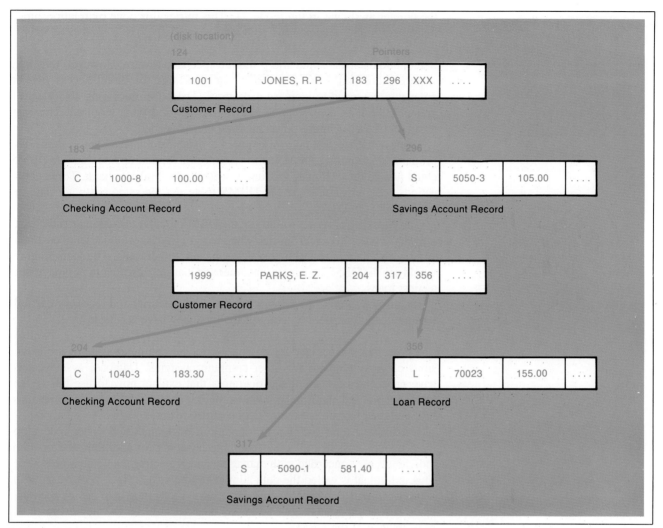

Two examples of using pointers to identify database relationships

Figure D3.21 shows some examples of these record types. The lines represent relationships. Relationships are identified by pointers. The **pointer** is an additional field in the record that contains the disk location of another record.

In figure D3.21, there are two pointers in Jones's customer record. The first pointer is the number 183, which identifies the associated checking account record. The second pointer identifies the location of the savings account record. The third pointer field is left blank because the customer does not have a loan through the bank. Customer Parks, the second example, has all three types of accounts.

In a database application, all this data, including the relationships, is sent to the DBMS for storage. Later, when an applications program asks for data about Jones's checking account, the DBMS retrieves the Jones record using

Hardware and Programs

the pointer as shown in figure D3.21. This retrieval is done by relationship—not by key value or sequential position.

Seldom do database applications require special hardware. However, they may require more hardware. Since database files must be direct access files, a company may need to increase disk space. Database processing also places a greater burden on the computer because of the processing required. This may mean that a larger, more powerful computer is needed.

Using database technology requires a database management system. The primary function of a DBMS is to store, retrieve, and update data. A DBMS could handle the customer account processing for Midstate bank. Three applications programs could use the DBMS to access the same customer data, as shown in figure D3.22.

The checking program would use the DBMS to refer to customer and checking data in order to cancel checks. The savings program would refer to customer and savings data in order to post deposits and withdrawals. The loan program would use the DBMS to access customer and loan data in order to post payments against loans.

In addition to this, the DBMS provides data security and recovery capabilities and can give users a listing of the data they have access to.

Procedures and Personnel

The procedures necessary for database-oriented computer systems are extensions of those required for other computer systems. Database systems must have procedures for users and operators that explain how to use the system under normal and abnormal operating conditions. In addition, procedures must be developed that utilize the DBMS security features.

Database systems have users, operations personnel, and systems development people, just like all other computer systems. In addition, one or more individuals are concerned with managing and protecting the database resource. This individual is called the data administrator.

Data administrators perform several jobs. First, they help design the database. Second, they manage day-to-day data activity. Third, they evaluate the performance of the DBMS.

Generally, data administrators are nontechnical people who have been in the company for some time. Although data administrators have responsibility for some technical matters, they are not computer systems experts. It is more important for data administrators to be diplomats than to be technical experts.

Characteristics of Database Processing

Database applications provide a number of ways to access data. One way of accessing records is by predefined relationships. Additionally, records can be accessed by any of several keys. We previously defined a key—or key field—as a field used to identify a record. Database systems expand upon this concept.

Finding Data in a Database

Several fields can be used as keys in a database system. Thus, customer records can be accessed by the bank's customer number or by the customer's social security number or by some other key. Also, database systems support **non-unique keys.** These keys identify a group of records, not just one. For example, a database system could display all the customers from one geographic area

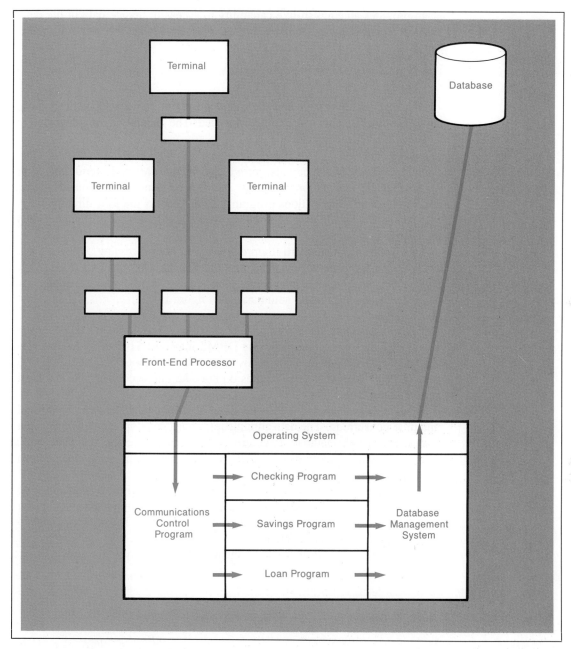

Program interaction during database processing

by using the zip code as a key. The zip code is a nonunique key because several customers will have the same zip code.

In addition to using multiple keys to access data, some database management systems provide a **query program** to complement the DBMS. This program provides an English-like capability to access or update data in the database. To print all the customer names in zip code 49442, the user could enter

```
SELECT    CUSTOMER _ NAME
FROM      CUSTOMER _ DATA
WHERE     ZIP CODE = 49442
```

By using multiple keys and the query program, someone like Fred could obtain the specific data Martha Baker needed. The data processing department would not have to be involved.

Program and Data Independence

Some database systems can also provide **program/data independence.** This means that the applications programs are independent of the data files. In a database system, applications programs do not access the files directly. They ask the DBMS for the data. Therefore, when the file format is changed, only the DBMS is affected.

This differs from standard file processing. In file processing, when a file is changed, all the programs that process the file are also changed. This could represent a large number of programs in some systems. The advantages to using database systems are summarized in figure D3.23.

Disadvantages of Database Management Systems

Database processing has several major disadvantages. First, it can be expensive. For mainframe computers, the DBMS may cost $100,000 or more. The cost of the DBMS is less for minis and micros at about $5000 and $1000, respectively. However, these figures do not take into account additional hardware and development costs.

A second disadvantage is that the initial design of a database can be difficult and time-consuming. The data administrator must develop and define the database structure. The database structure must support the needs of all users while dealing with the limitations of the DBMS. Because of this, awkward compromises are sometimes necessary.

The vulnerability of the database system is a third disadvantage. In a file processing system, if one file is accidentally destroyed, applications programs using another file can still run. However, when something happens to a database file, no applications can operate.

We are at a point in the development of computer systems where we are

Advantages	Disadvantages
Elimination or reduction of duplicated data	Expensive DBMS
Integrated processing	More hardware
Generalized access to data	Development costs high
Program/data independence	Higher risk
	Difficult initial development
	Vulnerability to crash

trading people resources for machine resources. A DBMS requires more from the computer system than a file processing system does. But once the database is defined, it enables people to work more efficiently. People's time has become increasingly expensive while computers have become cheaper, so trade-offs of this kind are often smart decisions.

STUDY OBJECTIVES

16. Define database processing, database, data base, pointer, DBMS, data administrator, nonunique key, and program/data independence.
17. Identify two disadvantages of file processing systems.
18. Describe how a pointer is used to identify an associated database record.
19. List three functions of a database management system.
20. Identify the responsibilities of a data administrator and describe desirable personal characteristics.
21. Briefly describe three ways of accessing database data.
22. Describe the function of a query program.
23. Identify four advantages and disadvantages of database processing.

SUMMARY

Computer systems can be expanded to include teleprocessing, distributed processing, and database processing. These advanced computer systems represent new areas of growth for computer technology.

A teleprocessing system is a computer system with one or more of its components connected through communication lines. Special hardware is used to help the computer handle this communications capacity. A communications control program assists the operating system in handling remote processing.

Special communications specialists in hardware and software are needed to support both teleprocessing and distributed processing systems. With distributed processing systems, applications processing takes place on more than one computer system. This raises questions about where to keep data. While local data always stays local, global data is either centralized on one system or scattered across several systems.

Special care must be taken in the development and documentation of distributed systems, since users are also distributed. In addition, remote users sometimes take over the responsibilities of computer professionals.

Database processing is a technique of organizing data under the control of a database management system. This system software retrieves data by identifying and following stored relationships between associated records.

The centralizing of data under a database management system requires the presence of a database administrator. The database administrator manages and protects this valuable resource.

U N I T E

Looking Ahead

Computers are a part of our future. The first part of this unit looks at the possibility of misusing computer technology. Types of computer crime are discussed along with ways of preventing them.

In the second part of this unit, you look at current computer applications and identify future trends. Computers now allow you to shop, bank, and even work at home. What next? Computer experts talk of creating intelligent machines. The need for controlling the impact computers are having on our lives is discussed along with ways to do it.

The last part of Unit E addresses education and careers in computing. Ways in which you can learn more about the use of computers are examined. Discussion also centers on professional organizations, the effect of computers on tomorrow's job market, and career paths for computer professionals.

CHAPTER E1
Computer Crime and Security

CHAPTER E2
Computer Industry and Society: Today and Tomorrow

CHAPTER E3
The Next Step: Education and Careers in Computing

CHAPTER E1

Computer Crime and Security

As computers expand into every nook and cranny of our society, we must take an in-depth look at the impact these machines are having. Many organizations could not function as they do without computers.

Beyond this fact lies another. Some companies could not survive if their data was tampered with or lost. Such an occurrence could have the same effect as a fire or earthquake without the smoldering ruins.

The data that computers store and manipulate is often priceless. Data security should therefore be of prime importance. However, organizations often take the attitude that disasters always strike the other guy. They are not prepared for computer crime when it happens.

MISUSING COMPUTER TECHNOLOGY

The image most people have of the common computer criminal adds to the misconception that "it can't happen here." But computer criminals are not thugs in leather jackets. Instead, they are highly skilled professionals who attend company picnics.

In some cases, these criminals are first-time offenders. They did not intend to commit crime or fraud, but circumstances led them to it. Unfortunately, Harold Johnson was one of these people. His tool was not a jimmy or a glass cutter, but a computer.

Harold Johnson, Computer Criminal

After working at Miracle Motors for four years, Harold Johnson applied for a programmer/analyst job at Modern Record Distributing Company—MODREC. He left Miracle Motors because he believed that the major challenges were over and he wanted to try something new.

Harold had lost none of his intensity over the years. He was still highly motivated, creative, and willing to spend long hours solving difficult problems. In short, he had matured into a superior systems developer.

At one time, MODREC had been a division of a large, traditional record manufacturer. A separate company was created when MODREC's sales exceeded $5 million. The directors of the parent company thought that it made sense to form a subsidiary. MODREC specialized in distributing rock music.

MODREC's first president was the son of one of the directors. He was promoted into his position through influence, not ability. Consequently, MODREC's sales began to slip, morale fell, and MODREC lost many sales opportunities.

MODREC's small data processing department was managed by the financial vice-president. He meant well, but he had many responsibilities and was uneducated about data processing. When Harold applied for the job, the financial V.P. was delighted. He made Harold an excellent offer and Harold accepted.

In the first year, Harold made many contributions to MODREC's data processing. The level of service vastly improved. Salespeople were given better information about their customers. The time needed to deliver an order was cut in half. Sales went up. In addition, the accounting systems were improved, and the accountants had better information than ever.

Unfortunately, Harold began to feel discontented. Nobody paid any attention to him. He felt that no one recognized the contributions he had made. However,

Harold and Joan plotting a computer crime

after a year, MODREC gave him a big pay increase, so he didn't move to another company. He thought he would have trouble earning as much money elsewhere.

As Harold worked with the accounting systems, he began to notice MODREC's large profits. This was possible in spite of inept management because MODREC had a very large markup. Harold decided that MODREC was ripping off their customers.

One day, Harold mentioned this to Joan Everest, the manager of a record store that ordered from MODREC. "Harold," said Joan, almost in jest, "why don't you reprogram your computer to offer special discounts to my store? Perhaps I could share the savings with you."

Harold was never quite the same. After being bored at work, the technical challenge of such special discounts excited him. He was also angry with the way MODREC had treated him. He believed it was unfair for them to make so much profit. Joan needed the financial help and MODREC could easily afford to lose $40,000 to $50,000 a year. In some ways he felt he was Robin Hood—stealing from the rich and giving to the poor.

Once Harold decided to cooperate, the technical aspects were easy. In fact, Harold was disappointed at the lack of challenge. He changed the pricing program to look for Joan's customer number. When the computer found it, her prices were reduced by 85 percent. Only he saw this special copy of the pro-

Type of Crime	Average Amount Stolen ($)
Larceny-Theft	150
Burglary	320
All Robberies	400
Branch Bank Robbery	2,000
Full-Service Bank Robbery	10,000
Conventional Bank Embezzlement	19,000
Computer-Related Embezzlement	430,000

Source: National Bureau of Standards

FIGURE E1.2

Average amount stolen in various types of crime, 1976.

gram. An unchanged version was kept in the program documentation library for appearances.

Harold Johnson was a typical computer criminal. He was also caught.

What Is Computer Crime?

No one knows for sure how many computer crimes have occurred. In an excellent book entitled *Crime by Computer,* Donn Parker estimates that $300 million is lost each year through computer crime. Figure E1.2 shows that in 1976, an average of $430,000 was lost per computer crime.

There are many stories of computer crime. Some seem absurd. It's hard to tell what is fact and what is fiction. However, the following three cases have been well documented.

Pacific Telephone

Jerry Schneider was a child prodigy who developed his own telecommunications system at the age of 10. By the time he was in high school, he had started his own electronics company.

While he was a part-time college student, Jerry found a way to steal electronic equipment from Pacific Telephone. He used a terminal in his home to order parts and not be charged for them. Old computer printouts and other documentation from a Pacific Telephone trash container had provided the correct account numbers, passwords, and procedures.

Jerry had expensive telephone components delivered to his home and other locations. To add excitement, he had the company deliver a $25,000 switchboard to a manhole cover at the intersection of two streets. He picked up the switchboard in the Pacific Telephone truck he bought at a company surplus auction.

Much of the equipment he stole in this way was resold to Pacific Telephone. In fact, he used their own information system to determine what they were low in so he would know what to steal.

Schneider was caught when one of his own employees informed on him. The employee wanted a pay raise and Jerry refused. When he was apprehended,

Former Students Indicted for Altering Grades

JAMAICA, N.Y.—Two former Queens College students—one who had been employed at the school's DP center—were indicted last month on charges of falsifying a total of 154 grades in the computerized records of 19 different students. The alterations allegedly took place from 1974 to 1977, with some students reportedly paying hundreds of dollars for the revised grades.

James Chin, 35, and Tom Tang, 26, voluntarily surrendered to New York police on the day the indictments were announced. At their arraignment later that day, both Chin and Tang plead not guilty.

Both were freed without bail since neither had any prior arrests and since they had voluntarily surrendered. The hearing was adjourned to Jan. 15, when a trial date may be set, according to a spokeswoman for the district attorney's office.

Queens District Attorney J.

Santucci said the indictments of Chin and Tang resulted from an investigation begun last spring by his office's Rackets Bureau and his detective squad, with the assistance of the city Department of Investigation, the Board of Higher Education's Office of General Counsel and the administration of Queens College.

Chin, formerly Queens College's senior computer operator, is employed by Printronics Corp. of America in New York. He was indicted on one count of falsifying business records, first degree; one count of bribe receiving, second degree; two counts of receiving a reward for official misconduct, second degree; and one count of violating a state education law section dealing with unlawful acts in respect to examinations.

Tang, a salesman for Burroughs Corp. in Warrendale Heights, Ohio, was not employed at the college during the period of his alleged crime, but was a student. He has

been indicted on one count of falsifying business records, first degree.

The Chin indictment charges him with 131 grade falsifications on the computer records of 15 students, including himself, and with receiving approximately $300 from one student for whom he falsified 22 grades and $100 from another for whom he falsified 11 grades.

The Tang indictment charges him with arranging for the falsification of 23 grades on the computer records of four students, including himself. Tang did not accept money for his part in the falsifications, according to the spokesman for the district attorney's office, and the 23 grade changes he is charged with arranging are separate from the 131 grade changes allegedly made by Chin. If convicted, Chin could receive a sentence of up to seven years in jail and Tang could get a four-year sentence.

By MARGUERITE ZIENTARA
Computerworld

FIGURE E1.3

Computer crime committed by students

Pacific Telephone did not believe he had stolen as much inventory as he claimed. He said he had stolen $800,000 to $900,000; they said $70,000.

Another famous computer crime concerned the Penn Central Railroad. In the early 1970s, someone modified a freight flow system to send boxcars to a small railroad company outside Chicago. There, the boxcars disappeared!

Apparently, the boxcars were repainted and sold to or used by other railroads. Estimates vary, but approximately 400 boxcars disappeared. Somehow the computer system was modified so that the missing railroad cars were not noticed.

Penn Central Railroad

Equity Funding Corporation

The Penn Central case is mysterious. For some reason, it was in Penn Central's interest to minimize attention to the crime. They refused to acknowledge that the boxcars were stolen. No prosecution occurred. There were rumors that organized crime was involved.

A third famous case also occurred in the 1970s. This large fraud involved the Equity Funding Corporation. Over 20 people were convicted on federal charges. Estimates of losses are as high as $2 billion.

Equity Funding was a conglomerate of companies that specialized in investments and insurance. Top-level management distorted the company's financial situation to lure investors. Also, they created artificial insurance policies.

The media described this crime as modern computer fraud. However, there is some debate about whether it can be blamed on the computer. Most of the criminal activity did not involve the computer. All of the phony accounting was done manually.

The Equity Funding case is very complex. Over 50 major lawsuits were filed. Basically, the fraud was accomplished by inflating the company's reported income. This was done in two ways. First, the company's officers declared income and assets that did not exist. They did this simply by writing them into the financial statements. The firm's auditors were severely criticized for not detecting this activity.

The second way income was inflated did involve the computer. Massive numbers of phony documents were generated by the computer system. These documents were supposed to be valid insurance policies. In fact, they were computer fabrications. The phony policies were sold to other insurance companies for cash.

The system was designed to print only valid policies during auditing. In retrospect, it is amazing that the phony documents were taken at face value. The insurance industry personnel accepted computer-generated documents. It didn't occur to them that the computer could produce phony data.

Types of Computer Crime

These three short stories represent only a few of the ingenious ways people have found to commit crimes with computer help. Most computer crimes fall into one of the five categories shown in figure E1.4.

Sometimes, the input to the computer is manipulated. This was done in the Pacific Telephone case. Other crimes are committed by changing computer programs. This was Harold Johnson's approach and the approach used to maintain the phony data for Equity Funding.

F I G U R E   E 1 . 4

Types of computer crime

Type of Crime
Manipulating computer input
Changing computer programs
Stealing data
Stealing computer time
Stealing computer programs

A third type of computer crime is stealing data. Such data might be the names and address of a company's customers. It might be proprietary designs and plans. Fourth, computer time can be stolen. the criminal either uses the time or sells it to others who may not be aware that the time is stolen. For example, a computer communications system may be used to transmit unauthorized data. In one case, a company's message-switching system was used daily to broadcast racing results.

Finally, computer programs can be stolen. Computer programs are very expensive and time-consuming to produce. They can give a company a competitive edge in the marketplace. Therefore, stealing programs is a criminal act.

The theft of computer data and programs is very hard to detect. Someone can steal data and programs simply by copying the computer program or data files. Since the original is not missing, companies have difficulty knowing that a crime has even been committed.

Many computer crime experts think that the cases we know about are only the tip of the iceberg. Some companies have been victims of crimes and have not acknowledged it. They wanted to avoid adverse publicity. A bank that lost money through computer crime would not want its customers to know.

Businesses do not want to advertise their vulnerability. They may not know how to prevent similar crimes in the future. Certainly, they do not want the crime advertised in the newspaper. Therefore, they do not prosecute.

Figure E1.5 shows 12 warning signs of computer crime. These are characteristics of companies in which crimes have occurred. We hope that in the course of your business career, you will not work for a company that has many of these signs. However, if you do, you should be aware of the possibilities of computer crime.

1. The computer seems to run the company; management just reacts.
2. Management expects computers to solve major existing problems.
3. Management does not (cannot) communicate with the DP staff.
4. Users are told how their systems will be designed.
5. There are no documented standards for the development of new applications or the maintenance of existing ones.
6. Technical management is actively involved in programming and troubleshooting.
7. Programmers are uncontrolled; they can do what they want with the computer.
8. DP staff has easy access to data and to program libraries.
9. Errors occur so frequently that adequate investigation is not possible.
10. Auditors treat the computer like a mysterious black box.
11. Management fails to implement audit recommendations.
12. No DP audits are performed.

Most of the characteristics listed in figure E1.5 indicate poor data processing management. Except for the items concerning audits, every one of these characteristics is a violation of a principle discussed in this text. Good data processing management is needed to build and use systems that are less susceptible to computer crime.

STUDY OBJECTIVES

1. Identify five types of computer crime.
2. Briefly describe one reason companies are reluctant to prosecute computer criminals.
3. List 12 warning signs of computer crime.

PREVENTING COMPUTER CRIME

Unfortunately, there is no such thing as a completely secure computer center. First, computer manufacturers do not provide completely secure computers. A smart programmer can find a way to modify the operating system. Once this is done, computer security features like passwords and account numbers are ineffective.

Second, many data processing departments are so busy just keeping on schedule that they do not adequately monitor computer security. Input to the computer is not as well controlled as it should be. Output is not checked for accuracy and completeness. Also, security issues are not considered when systems are designed or when programs are written. Most organizations take the attitude that computer crime won't happen to them.

Finally, effective security can be costly. It takes time and resources to build a secure system. The system may be more expensive to operate because of security features. If a user must spend half of each working day verifying outputs, then half of the person's salary is spent on security.

Good security on the computer will mean that programs operate more slowly. More instructions must be processed for security functions. Therefore, more computer power will be required.

Most organizations must strike a balance between no security at all and nearly perfect security. How much security is needed depends on the potential loss. An accounts payable system probably needs more security than a system producing company telephone lists.

In *Crime by Computer,* Parker reports a surprising and distressing fact. Most computer crimes are discovered by accident. In some cases, the computer failed and the irregularities were discovered while someone was fixing it.

In other cases, people consistently spent more money than was earned. The source of the additional money was traced back to a computer system. The Internal Revenue Service has caught some of these people not paying taxes on their criminal earnings. The FBI has caught others in illegal gambling activities.

The sad part of this discussion is that few crimes are caught as a result of controls in the computer system. Apparently few systems provide protection against computer crime. However, this need not be the case. Systems can be designed to stop unauthorized activity.

Categories	Related System Component
Management	People/Procedures/Data
Organizational	People/Procedures/Data
Computer Center Resources	Hardware/Programs/Procedures/Data
Input/Processing/Output	Programs/Procedures/Data
Data Administration	Procedures/Data
Systems Development	Programs/Procedures

FIGURE E1.6

Categories of EDP controls

Professionals Call for Tighter Computer Security

The American Institute of Certified Public Accountants has recognized the possibility of computer crime. This organization has issued an official statement—called SAS-3—directing CPAs to be more alert when auditing business computer systems. As a result of this statement, data processing departments and personnel are now under closer scrutiny by auditors.

Groups of auditors and data processing personnel have worked together to develop recommended procedures or controls over data processing operations. In the remainder of this chapter, we will discuss these controls. To show their usefulness, they will be related to the MODREC case.

The term **EDP controls** started with accountants and auditors. EDP is an accounting term that means **electronic data processing.** EDP controls are features of any of the five components of a computer system that reduce the chance of unauthorized activity. Figure E1.6 summarizes the basic categories of EDP controls.

Management Controls

Harold Johnson was dissatisfied with MODREC management. He felt unappreciated. Since his boss was the financial vice-president, Harold was buried in the finance department. Neither he nor anyone else in data processing had access to top management.

Top management did not have access to Harold or data processing. They knew little of what he was doing and had only a limited idea of how data processing operated. They spent considerable money on data processing operations, but they did not know how it was used. In short, there was a large gulf between top-level management and data processing.

Over the years, professionals have learned that such a situation is an invitation to trouble. Senior management should take an active part in the management of the data processing function. This does not mean that they should be in the computer center mounting tapes. However, they should recognize the importance of data processing. They should set the direction and be actively involved in data processing plans.

You may be surprised that this even needs to be said. However, in the past, too many managers have washed their hands of data processing. They have stayed as far away from the computer as possible. Perhaps they didn't understand or were afraid of computing. Perhaps it was because the data processing personnel spoke in strange ways.

So data processing went its own way. In some cases, like Harold's, data processing personnel felt disassociated with the company. They felt rejected and unappreciated. A computer crime could then result.

Senior management can supervise data processing in several ways. First, they can demonstrate an appreciation for and interest in the data processing function. Occasional visits to the computer staff, recognition in a newsletter, and references to data processing in reports are ways of showing interest.

In addition, data processing can be recognized in another important way. Companies can place data processing high in the organizational structure, instead of burying it somewhere in accounting or finance, where senior managers never hear of it. They can make it a department equal with other departments. Figure E1.7 shows two ways that data processing can be placed in a business to gain the attention it deserves.

Next, management should understand the organization's vulnerability to computer crime. Then they can communicate the importance of controls to everyone. As we shall see, controls on the data processing function involve more than just data processing. To encourage other departments to help, management must be very positive about the need for controls.

Another responsibility of management is to form a steering committee. Like the steering committee at Miracle Motors, this group controls data processing development efforts. They receive reports about the project status and make appropriate decisions.

Finally, management can take a role in data processing by requesting and paying attention to periodic operations reports. Management should know how well the computing resources are being used. They should have a feel for how happy or unhappy users are with data processing. They should be aware of the major data processing problems.

Operations reports increase communication between data processing and management. Management control responsibilities are summarized in figure E1.8.

Organizational Controls

Harold Johnson had free access to the computer and all of its resources. When he needed a tape file to determine Joan's account number, he went into the tape library and got it. When he wanted to obtain the pricing program, he instructed the computer to print a copy of it. After he made the changes, Harold put the changed program into the program library. No one checked Harold's authority to do these things.

Organizational controls concern the structure of the company. We have already mentioned that data processing should be equal to other functions. In addition, the company should be structured so that there is separation of authorities and duties.

The MODREC case is a good example of what can happen when there is no separation. Data processing employees had unlimited access to the computer. MODREC should have had at least two categories of data processing personnel: operations and development. These groups could have provided checks and balances on each other.

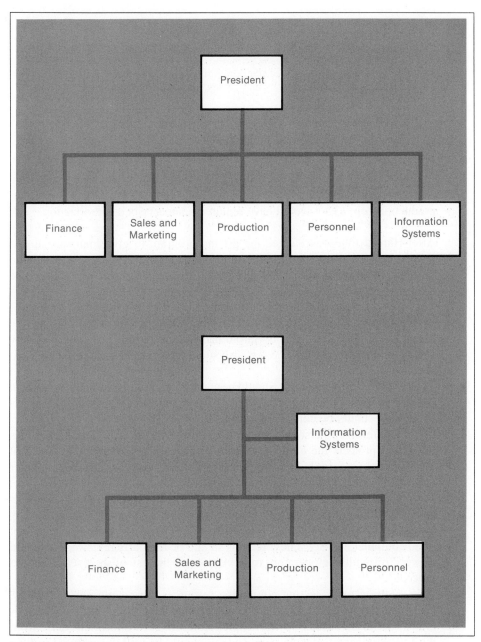

FIGURE E1.7

Two places for the data processing
department in an organization's structure

The operations group would control the equipment and applications programs in use. The development group would create new programs in accord-
ance with requirements. This group would not have access to the stored programs or data.

1. Data processing is placed at high organizational level.
2. Senior management demonstrates knowledge and good attitude toward data processing.
3. Data processing steering committee takes active role in DP.
4. Management requests and reviews periodic reports.

If this had been the case at MODREC, Harold still could have made the changes to the program, but he would not have had the authority to change the production copy. That would have required a supervisor's authorization.

Computer Center Resource Controls

After Harold Johnson changed the pricing program to give Joan special discounts, he wanted to test it. After all, he didn't want to make a mistake and give the discount to the wrong customer. However, to test the change, he needed to mount the customer and price files on the tape drives.

To avoid suspicion, Harold stayed after work the next week. Since none of the managers paid any attention to data processing, no one asked what he was doing. After three short nights Harold had fully tested his program. Not only was he sure it would work, he was also sure no one could trace the changes to him.

Computer center resources should be controlled. Use of computer equipment must be restricted to authorized personnel and records kept on who used what. Processing should be controlled by schedules.

Only authorized personnel should be allowed in the computer room. This restriction protects the equipment from damage. It also helps to ensure that output is delivered only to the right people. Limiting access to the computer room reduces the level of chaos and helps eliminate operator errors.

Computer operations should be controlled as well. Procedures and job schedules should be documented and followed. Operations should be examined by a supervisor to ensure that the procedures are followed. Records should be kept of all computer activity. These records should be regularly reviewed. It should be very difficult for operators to deviate from the established schedule and procedures.

In addition to protecting computing resources during normal operations, plans and procedures must exist to recover from problems. All files and programs should be backed up with copies stored in secure locations away from the computer center. Recovery procedures should be well documented and the staff trained to follow them.

There should also be a disaster recovery plan that explains what to do in case of fire, flood, earthquake, or other disaster. Some organizations should consider having backup hardware and programs available in other locations. The procedures and data necessary to use the hardware should be available in the backup location. Computer center resource controls are summarized in figure E1.9.

1. Access to computer center is controlled.
2. Operating procedures are documented.
3. Program libraries are secure.
4. Backup and recovery procedures exist.
5. There is protection from natural hazards.
6. There are documented emergency procedures.

FIGURE E1.9

Computer center controls

Harold Johnson did not have to modify program input. He found a way to provide special discounts by changing the processing. This process changed only the output. If anyone had ever examined the invoices printed by the pricing program, they would have seen that something was wrong. Luckily for Harold, MODREC had no policy to examine output.

In general, there should be controls over input, processing, and output. First, the authorized form of input data should be documented. The operations personnel should not accept improper input data. Second, data processing personnel should not make changes to input data. These changes are the user's responsibility.

When appropriate, **control totals** should be used. Control totals are calculations made independently of the computer system. They are then used to double-check the accuracy of the figures produced by the computer system.

For example, when users send the weekly payroll to data processing, they should calculate—independently—the sum of the hours worked or a similar total. The payroll program should be written to calculate and print a summary report with the total number of hours worked. The report should be examined by the payroll department after the payroll is run to ensure that the manual and computer-generated totals match.

Similar totals can be kept on changes to other files. Users must be trained to compute these totals and to treat them seriously. They can be the most important control in a computer system.

Input into teleprocessing applications is harder to control. A program must be written to accept only certain input from designated users or locations. However, it is possible to fool such a program. Therefore, the use of terminals must be limited to certain individuals at specified times. The supervisors need to be trained to review their employees' terminal activity.

There must also be controls over the processing of data. As stated earlier, all operating procedures should be documented and followed. The performance of the operators should be monitored.

The operations department should keep records of all errors and system failures. Each correction should be documented. These records should be reviewed by data processing supervisors to determine whether or not the problems could relate to—or cover up—unauthorized activity. These records can also be used to evaluate employee performance and to determine if additional training is needed.

Input, Processing, and Output Controls

379

Category	Type of Control
Input	Documentation of authorized input format Separation of duties and authorities Verification of control totals Online system input controls
Processing	Documented operating procedures Reviews of processing logs Adequate program testing
Output	Documented output procedures Control over disposition of output Users trained to examine output

F I G U R E   E 1 . 1 0

Input/processing/output/controls

Finally, the output from all data processing activities should be controlled. Procedures for distributing output should be documented and followed. Output should be given only to authorized users. Users should examine the output for completeness and accuracy. Control totals should be checked against each other.

Output from online systems is hard to control. When data is changed online, it can be very difficult to trace. For example, a price might be changed several times without producing any written records. The absence of records can make an auditor's job impossible. Consequently, online programs are often programmed to copy each transaction on an **activity log.** This log is a summary of the online activity. The activity log is saved and used to correct errors or for audits. Figure E1.10 summarizes input, processing, and output controls.

Other EDP Controls

Some EDP controls are not oriented toward preventing criminal activity. Instead, their purpose is to encourage effective use of EDP systems. Data administration controls are one example. Controls over systems development are another. We have discussed these controls in other chapters and will not repeat them here. Needless to say, they are important to system designers and auditors. If you make either of these professions your career, you will learn more about them.

MODREC: The End of the Story

Harold Johnson and Joan Everest were able to continue their crime for 18 months. During that time, they obtained $150,000 worth of records for $22,500. The crime would have gone on longer, except for a change of MODREC management.

A new president was hired and he expected better performance from the entire company. As part of his improvement program, the sales force was required to increase sales. When one of the new sales managers reviewed the performance of the region covering Joan's store, he detected something suspicious. It seemed that the volume of sales should have netted larger income. He examined the sales invoices over the last year and saw what was going on. He contacted the new president and the game was up.

Harold was actually relieved. The strain of the crime had begun to wear on him. He was also frustrated. He liked to brag about his creations and he wanted to tell his friends about the crime. He thought it was clever and wanted credit for it.

MODREC threatened to sue for damages, but a settlement was made out of court. Harold and Joan paid MODREC $50,000 and Joan turned over a sizable part of her record inventory. Surprisingly, Harold had all but a few hundred dollars of the money Joan had paid him. He really was not in it for the money.

Criminal action was taken. Since both Harold and Joan were first-time criminals, they received light sentences. Each spent 60 days in jail and was fined $5000.

STUDY OBJECTIVES

4. Describe how computer crimes are usually discovered.
5. Define EDP and activity log.
6. List six types of EDP controls.
7. Describe how control totals are used to double-check output accuracy.
8. Briefly describe the four EDP controls oriented toward preventing criminal activity.

SUMMARY

Computer crime is an important issue. Thousands of dollars are lost each year because of it. Five types of computer crime were covered in this chapter: manipulating input, changing programs, stealing data, stealing computer time, and stealing programs.

The characteristics of companies that are vulnerable to computer crime are known. Most of these characteristics reflect bad data processing management and violate the principles of effective data processing discussed in this book.

To prevent crime, organizations need to develop better controls. These controls fall into several areas: management, organizational, computer center resource, input/processing/output, data administration and systems development. While EDP controls cannot eliminate computer crime completely, they can reduce the likelihood of crime.

CHAPTER E2

Computer Industry and Society: Today and Tomorrow

We are on the threshold of a new era. Technological advancements that are on the drawing board today will profoundly affect tomorrow's life-style.

Computers will be a part of this change. They will be an integral part of a new generation of consumer products. Computer use will be interwoven into many activities at work and at home.

The exciting thing about these changes is that they feed upon themselves. One technological breakthrough leads to another. For example, early work with integrated circuits led to the development of the hand-held calculator and digital wristwatch.

TECHNOLOGICAL TRENDS

The impact that rapid change has on society leads some people to complain about "runaway technology." They fear that the social impact of many new advancements will not be given enough thought. Currently, the robotics industry is the focus of this type of analysis.

In the long run, an in-depth analysis is good for any new industry. This is especially true for the computer and electronics industries, which are experiencing explosive growth.

Two Old Friends Meet Again

Peter Clark passed through security clearance with a minimum of trouble. His work in robotics over the last 11 years had brought him into constant contact with many types of security systems.

The hallway opened up into a huge building complex. This was the research and manufacturing facility of the Krasnor Aircraft Company. They were designing the navy's newest generation of weather satellites.

Several classified projects were being assembled in the large hangar Pete entered. It took him another 15 minutes to walk to the area that housed three massive robotic arms. Pete was Krasnor's design expert and had come to inspect the partially built arms.

As Pete neared the area, a uniformed man stood to greet him. Chief Petty Officer John LaFriend had been assigned to the project as one of the navy's technical experts. The two high school friends had taken different career paths to get to this point in time. Not surprisingly, computers were the common denominator in the work they did now.

Computer-Supported Services

Pete, John, and the others have grown up with computer technology. As their needs became more sophisticated, so did the computer's abilities to support these needs. Let's examine several computer-supported services that are affecting our lives today and certainly will tomorrow.

Information Utilities

The growing number of personal computers has brought about a variety of support services. Some of these services allow the owners of small computers or terminals to access data in large, remote data bases. Like the gas and electric companies, these **information utilities** charge for their services.

Users pay for access to data from the information utility through a minimum monthly fee, usage charge, and/or initiation fee. The usage charge is based on the time of day and connect time. Accessing the data base during business hours—called prime time—costs the most, while evening, early morning, and

weekend hours cost less. Users usually receive a password and user documentation for the system after paying the initiation fee.

Access to these systems can be through telephone lines, cable-TV, or communications satellites. All the user needs is a personal computer or terminal, a communications control program, and a modem.

Once connected to the system, the user identifies what is wanted and the computer searches through the data to find the requested information. These services provide greater flexibility than newspapers, magazines, and other sources of information. Some systems will even let users leave messages for others, write programs, and store data.

Information utilities, like other sources of information, provide different types of information. Some specialize in a single service, like stock market information, while others provide a wide range of capabilities. These services include national and international news; reference sources from magazines, journals, and encyclopedias; games; electronic mail; banking; catalog shopping; and travel information.

FIGURE E2.2

Information utilities provide a wide variety of services (Courtesy Compuserve)

FIGURE E2.3

Accessing information utility at home (Courtesy AT&T)

1. Stock Market Closings
2. News
3. Reference Sources
4. Games
5. Electronic Mail
6. Home Banking
7. Catalog Shopping
8. Travel Reservations
9. Weather

VIEWTRON/WEATHER   4b

FIVE-DAY FORECAST/MIAMI

DAY	FRI	SAT	SUN	MON	TUE
HI F/C	75/24	70/21	75/24	80/27	80/27
LO F/C	70/21	65/18	70/21	70/21	75/24
RAIN %	30-40	80-90	30-40	10-20	10-20

The leading edge of a cold front will bring some thundershowers Saturday

FIGURE E2.4

Several services provided by information utilities, and an example of a weather report (Courtesy Knight-Ridder Newspapers, Inc.)

Working at Home

The ability to access information networks has forced a lot of people to re-evaluate how work will be done in the future. Already, some people's work takes them away from the office. For example, traveling salespeople work away from the office when they are covering their territories. With the ability to link people together through computer networks, it is now feasible to allow others to work away from the office.

Some professionals, like computer programmers, can work at home using a personal computer. Electronic mail systems allow them to keep in touch with the office. This type of flexibility has special appeal to workers with small children. The ability to work at home allows them to raise a family without sacrificing their careers.

The idea of people working at home is not new. Before the industrial revolution, most farmers and crafts people worked out of their homes. Historians refer to this as **cottage industry.** The futurist Alvin Toffler coined the term **electronic cottage** in his book *The Third Wave*, referring to people working with computers at home instead of at the office or factory.

Entertainment

Harold Johnson once again found himself in a tight spot. The dense jungle was alive with fearsome sounds. He could see only a few feet in any direction and was low on ammunition. Moving slowly ahead with his gun cocked and ready, he heard only the faint whisper of a heavy object falling through the trees from behind. That was enough. Harold wheeled right and fired a single shot. He couldn't afford to waste any ammunition.

Harold's single shot was enough. He bagged his second black panther of the day—worth 500 points—and was well on his way to the forgotten diamond mine. There would be other obstacles ahead, but he wasn't worried. Harold had programmed the game.

The 60 days Harold spent in jail gave him some badly needed time to think. He realized that his criminal record was going to make it difficult to get another

Harold on the hunt

computer-related job in business. It was time for him to take stock of himself. He thought about past mistakes and forced himself to remember past successes.

This was the first time in years that Harold had an opportunity to relax and think without the pressures of an ever-present deadline. Harold's old love for video games and new understanding of computer technology came together as an idea for a new arcade game.

The result was a new 360°, three-dimensional adventure game called Survival. The player could either sit or stand inside the game. The images were projected all around the player and on the ceiling. The game was an instant success when it hit the market.

Those in the entertainment industry, especially electronic game manufacturers, have been instrumental in bringing computer technology home. There is no reason to suspect that they will not continue to do so.

The next generation of electronic games will make better use of sound, color, and three-dimensional images. Information utilities currently let players from around the country challenge one another at various games. In some cases, teams of players compete, with the computer acting as moderator or referee. New game programs will be more sophisticated.

Another service that information utilities may provide in the future is the ability to review movies or games before purchase. If consumers like what they see, they can downline load the movie or game to their personal computer or video recorder. The utility will then bill them for the movie or game.

Computer technology has also been transferred to amusement parks. Besides helping with the business functions, computers are controlling the rides and animated characters that inhabit these parks.

In Walt Disney World's Epcot Center, computer technology has become the focus of attention. At Epcot's computer central, visitors receive a demonstration of the role computers are playing in their lives now and in the future.

The banking industry has developed a communications network that will help minimize the work involved in transferring money between banks. The **Electronic Funds Transfer (EFT)** system is having a major impact on society.

The existing checking and banking system is expensive to operate. Consider this example. Suppose you live and bank in New York and have a grandmother who lives and banks in Los Angeles. When she sends you a check as a birthday present, the processing shown in figure E2.6 occurs.

Much of this processing involves physically handling the check. People are needed for data entry, sorting, distributing, and mailing. Since people's time is expensive, the process is expensive.

Electronic Funds Transfer

Several schemes have been proposed to reduce the expense of transferring funds. Some people have recommended a **cashless society.** Instead of using physical checks, we would make all our purchases as electronic transactions.

Individuals and businesses would have national account numbers. When someone wanted to make a purchase, the merchant would input both the customer's account number and the store's account number along with the amount of the purchase. This amount would be electronically deducted from the customer's account and added to the store's account—minus a processing charge. This is an extension of the VISA and MasterCard systems.

Deposits would be handled the same way. When workers were to be paid, their employers would make electronic deposits to employee accounts. At the same time, the employer's account would be reduced.

If this system were operational, there would be no obvious need for money. This could lead to a cashless society. In such a society, checks and money would be eliminated. All purchasing and payments would be handled electronically.

A Cashless Society

Other forms of EFTS have been proposed. **One-way checks** would be physically moved only to the bank of first deposit. In figure E2.6, that would be your bank in New York. The check would not physically go beyond step 3. Your bank would create an electronic transaction that would speed up steps 4 through 11. Canceled checks would not be returned. Instead, your grandmother

One-Way Checks

Step	Processing Action

1. Your grandmother deposits money in her Los Angeles checking account for your birthday present.

2. She writes a check and encloses it in your birthday card.

3. You deposit the check in your New York bank.

4. The New York bank deposits the check for credit in the Federal Reserve Bank of New York.

5. The Federal Reserve Bank in New York sends the check to the Federal Reserve Bank in Los Angeles for collection.

6. The Federal Reserve Bank in Los Angeles forwards the check to your grandmother's Los Angeles bank. The amount of the check is deducted from her checking balance.

7. Grandma's Los Angeles bank tells the Federal Reserve Bank in Los Angeles to deduct the amount of the check from its deposit account.

8. The Los Angeles Federal Reserve Bank pays the New York Federal Reserve Bank for the amount of the check.

9. The New York Federal Reserve Bank pays your bank in New York.

10. Your bank credits your account.

11. Grandma's Los Angeles bank photographs the check and sends her the canceled check at the end of the month.

FIGURE E2.6

Existing system for processing checks

would receive a monthly printout of the recorded transactions. This is sometimes called **truncated check flow.**

The one-way check system is a compromise between existing systems and the cashless society. It would save physical processing and yet be similar to the existing system. This similarity is important to bank customers.

There is always some resistance to changing old ways. Research and experience show that people will not regularly use credit cards in place of checks. In January of 1980, Seattle First National Bank had to offer 5 percent discounts to encourage use of its checkless system. Even then the response was hardly overwhelming. People like checks. But in spite of this preference, EFT is even now a part of the way banks do business.

Clearly, there are substantial problems to overcome before these advanced EFT systems become a reality. Congressional hearings have been held on the subject, and it is hoped that most of the problems will be solved before new EFT systems are implemented. In the meantime, don't throw out the family checkbook.

1. Briefly describe an information utility.
2. Identify three ways users pay for access to an information utility.
3. List eight services provided by information utilities.
4. Briefly explain the "electronic cottage."
5. Describe three entertainment uses of computers.
6. Identify four ways the next generation of computer games will improve.
7. Define EFT and one-way checks.
8. Briefly describe how a cashless society would work.

Work is already in progress on the development of the next generation of computers. Computer scientists around the world are researching new hardware and software ideas that will eventually merge to become **fifth-generation computer** systems.

Artificial Intelligence

One of the most fascinating areas of research is the effort to build machines that think. The capability of these machines goes beyond the logical and arithmetic activity normally associated with computers. In some ways, these machines appear humanlike.

"The brain," said Marvin Minsky of the Massachusetts Institute of Technology (MIT), "happens to be a meat machine." Many scientists agree with this philosophy. Some take it one step further. If the brain is a machine, then it may be possible to build an electronic machine that has the same or even greater capability.

Computer scientists around the world are building systems that can learn from experience and are able to apply this information to new situations. This area of research is called **artificial intelligence.**

Early Work in Artificial Intelligence

Research in artificial intelligence began in the mid-1950s. Results were slow at first. There were early programs that could play easy games like tic-tac-toe. There were also programs that could play reasonable games of checkers.

Promises were made that there would soon be chess-playing programs, but this was overly optimistic. Respectable chess-playing programs have only recently become available.

Language translation was also harder than expected. In the 1950s people said it would only be a short time until computers could translate English into another language, like French. However, they discovered that human language is very complex.

Early **language translators** simply substituted a word in one language for an equivalent word in another. With this procedure the phrase "The spirit is willing but the flesh is weak" was translated to "The booze is good, but the meat is rotten." One scientist said that programs had to be taught that when Mary had a little lamb, she didn't have it for lunch!

The attempt to translate human language by computer led to a greater understanding of language. New language theories resulted from this work. Today, there are programs that can do limited forms of translation.

391

FIGURE E2.7

Chess-playing computers (Courtesy Bruce Helm/U.S. Chess Federation)

Conversational Computers

One subset of artificial intelligence is oriented toward simulating human conversation. In 1963 at MIT, Dr. Joseph Weizenbaum decided to build a system that would simulate the conversation between a psychoanalyst and a patient.

Weizenbaum's program was called ELIZA. This program was enhanced by Dr. Kenneth Colby and renamed DOCTOR. The following conversation between DOCTOR and a distinguished foreign visitor was reported:*

Doctor: Good afternoon. Please type in your name.
(This visitor typed his name.)

Doctor: What brought you here to see me today?

Visitor: Oh, nothing much. I'm feeling a bit tired, that's all.

Doctor: Why do you think you're feeling a bit tired?

Visitor: Well, I've been traveling a lot and away from home.

Doctor: Tell me about your family.

According to Ms. McCorduck, the conversation continued in a personal manner. Even though the visitor knew he was talking with a machine, he continued to reveal his personal fears and concerns.

Scientists debate whether this program has any therapeutic value. Weizenbaum says it does not. He says that he wrote it only to simulate conversation. Others think it may provide some therapy.

The work in artificial intelligence continues. Many of the problems have been more difficult than anticipated. A keen appreciation for the human mind has resulted.

Many experts, especially in Japan, think that the development of artificial intelligence is central to the next generation of computers. Based on this belief, Japanese industry and government have launched a concentrated effort to develop the next computer generation.

---

*From *Machines Who Think* by Pamela McCorduck, San Francisco: W. H. Freeman, 1979, p. 254.

In 1981, the Japanese government pooled resources with eight of the country's largest electronic firms to create a fifth-generation computer. The Institute for New Generation Computer Technology was formed to develop the hardware and software technology needed to complete the project by 1992.

The institute's goal is to design a machine that can perform the following:

- Accept spoken instructions along with traditional forms of input
- Use graphic images—like diagrams and photographs—for input
- Collect, select, and store useful data given newspapers, books, tape-recorded speeches, and other common sources of data
- Translate foreign languages
- Research and provide answers to questions by using all available data
- Learn from its own experience
- Program itself

To achieve this goal, the Japanese want to build upon artificial intelligence research. Two applications that will incorporate these concepts are language translators and **expert systems.**

Expert systems also go by the name **knowledge engineering** in Japan or **knowledge-based systems** in the United States. These systems are built around large databases for specialized topics, such as medical diagnosis or molecular genetics.

These databases take the capability of database management system one step further. They not only contain data and data relationships, but also contain instructions on how to use them—the knowledge base.

An expert system is the application of artificial intelligence. New conclusions are drawn from the database and added to this knowledge base. Through its own efforts, the computer system becomes more intelligent. The idea is to design an expert system that can draw from a wide variety of specialized data. The user would simply need to ask the right question.

To support the large databases and processing speeds needed by these systems the development of new hardware is required. The state-of-the-art large-scale integrated circuits must now advance one step further.

Fifth-generation computers will integrate independent processing hardware into one machine. Some computers already have several control and arithmetic/logic units processing instructions at the same time. This is called **parallel processing.**

These advanced computers will contain thousands of chips. In turn, each chip will contain processing hardware, memory, communication links, and other circuits. The challenge is to combine all these chips with the other components of a computer system.

Work is also under way in the United States to develop fifth-generation computers. While the research and development (R & D) is not coordinated by the government as it is in Japan, the U.S. government does play a role.

Latest generation of very large scale
integrated circuits manufactured in USA
(Courtesy Trilogy Systems Corporation)

The Department of Defense had been the driving force behind the R & D of several computer-based technologies. In particular, they backed the early work on artificial intelligence. Communication between artificial intelligence researchers was supported by the Department of Defense's Advanced Research Projects Agency (ARPA). ARPA is a telecommunications network that connects research computers.

The expert systems being developed in the United States and elsewhere are based on this early research in artificial intelligence. In the United States, expert systems are being developed independently at universities and private companies.

At least three problems confront researchers developing expert systems. First, they need to develop the software that can make assumptions based on a given set of data.

Second, they need to collect the data. Creating an "expert" system means identifying all the knowledge—data and data relationships—an expert uses to make decisions. The identification of this data is not easy. The identification of relationships is even harder. Often, the experts cannot describe all the data they use to make decisions. Their expertise is based on years of experience and the ability to interrelate these experiences.

The third problem relates to hardware. The programs used in an expert system require access to huge databases and many cross-references between data. Fourth-generation hardware, as fast as it is, may not adequately handle the processing needs of sophisticated expert systems. A new generation of hardware will have to be developed, providing users with faster response time.

Solutions to these problems are being sought in several countries. Those that find the solutions will have the upper hand in coming years. They will be the knowledge brokers of the world.

9. Define artificial intelligence and parallel processing.
10. List seven characteristics of Japan's proposed fifth-generation computer.
11. Describe an expert system.
12. Identify three problems in developing expert systems.

NEGATIVE ASPECTS TO USING COMPUTERS

Unfortunately, the impact of computers has not been entirely positive. There have been social costs to the application of computer technology. These are summarized in figure E2.9.

Some aspects of computing have lowered the quality of life. First, computers have eliminated jobs. While it is true that they have created other jobs, these new jobs are not always available to the people whose jobs were eliminated.

In addition, computers have changed the environment of business activities. To some extent, business has become impersonal. People are frequently treated as numbers instead of human beings.

Actually, this treatment should not be blamed on computers. Computers do not make business more impersonal. People do. Blaming the computer is like placing the blame for murder on the weapon.

However, some people will always use the computer as a scapegoat. But the next time someone says, "The computer won't let me do that," why not ask "Who programmed the computer?"

Improper Use Of Computers

In addition to the disadvantages already mentioned, there is also the problem of computer abuse. The abuse stems from two sources: improper data handling and bad systems design.

Data is relatively easy to collect and store. Once data is in magnetic form, billions of characters can readily be sent from one computer to another—across the nation or across the world. The data doesn't wear out either. It doesn't fade with time as people's memories do.

Under these conditions, it is hard to have any privacy. If someone defaults on a home mortgage, a record of the default may be distributed across the nation. It may be available to credit bureaus for years.

Lenders may consider this capacity an advantage, but many people do not. People change and grow. Some people feel that we all have something in our past we would prefer to forget. With computer technology, forgetting about the past may be impossible.

FIGURE E2.9

Social costs of computing

1. Elimination of jobs
2. Impersonalization of business
3. Human abuse caused by
   Improper data handling
   Poor systems design

In addition, the potential for unwanted government control is tremendous. It is technically possible to gather data about the earning and spending habits of every person in the nation. With EFT, it is possible to prohibit certain people from making certain purchases or from living in certain areas or from working at certain jobs.

Dangers in Using Bad Data or Misusing Good Data

Perhaps the most common abuse occurs when computer systems produce inaccurate information. There are many stories about people who have been refused employment or credit. Some people have had these problems because their records were in error or they were confused with someone having the same name. The individuals who learned about such errors were the lucky ones. The unlucky ones did not receive the job or credit and never knew why.

Sometimes, people are abused by computers when they are unable to obtain services they need or desire. There are cases of utility companies terminating service to homes because computer systems incorrectly "figured" that the bills were overdue.

The worst abuse may develop when computers are used to intimidate people. Computer-generated letters that look and sound official sometimes cause people to do things that they are not required to do. People who do not know their rights or who do not know how to deal with computer errors are likely victims.

All such cases of systems abuse are preventable. When they occur, they reflect poor systems design or personnel errors. The computer is almost never at fault. The problems lie with incomplete or inaccurate procedures or poorly trained personnel.

STUDY OBJECTIVE

13. Briefly describe three social costs of computing.

CONTROLLING COMPUTER IMPACT

Computers have the capacity to be a boon to humankind and to help us solve our greatest difficulties. However, they also have the capacity to be destructive, to limit personal freedom, and to eliminate personal privacy. How can we best obtain the benefits of computer technology while minimizing the dangers?

Consumer Knowledge

First, the greatest strength we have is knowledge. As you take courses like this one, you will learn what computer systems should be. You will also learn what the dangers of computer technology are and what we can do to avoid these pitfalls. Never underestimate the power of education.

We hope you will not believe anyone who says, "The computer won't let me." If you hear that statement, let the supervisors know you are aware that people often hide behind the computer to avoid responsibility. Encourage them to take control over their organization. Computers are not supposed to be dictators. They are supposed to be servants.

As more people learn how to deal with computers, they will exercise more power as consumers. They will learn to observe the quality of computer service and will choose to do business with companies that have good systems. As time passes, competition in the marketplace will eliminate companies that operate substandard computer systems.

Legislation will also help to eliminate computer abuse. Several laws have already been passed. The **Fair Credit Reporting Act of 1970** gives individuals the right to see credit data that is maintained about them. This act stipulates that people can challenge the credit data and that the data must be changed if it is wrong. The **Freedom of Information Act of 1970** gives individuals access to data collected by government agencies.

Another law gives citizens rights with respect to data gathered by the government. The **Privacy Act of 1974** stipulates that individuals must be able to learn what information the government collects about them. The government must also state what the data will be used for. Figure E2.10 shows the form used to request information from the Social Security Administration.

According to this act, data gathered for one purpose cannot be used for a different purpose without permission of the individual. In addition, individuals have the right to have wrong data changed. Finally, this act clearly puts the responsibility for maintaining correct data on the organization that keeps it. The responsibility for ensuring that data is not misused lies with the government.

Unfortunately, this act applies only to government agencies. Legislation that applies to private organizations is yet to be adopted. Some states have passed such legislation and others are considering it. Such laws are not popular with many businesses because the cost of compliance will be high.

Knowledge and legislation are the tools we have to control the impact technology has on society. As citizens, we have the responsibility to make our voices heard when abuses occur. We can do this through consumer power and by knowing and insisting on our rights.

If you become involved with the design or operation of computer systems, you will have the opportunity to ensure that the system is responsibly designed and used.

STUDY OBJECTIVES

14. List two means of controlling computer impact.
15. Briefly describe the rights defined by the Fair Credit Reporting Act of 1970, the Freedom of Information Act of 1970, and the Privacy Act of 1974.

SUMMARY

Technological advancements are in the making today that will change the way we live tomorrow. Computer-supported services like information utilities and electronic funds transfer speed up the interchange of ideas and reduce paperwork. Some people are working at home with personal computers. Many leisure activities like games and amusement parks use computers.

REQUEST FOR STATEMENT OF EARNINGS
(PLEASE PRINT IN INK OR USE TYPEWRITER)

FOR SSA USE ONLY
AX
SP

I REQUEST A SUMMARY STATEMENT OF EARNINGS FROM MY SOCIAL SECURITY RECORD

NH Full name you use in work or business

First	Middle Initial	Last

SN Social security number shown on your card

Your date of birth

DB | Month | Day | Year | **A**

MA Other Social Security number(s) you have used

Your Sex

SX ☐ Male ☐ Female

AK Other name(s) you have used (Include your maiden name)

PRIVACY STATEMENT

The Social Security Administration (SSA) is authorized to collect information asked on this form under section 205 of the Social Security Act. It is needed so SSA can quickly identify your record and prepare the earnings statement you requested. While you are not required to furnish the information, failure to do so may prevent your request from being processed. The information will be used primarily for issuing your earnings statement.

I am the individual to whom the record pertains. I understand that if I knowingly and willingly request or receive a record about an individual under false pretenses I would be guilty of a Federal crime and could be fined up to $5000.

Sign your name here: (Do not print)	Date

I AUTHORIZE YOU TO SEND THE STATEMENT TO THE NAME AND ADDRESS BELOW: *(To be completed in all cases)*

PN Name of the addressee

AD Street number and name

City and state	**ZP**	Zip Code

Form **SSA-7004 PC** OP 3 (9-82) Previous Editions are Obsolete

FIGURE E2.10

Request for social security summary of earnings

The next computer generation will bring us computers that think. Even now, expert systems using the latest hardware technology are helping specialists solve problems. The developers of these systems will become the knowledge brokers of the world. They will bring the knowledge revolution to full life.

However, people should not be blindly led into this knowledge revolution. They must be alert to some of the negative aspects of using computers. Some jobs will be eliminated. Organizations could become more impersonal. Abuses using computers will occur unless people are concerned enough to stand up for their rights.

To prevent runaway technological growth, people will have to be knowledgeable about these changes and support legislation that will control its impact on society.

CHAPTER E3

The Next Step: Education and Careers in Computing

There is a saying that "there is only one constant in life . . . change." It is appropriate for the computer industry in the next decade. Those of us who want to grow with the rapid advancements in computer technology must understand that education will be an important part of our lives.

We use the term education in the broadest sense. Education can be on-the-job training or attendance at professional seminars. It can also mean going back to school for advanced degrees. One way or another, new ideas and skills are needed to prosper in tomorrow's job market.

EDUCATION

There will come a time when you will need to know more about a new applications package, operating system, piece of hardware, or design technique. The best way to get this additional knowledge is to go to a source with the necessary information. This source could be a book, a videotape, a computer program, or another person. Sometimes, a more structured method of learning is needed.

Several educational options are available. Each helps you make the most of your study time.

On-the-Job Training

New employees are often assigned to an experienced employee when they start a job. The experienced employee will show them how the job is done and where to go for help. Eventually, the new employees can do the job themselves. The experienced employee can then supervise, making sure that everything is done correctly. Later, the new employees will be left on their own. They will be responsible for getting the job done correctly and on time.

Seminars and Conferences

When new equipment or techniques are brought into an organization, there might not be an "experienced" employee to help train people. Sometimes the organization sends selected people to training seminars or conferences. In other cases, speakers are brought in-house to provide the training.

A **training seminar** concentrates on a single topic. It can last from a few hours to several weeks. In many ways, seminars are like formal schooling. There are lectures, demonstrations, and materials to read. However, the participants are usually not tested or graded.

Conferences usually concentrate on broader subjects. Many speakers discuss different aspects of a subject over several days. Presentations at conferences are usually one to two hours long, and several can occur at the same time. There is often a special area where salespeople set up demonstrations for related products.

Vocational Training

When individuals need new job skills, they can acquire them through **vocational training.** A vocational school usually provides training for entry-level jobs. These jobs do not require prior work experience.

Many school districts, community colleges, and private institutions provide vocational training. These training programs emphasize hands-on experience. Although students attend lectures and have reading assignments, much of their time is spent working with equipment.

Seminars as a source of on-the-job training (Courtesy George Riley)

When you shop around for a vocational school, ask if the school is accredited, has a job placement service, and provides on-the-job or co-op experiences. These features are not required, but they can help when looking for a job. If possible, talk to former students and ask them about the school's training program.

Military Service

The armed forces also provide vocational and technical training. For example, figure E3.2 shows a young recruit training in the navy. New recruits can request special training as part of enlistment contracts. A number of military programs even allow individuals to continue their formal education while in the service.

In many instances, the education people receive in the service is useful after they are discharged. This training provides on-the-job experiences that employers like. Colleges and universities will even award college credit for some of these experiences. In addition, the armed forces provide educational assistance programs for people who wish to continue their formal education after leaving the service.

Two-Year College Programs

Community or junior colleges provide associate degrees for two years of college-level training. These institutions offer both vocational and transfer programs. The objective of a vocational program is to provide the necessary training for a job after graduation. A two-year transfer program is designed to be the first part of a four-year bachelor's degree.

403

Two-year colleges are usually located near a student's home. The idea is to let the student take advantage of the college's lower tuition while living at home.

After receiving their associate degree, students can transfer to a four-year college or university to complete their bachelor's degree. Most two-year colleges offer associate degrees in areas that match programs offered at four-year colleges. Special care should be taken to ensure that classes will transfer to the four-year college. Counselors at both schools can provide such information.

Four-Year College Programs

Universities and four-year colleges award bachelor's degrees in arts or science. To obtain a bachelor's degree, a student must specialize in particular fields of study in addition to taking required courses.

A student's fields of specialization are called **majors** and **minors.** A major will require more class work than a minor. Most bachelor's degrees require at least one major and one minor.

To receive a major or a minor in a subject area, students must take a required group of classes. In addition, they select several **electives.** Electives are a set of optional classes from which the student can choose. Students either select electives recommended by their faculty advisor or get permission to attend other classes.

Three different types of computer-related majors are found at four-year colleges: **computer science, computer engineering,** and **information systems.** Most schools also offer minors in these areas. These majors may be called by different names at various schools. Whatever the titles, they represent three distinct areas of study.

Computer Science

The course work in a computer science major concentrates on the working relationship between computer hardware and system software.

JAMES STULZ
Lab Tutor/Computer Science Major

RESPONSIBILITIES

Actually, they call me a "software consultant," but what I do is help students with their computer assignments and any problems they are having with the system. I'm a senior, majoring in computer science. There is no information systems or business department on campus—just computer science. The students here are very fortunate. They receive a free access account to use one of the VAX computer terminals. We also have a number of micros that are used for computer graphics courses and the introductory BASIC and PASCAL courses. I need to know quite a bit about both the hardware and software on campus

MY BACKGROUND

After a year at a junior college, I enrolled here as a chemistry major. I learned to use the computer pretty much on my own. I used various software packages on the system for my chemical analysis assignments. When I was a sophomore I answered an ad on a bulletin board for a job as computer operator in the computer center. That really helped. I had access to a lot of help and advice for the first computer science course I was taking, and then later on for many other courses.

I was bored with chemistry. Computers were more exciting. In high school I was a B student, but I didn't try very hard. I tested as a strong aptitude in math. In junior college I took an introduction to data processing course that emphasized history, number systems, and hardware. It wasn't very helpful though, because we never had an understanding of systems and applications, or what it takes to use computers.

SKILLS REQUIRED

For computer science, math aptitude is important. Or at least you have to have an interest in games or game theory, probability, logic, and that stuff. Applications such as computer graphics, which are exciting, actually require understanding matrices, functions, and other math. Here you concentrate on one of four areas within computer science: (1) straight computer science, emphasizing software development; (2) artificial intelligence; (3) coding theory and applied algebra; and (4) heavy mathematics with some computer science.

MY FUTURE

Society is changing. A couple of years ago, everyone thought the computer science students were strange. Now it seems to be the way to go. One thing I like is the flexibility of the hours and, of course, the money. All my friends that graduated last year got jobs—ranging from $24,000 to $30,000. I'm interviewing companies now. I'm from Hawaii, and I would really like to get back to a warmer climate.

Computer Science (CS)

Computer Science is the study of the uses of digital computers for the effective processing of information. Degree programs offered are primarily concerned with the uses of computers (software aspects) rather than the physical construction of computers (hardware aspects). Several introductory courses in computer programming are offered as well as complete programs which provide a major or minor in computer science.

Students considering a major or minor in computer science should make an appointment with the departmental office to see an adviser as soon as possible certainly within the second semester the student is enrolled in computer science courses. Eligibility requirements for admittance to a major or minor program are available from a computer science adviser.

Students majoring in computer science are required to complete a minor in mathematics. In addition, students in this program are urged to consider completion of a second minor in some application field of interest to them. Graduates of this program should be qualified for jobs in industry and government as well as in computer consulting and software firms.

The minor in computer science is appropriate for students in a variety of fields. Graduates holding minors should be particularly qualified for applications programming positions in their major areas.

Major

Computer Science Courses		Mathematics Courses	
CS 111 Computer Programming I	3	Calculus through Math 123	8
CS 112 Computer Programming II	3	Math 230 or 374	4
CS 215 Structured COBOL	3	Math 310	3
CS 223 Computer Organization	3	Math 362 or 364	3-4
CS 224 Assembly Language	3	Electrical Engineering	
CS 331 Data Structures & Algorithms	3	EE 250	3
CS 342 Software and File Systems	3		
CS 485 Programming Languages	3	Approved electives can be CS 495, 506, 527, 542, 544, 554, MATH 440, 507, 574, PHIL 520 Electives should be approved in advance by the student's adviser.	
CS 499 Senior Seminar	1		
Approved Electives	6		

Minor

Computer Science Courses		Mathematics Courses	
CS 111 Computer Programming I	3	Math 122 or 200	4
CS 112 Computer Programming II	3	The elective is normally CS 115 or 506. Students in the CSE curriculum may substitute CS 485 for CS 224 in the minor program.	
CS 223 Computer Organization	3		
CS 224 Assembly Language	3		
CS 331 Data Structures & Algorithms	3		
Approved elective	3		

FIGURE E3.3

Portion of a college catalog showing computer science curriculum (Courtesy Western Michigan University)

Students take several programming classes. Depending upon the school, they will learn about file structures, systems development, and operating systems. Students will also be expected to take selected mathematics courses. Figure E3.3 is a portion of a college catalog outlining classes offered as part of a computer science major or minor. Electives can cover a wide range of topics from computer graphics to artificial intelligence or compiler design.

1. On-the-job Training

2. Seminars and Conference

3. Vocational Training

4. Military Training

5. Two-year College Programs
   - Vocational
   - Transfer

6. Four-year College Programs
   - Computer Science
   - Computer Engineering
   - Information Systems

FIGURE E3.4

Educational options

Computer Engineering

Students majoring in computer engineering will learn about the design and development of computer hardware. They will take classes in digital logic, programming, and circuit design. Some computer science courses will be required along with mathematics courses.

Information Systems

The emphasis of an information systems major is on the development and use of computer systems. Students will be expected to supplement computer classes with background courses in business. Different schools may have different names for this major. It can be called computer information systems or management information systems, for example.

As with the other computer majors, students getting an information systems major will take several programming courses. In addition, they will take classes in file organizations, systems analysis, and design, along with database development. Electives vary from distributed processing concepts to data communications and office automation.

Figure E3.4 summarizes the educational options available to people wanting to acquire or update skills.

STUDY OBJECTIVES

1. Identify six options available to those wanting to further their education.
2. Define electives, college major, and college minor.
3. Describe three college degrees related to computer technology.

PROFESSIONAL ORGANIZATIONS

Professional organizations provide a way to get people with the same interests together. These groups also help members update their professional skills by organizing seminars and conferences. Some organizations are even involved in setting professional standards for their members. They do this by identifying skills and ideas that are important to their area of expertise.

There are several professional computer organizations. The Association of Computing Machinery (**ACM**) and Data Processing Managers Association (**DPMA**) are two of the larger organizations. They are actively involved in getting computer professionals together for seminars. Both organizations have identified the skills and ideas that future professionals will need.

The ACM and DPMA support student activities and have student members. These organizations have established model college curricula that include courses each organization considers important for students majoring and minoring in computer science or information systems.

The Institute for Certification of Computer Professionals sponsors a Certificate in Data Processing (**CDP**). To receive a CDP, individuals must pass a five-part examination and have five years of work experience with computerized information systems. Two years of college work can substitute for two years of work experience.

The student must pass all five sections within three years. Once a section has been passed, it does not have to be taken again. If a section is failed, it can be retaken. The five sections of the exam are:

1. Data processing hardware
2. Computer programming and software
3. Principles of management
4. Quantitative methods and accounting
5. Systems analysis and design

Individuals who have received a CDP place these initials following their name to show others their professional certification.

FIGURE E3.5

CDP certificate

408

4. Identify three functions of a professional organization.

5. Describe two ways ACM and DPMA support computer education.

6. Briefly describe how someone can be certified in data processing.

CAREERS IN DATA PROCESSING

Job opportunities in data processing are expanding as people find more uses for computers. Each job has the potential to lead into other job opportunities if individuals perform well and prepare themselves for new responsibilities.

Data Entry Operator

Data entry operators are responsible for transferring data from source documents onto machine-readable media such as cards, tapes, or disks. In some cases, they enter the data directly into the computer for processing.

FIGURE E3.6

Data entry operators (Courtesy Sperry Univac, a Division of Sperry Rand Corporation)

Since these operations are using a keyboard to enter the data, fast and accurate typing skills are necessary. In addition, experience with keypunches, key-to-tape devices, or key-to-disk devices is desirable. To increase their chances for new jobs, some data entry operators are also familiar with the operation of word processing equipment.

Most employers want data entry operators to have at least a high school diploma. Working as a data entry operator is considered an entry-level job. People can receive their training on-the-job or through vocational programs.

Working as a data entry operator could lead to other jobs within an organization, as seen in figure E3.7. Large computer centers often have data entry

FIGURE E3.7

Career paths for computer professionals, part 1

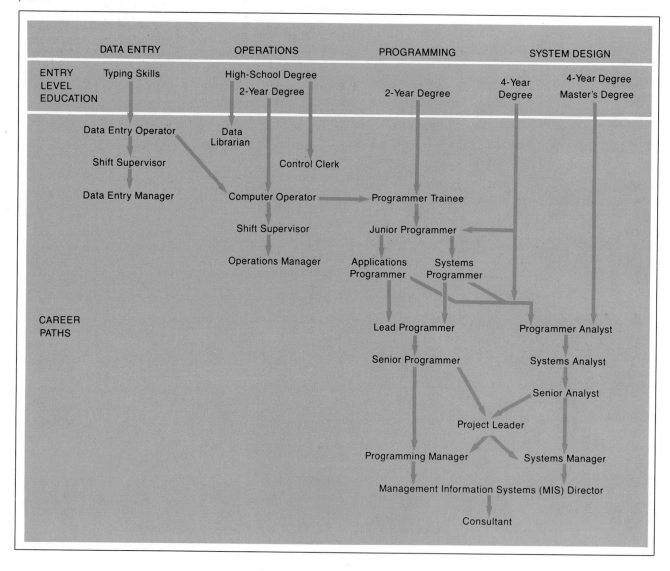

operators working at different times or shifts. Therefore, a **shift supervisor** is needed to assign job responsibilities and oversee data entry operations. When a new shift supervisor is needed, one of the data entry operators is often selected to fill the position.

Control Clerk and Data Librarian

The jobs of **control clerk** and **data librarian** are also considered entry-level positions. These people are responsible for keeping the computer center organized and operating smoothly. Usually, a high school degree is needed for both positions, and training is on-the-job.

Control clerks oversee requests as they come into the computer center. They make sure that reports are sent to the appropriate users. All incoming source documents are recorded by control clerks. They inform the data entry supervisor of upcoming work assignments. They also schedule jobs for processing.

Data librarians are responsible for tapes and disks when they are not in use. They catalog and maintain the storage media and place them in a tape/disk library. Librarians are also responsible for organizing all stored programs and program documentation.

Both positions require organizational skills and the ability to read and write clearly. Control clerks should be friendly, outgoing people because they interact with users.

Computer Operator

In some organizations, data entry operators can be asked to become **computer operators.** Computer operators are usually required to have at least a high school degree and are often expected to have an associate or bachelor's degree. A job in computer operations is also considered an entry-level job.

Computer operators run the computer, mount tapes and disks, load paper into the printer, and troubleshoot any problems that arise. They are given a schedule of when to run programs and are expected to maintain that schedule.

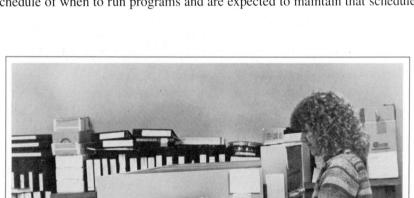

To operate the equipment and maintain production schedules, operators must be able to read manuals and follow written instructions. Good communications skills are needed, since operators must describe problems to service technicians. They can receive their training on-the-job, at vocational schools, or at two-year colleges.

In large computer centers, several operators will work on the same shift. Each will be responsible for one part of the IPO cycle. An **operations supervisor** is also needed to coordinate work during the shift. One of the computer operators is usually promoted to operations supervisor when a position opens (see figure E3.7).

Computer Programmer

Jobs in computer programming will be in demand for some time. Computer programmers are either **applications programmers** or **systems programmers.** Both jobs usually require a bachelor's degree. However, people with associates degrees or on-the-job training have been hired as programmers.

An applications programmer works with a systems analyst and users in defining the IPO cycle for a specific need. The applications programmer then designs the program, writes it in a high-level language, and tests the final results. Bachelor's degrees in information systems are designed to teach skills needed for applications programming.

Systems programmers work behind the scenes designing, writing, and testing systems programs. These programs can be compilers, interpreters, supervisors, or data utilities. Systems programmers often have majors in computer science.

FIGURE E3.9

Computer programmer

As programmers gain more experience, they receive different job titles. These titles vary from organization to organization. If the individuals are trained on-the-job, they have the title **programmer trainee.** After moving out of the training program, they are called **junior programmers.** Programmers who have proved themselves are promoted to **staff programmers.**

The programming profession is a wide-open field to those who have the aptitude for taking complex problems and breaking them down into step-by-step computer instructions. People with physical handicaps are not limited in their advancement opportunities. In addition, programming can be done at home with a terminal or personal computer.

Experienced programmers working in applications development teams will also oversee the work of other programmers on the team. The title of **lead programmer** is reserved for people who supervise the work of others.

Systems analysts will also be in demand. To be effective, systems analysts must be organized and people oriented. They must have excellent communications skills.

To become a systems analyst, a person must have a college degree or work experience. Knowledge of the organization is also vital to the success of any systems analyst. Analysts working for a business often have a business background; those working for an engineering firm have an engineering background; and so forth.

Systems analysts interview users who need output from an organization's computer resources. They then define and design the system. It is their responsibility to perform the feasibility study. In addition, they must keep management informed of the project's status.

If management approves a project proposal, the systems analysts work with programmers to develop and test the system. They help write documentation and train users. Finally, they evaluate the finished system to determine if it is performing as expected.

While systems analysts work with the operations staff in designing a system, they are not involved with the day-to-day operation of the computer. Their job is to prepare the users and the system for operation. After that, the operations staff and maintenance programmers take over. The systems analyst goes on to another project.

Figure E3.7 shows a career path for systems analysts. As with computer programmers, systems analysts will usually have several job titles over many years of work. Experienced systems analysts are often promoted to **senior systems analysts** or possibly **project leader.** Both positions require the analyst to supervise the work of others.

The titles of **engineer** or **technician** are placed on many job descriptions. There are service technicians, electronic technicians, and other jobs involving the repair or assembly of hardware (see figure E3.10). Traditionally, technicians have high school or two-year degrees and are trained on-the-job.

There are also computer engineers, electrical engineers, and other jobs dealing with design and manufacturing. Engineers usually have at least a bachelor's

Systems Analyst

Technician and Engineer

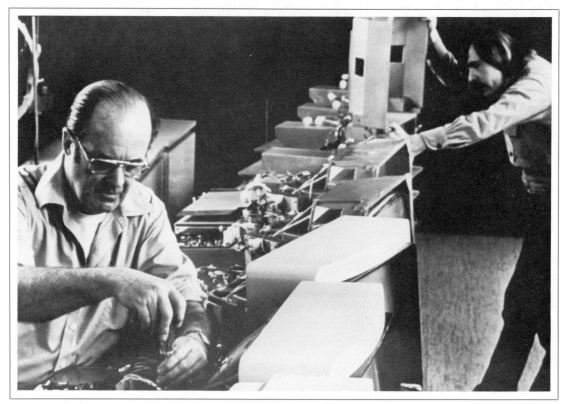

Technicians assembling display terminals
(Courtesy Calcomp, Anaheim, California)

degree. Generally, the difference between the two titles is in the level of education and the amount of responsibility.

Technicians must have good eye-hand coordination to work with instruments and assemble parts. Both technicians and engineers need good reading comprehension for using technical documents. In addition, engineers need to be able to write clearly when organizing design specifications.

Salesperson

A **salesperson's** livelihood is based on his or her ability to match a customer's need with a product. As shown in figure E3.11, a salesperson's career path depends on whether the individual works out of a retail store or a manufacturer's branch office.

In either case, the skills that are needed are not unlike those of systems analysts. In discussing a customer's need, the salesperson must be able to define a system that provides the best solution.

The educational requirements for a salesperson will vary. Some companies will require a college degree. Others are more interested in previous work experience. The ability to communicate with people is of prime importance.

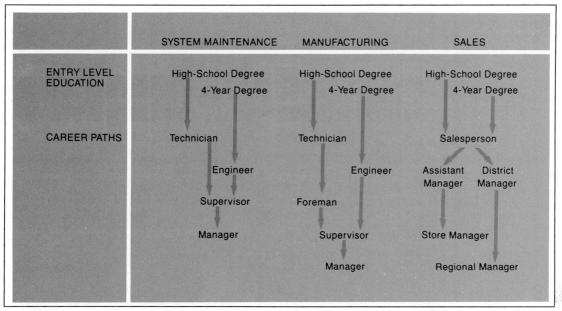

	SYSTEM MAINTENANCE	MANUFACTURING	SALES
ENTRY LEVEL EDUCATION	High-School Degree / 4-Year Degree	High-School Degree / 4-Year Degree	High-School Degree / 4-Year Degree
CAREER PATHS	Technician → Engineer → Supervisor → Manager	Technician → Engineer / Foreman → Supervisor → Manager	Salesperson → Assistant Manager / District Manager → Store Manager / Regional Manager

FIGURE E3.11

Career paths for computer professionals, part 2

Those salespeople who can ask the right questions and then clearly describe their solution will be the most successful.

Managers by definition are people-oriented individuals. Their ultimate responsibility is to make sure that the jobs assigned to them get done correctly, on time, and within budget. To do this, they must be able to work with the people under them.

Sometimes, people who manage other workers have other titles. A technician may report to a foreman. The foreman manages people even though the job title does not say so. Shift supervisors, lead programmers, and project leaders also manage people. Most organizations have several levels of management.

Figures E3.7 and E3.11 identify the management positions for all the jobs previously described. At large computer centers, a data entry shift supervisor reports to the data entry manager. The operations supervisor reports to the operations manager. Senior programmers and systems analysts report to their respective managers. Salespeople report to a store or branch manager.

Management-level personnel are often promoted from related jobs, but not always. While a manager's prior experience and ability to work with people are important, educational background also plays an important role. For some managers, salary and future promotions depend on his or her educational background.

Manager

7. Describe the responsibilities of a data entry operator, a data entry supervisor, a control clerk, a data librarian, a computer operator, an operations supervisor, a computer programmer, a lead programmer, a systems analyst, a technician, an engineer, a salesperson, and a manager.

8. Identify the skills and formal education needed to become a data entry operator, a control clerk, a data librarian, a computer operator, an applications programmer, a systems programmer, a systems analyst, a technician, an engineer, and a salesperson.

9. Briefly describe one possible career path for a newly hired programmer trainee.

10. Identify three possible prerequisites for promotion to a management position.

CAREER PATHS

A job does not make a career. Those of us with an eye toward the future can make the most of work by realizing that our careers will probably be a series of related jobs or a **career path.**

If we identify long-term goals, then we can select a career path that will lead us to those goals. Otherwise, we could wander in circles like someone lost in the woods. Or worse yet, we could stay in the same place because we have nowhere else to go.

Career Paths for Computer Professionals

Career goals are never easy to choose and are certainly subject to change. But having a career goal in mind does help in selecting majors and minors in college. It also helps when we are looking for a new job. Peter Clark and Harold Johnson both followed career paths as computer professionals.

Entry-Level Jobs

People looking for entry-level jobs in data processing can find positions as data entry operators, computer operators, technicians, and programmers. Having career goals will help individuals determine the type of entry-level position they should be seeking. Figures E3.7 and E3.11 outline some potential career paths for computer professionals.

Organizations will have different policies for job advancement. Some like to promote from within. This means that they would rather promote someone currently working for them rather than hire someone new.

In some organizations, it is possible to hire in as a data entry operator and advance into operations, programming, and even systems design. Therefore, during a job interview, it is worthwhile to ask the interviewer about the organization's promotion policies.

Many computer professionals find it to their advantage to periodically move to new jobs in a different organization. After obtaining an entry-level position, they continue their education and after several years move to a new position. Usually, this move is accompanied by a pay increase and a change in job title.

Peter Clark

Pete used his high school degree and interest in machines to acquire an entry-level job as a service technician. His training was on-the-job and through company-sponsored seminars.

FIGURE E3.12

Peter Clark

To improve his chances for promotion, Pete took advantage of the company's educational benefits. These benefits paid for some of the cost of going back to school. Pete initially took classes at a community college close to his home. Later, he finished his engineering degree at a nearby university.

Pete's college degree and good work record helped dictate the next step in his career path. When the company decided to produce industrial robots, Pete became involved in the initial stages of the program. His up-to-date skills in hydraulics and computer technology made him a logical choice.

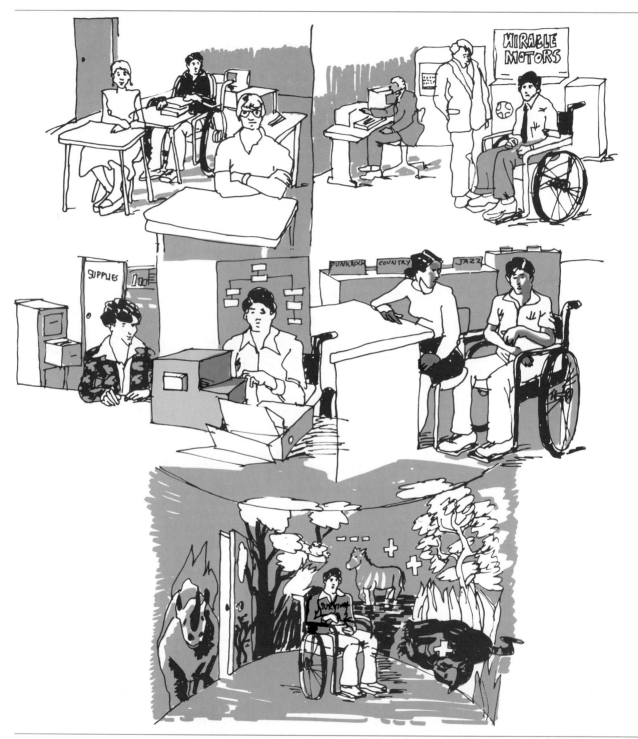

As often happens with successful careers, Pete eventually worked his way into a supervisory position. The company felt that his knowledge and skills could be better used if he were coordinating others instead of doing the work himself. In this new position, Pete was sent to a plant with design specifications and a crew of technicians and engineers. He was responsible for coordinating the activities of these people and troubleshooting any problems.

Pete's next career step will depend on how well he can make the transition from a machine-oriented engineer to a people-oriented supervisor. If he is successful, he will eventually be promoted to the next management-level position.

Another career option for Pete would be to leave the company and become a private **consultant.** Pete's skills are special and in great demand as businesses automate their production facilities. He could sell his services to businesses that need a specialist for designing new systems or troubleshooting special problems with working systems.

Harold Johnson's first career decision was to attend college before looking for a job. While it was expensive, his college education allowed Harold to start at a salary far higher than he could have expected right out of high school.

Not all programmers start as maintenance programmers like Harold. However, companies will evaluate new programmers during the first months on the job, perhaps while the programmers take part in an in-house training program. Programmers will also be evaluated when they become members of an applications development team or maintenance programmers.

Promotion rate and salary are based on the ability to get programs written correctly, on time, and with good documentation. Programmers will also be evaluated on how well they work with users and other professionals.

Harold left his staff programmer position to become a programmer/analyst at MODREC. This was an important career decision for him. Most programmers face the same decision at some time in their career. The decision is whether to stay behind the scenes working as a machine-oriented programmer or to move into a people-oriented systems analyst position.

Unfortunately, Harold's career took a turn for the worse before getting back on the right track. If Harold had stayed in programming, however, any further advancements would have placed him in a supervisory role of some type, perhaps as a lead programmer or a programming manager. A lead programmer or programming manager works with other technical people. As a systems analyst Harold worked with nontechnical users as well.

Figure E3.7 depicts possible career paths for programmers and systems analysts. Individuals can stop at any point along these career paths. Obviously, not everyone can or wants to become a manager. To get the most job satisfaction, people must do a little soul-searching. Those people who like the challenge of computer programming and don't like to supervise others may not want to become a lead programmer or programming manager.

Large computer centers have managers for each job area. These managers report to a **management information system (MIS) director.** Long hours and a fair amount of stress come with this job. Therefore, only a few highly motivated managers will move into this level of management. The MIS director works with the organization's executives in determining long-range plans.

Harold Johnson

FIGURE E3.14

Sue McKnight

Consulting is another career option available to highly motivated computer professionals. To be successful, a consultant must be able to work well with people. Happy clients are a consultant's best advertisements. Since consultants jump from one job to the next, they must be organized enough to have a steady stream of clients. Time between jobs represents periods of no income.

Harold put his computer skills and creativity into his own video game. People who organize and manage their own businesses are called **entrepreneurs.** To be successful, they must have financial backing and organizational skills. Often, groups of investors will support new businesses and help manage them for a portion of the profits.

Certainly, the idea of career paths can apply to any occupation. No matter what the occupation, an understanding of computer technology will help in career advancement.

An understanding of computers helped Sue McKnight, John LaFriend, and Martha Baker. While they are not computer professionals, computers play an important role in their work every day.

Sue was right when she said "Computers are being used everywhere in medicine." Her first exposure to computers in Mrs Dingman's class and at her father's pharmacy was only the beginning. Computer technology was a part of Sue's medical education and a tool she used while finishing her internship and residency. As a doctor, she attends professional seminars that describe the latest advancements in computer technology as they relate to medicine.

The next decade will bring some spectacular tools to the health professions. The development of expert systems to help doctors diagnose illnesses is of particular importance.

Databases containing medical information about organ donors are of great assistance to doctors looking for ways to save critically ill patients. Each advancement requires Sue and her colleagues to take the time to educate themselves about its impact on their profession.

John's work in the U.S. Navy brings him into contact with the latest computer technology. The armed services spend a lot of time and money keeping people's skills up-to-date.

Mrs. Dingman's class and John's short stint as a rock musician provided him with his early computer training. However, the navy's vocational training and on-the-job experience with computer technology really gave John a sense of direction.

John's promotions from seaman up through the ranks to chief petty officer were preceded by additional education. His work with Peter Clark was the latest project that used computer education.

Martha's career path demonstrates that all jobs do not have to be natural extensions of one another. Employers often like to hire individuals that have a wide range of experiences.

Career Paths for Other Occupations

Sue McKnight

John LaFriend

Martha Baker

FIGURE E3.15

John LaFriend

In Martha's case, she was able to get an entry-level job as a data entry/
computer operator. This job was made available to her through a friend of the
family. Keep this in mind when you are looking for a job. Personal contacts
like family friends or relatives can often provide the valuable "foot in the door"
that is needed to get a job interview.

Martha Baker

As it turned out, Martha's job in data processing was not the start of a career path as a computer professional. Instead, the experience helped her understand what she really wanted to do. In addition, it allowed her to earn money for a college degree in accounting.

Martha changed career paths again after working several years at the bank. She left her job as an accountant to become one of the bank's credit analysts. This job brought her into contact with the bank's customers, which is what she wanted.

Several years later, Martha was promoted to the position of loan officer. An officer at a bank is considered a management-level position. Martha was later offered the new position of data administrator. After seriously considering the offer, she decided to turn it down.

Martha turned the job down for two reasons. First, she liked working with the customers. The new position would have had her working more with bank personnel than with customers.

Second, she had aspirations of moving further up in the bank's management. Traditionally, people who work directly with an organization's customers or products move up in the organization the fastest. These positions are called **line positions.**

People who work in areas that support the organization by performing accounting, data processing, hiring, or other functions are called **support positions.** People in support positions often have a harder time getting promoted to upper-level management.

Since a data administrator is considered a support position, Martha felt it would be wiser to stay in her line position as a loan officer. Martha's understanding of both her career goals and company policy helped her make a career path decision.

STUDY OBJECTIVES

11. Define career path and entrepreneur.

12. Describe the responsibilities of a consultant and an MIS director.

13. Explain the difference between line position and support position.

SUMMARY

Rapid advancements in the fields of computers and electronics are creating many new products and services. Education is important in preparing people for these new jobs. Preparation for new job opportunities is now taking place on-the-job, at professional seminars and conferences, in the military, and at two- or four-year colleges. Organizations like the ACM and DPMA are helping identify the skills that future professionals will need.

There are many careers for people interested in working with computers. Positions for data entry operators, control clerks, data librarians, computer operators, computer programmers, salespeople, and technicians are considered entry-level jobs. People interested in becoming systems analysts, engineers, and managers need additional experience and more education.

Whether people are looking for jobs as computer professionals or in other occupations, they must consider long-range career goals. These career goals will help them select a major at school and help them plan a career path. Their career path will probably include several jobs before they reach their final career goals. In some cases, career goals will change along the way.

THE COMPUTER INDUSTRY AND CAREERS

Gold Rush of the 1980s

The computer industry is the gold rush of the 1980s—Apple Computer achieves $1 billion in sales in less than 10 years, after two young graduate students build a computer in their garage. IBM exceeds $36 billion in sales. People in their 20s have a bright idea, start a company or write software, and become wealthy overnight. So far, few roadmaps through this golden frontier exist.

HARDWARE, SOFTWARE, AND SERVICES

The computer industry is the gold rush of the 1980s. People in their 20s have a bright idea, start a company, and become millionaires overnight. Apple Computer achieves $1 billion in sales in less than 10 years of existence. IBM exceeds $36 billion in sales.

The computer gold rush involves three types of companies: hardware vendors, software vendors, and service vendors. The characteristics of these vendors vary. Hardware companies have different opportunities and working environments than software vendors. Service organizations are different still. Although most companies specialize in either hardware, software, or services, some companies do provide products from more than one of these categories.

Computer hardware vendors are similiar to traditional manufacturers. They design, develop, manufacture, sell, and support physical products. Some sell computer parts, like chips. Others sell complete components, like terminals and disk units. Still others sell complete computer systems.

Hardware vendors have four basic internal functions. In *product development*, engineers and engineering technicians design new products or changes to existing products. In addition to design, this work may involve research and development into new technologies. In *manufacturing*, the personnel build products according to the designs provided by product development.

A computer hardware vendor uses product development teams of computer scientists and engineers to design new products.

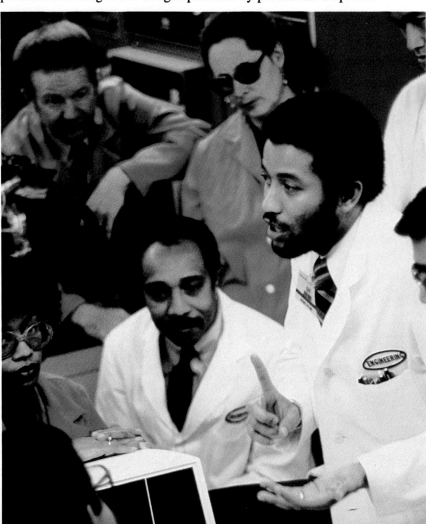

Sales is a third function of hardware vendors. Sales activity varies according to product. The sale of mainframes is usually made directly from the vendor to the customer. Minicomputer sales can be made directly, but they are also made indirectly via third-party companies, called OEMs (original equipment manufacturers). OEMs add value to the minicomputer hardware by adding more hardware, programs, or services. OEMs sell directly to their customers. Microcomputer sales are almost never made directly from manufacturer to customer. They are usually made from retail computer stores, business supply stores, and department stores. Microcomputers are often sold as computer appliances.

The fourth function, *product support*, involves assistance to customers after sales have occurred. Product support personnel provide education in the use and care of equipment. The product support organization also maintains and repairs equipment when necessary. A difficult product support task is to maintain an inventory of spare parts. Over the years, a company may have hundreds of products and variations on products. Knowing which parts are in which versions of which products can be difficult. Keeping a cost-effective inventory of spares can be nearly impossible.

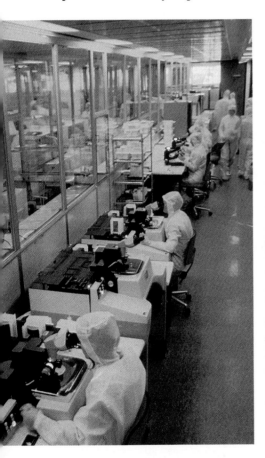

Chip manufacturing and fabrication jobs often require that work be done in dust-free, clean rooms ...

Almost as clean is a typical computer vendor's maze of office compartments.

The chart on this page shows projected dollar sales of computer systems from 1981 to 1986, broken down by type. By 1986, total hardware sales are expected to be over $62 billion—an increase of over $6 billion per year between 1981 and 1986. Observe that most of that growth is for minis and micros. Mainframe sales are expected to increase only slightly.

For hardware vendors, manufacturing and distribution can occur all over the world. This IBM plant is in Scotland.

The position of sales representative in the computer industry can offer an excellent income, as well as considerable contact with people.

PROJECTED GROWTH OF THE
COMPUTER INDUSTRY, 1981 TO 1986

World-Wide Hardware Sales	1981	1986
Mainframes	$17.4	$24.7
Minis	6.2	15.4
Micros	5.8	22.3
	$29.4 Billion	$62.4 Billion

SOURCE: International Data Corporation

Hardware manufacturers may manufacture computers or "peripherals," such as these printers.

Quality control of their disk surfaces is important to RCA to assure consistent storage capability.

Even the seven colors offered in these IBM terminals must undergo quality control checking.

Computer system vendors, such as Apple, sell both hardware and software.

Today the most important part of a microcomputer system is its software, and software vendors emerge overnight.

PROJECTED GROWTH OF THE
COMPUTER INDUSTRY, 1981 TO 1986

The second type of computer company in the software vendor. Software vendors are a new phenomenon in business. In a sense, they are manufacturers, but they do not manufacture anything physical. They manufacture programs, which are "thought-stuff." Software vendors are manufacturers of logical poetry.

Once a computer program is developed, the cost of production is very, very low. A computer program to do word processing, for example, may sell for a retail price of $495. The manufacturer may net, say, $250 of this amount. The cost of producing a copy of the program and its documentation may be only $15. This is an incredibly high gross margin.

Software vendors have the same four internal functions that hardware vendors have. The characteristics of the functions are different, however. Product development for software companies consists of the analysis, design, and construction of programs. The vendor identifies a need, determines the requirements for programs to meet that need, designs programs, and builds and tests them. Documentation is also a product development function.

The manufacturing function of a software vendor is simple, at least as compared to hardware manufacturing. Copies of the program are made on floppies or other media, and then the floppy is packaged with documentation—period.

Sales activity for software vendors is similar to sales activity for hardware vendors. For programs to be run on mainframe computers, direct sales to customers are common. For minicomputer programs, both direct and OEM sales strategies are used. Microcomputer program sales are nearly always made via a third party. Microcomputer retail stores, business supply stores, and department stores all sell programs for micros.

Distribution of microcomputer programs is emerging as a new area of the computer industry. Such distributors buy programs from vendors and resell them to retail stores. They provide sales assistance and sales training as well.

Some companies, called *software houses*, develop computer programs on a custom basis. These companies either alter existing programs to meet specific needs, or they design and build entirely new programs.

The chart on this page shows anticipated growth in program sales. In 1981, the great bulk of program revenue was for mainframe applications. By 1986, that is expected to change. More and more program revenues will stem from microcomputer applications.

The third type of computer company provides services. Computer service companies vary widely. Some companies provide computer processing service. This service can be a specific one, such as processing deposits, checks, and teller transactions for credit unions. Such a service provides a complete pack-

World-Wide Software & Services	1981	1986
Time Sharing	$ 7.9	$15.0
Software Packages	3.6	16.3
Professional Services	3.5	10.3
Systems Houses	1.5	5.2
	$16.5 Billion	$46.8 Billion

SOURCE: International Data Corporation

age, including processing hardware, programs, personnel, forms, training, and so forth. Other companies provide less comprehensive service.

Consulting companies provide information as a service. Consultants analyze needs and help their customers to select and acquire hardware, programs, or other resources. They provide education and training. Consultants also serve as advisers to management.

Some consultants, called *EDP auditors*, provide expertise to CPAs in conjunction with annual audits. These consultants evaluate the completeness and effectiveness of controls over accounting systems. They also do an evaluation of emergency and disaster recovery plans.

Customer training for a new computer system is provided by the customer service department.

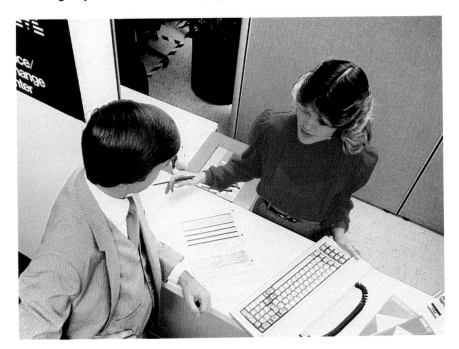

This IBM service center offers customers product support in a wide variety of forms.

A *consultant* provides analysis and advice to a computer user.

COMPUTER CAREERS

As computer applications have spread throughout society, the number and type of computer-related jobs have increased dramatically. At one time, there were only a few different types of jobs. Today, there are dozens of job titles, and, unfortunately, there are few standard meanings for the titles that exist. The chart below shows computer industry job titles broken down by employer—vendor versus user.

A *computer scientist* at a major university conducts research funded by a hardware vendor in a continuing search for new technology.

COMPUTER INDUSTRY JOB TITLES

Vendors			Users	
Hardware	*Software*	*Service*	*Data Processing Department*	*End Users*
Computer engineer	Software engineer	Consultant	Computer operator	Word processing
Electrical engineer	Systems analyst	Computer operator	Data entry operator	operator
Engineering aid	Programmer	Data entry operator	Applications	Office administrator
Quality assurance	Quality assurance	EDP auditor	programmer	Architect
technician	technician	Technical writer	Systems analyst	Product engineer
Industrial engineer	Production supervisor	Salesperson	Data administrator	Graphic artist
Production supervisor	Technical writer	Customer service	Management	Scientist
Technical writer	Salesperson	technician		Lawyer
Salesperson	Product support	Management		Consultant
Maintenance	technician			Liaison with
technician	Management			computer personnel
Product support				Teacher
technician				
Management				

Vendors Hardware vendors employ people to design, produce, sell, and support hardware products. Computer and electrical engineers are the top echelon of their personnel. Other positions in this area are quality control engineer, industrial engineer, and production engineer. In addition, supporting personnel include engineering aids, production assistants, and quality control supervisors. Hardware vendors, like all of the vendor types, also employ technical writers, salespeople, support personnel, and managers.

Software vendors employ people to design, produce, sell, and support programs. Typical job titles include programmer, systems analyst, and software engineer. The latter job title refers to someone who designs, programs, and tests software products. Quality control personnel test programs to verify that they perform according to specifications.

The personnel in a computer service company vary according to the company's products. A processing service company would have computer operators, programmers, systems analysts, salespeople, and account support representatives. Account support personnel serve as a technical liaison between the customer and the service company.

A consulting company employs consultants. These people need to have expertise in one or more specialties. They also need to be superb communicators and good judges of people.

Programmers and systems analysts may spend little time at a computer terminal. Instead, they are involved in designing program solutions to problems, sometimes in small teams.

Computer engineers at Intel design and modify products.

Users Career opportunities among companies that use computer products can be divided into two categories. The first is traditional data processing. People in operations run the computer equipment and perform limited routine maintenance. Data entry personnel convert computer data into machine-sensible form. Usually, but not always, this process involves operating some type of keyboard device. Systems analysts and programmers build new computer systems or maintain existing systems.

Data administration personnel standardize and protect the usage of computer data. Computer managers plan, organize, and control some aspect of the computer department.

End users are people who use computer-based products to perform their jobs. Word processing systems are used both by secretaries and by professionals, such as attorneys, consultants, authors, and architects. Office administration personnel manage the information resources of an office.

Engineers use computer systems to facilitate design. Products for computer-assisted design and manufacturing (CAD/CAM) and computer-assisted engi-

Data entry clerks key program statements and input data.

Computer operations personnel run and maintain computer center equipment.

neering (CAE) allow engineers to design on computer screens. The designs are stored on computer media. Later, approved designs are input to other computer-based systems that control and operate machinery.

Robots are beginning to be used in manufacturing. Robots perform repetitive work without error and can work in undesirable or dangerous environments. The use of robots has led to a new job title. A *production automation specialist*, with knowledge of manufacturing *and* computing, oversees the application of robots.

Scientists use computers to analyze and store data. Computers are used as sensing devices in laboratories, and they facilitate experiments in other ways. The space program would have been impossible without computers.

Computers are being used in more and more products. They are being used in automobiles, for example, to monitor fuel flow as well as to perform other functions. Talking soda machines have microprocessors, as do microwave ovens and washing machines. Consequently, engineers of all sorts of products increasingly need to understand computer technology.

Systems analysts find that communication skills and knowledge of the organization are as important as technical knowledge.

A *data administrator* standardizes data and develops computer security procedures.

CAREER PLANNING

A *computer department manager* combines technical knowledge with skill in planning, organizing, and controlling.

The chart on this page shows entry-level job titles for college majors in information systems, computer science, and computer engineering. Differences in salary are shown for two- and four-year degree graduates. The salaries shown are estimates of entry-level positions in 1984. Inflation, demand, company size, and local economic conditions greatly influence these salaries.

Because this chart shows only entry-level positions, some computer careers are omitted. Specifically, project leader and other management positions are not shown. Although exceptions occur, such management positions are more readily offered to experienced employees.

Selecting a Job—for You   The computer industry is expected to grow from a \$46-billion industry in 1981 to a \$99-billion industry in 1986. In an industry growing at such a rate, there are obviously many jobs. Because this is true, you should take some time to decide which of these many jobs will be best for you. With this objective, you can obtain the education most appropriate for the type of job you want.

First, as much as you are able, determine what you want. You are unique, and the best job for you will be different from the best job for someone else. Do you like to be with people? Do you enjoy interaction with your fellow students? Is it hard for you to work for long periods of time on your own? If so, sales, product support, and systems analysis, consulting, and management jobs may be appropriate for you. Each of these jobs will bring you into contact with people, and, in all of them, good communication skills are essential.

JOB TITLES AND ENTRY-LEVEL SALARIES (in \$)

		College Major		
		Information Systems (Business)	*Computer Science*	*Computer (Electrical) Engineering*
Two-year Degree	*Vendor*	Programmer (20,000) Product support (18,000) Sales (20,000 +) Technical writer (18,000)	Programmer (20,000) Systems programmer (23,000) Product support (18,000) Technical writer (18,000)	Engineering aid (16,000) Production technician (18,000) Maintenance technician (20,000) Technical writer (18,000)
	User	Programmer (18,000) Junior analyst (23,000) Data administration ass't. (21,000) Computer operator (14,000)	Programmer (18,000) Systems programmer (23,000)	Maintenance technician (18,000)
Four-year Degree	*Vendor*	Programmer (25,000) Product support (23,000) Sales (25,000 +) Consultant (30,000 +) Technical writer (22,000)	Programmer (25,000) Systems programmer (27,000) Software engineer (27,000) Product support (23,000) Technical writer (22,000)	Computer engineer (32,000) Production supervisor (26,000) Support engineer (28,000) Maintenance engineer (28,000) Technical writer (22,000)
	User	Programmer (23,000) Systems analyst (28,000) Data administrator (27,000) Operations manager (24,000)	Programmer (23,000) Software engineer (25,000) Systems programmer (27,000)	Data communications specialist (30,000) Computer facilities maintenance supervisor (27,000)

Partly based on *Infosystems*, June 1983.

If you do not enjoy the company of other people in your work, then you will probably find more solitary jobs satisfying. Programming, operations, engineering, and other technical jobs may be your forte. If you are in the middle of this continuum—if you like people and also enjoy working on your own— then jobs that involve both solitary and group activities may be appropriate. Applications programming, systems analysis, product support, technical writing, and project management are possible jobs for you.

Did this farmer at an Alberta, Canada, wheat cooperative think he would want to learn to use a computer?

Banks and similar businesses may train employees at every level to use the computer.

Offices are becoming more automated as they implement word processing systems.

Women have found the computer industry full of opportunities—perhaps because of the youth of this industry.

Your First Job   The best jobs come to those who actively seek them. Unless you develop a wide reputation and considerable expertise, the perfect job will not come looking for you. Begin to prepare while you're a student. If possible, seek out part-time employment at various jobs. See what you like to do and what you do not. Such part-time employment will also make your résumé more interesting when the time comes to find a job.

When selecting your first job, pick not only the work but also the people with whom you will work. Work for someone from whom you can learn. You may think you learned a lot in school, but, after one year on the job, you'll be amazed at how little you knew when you graduated.

Perhaps the best career advice was offered by a cross-country coach who told his runners, "On the bottom line, running should be fun. If you don't enjoy it, if, at some point, you don't get into it so much that you're not even aware you're running, then you should find another sport." A young product support engineer said that his job was so much fun, he felt guilty getting paid for it. If you can find a job like that for yourself, you'll be good at it, and your career will be exceedingly successful.

Once you find a job, take it seriously. If first impressions are not lasting, they are at least very powerful. When you accept a job, arrange your personal affairs so that you can work just as hard as you must to make an excellent

JOB TITLES BY INTEREST AND DESIRE TO WORK WITH PEOPLE

Area of Interest	Desire to Work with People		
	Low	Medium	High
Systems/applications orientation (information systems degree recommended)	Applications programming Maintenance programming Computer operations	Applications programming Systems analysis Technical writing Quality assurance Project management	Systems analysis Data administration Sales Customer support Education and training Project management Teaching Data processing management
Technical/software orientation (computer science degree recommended)	Programming Systems programming	Programming Systems programming Technical writing Quality assurance	Sales Customer support Systems analysis Programming/analysis Education and training Project management Teaching
Hardware design orientation (computer engineering degree recommended)	Engineering Engineering support Equipment maintenance Data communications	Engineering Engineering support Customer support Equipment maintenance Quality assurance Technical writing Project management	Sales Customer support Education and training Project management Teaching

impression. If you make that impression, it will carry you through all sorts of ups and downs. Be the last person out of the office four nights out of five. Read documentation, read standards, and learn all you can. Be courteous, helpful, agreeable, ambitious, competent, and sincere. Do more than you are supposed to do. Aim to be the best employee at your level.

If you have mechanical skills and enjoy working by yourself, then engineering technology may be your career.

Word processing skills are in increasing demand for new employees.

If you enjoy working with people, then customer sales and training can be an exciting career.

The spread of microcomputers has greatly expanded the opportunities for computer store retail salespeople.

Teachers in computer education are needed in high schools, community colleges, and universities.

QUESTIONS

1. What are the three major segments of the computer industry? Describe differences in these segments.

2. Summarize projected sales growth in the computer industry between 1981 and 1986.

3. Name three job titles to be found in a hardware vendor.

4. Name three job titles to be found in a software vendor.

5. Name three job titles to be found in a services vendor.

6. Think about what you like to do. How important is working with other people? How important is working with hardware, software, or systems? Once you have answered these questions, list three or four jobs that might be appropriate for you.

7. What can you do today to prepare for a job you will like?

U N I T   F

BASIC on Microcomputers Step-by-Step

Many people now have access to small, powerful computers. To have full control of this resource requires knowledge of how to design and write computer programs. Unit F introduces the BASIC programming language step-by-step as used on four popular microcomputers.

Each step provides you with an understanding of how computer programs are developed using BASIC. Step 0 starts you off with learning how to operate your computer. Steps 1 through 11 then take you from an introduction to simple BASIC statements like PRINT and INPUT all the way to arrays and subroutines. Program design is presented through the use of flowcharting techniques.

Before you start programming, a quick review of microcomputer hardware is in order. There is input hardware, processing hardware, output hardware, and storage hardware. A microcomputer is the processing hardware. Like all computers, it is composed of three units: memory, control, and arithmetic/logic. These units are placed on integrated circuits—chips—that are interconnected on a wiring board. The wiring board is then placed inside a metal or plastic housing that is "the computer."

Input is primarily from a keyboard. A color or black-and-white screen (CRT) acts as the output hardware. Storage hardware is either a cassette tape recorder or a floppy disk drive. The keyboard, CRT, tape recorder, and disk drive are either built into the computer or attached by a cable. Hardware attached by a cable usually has its own on/off switch.

One of the difficulties in learning BASIC programming is that computers differ. Each computer manufacturer has designed its hardware a little differently. Once in a while, you will need to refer to the user's manual to find out how something special is done with your type of computer.

People using Apple, Commodore, IBM, or Radio Shack microcomputers will get additional help. The differences between these computers will be identified in the text.

STEP 0

Turning on the computer and attached equipment provides the first place where machines differ. If you are using an Apple computer, turn to appendix A; a Commodore computer, turn to appendix B; an IBM computer, turn to appendix C; a Radio Shack Model I, II, III, IV, or color computer, turn to appendix D. Otherwise, ask for the user's manual for the computer you are working with.

STUDY OBJECTIVES

1. Identify the primary input-output and storage hardware used by the microcomputers at your school.
2. Demonstrate how to turn on the school's microcomputer and attached equipment.
3. Define cursor and nondestructive cursor movement.
4. Demonstrate how to erase characters, insert characters, and move the cursor left or right.
5. Depending on the computer you are using, describe the function of the Return or Enter key, or ⏎ key.

STEP 1

After the computer is on, enter the following program. Put your own name inside double quotes. Press the Return, Enter, or ⏎ key after completing each line.

```
10 PRINT    "your name"
20 END
```

Remember, when you press the Return, Enter, or ⏎ key the line is entered into the computer's memory.

Using the instructions on the right, clear the screen.

Although you can no longer see the program, it is still in the memory.

APPLE:	press and	ESC and @/p and SHIFT
COMMODORE:	press	SHIFT and CLR HOME
IBM:	press	CNTL and HOME
RADIO SHACK:	press	CLEAR

Recall it to the screen by typing **LIST.** Don't forget to press the Return, Enter, or ⏎ key.

```
LIST
 10 PRINT "JOE SMOE"
 20 END
 ▨
```

Now make the computer follow the program instructions. Type in **RUN.** What happens?

```
LIST
 10 PRINT "JOE SMOE"
 20 END
RUN
JOE SMOE
 ▨
```

Our program consists of two lines of instruction—the **program code.** The **PRINT** statement in line 10 tells the computer to display the information in quotes—called a **string constant** or **string**—on the screen. A string can contain any combination of numbers, letters, or special characters.

The **END** statement in line 20 tells the computer to stop. Every BASIC program should have an END statement.

Notice that both lines of code begin with a **line number.** Every line in a BASIC program starts with a line number. It identifies each instruction or **BASIC statement.** The computer will wait until the user types RUN before following the BASIC statements. Line numbers indicate to the computer the order in which the instructions will be performed.

Some instructions are immediately followed by the computer. Instructions like LIST and RUN are called **commands.** The computer will follow these commands as soon as the user presses the Return, Enter, or ⏎ key.

Now enter this line:

```
10 PRINT "HQ#$4"
```

(Don't forget to press the Return, Enter, or ⏎ key.)

429

Clear the screen and RUN the program. What happens?

```
RUN
  HQ#$4
▱
```

LIST the program. What is in line 10?

_____

```
RUN
HQ#$4
LIST
  10 PRINT "HQ#4"
  20 END
▱
```

Three new things can be seen here:

1. You don't have to LIST a program before you RUN it.
2. To replace a line, just retype the line number followed by the new line. Notice that the PRINT statement with your name is no longer in memory.
3. Anything within quotes in a PRINT statement will be displayed. A string can be any combination of numbers, letters, symbols, and blank spaces—even misspelled words!

_____

By replacing line 10 you have actually created a new program. Another way to enter a new program is to erase the old program by clearing the memory. Type in NEW.

LIST the program. What happens?

```
LIST
▱
```

_____

NEW clears the memory and the screen with some computers. It is now ready for a new program.

WARNING: Once you enter the NEW command, you cannot recall your old program!

STUDY OBJECTIVES

6. Describe the functions of PRINT, END, LIST, RUN, and NEW.
7. Identify the difference between a BASIC statement and command.
8. Define string and program code.

9. Describe how the computer uses line numbers.

10. Briefly describe how a programmer can enter and replace a line of a BASIC program.

STEP 2

Clear the memory using the NEW command and enter this program. Make your first name the first string and your last name the second string.

```
10 F$ = "FIRST NAME"
20 L$ = "LAST NAME"
30 PRINT F$,L$
40 END
```

Now RUN the program.
What happens?

```
10 F$ = "ABE"
20 L$ = "LINCOLN"
30 PRINT F$,L$
40 END
RUN
ABE        LINCOLN
```

⌷

*VARIES BETWEEN COMPUTERS

F$ and L$ are called **string variable names** because they identify strings. All string variable names consist of one or two letters of the alphabet followed by a $ sign. Some computers will allow string variable names to be longer.

The two strings are displayed in order from left to right as found in the PRINT statement on line 30.

Now add line 35.

```
35 PRINT F$;L$
```

Clear the screen, LIST the program, and RUN it. What happens?

```
LIST
 10 F$ = "ABE"
 20 L$ = "LINCOLN"
 30 PRINT F$,L$
 35 PRINT F$;L$
 40 END
RUN
ABE        LINCOLN
ABELINCOLN
```

⌷

*VARIES BETWEEN COMPUTERS

431

When a comma is used in a PRINT statement to separate two strings, the second string is printed using a preset tab. The preset tab will vary between computers.

When a semicolon separates the two strings, they are displayed next to each other.

There is another way to control the spacing in a PRINT statement. Enter:

```
30 PRINT F$;TAB(20);L$
35
```

Clear the screen and LIST the program.

Notice that the new line 30 is in the program and line 35 has been deleted. You can delete any line from a BASIC program by entering the line number and pressing the Return, Enter, or ⏎ key.

RUN the program.
What happens?

The **TAB** function works just like the one on a typewriter. It skips to the specified column number—column 20 in this program—before displaying the second string.

Replace line 30 with this statement:

```
30 PRINT L$;",_";F$
```

Note: ___ means a blank space.

Clear the screen, LIST and RUN the program. What happens?

PRESET TABS

APPLE:	16 columns —	1, 17, 33 . . .
COMMODORE:	10 columns —	1, 11, 21 . . .
IBM:	14 columns —	1, 15, 29 . . .
RADIO SHACK:	16 columns —	1, 17, 33 . . .

```
LIST
  10 F$ = "ABE"
  20 L$ = "LINCOLN"
  30 PRINT F$;TAB(20);L$
  40 END
▨
```

```
LIST
  10 F$ = "ABE"
  20 L$ = "LINCOLN"
  30 PRINT F$;TAB(20);L$
  40 END
RUN
ABE                 LINCOLN
▨
```

```
LIST
  10 F$ = "ABE"
  20 L$ = "LINCOLN"
  30 PRINT L$;",_";F$
  40 END
RUN
LINCOLN, ABE
▨
```

This program demonstrates two things:

1. The order in which strings are displayed is dictated by the PRINT statement.

2. A PRINT statement can contain a mixture of string variable names and string constants like ",___" in this program.

STUDY OBJECTIVES

STEP 3

Clear the memory and enter this program:

```
10 INPUT N$
20 PRINT "HI  ";N$
30 END
```

RUN the program. When the ? appears, enter your name. What happens?

```
RUN
?ABE
HI  ABE
▨
```

Now RUN the program again. When the ? appears, enter a different name. What happens?

```
RUN
?ABE
HI  ABE
RUN
?GEORGE
HI  GEORGE
▨
```

In the previous steps, you put your name into the program as a string constant. That meant that each time you ran the program, the same name was always displayed.

The **INPUT** statement allows the user to change the value associated with a string variable name—like N$—each time the program is run. Any string value that can be changed by the user is called a **string variable.**

Now add lines 15 and 25:

```
15 INPUT C$
25 PRINT "YOU LIVE IN ";C$
```

Clear the screen. LIST and RUN the program. Enter your name after the first ? and your hometown after the second ?. What happens?

A BASIC program can contain any number of INPUT statements. When an INPUT statement is executed, a ? will appear on the screen to let the user know that the computer is waiting for data.

Each time a string variable needs to be changed, use an INPUT statement. Once the string has been INPUT, you can display it along with other constants and variables by using the PRINT statement.

Delete line 15 and enter line 10:

```
10 INPUT N$,C$
```

Clear the screen. LIST and RUN the program, entering your name after the ?, followed by a comma and your hometown. What happens?

The INPUT statement allows the user to put in more than one variable at a time. To keep the variables separate, a comma—called a **delimiter**—is used. The computer associates the characters before the delimiter with the first string variable name, and the characters after the delimiter with the second variable name. Any spaces contained within the string will be retained.

```
LIST
 10 INPUT N$
 15 INPUT C$
 20 PRINT "HI ";N$
 25 PRINT "YOU LIVE IN ";C$
 30 END
RUN
?ABE
?WASHINGTON D.C.
HI ABE
YOU LIVE IN WASHINGTON D.C.
▨
```

```
LIST
 10 INPUT N$,C$
 20 PRINT "HI ";N$
 25 PRINT "YOU LIVE IN ";C$
 30 END
RUN
?THOMAS,MONTICELLO
HI THOMAS
YOU LIVE IN MONTICELLO
▨
```

434

RUN the program again. This time when the ? appears, enter the city, a comma, and then your name. What happens?

```
RUN
?THOMAS,MONTICELLO
HI  THOMAS
YOU  LIVE  IN  MONTICELLO
RUN
?MONTICELLO,THOMAS
HI  MONTICELLO
YOU  LIVE  IN  THOMAS
▨
```

The order in which the strings are entered must match the order of the string variable names in the INPUT statement. In this program, N$ was used for the name and C$ for the city. Since N$ appears first in the INPUT statement, it must be the first string value entered.

To help the user, a programmer uses a PRINT statement to explain what data must be entered. This explanation or request for data is called a **prompt.**

Enter this prompt:

```
6 PRINT "ENTER NAME AND HOMETOWN"
8 PRINT " SEPARATED BY A COMMA"
```

Clear the screen. LIST and RUN the program. What happens?

```
LIST
  6 PRINT "ENTER NAME AND HOMETOWN"
  8 PRINT " SEPARATED BY A COMMA"
 10 INPUT N$,C$
 20 PRINT "HI ";N$
 25 PRINT "YOU LIVE IN ";C$
 30 END
RUN
ENTER NAME AND HOMETOWN
 SEPARATED BY A COMMA
?THOMAS,MONTICELLO
HI  THOMAS
YOU  LIVE  IN  MONTICELLO
▨
```

In a well-written program, each INPUT statement should be preceded by a prompt for the user.

Add these three lines, putting today's date in line 3:

```
1 REM STEP 3 - PROGRAM #1
2 REM AUTHOR: T. TRAINOR
3 REM DATE WRITTEN: 9/8-
```

Clear the screen. LIST and RUN the program, following the prompts. What happens?

```
LIST
 1 REM STEP 3 - PROGRAM #1
 2 REM AUTHOR:T. TRAINOR
 3 REM DATE WRITTEN:9/8-
 6 PRINT "ENTER NAME AND HOMETOWN"
 8 PRINT " SEPARATED BY A COMMA"
 10 INPUT N$,C$
 20 PRINT "HI ";N$
 25 PRINT "YOU LIVE IN ";C$
 30 END
RUN
ENTER NAME AND HOMETOWN
 SEPARATED BY A COMMA
?SANDRA,PHOENIX
HI SANDRA
YOU LIVE IN PHOENIX
▨
```

Lines 1, 2, and 3 are called **REM**—remark—statements. They are notes to the programmer or anyone LISTing the program about what the program does, who wrote it, and other useful information.

REM statements are ignored by the computer and only appear in a LISTing of the program. They will not be displayed when the program is run.

REM statements can appear anywhere and can be used as many times as needed in a program. They start with the letters REM followed by any combination of characters you wish. Use them frequently!!!

Since the computer's memory is cleared when NEW is entered or the machine is turned off, programs need to be saved in order to avoid typing them into the computer again.

Cassette tapes and floppy disks are common storage media. The command to copy a program from memory to a storage medium differs slightly among computers.

Usually, it is a form of the word **SAVE** followed by the program name. The **program name** is a short one- or two-word description assigned by the programmer. For example: SAVE "STEP3-1"

APPLE:	SAVE program name
COMMODORE:	SAVE "program name" for tape recorders
	DSAVE "program name", D0 for disk drive 0
	DSAVE "@program name", D0 when a program by that name is already on disk in drive 0
IBM:	SAVE "A: program name" for disk drive A
RADIO SHACK:	SAVE "program name" for disk drives
	CSAVE "program name" for tape recorders

436

To ensure accuracy, some computers allow the user to compare (**VERIFY**) the copy against the original in memory. Commands for SAVEing and VERIFYing programs can be found at the right. More detailed information is in the user's manual.

APPLE:	not available
COMMODORE:	VERIFY "program name" for tape recorders
IBM:	not available
RADIO SHACK:	CLOAD? "program name" for tape recorders

With the help of the user's manual, SAVE and VERIFY—if possible—this program on tape or disk.

To make sure it worked, clear the memory using the NEW command. The program can be copied from the tape back into memory using the **LOAD** command.

APPLE:	LOAD program name
COMMODORE:	LOAD "program name" for tape recorders
	DLOAD "program name", D0 for disk drive 0
IBM:	LOAD "A: program name" for disk drive A
RADIO SHACK:	LOAD "program name" for disk drives
	CLOAD "program name" for tape recorders

A word of caution needs to be added. The program name must be spelled *exactly* the same as it was originally SAVEd. Otherwise, the computer will not find it.

LOAD Step 3 – Program #1 back into memory using the LOAD command. LIST the program to double-check that it is the same as before.

---

14. Define string variable, prompt, and program name.
15. Describe the function of INPUT, REM, SAVE, VERIFY, and LOAD.
16. Identify the meaning of a ? on the screen when running a BASIC program.
17. Demonstrate the use of a single INPUT statement to accept two or more string variables, and describe the purpose of a delimiter when entering more than one string on a single line.
18. Demonstrate how to SAVE and LOAD a program on/from tape or disk.

STUDY OBJECTIVES

Clear the memory and enter this program:

```
10 REM STEP 4 - PROGRAM #1
20 REM  USING + WITH STRINGS
30 A$ = "1"
40 B$ = "2"
50 PRINT A$ + B$
60 END
```

RUN the program.
What happens?

```
RUN
12
▨
```

Looking at the PRINT statement in line 50, we might expect the computer to add the two numbers—1 and 2—to get 3.

However, string constants and variables cannot be used as part of any arithmetic calculation. If the values 1 and 2 are to be treated as numbers—to be used in calculations—they must be identified as **numeric data.**

Numeric data can only contain numbers, a decimal point (.), and either a plus (+) or a minus (−) sign.

Clear the memory and enter this program:

```
10 REM STEP 4 - PROGRAM #2
20 REM  USING NUMERIC DATA
30 A = 1
40 B = 2
50 PRINT A + B
60 END
```

RUN the program.
What happens?

```
RUN
3
▨
```

In this program, A and B are **numeric variable names** because they identify numbers.

438

Numeric variable names consist of one or two letters of the alphabet. The difference between a string variable name and a numeric variable name is that the numeric variable name does not have a $ sign.

Add these statements to your program:

```
52  PRINT A;B;3
54  PRINT A,B,3
56  PRINT A;TAB(15);B;TAB(30);3
```

Clear the screen. LIST and RUN the program. What happens?

```
LIST
 10  REM STEP 4 - PROGRAM #2
 20  REM   USING NUMERIC DATA
 30  A = 1
 40  B = 2
 50  PRINT A + B
 52  PRINT A;B;3
 54  PRINT A,B,3
 56  PRINT A;TAB(15);B;TAB(30);3
RUN
 3
 1  2  3
 1              2           3 ⁑
 1                   2                3
☑
```

⁑DEPENDS ON PRE-SET TABS

This program demonstrates that **numeric constants** do not have double quotes around them. The quotes distinguish a string constant from a numeric constant.

Remember, only numbers stored as numeric variables or constants can be used in calculations.

In addition, this program shows that ; , and TAB work the same in spacing numeric data as they do in spacing strings.

However, there are a few differences. Most computers will reserve a space in front of the number for a plus or minus sign, even when a + or − is not used. A space is also reserved after the number. Even when using a semicolon, there are spaces between 1 2 3.

439

To do mathematical computations, the computer uses the following symbols with numeric variables and constants:

+	addition
−	subtraction and negative numbers
*	multiplication
/	division
↑ or ^	exponentiation (raise to a power)

Enter and RUN this program after clearing the memory:

```
10 REM STEP 4 - PROGRAM #3          RUN
20 REM   MATH OPERATIONS              12
30 A = 10                              8
40 B = 2                              20
50 PRINT A + B                         5
60 PRINT A - B                       100
70 PRINT A * B                       120
80 PRINT A / B                        ▨ .
90 PRINT A ↑ B
100 C = A * (A + B)
110 PRINT C
120 END
```

Program #3 demonstrates the complete range of computations the arithmetic/logic unit is capable of performing. All complex calculations use these simple operations.

Clear the memory and enter this program:

```
10 REM STEP 4 - PROGRAM #4
20 REM   USE OF PEMDAS
30 A = 4 + 20 / 2 ↑ 2
40 B = 4 + (20 / (2 ↑ 2))
50 C = 4 + ((20 / 2) ↑ 2)
60 PRINT A,B,C
70 END
```

RUN the program.
What happens?

```
RUN
  9         9         104*
  ▨

*DEPENDS ON PRE-SET TABS
```

440

Look at line 30. The numeric variable name associated with the answer is *always* placed on the left side of the equals sign. Now, if the equation were computed left to right, we would get

```
A = 4 + 20 / 2 ↑ 2
  = 24 / 2 ↑ 2
  = 12 ↑ 2
  = 144
```

However, this is not the correct answer! When there is more than one mathematics symbol in an equation, the computer performs the operations in a specific order—called the **order of precedence.** This order is:

LEVEL	OPERATION
1	**P**arentheses (innermost first)
2	**E**xponentiation
3	**M**ultiplication and **D**ivision (whichever comes first)
4	**A**ddition and **S**ubtraction (whichever comes first)

The computer scans the equation and performs all level 1 operations first. It performs the remaining computations according to the order of precedence. Multiple occurrences of the same operation, such as multiplication, are performed from left to right. Operations from the same level, such as addition and subtraction, are also performed from left to right. Using the acronym **PEMDAS**—or **P**lease **E**xcuse **M**y **D**ear **A**unt **S**ally—may help you remember.

Line 40 reflects the order of precedence by using parentheses. Notice that A and B are equal. Working from the innermost set of parentheses out,

```
B = 4 + (20 / (2 ↑ 2))
  = 4 + (20 / 4)
  = 4 + 5
  = 9
```

Sometimes the operations must be performed in a way that doesn't follow the order of precedence. By using parentheses, the programmer can "force" the computer to do certain operations first. For example, in line 50,

```
C = 4 + ((20 / 2) ↑ 2)
  = 4 + (10 ↑ 2)
  = 4 + 100
  = 104
```

The outer set of parentheses is not really necessary. The computer would perform exponentiation second anyway. However, using the parentheses may help the programmer in understanding and checking the equation.

You can use as many parentheses as you wish in an equation. Just make sure you have a right parenthesis for every left parenthesis and vice versa.

STUDY OBJECTIVES

19. Define numeric data.
20. Explain the difference between a string variable name, string constant, numeric variable name, and numeric constant.
21. Identify the symbols associated with addition, subtraction, multiplication, division, and exponentiation.
22. Describe the computer's computational order of precedence by using the acronym PEMDAS.

STEP 5

A BASIC statement is made up of three parts: statement or line number, verb, and object of action. For some statements, all three parts may not be apparent. Here is a program with each statement broken down into the three parts:

```
LINE                        OBJECT
NUMBER      VERB           OF ACTION

  10        REM      SQUARES PROGRAM
  20        PRINT    "ENTER NUMBER"
  30        INPUT    N
  40        (LET)    M = N * N
  50        PRINT    N;"SQUARED IS";M
  60        END      (PROGRAM)
```

Of all the statements discussed so far, only mathematical statements and END do not seem to have three parts. In line 40, the equation M = N * N is actually the object of the implied verb **LET.** Earlier versions of BASIC required the use of LET. Using this form, line 40 would read

```
40 LET M = N * N
```

This form is now considered archaic—old-fashioned—and will not be used in this text.

Line 60 is the END statement required for every well-written program. The object of ENDing is always the program, so "program" is not written.

The computer needs all three parts of a statement to be able to follow it. If you leave out a part, misspell it, or use symbols the computer doesn't recognize, the translator program will not be able to convert it into machine language. These types of errors are called **syntax errors.**

Clear the memory and enter this program *exactly* as written.

```
10 REM STEP 5 - PROGRAM #1
20 REM  SYNTAX ERRORS
30 PRNT "ENTER NAME"
```

RUN the program.
What happens?

APPLE:	?SYNTAX ERROR IN 30
COMMODORE:	?SYNTAX ERROR IN 30
IBM:	Syntax error in 30
RADIO SHACK:	?SN Error in 30

The error message displayed on the screen is called a **diagnostic message.** It is a description of the type of error found in the program. Usually, the location—line number—is also given.

In this case, the syntax error is in line 30. To look at just line 30, type in LIST 30. What happens?

```
LIST 30
 30 PRNT "ENTER NAME"
 ▨
```

When the computer uses a BASIC interpreter, it will only print a diagnostic message for the first error it finds. Therefore, that error must be corrected before others are found.

If you do not understand an error message, check the user's manual. A list of all possible diagnostics and further explanations should be available there.

Consider the following program.

```
10 REM STEP 5 - PROGRAM #1
20 REM  SYNTAX ERRORS
30 PRNT "ENTER YOUR NAME"
INPUT N$
50 PRINT, HI; N$"
60 END PROGRAM
```

Using what you know about BASIC programming, correct any errors in the preceding program. Write the correct program code on a separate piece of paper, enter the state-

ments, and RUN the program before checking the correct
answer on the right.

```
10  REM STEP 5 - PROGRAM #1
20  REM   SYNTAX ERRORS
30  PRINT "ENTER YOUR NAME"
40  INPUT N$
50  PRINT "HI ";N$
60  END
```

Clear the memory and enter this program *exactly* as written:

```
10  REM STEP 5 - PROGRAM #2
20  REM ADDITION OF 2 NUMBERS
30  PRINT "ENTER TWO NUMBERS"
40  PRINT " SEPARATED BY A COMMA"
50  INPUT A,B
60  C = A - B
70  PRINT A;" + ";B;" = ";D
80  END
```

RUN the program entering 6 for A and 3 for B. What
happens?

```
RUN
ENTER TWO NUMBERS
 SEPARATED BY A COMMA
?6,3
 6 + 3 = 0
▨
```

Notice that although there are no diagnostic messages
displayed, the answer is still wrong. The program contains one or more **logic errors.**

A logic error results when the computer does what the
programmer told it to do instead of what the programmer
meant it to do. A statement with a logic error has proper
syntax but is not appropriate for the program to work
correctly.

Logic errors are the hardest to find. The best approach to
finding them is to go through the program line by line
just like the computer would.

One logic error is in line 60. The minus sign should be a
plus sign. Substitution—mistyping—is a common source
of logic errors. Change line 60 to

RUN the program again. What happens?

```
RUN
ENTER TWO NUMBERS
 SEPARATED BY A COMMA
?6,3
 6 + 3 = 0
 ▱
```

There is still a logic error. Searching further shows that the answer is assigned to the numeric variable name C while the PRINT statement uses a D. Since the variable name D had never been assigned a numeric value, the computer displays a zero.

Change D to C in line 70 and RUN the program again. What happens?

```
RUN
ENTER TWO NUMBERS
 SEPARATED BY A COMMA
?6,3
 6 + 3 = 9
 ▱
```

The process of eliminating syntax and logic errors—called **debugging**—can be time-consuming. Careful coding and entering of a program will reduce debugging time and make programming less frustrating.

23. Identify the three parts of a BASIC statement.
24. Describe the functions of LET, diagnostic messages, and debugging.
25. Define syntax error and logic error.
26. Identify one reference source for additional explanations of diagnostic messages.

The programs discussed so far have been short, simple, and **linear.** With linear programs, the computer goes straight through each line of code without stopping or deviating along the way. Most computer programs are neither linear nor short. Therefore, programmers have developed design techniques to help in program writing.

Programmers follow five phases when organizing ideas and designing programs: **definition, design, writing, testing/debugging,** and **documentation.** These phases provide a systematic approach to problem solving.

445

Let's start by defining the problem. You are asked to write a program that lists sources of emergency help. The user should be able to select a single item from a list—**menu**—of available telephone numbers. The computer should then display the corresponding telephone number. To keep things simple, consider displaying only the numbers for an ambulance dispatch and the poison center.

The next phase is to design possible alternatives. A list of steps can help you design the program:

1. Display menu
2. Prompt user to select one item
3. Input selection
4. Find corresponding telephone number
5. Display telephone number

Consider these steps in respect to the IPO cycle.

FIGURE F6.1

INPUT	PROCESSING	OUTPUT

1. Display menu
2. Prompt user to
    select one item
3. Input selection
	4. Find corresponding
	    telephone number
		5. Display telephone
		    number

Symbols are frequently used to identify each step of the IPO cycle.

When linked with arrows to identify the flow of the program logic, the resulting chart is called a **program flowchart.** Programmers use flowcharts to show the order of instructions in a proposed program and to document the finished program. Other times, English-like sentences called **pseudocode** are used.

FIGURE F6.2

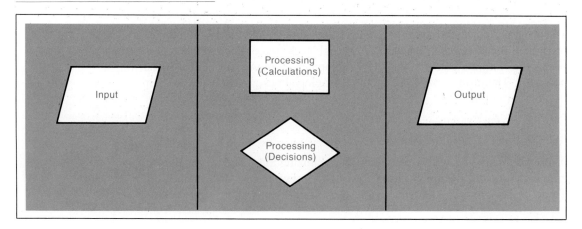

446

A flowchart using the steps defined earlier would look like this:

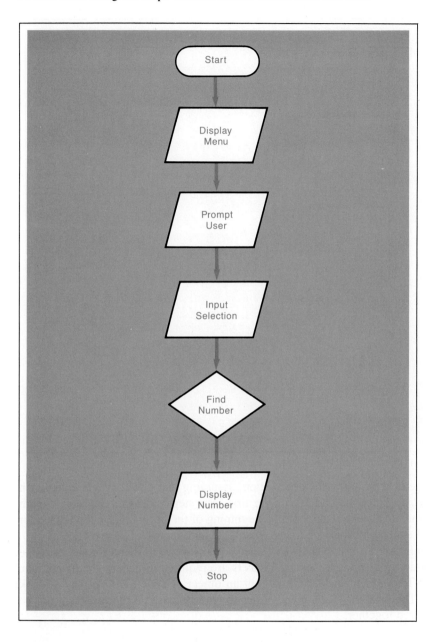

Note these features of a program flowchart:

1. Each step is contained in a separate box, varying in shape.
2. Each box contains a very short summary of the step, not a detailed explanation.
3. The flowchart begins at the top and proceeds downward with all boxes connected by an arrow showing direction.
4. START and STOP boxes are included.

The meaning of the symbols used in program flowcharts are as follows:

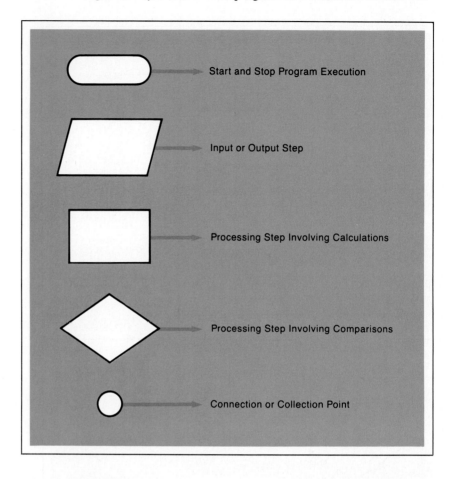

The program must then be written, assuming that it is beneficial and worth the cost. Enter the coding for the first four steps. Remember that although there is no START statement, the beginning of the program is a good place for REM statements that document what is being done (see figure 6.5).

Note that each flowchart box does not always correspond to only one line of code. For example, several PRINTs are required to display the menu. The PRINT statement in line 50 without an object of action will display a blank line. This will make the menu easier to read because all the lines will not be clustered together.

The next step in the flowchart requires the appropriate telephone number to be found and displayed. The computer decides which number to display based on the value of variable A, which contains the user's choice. In other words, if A is 1, the ambulance dispatch number will be PRINTed. If A is 2, the poison center number will be PRINTed (see figure 6.6).

As you can see, this step really involves two separate comparisons or decisions. The remainder of the flowchart should be changed to reflect these decisions.

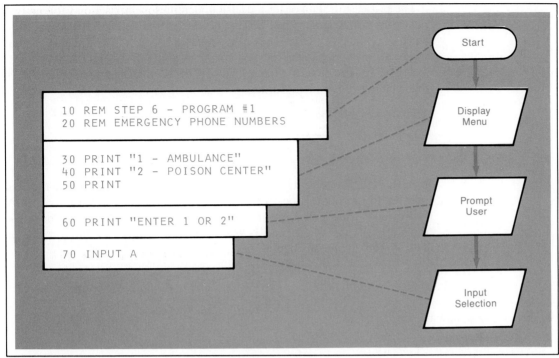

```
10 REM STEP 6 - PROGRAM #1
20 REM EMERGENCY PHONE NUMBERS

30 PRINT "1 - AMBULANCE"
40 PRINT "2 - POISON CENTER"
50 PRINT

60 PRINT "ENTER 1 OR 2"

70 INPUT A
```

FIGURE F6.5

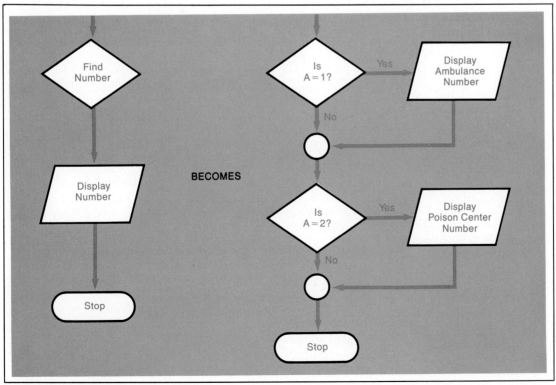

FIGURE F6.6

449

The processing symbol for a decision identifies a comparison between two values. In this program, one decision is whether the variable A is equal to 1. Either A is equal to 1 (true) or A is not equal to 1 (false). The decision symbol is used with two separately labeled arrows pointing to different actions.

In BASIC, decisions are made using **IF/THEN** statements. Each IF/THEN statement has this general form:

IF (comparison) THEN (action when comparison is true)

For example:

```
IF A = 1 THEN PRINT "555-2751"
```

In an IF/THEN statement, the computer will check to see if the comparison is true. For this example, does A equal 1? When the condition is true—when A does equal 1—the ambulance number is displayed. When the condition is not true—when A does not equal 1—the computer proceeds to the next line of code without taking any action.

The remainder of the flowchart can now be coded:

```
80 IF A = 1 THEN PRINT "555-2751"
90 IF A = 2 THEN PRINT "800-442-4571"
100 END
```

Enter these three lines to complete the program. Clear the screen. LIST the program and check for typing errors.

```
LIST
10 REM STEP 6 - PROGRAM #1
20 REM  EMERGENCY PHONE NUMBERS
30 PRINT "1 - AMBULANCE"
40 PRINT "2 - POISON CENTER"
50 PRINT
60 PRINT "ENTER 1 OR 2"
70 INPUT A
80 IF A = 1 THEN PRINT "555-2751"
90 IF A = 2 THEN PRINT "800-442-4571"
100 END
▨
```

RUN the program entering a 1. What happens?

```
RUN
1 - AMBULANCE
2 - POISON CENTER

ENTER 1 OR 2
?1
555-2751
▨
```

RUN the program entering a 2. What happens?

```
RUN
1 - AMBULANCE
2 - POISON CENTER

ENTER 1 OR 2
?2
800-442-4571
▱
```

RUN it again, entering any number but 1 or 2. What happens?

```
RUN
1 - AMBULANCE
2 - POISON CENTER

ENTER 1 OR 2
?6
▱
```

RUN it a fourth time, entering any letter or symbol. What happens?

APPLE:	?REENTER
COMMODORE:	?REDO FROM START
IBM:	?Redo from start
RADIO SHACK:	?REDO

In the first two cases, the correct telephone number was printed. In the third case, the program stops without displaying any useful information. Most computers will not continue in the fourth case until a numeric value is entered.

In designing a program, the programmer should expect users to make mistakes and should write the program to handle errors adequately. In this example, any number besides 1 or 2 will stop the program without providing an emergency telephone number.

Since invalid input causes the computer to proceed through both IF/THEN statements without performing any action, adding these two statements will check for data entry errors:

```
93 IF A < 1 THEN PRINT "INVALID RESPONSE"
95 IF A > 2 THEN PRINT "INVALID RESPONSE"
```

Now the testing/debugging phase is complete. Clear the screen. LIST and RUN the program entering an invalid number. What happens?

```
LIST
10 REM STEP 6 - PROGRAM #1
20 REM   EMERGENCY PHONE NUMBERS
30 PRINT "1 - AMBULANCE"
40 PRINT "2 - POISON CENTER"
50 PRINT
60 PRINT "ENTER 1 OR 2"
70 INPUT A
80 IF A = 1 THEN PRINT "555-2751"
90 IF A = 2 THEN PRINT "800-442-2571"
93 IF A < 1 THEN PRINT "INVALID RESPONSE"
95 IF A > 2 THEN PRINT "INVALID RESPONSE"
100 END
RUN
1 - AMBULANCE
2 - POISON CENTER

ENTER 1 OR 2
?6
INVALID RESPONSE
▨
```

Notice that by including the REM statements as internal documentation, you have completed the five phases of program design. SAVE this program on tape or disk.

Six different types of comparisons are allowed in the IF/THEN statement:

```
CONDITION    SYMBOL   EXAMPLE
EQUAL           =     IF A$ = "B" THEN . . .
NOT EQUAL      <>     IF S$ <> "NO" THEN . . .
LESS THAN       <     IF NY < 40 THEN . . .
LESS THAN      <=     IF X <= .5 THEN . . .
  OR EQUAL TO
GREATER THAN    >     IF Z < Y THEN . . .
GREATER THAN   >=     IF T <= 100 THEN . . .
  OR EQUAL TO
```

The IF/THEN statement is very powerful and can be used to represent a variety of comparisons and resulting action. Special rules guide the program-

```
```

mer in formulating the IF/THEN statement. Each symbol used to represent a comparison must be preceded and followed by a variable or constant. Variables and constants must match—both must be string or both numeric.

For example, IF A = "NO" THEN . . . is not acceptable because a numeric variable cannot be compared with a string constant. This is a special type of syntax error called a **mismatch error.**

Only certain statements may follow the THEN in an IF/THEN statement: PRINT, INPUT, a mathematics statement, or END. A REM or another IF cannot be used as the action after THEN.

27. List the five phases of program design.
28. Define linear program, program flowchart, menu, and mismatch error.
29. Identify the meaning of the following flowcharting symbols:

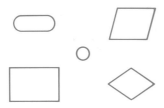

30. Briefly describe the BASIC code to display a blank line.
31. Demonstrate the use of flowchart symbols by outlining the logic of a BASIC program.
32. Describe the formatting rules for IF/THEN statements.
33. Identify the symbols for equal, not equal, less than, less than or equal to, greater than, and greater than or equal to.

STEP 7

Sometimes , using parts of a program again can save time. Step 6 – Program #1 is a good example. It would be more convenient in an emergency to provide the user with another chance when an invalid menu selection was entered.

There are several ways to repeat instructions in BASIC. One way is to actually rewrite the code each time. However, this takes time and makes the program unnecessarily long and redundant. A better way is to send the computer back—**transfer control**—to the code that needs to be used again. This looping action is handled in BASIC by the **GO TO** statement.

LOAD Step 6 – Program #1. Change these lines to allow the user another chance to enter the correct selection:

```
10 REM STEP 7 - PROGRAM #1
93 IF A < 1 THEN PRINT "INVALID RESPONSE": GO TO 50
95 IF A > 2 THEN PRINT "INVALID RESPONSE": GO TO 50
```

LIST and RUN the program, entering an invalid selection. What happens?

```
LIST
 10 REM STEP 7 - PROGRAM #1
 20 REM  EMERGENCY PHONE NUMBERS
 30 PRINT "1 - AMBULANCE"
 40 PRINT "2 - POISON CENTER"
 50 PRINT
 60 PRINT "ENTER 1 OR 2"
 70 INPUT A
 80 IF A = 1 THEN PRINT "555-2751"
 90 IF A = 2 THEN PRINT "800-442-4571"
 93 IF A < 1 THEN PRINT "INVALID RESPONSE"
 :GO TO 50
 95 IF A > 2 THEN PRINT "INVALID RESPONSE"
 :GO TO 50
 100 END
RUN
1 - AMBULANCE
2 - POISON CENTER

ENTER 1 OR 2
?6
INVALID RESPONSE

ENTER 1 OR 2
?
```

Placing GO TO 50 at the end of lines 93 and 95 has several advantages. Using the blank line and redisplaying the prompt leave the screen uncluttered while reminding the user of the correct selections. The programmer uses the prompt as an error message. It also allows the programmer to reuse existing code, which saves time.

The colon (:) is used to allow more than one statement—PRINT "INVALID RESPONSE" and GO TO 50—on the same line. In this way, several actions can follow the comparisons of the IF statement in lines 93 and 95. Generally, the colon is used to combine any two or more BASIC statements on a single line.

Stop the program run by entering either 1 or 2.

The placement of a GO TO is very important. Take out the :GO TO 50 in line 93 and add

```
94 GO TO 50
```

454

Clear the screen and RUN the program. Enter a valid number. What happens?

```
RUN
1 - AMBULANCE
2 - POISON CENTER

ENTER 1 OR 2
?2
800-442-4571

ENTER 1 OR 2
?
```

Although the commands are in the same order—IF followed by GO TO—the computer acts differently. When we enter a valid response, the correct telephone number is PRINTed. However, the PRINT in line 93 is not used and the GO TO in line 94 is still followed. The computer unconditionally goes to line 50 after reaching line 94, even when *valid* responses are entered. In other words, this program is in a continuous loop and is another example of a logic error.

To interrupt this or any program run each machine has a Break or Stop key. When pressed, this key will stop the execution of the program, but will not erase it from memory. Usually, the last line number executed before the program stops is displayed on the screen. This allows the programmer to locate and fix logic errors. Consult the user's manual for more information.

APPLE: ⌷CTRL⌷ and ⌷C⌷ and ⌷RETURN⌷
COMMODORE: ⌷RUN STOP⌷ and ⌷RETURN⌷
IBM: ⌷Ctrl⌷ and ⌷Scroll Lock⌷
RADIO SHACK: ⌷BREAK⌷

Use this key to stop the program execution. What happens?

APPLE: BREAK IN 70
COMMODORE: READY
IBM: Break in 70
RADIO SHACK: Break in 70

Many programs always return the user to the menu. When many things happen in a program, it makes it easier to design and change if you only allow the user to stop the program run through a menu selection.

Delete line 94, then add :GO TO 50 back to the end of line 93 like it was before. Now, add these lines:

```
23 PRINT
25 PRINT "0 - STOP PROGRAM RUN"
60 PRINT "ENTER 0, 1 OR 2"
75 IF A = 0 THEN GO TO 100
97 PRINT:PRINT"ENTER ANY LETTER TO CONTINUE"
98 INPUT XX$
99 GO TO 23
```

Clear the screen. LIST and RUN the program entering a valid selection. What happens?

```
LIST
 10 REM STEP 7 - PROGRAM #1
 20 REM   EMERGENCY PHONE NUMBERS
 23 PRINT
 25 PRINT "0 - STOP PROGRAM RUN"
 30 PRINT "1 - AMBULANCE"
 40 PRINT "2 - POISON CENTER"
 50 PRINT
 60 PRINT "ENTER 0, 1 OR 2"
 75 IF A = 0 THEN GO TO 100
 80 IF A = 1 THEN PRINT "555-2751"
 90 IF A = 2 THEN PRINT "800-442-4571"
 93 IF A < 1 THEN PRINT "INVALID RESPONSE"
 :GO TO 50
 95 IF A > 2 THEN PRINT "INVALID RESPONSE"
 :GO TO 50
 97 PRINT:PRINT "ENTER ANY LETTER TO CON
 TINUE"
 98 INPUT XX$
 99 GO TO 23
 100 END
RUN
0 - STOP PROGRAM RUN
1 - AMBULANCE
2 - POISON CENTER

ENTER 0, 1 OR 2
?1
555-2751

ENTER ANY LETTER TO CONTINUE
?
```

Next, enter C and press Return, Enter, or ⏎ . What happens?

```
ENTER ANY LETTER TO CONTINUE
?C

0 - STOP PROGRAM RUN
1 - AMBULANCE
2 - POISON CENTER

ENTER 0, 1 OR 2"
?
```

The menu now contains an option that allows the user to terminate the run. To support this new option, the IF statement in line 75 was added. Most BASIC translators will allow the programmer to forgo the GO TO in statements like this. Therefore, another variation of line 75 is also acceptable:

```
75 IF A=0 THEN 100
```

The addition of line 99 puts the program into a loop. However, this does not represent a logic error because the user has a menu selection to stop the program run.

Enter 0 to stop the program run and LIST the program again.

Since the computer will patiently wait for a user to enter data, lines 97 and 98 demonstrate using an INPUT statement to hold the program run until the user is ready to go on.

The idea is to let the user tell the computer when he or she is ready to continue. The value entered for XX$ is called a **dummy.** It does not matter what you enter because it is not used later in the program. Still, the computer will wait for the user to enter a value for XX$ before sending execution back to line 23.

Finally, programmers like to fit the displays on a single screen. When the screen is filled, it will be cleared before more information is displayed. This is called **paging.**

With this program, it would be appropriate to clear the screen before displaying the menu. Line 23 should be changed to the BASIC statement used by your computer to clear the screen.

APPLE:	Home
COMMODORE:	PRINT " ☑ " ***The ☑ appears when the SHIFT and HOME are used after typing the first double quote
IBM:	CLS
RADIO SHACK:	CLS
	CLR HOME

RUN the program and enter the value 1. What happens?

```
0 - STOP PROGRAM RUN
1 - AMBULANCE
2 - POISON CENTER

ENTER 0, 1 OR 2
?1
555-2751

ENTER ANY LETTER TO CONTINUE
?
```

_____

Enter any letter and then select option 3. What happens?

```
0 - STOP PROGRAM RUN
1 - AMBULANCE
2 - POISON CENTER

ENTER 0, 1 OR 2
?3
INVALID RESPONSE

ENTER 0, 1 OR 2
?
```

_____

Enter a 2 and then return the program to the menu. Now, stop the program run by entering 0.

SAVE this program on tape or disk. You will use it later.

STUDY OBJECTIVES

34. Define transfer control, dummy value, and paging.

35. Describe the function of GO TO.

36. Demonstrate the use of a colon when two BASIC statements are to be included on the same line.

37. Describe the purpose of the Break or Stop key.

STEP 8

Computers are at their best when performing computations on a series of numbers.

Clear the memory and enter the following program:

```
10 REM STEP 8 - PROGRAM #1
20 REM LIST OF SQUARES
30 C = 10
40 PRINT "NUMBER";TAB(12);"SQUARE"
50 S = C ↑ 2
60 PRINT TAB(2);C;TAB(13);S
100 END
```

RUN the program. What happens?

To find the squares of the numerals 10 through 20, the variable C needs to be incremented—increased—by 1 until 20 is reached. The computation and PRINT statement—lines 50 and 60—must be repeated for each value of C.

Form a loop by adding

```
90 GO TO 50
```

To increase C each time, add

```
80 C=C+1
```

Notice that C is assigned a starting value in line 30 and incremented only after the previous value has been squared and PRINTed.

The variable C in line 80 is called a **counter.** A counter is a numeric variable used to keep track of repeating program sequences. Counters can identify the number of passes through a loop or the number of lines on a page.

Line 80 may look strange because the counter C appears on both sides of the equals sign. Although this equation is impossible in algebra, it is a permissible BASIC statement. Think of the equals sign as a backward arrow—←. The old value of C has 1 added to it and is stored back in the counter C.

Make sure that only 11 values of C are printed by adding

```
70 IF C=20 THEN GO TO 100
```

Clear the screen. LIST and RUN the program. What happens?

```
RUN
NUMBER       SQUARE
   10          100
   ▱
```

```
LIST
 10 REM STEP 8 - PROGRAM #1
 20 REM  LIST OF SQUARES
 30 C = 10
 40 PRINT "NUMBER";TAB(12);"SQUARE"
 50 S = C ↑ 2
 60 PRINT TAB(2);C;TAB(13);S
 70 IF C = 20 THEN GO TO 100
 80 C = C + 1
 90 GO TO 50
 100 END
RUN
NUMBER       SQUARE
   10          100
   11          121
   12          144
   13          169
   14          196
   15          225
   16          256
   17          289
   18          324
   19          361
   20          400
   ▱
```

The flowchart for Step 8 – Program #1 would look like this:

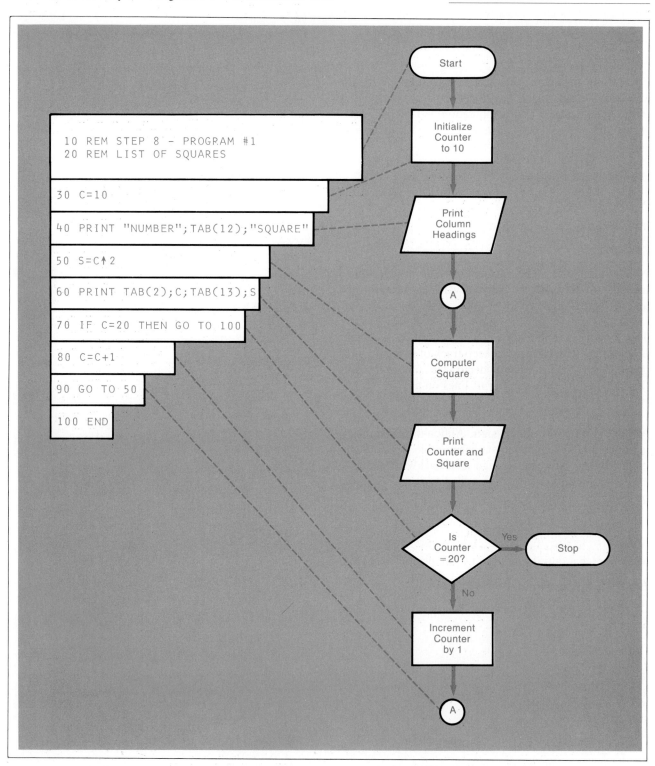

```
10 REM STEP 8 - PROGRAM #1
20 REM LIST OF SQUARES

30 C=10

40 PRINT "NUMBER";TAB(12);"SQUARE"

50 S=C↑2

60 PRINT TAB(2);C;TAB(13);S

70 IF C=20 THEN GO TO 100

80 C=C+1

90 GO TO 50

100 END
```

Notice that line 70 is represented by a decision diamond for the comparison and an arrow to either a stop symbol or a processing box. A shorter form of "INITIALIZE COUNTER TO 10" would be to write the BASIC statement C = 10. In addition, "INCREMENT C BY 1" can be shortened to C = C + 1.

Using the logical progression of assigning a starting value to a counter (C = 10), testing for an ending value (IF C = 20 THEN GO TO 100), and incrementing it (C = C + 1) is a common and very important programming tool.

Take a moment to modify this program. Change the starting, stopping, and incremental values.

Can you print all the squares from 1 to 25?
How about the even squares from 50 to 75?
Or the squares of all the multiples of 5
—5, 10, 15, 20 . . .—less than 100?

In looking back at the original version of Step 8—Program #1, the variable C was incremented within a loop. The variable and its square were then displayed. This process was then repeated 10 more times. The loop is determined by four lines of code:

GO TO 50—transfers control back to beginning of loop
C = 10—the starting value of C
IF C = 20 THEN GO TO 100—the ending value of C
C = C + 1—the increment or step size of C

The BASIC language has a shorter way of controlling a loop and the value of the counter within that loop—the **FOR/NEXT** statement.

Enter this program using the FOR/NEXT statement to produce the same output as Program #1 of Step 8:

```
10 REM STEP 8 - PROGRAM #2
20 REM USE OF FOR/NEXT TO LIST
30 REM SQUARES OF NUMBERS 10 TO 20
40 PRINT"NUMBER";TAB(12);"SQUARE"
50 FOR C = 10 TO 20 STEP 1
60 S = C ↑ 2
70 PRINT TAB(2);C;TAB(13);S
80 NEXT C
90 END
```

461

RUN the program.
What happens?

```
RUN
NUMBER      SQUARE
  10          100
  11          121
  12          144
  13          169
  14          196
  15          225
  16          256
  17          289
  18          324
  19          367
  20          400
  ▱
```

The FOR/NEXT statement is actually made up of two lines of code. Line 50 contains the FOR and identifies the variable C and the starting, ending, and increment values for C. Line 80 contains NEXT and the incremented variable C. A loop is formed by these two statements.

The action of the FOR/NEXT statement is most easily explained by following the program. When the computer first reaches line 50, C is set equal to 10 with the words *FOR C = 10*. Then lines 60 and 70 are performed with C having a value of 10.

When execution reaches line 80—NEXT C—control is automatically transferred back to line 50. At this time, the value of C is incremented. **STEP** 1 in line 50 means 1 is added to C and the loop is performed again.

This process continues until line 80 is reached with C equal to 20. Execution is transferred back to line 50 and C incremented to 21. The value of C is tested against the ending value identified by FOR C = 10 *TO 20* STEP 1. Since C is now greater than 20, control is transferred to the line after NEXT C. In this example, that is line 90.

Actually, the comparison of C against the ending value is performed for each pass through line 50, but it is only true on the twelfth pass.

Like all BASIC statements, FOR/NEXT has several restrictions and variations:

1. Each FOR statement must have a corresponding NEXT statement using the same variable. NEXT must be located after the FOR.

2. Only numeric variables can be used as counters in FOR/NEXT statements.

3. The starting, ending, and step values may be numeric variables or constants, positive or negative.

Example. `100 FOR EX = 5 TO N STEP -.5`

            .
            .
            .

`300 NEXT EX`

4. If a FOR/NEXT loop is left before all the values of the counter are completed, the counter retains the last value when leaving the loop.

5. Each FOR/NEXT loop is performed at least once.

Clear the memory and enter this program:

```
10 REM STEP 8 - PROGRAM #3
20 REM  FOR/NEXT WITH VARIABLES
30 PRINT "ENTER START, END AND"
40 PRINT "STEP SEPARATED BY COMMAS"
50 INPUT S,E,SP
60 FOR C = S TO E STEP SP
70 PRINT "COUNTER =";C
80 NEXT C
90 END
```

Clear the screen. RUN the program using the values 5, 10, 2.
What happens?

```
RUN
ENTER START, END AND
STEP SEPARATED BY COMMAS
?5,10,2
COUNTER = 5
COUNTER = 7
COUNTER = 9
▨
```

_____

Using these values, the loop is completed three times and the odd digits 5, 7, and 9 are displayed. On the fourth pass, C equals 11, which is greater than the desired ending value of 10. C never actually equals 10, but a value of 11 will complete execution of the FOR/NEXT loop.

_____

Clear the screen. RUN the program using the values 10, 0, −1.
What happens?

```
RUN
ENTER START, END AND
STEP SEPARATED BY COMMAS
?10,0,-1
COUNTER = 10
COUNTER = 9
COUNTER = 8
COUNTER = 7
COUNTER = 6
COUNTER = 5
COUNTER = 4
COUNTER = 3
COUNTER = 2
COUNTER = 1
COUNTER = 0
▨
```

Clear the screen again. RUN the program using the values
− 3, 2, .5.
What happens?

```
RUN
ENTER START, END AND
STEP SEPARATED BY COMMAS
?-3,2,.5
COUNTER = -3
COUNTER = -2.5
COUNTER = -2
COUNTER = -1.5
COUNTER = -1
COUNTER = -.5
COUNTER =  0
COUNTER = .5
COUNTER = 1
COUNTER = 1.5
COUNTER = 2
▨
```

Only numeric variables can be changed as part of the FOR/NEXT statement. However, the variable does not have to be displayed or used in a computation. It can just act as a counter to guarantee that the instructions in a loop are performed the requested number of times.

Change line 70 to

```
70 IF C = 1000 THEN PRINT "HALF WAY"
```

Clear the screen. RUN the program using the values 1, 2000, 1.
What happens?

```
RUN
ENTER START, END AND
STEP SEPARATED BY COMMAS
?1,2000,1
HALF WAY
▨
```

STUDY OBJECTIVES

38. Define counter.

39. Identify the four parts of a program loop.

40. State the reason C = C + 1 is a valid BASIC statement and explain what is meant by "incrementing a variable."

41. Describe the function of FOR, NEXT, and STEP.

42. Identify the five rules associated with FOR/NEXT statements.

Consider this problem. A program needs to be written that allows users to INPUT and PRINT any number of names for nametags. When a name is entered, the nametag should be immediately PRINTed. The IPO cycle for this program looks like this:

INPUT	PROCESSING	OUTPUT
1. Prompt and input desired number of nametags		
	2. Check to make sure input is greater than zero	
3. Prompt and input a name		
	5. Return to Step 3 the requested number of times	4. Print nametag

Since the action of INPUTing and PRINTing a name must be repeated, a FOR/NEXT loop can be used. One possible design for this program is outlined in figure 9.2.

Now enter the BASIC code for this problem:

```
10 REM STEP 9 - PROGRAM #1
20 REM NAMETAG PRINTING PROGRAM
30 ( CLEAR SCREEN )
40 PRINT
50 INPUT "REQUESTED NO. OF NAMETAGS";NO
60 IF NO <= 0 THEN PRINT "REQUEST MUST BE > ZERO": GO TO 40
70 FOR TG = 1 TO NO STEP 1
80 PRINT
90 INPUT "NAME";NA$
100 PRINT
110 PRINT "*********************"
120 PRINT
130 PRINT TAB(10);NA$
140 PRINT
150 PRINT "*********************"
160 NEXT TG
170 END
```

465

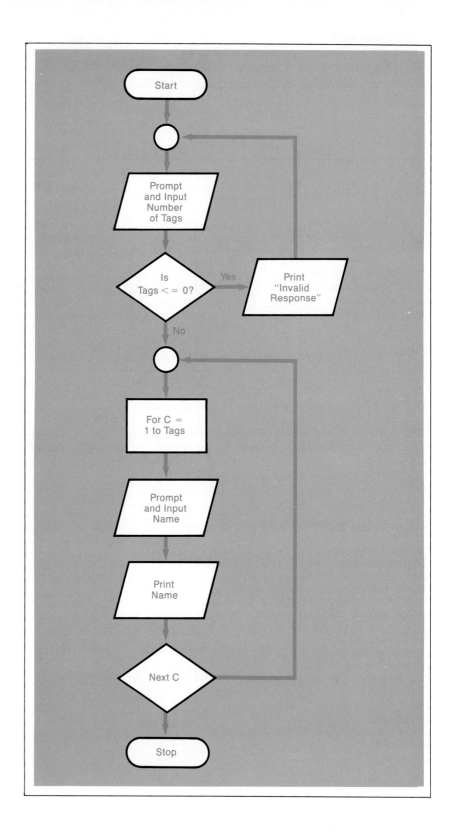

RUN the program.
What happens?

REQUESTED NO. OF NAMETAGS?2
NAME?TIM

※※※※※※※※※※※※※※※※※※※※※※※※※※※※※※※

            TIM

※※※※※※※※※※※※※※※※※※※※※※※※※※※※※※※

NAME?DAVE

※※※※※※※※※※※※※※※※※※※※※※※※※※※※※※※

            DAVE

※※※※※※※※※※※※※※※※※※※※※※※※※※※※※※※
☑

This program contains several new ideas besides the FOR/
NEXT loop. Lines 50 and 90 use an INPUT statement
that contains the prompt. Since every INPUT should be
preceded by a prompt, most BASIC translators will allow
the prompt as part of the statement. Two rules must be
followed:

1. The prompt must be in double quotes like any string
   constant
2. A semicolon (;) must separate the prompt from the
   variable name

As seen before, the PRINT verb alone, as in lines 80 and
100, will display a blank line. It is used to make the
nametag more legible. Also note that the variable NO that
is associated with the requested number of nametags is
used in the FOR/NEXT statement.

Step 9 – Program #1 is useful for entering a small number
of names. If the user wanted 100 nametags for a party or
wanted several sets of tags, time would be wasted entering
names one at a time and waiting for them to be printed.

A better method would be to store the names in the program as string constants. The user could then start the
program and leave. This logic has its disadvantages, since
every run would produce the same set of tags. However,
this may be beneficial in some applications and provides
an interesting example.

467

To store five names as a data bank in the program, delete line 50 and add or change these lines:

```
60 READ NO
90 READ NA$
165 DATA 5,PETE,SUE,JOHN,MARTHA,HAROLD
```

Clear the screen. LIST and RUN the program. What happens?

```
(1ST SCREEN WITH LISTING)
LIST
 10 REM STEP 9 - PROGRAM #1
 20 REM  NAMETAG PRINTING PROGRAM
 30 (CLEAR SCREEN)
 40 PRINT
 60 READ NO
 70 FOR TG = 1 TO NO STEP 1
 80 PRINT
 90 READ NA$
100 PRINT
110 PRINT "xxxxxxxxxxxxxxxxxxxxxxxxxxxxxxx"
120 PRINT
130 PRINT TAB(10);NA$
140 PRINT
150 PRINT "xxxxxxxxxxxxxxxxxxxxxxxxxxxxxxx"
160 NEXT TG
165 DATA 5,PETE,SUE,JOHN,MARTHA,HAROLD
170 END
```

```
(2ND SCREEN WITH OUTPUT)

xxxxxxxxxxxxxxxxxxxxxxxxxxxxxxx

          PETE

xxxxxxxxxxxxxxxxxxxxxxxxxxxxxxx

xxxxxxxxxxxxxxxxxxxxxxxxxxxxxxx

          SUE

xxxxxxxxxxxxxxxxxxxxxxxxxxxxxxx

xxxxxxxxxxxxxxxxxxxxxxxxxxxxxxx

          JOHN

xxxxxxxxxxxxxxxxxxxxxxxxxxxxxxx

xxxxxxxxxxxxxxxxxxxxxxxxxxxxxxx

          MARTHA

xxxxxxxxxxxxxxxxxxxxxxxxxxxxxxx

xxxxxxxxxxxxxxxxxxxxxxxxxxxxxxx

          HAROLD

xxxxxxxxxxxxxxxxxxxxxxxxxxxxxxx
```

To store values as part of the program, BASIC uses **READ/DATA** statements. Line 165 stores one numeric and six string constants separated by commas. Line 60 instructs the computer to assign the first data value—5— to variable name NO. When line 90 is reached, the next data value—PETE—is assigned to NA$. The next time line 90 is executed, SUE is assigned to NA$, and so on.

Change the 5 in line 165 to 3 and RUN the program. What happens?

```
:::::::::::::::::::::::::::::::::::::::::::::::::

            PETE

:::::::::::::::::::::::::::::::::::::::::::::::::

:::::::::::::::::::::::::::::::::::::::::::::::::

            SUE

:::::::::::::::::::::::::::::::::::::::::::::::::

:::::::::::::::::::::::::::::::::::::::::::::::::

            JOHN

:::::::::::::::::::::::::::::::::::::::::::::::::
☑
```

Now change the 3 in line 165 to a 7 and RUN the program again. What happens?

```
:::::::::::::::::::::::::::::::::::::::::::::::::

            PETE

:::::::::::::::::::::::::::::::::::::::::::::::::

:::::::::::::::::::::::::::::::::::::::::::::::::

            SUE

:::::::::::::::::::::::::::::::::::::::::::::::::

:::::::::::::::::::::::::::::::::::::::::::::::::

            JOHN

:::::::::::::::::::::::::::::::::::::::::::::::::

:::::::::::::::::::::::::::::::::::::::::::::::::

            MARTHA

:::::::::::::::::::::::::::::::::::::::::::::::::

:::::::::::::::::::::::::::::::::::::::::::::::::

            HAROLD

:::::::::::::::::::::::::::::::::::::::::::::::::
```

APPLE:	?OUT OF DATA ERROR IN 90
COMMODORE:	?OUT OF DATA ERROR IN 90
IBM:	Out of DATA in 90
RADIO SHACK:	?OD Error in 90

The numeric value that identifies the number of elements in the data base is called a **header.** The effect that the header and READ/DATA have depends on the value of the header and how many times the READ statement is executed.

If the number of times the READ statement is executed equals the number of data values in the DATA statement, there is no error.

If there are more data values, not all will be used, but no error message is printed. This is sometimes a logic error.

If there are fewer data values, the computer stops and warns that it is out of data.

The data can actually be split up into several DATA statements. Here is another way of coding the data listed in line 165:

```
163 DATA 5
165 DATA PETE,SUE,JOHN
167 DATA MARTHA,HAROLD
```

Add these lines to the program and RUN it. Is there any difference?

```
※※※※※※※※※※※※※※※※※※※※※※※※※※※※※※
             PETE
※※※※※※※※※※※※※※※※※※※※※※※※※※※※※※

※※※※※※※※※※※※※※※※※※※※※※※※※※※※※※
             SUE
※※※※※※※※※※※※※※※※※※※※※※※※※※※※※※

※※※※※※※※※※※※※※※※※※※※※※※※※※※※※※
             JOHN
※※※※※※※※※※※※※※※※※※※※※※※※※※※※※※

※※※※※※※※※※※※※※※※※※※※※※※※※※※※※※
            MARTHA
※※※※※※※※※※※※※※※※※※※※※※※※※※※※※※

※※※※※※※※※※※※※※※※※※※※※※※※※※※※※※
            HAROLD
※※※※※※※※※※※※※※※※※※※※※※※※※※※※※※
☑
```

DATA statements can appear anywhere in a program, even before the READ statement. The order in which the data values appear from top to bottom will determine the order in which they are accessed.

Step 9–Program #1 PRINTs only one set of five name-tags. To allow the user to request multiple sets, add or change these lines:

```
45 INPUT "ENTER NO. OF SETS";NS
50 IF NS < = 0 THEN PRINT "REQUEST
MUST BE  >  ZERO":GO TO 40
55 FOR SE = 1 TO NS STEP 1
161 RESTORE
162 NEXT SE
```

Clear the screen. LIST and RUN the program. What happens?

The variable NS represents the number of nametag sets needed. An additional FOR/NEXT loop including lines 55–162 is used to PRINT the set the requested number of times. Inside this loop is the second FOR/NEXT loop for READing each name. This is called a **nested loop.**

When using nested loops, be sure that both the FOR and NEXT of the second loop are *inside* the first FOR/NEXT loop. Otherwise, unpredictable results can occur.

The **RESTORE** statement in line 161 resets the pointer for the READ statement so that after the fifth name is read, the computer returns back to the first DATA statement. The placement of the RESTORE statement is critical. It must be positioned after the completion of the inside loop and before the NEXT statement for the outside loop. This programming tool, READ/DATA/RESTORE, is useful for repeated processing of the same data base.

```
LIST
 10 REM STEP 9 - PROGRAM #1
 20 REM  NAMETAG PRINTING PROGRAM
 30 (CLEAR SCREEN)
 40 PRINT
 45 INPUT "ENTER NO. OF SETS";NS
 50 IF NS <=0 THEN PRINT "REQUEST MUST BE
 > ZERO":GO TO 40
 55 FOR SE = 1 TO NS
 60 READ NO
 70 FOR TG = 1 TO NO STEP 1
 80 PRINT
 90 READ NA$
100 PRINT
110 PRINT "✕✕✕✕✕✕✕✕✕✕✕✕✕✕✕✕✕✕✕✕✕✕✕✕✕✕✕✕✕✕"
120 PRINT
130 PRINT TAB(10);NA$
140 PRINT
150 PRINT "✕✕✕✕✕✕✕✕✕✕✕✕✕✕✕✕✕✕✕✕✕✕✕✕✕✕✕✕✕✕"
160 NEXT TG
161 RESTORE
162 NEXT SE
163 DATA 5
165 DATA PETE,SUE,JOHN
167 DATA MARTHA,HAROLD
170 END

ENTER NO. OF SETS?

✕✕✕✕✕✕✕✕✕✕✕✕✕✕✕✕✕✕✕✕✕✕✕✕✕✕✕✕✕✕

        PETE

✕✕✕✕✕✕✕✕✕✕✕✕✕✕✕✕✕✕✕✕✕✕✕✕✕✕✕✕✕✕

✕✕✕✕✕✕✕✕✕✕✕✕✕✕✕✕✕✕✕✕✕✕✕✕✕✕✕✕✕✕

        SUE

✕✕✕✕✕✕✕✕✕✕✕✕✕✕✕✕✕✕✕✕✕✕✕✕✕✕✕✕✕✕

✕✕✕✕✕✕✕✕✕✕✕✕✕✕✕✕✕✕✕✕✕✕✕✕✕✕✕✕✕✕

        JOHN

✕✕✕✕✕✕✕✕✕✕✕✕✕✕✕✕✕✕✕✕✕✕✕✕✕✕✕✕✕✕

✕✕✕✕✕✕✕✕✕✕✕✕✕✕✕✕✕✕✕✕✕✕✕✕✕✕✕✕✕✕

        MARTHA

✕✕✕✕✕✕✕✕✕✕✕✕✕✕✕✕✕✕✕✕✕✕✕✕✕✕✕✕✕✕

✕✕✕✕✕✕✕✕✕✕✕✕✕✕✕✕✕✕✕✕✕✕✕✕✕✕✕✕✕✕

        HAROLD

✕✕✕✕✕✕✕✕✕✕✕✕✕✕✕✕✕✕✕✕✕✕✕✕✕✕✕✕✕✕
```

Repeated Requested Number of Times

43. Be able to flowchart a FOR/NEXT loop.

44. Identify the rules associated with including a prompt as part of an INPUT statement.

45. Describe the function of READ, DATA, and RESTORE.

46. Define header.

47. Briefly describe the effect of having more data values than executed READ statements and of executing more READ statements than there are data values in a program.

48. Identify the rules associated with the placement and access of DATA statements.

49. Demonstrate the use of nested FOR/NEXT loops in a BASIC program.

STEP 10

Several operations occur frequently in BASIC programs. Some, like finding a square root or generating a random number, require complicated code. To reduce the need to recreate these complicated routines, BASIC translators contain a series of preprogrammed instructions—called **functions**—for common operations. Each function is given a name that reflects the type of operation it performs. The general form of a function is

```
FUNCTION NAME (ARGUMENT 1, ARGUMENT 2, . . . )
```

The **arguments** are the constants or variables used by the function. For example, to compute the square root of 144 would require

```
A = SQR(144)
```

SQR is the function name and 144 the single argument used in the square root function.

Although there are slight differences between computers, BASIC translators contain functions to handle numeric operations and string manipulations and to generate random numbers. Common functions are listed in appendix F. Additional functions are explained in the user's manual.

Note these features:

1. The name of the function indicates the type of result to be returned. For example, STR$ contains the $ found in string variable names and returns a string value.

2. Depending on the specific form, each function requires a certain number and type of argument. For example, COS requires one numeric value. LEFT$ requires two arguments, a string followed by a numeric value.

3. An argument can be a constant or a variable.

4. Functions are found only on the right side of the equals sign.

5. Functions may be used in a PRINT statement.

   Example: `10 PRINT VAL(A$)`

6. More than one function may be used in a statement, and a function value can be used as the argument in another function.

   Example: `25 EM = ABS(Y) + INT(SQR(14))`

The following program uses the numeric functions INT, ABS, and SGN. These functions will produce a table of integer values (numbers without decimal point values), absolute values, and signs of the numbers from −5.5 to 5.5.

```
10 REM STEP 10 - PROGRAM #1
20 REM  EFFECT OF INT, ABS AND SGN
30 PRINT TAB(9);"INTEGER";TAB(19);"ABSOLUTE"
40 PRINT " NO.";TAB(10);"VALUE";TAB(20);"VALUE";TAB(30);"SIGN"
50 FOR N = -5.5 TO 5.5
60 PRINT N;TAB(11);INT(N);TAB(20);ABS(N);TAB(31);SGN(N)
70 NEXT N
80 END
```

Clear the memory. Enter this program and RUN it. What happens?

```
RUN
           INTEGER   ABSOLUTE
    NO.     VALUE     VALUE     SIGN
   -5.5      -6        5.5       -1
   -4.5      -5        4.5       -1
   -3.5      -4        3.5       -1
   -2.5      -3        2.5       -1
   -1.5      -2        1.5       -1
   -.5       -1         .5       -1
    .5        0         .5        1
   1.5        1        1.5        1
   2.5        2        2.5        1
   3.5        3        3.5        1
   4.5        4        4.5        1
   5.5        5        5.5        1
   ▨
```

In producing the table, a FOR/NEXT loop is used to generate the numbers. Notice that there is no STEP value in line 50. STEP 1 is assumed when STEP is left out.

The next program uses string functions to manipulate strings. The function LEFT$ isolates a single character from the string. The following code will allow the user to enter any string beginning with Y, like YES, YEP, or YEAH, and have it accepted as a positive answer. Also, any string beginning with N will be considered a negative answer.

```
10 REM STEP 10 - PROGRAM #2
20 REM  ONE-ARMED BANDIT
30 ( CLEAR SCREEN )
70 PRINT
80 INPUT "DO YOU WISH TO PLAY ";A$
90 IF LEFT$(A$,1) = "Y" THEN GO TO 140
100 IF LEFT$(A$,1) = "N" THEN GO TO 340
110 PRINT "ANSWER YES OR NO"
120 GO TO 70
140 ( CLEAR SCREEN )
150 PRINT "THE ONE-ARMED BANDIT"
340 END
```

Clear the memory. Enter this program. RUN it and answer YES to the question. What happens?

————————————

RUN the program again and answer NAW to the question. What happens?

————————————

RUN the program one more time and answer OK to the question. What happens?

————————————

Stop the program and then LIST it. Lines 90 and 100 isolate the leftmost character and compare it with Y or N. If a match is found, control will be sent to the appropriate line.

If line 140 is reached, neither Y nor N began the input string and another chance is given to the user. The idea

```
(1ST SCREEN)
DO YOU WISH TO PLAY ?YES

(2ND SCREEN)
THE ONE-ARMED BANDIT
▨


DO YOU WISH TO PLAY ?NAW
▨


DO YOU WISH TO PLAY ?OK
ANSWER YES OR NO

DO YOU WISH TO PLAY ?
```

is to provide the user with single-letter entries that allow easy passage through the program while minimizing the effect of data entry errors.

The randomizing function—RND—performs a unique operation. Using the argument of the function as a starting or **seed value,** it generates a single random number each time it is used.

The RND function acts differently in each machine. Some will produce a number between 0 and 1 based on the seed. Others will produce whole numbers between 0 and the seed number.

APPLE:	RND (1)*
COMMODORE:	RND (TI)*
IBM:	RND (−1)*
RADIO SHACK:	RND (0)*

*User's manual provides other alternatives

Complete Step 10–Program #2 as follows. This program uses the RND function to generate three random numbers from 0 to 9. It then checks to see if they match each other. If all three match, the user wins the jackpot, which is all the money paid in plus $25. If no match occurs, the user loses 25 cents. Lines 170–190 may be different, depending on how RND is used in your computer.

```
10 REM STEP 10 - PROGRAM #2
20 REM  ONE-ARMED BANDIT
30 ( CLEAR SCREEN )
40 TL = 25
50 PRINT "EACH PLAY COSTS 25 CENTS"
60 PRINT "YOUR POSSIBLE WINNINGS ARE NOW $";TL
70 PRINT
80 INPUT "DO YOU WISH TO PLAY ";A$
90 IF LEFT$(A$,1) = "Y" THEN GO TO 140
100 IF LEFT$(A$,1) = "N" THEN GO TO 340
110 PRINT "ANSWER YES OR NO"
120 GO TO 70
130 REM GENERATE AND DISPLAY NUMBERS
140 ( CLEAR SCREEN )
150 PRINT "THE ONE-ARMED BANDIT"
160 TL = TL + .25
170 N1 = INT(RND(?) * 10)
180 N2 = INT(RND(?) * 10)
190 N3 = INT(RND(?) * 10)
200 PRINT
```

```
210 PRINT "YOUR NUMBERS ARE . . . . ."
220 FOR C = 1 TO 1500: NEXT C
230 PRINT N1;TAB(10);
240 FOR C = 1 TO 1500: NEXT C
250 PRINT N2;TAB(20);
260 FOR C = 1 TO 1500: NEXT C
270 PRINT N3: PRINT
280 REM CHECK FOR MATCH & PRINT RESULT
290 IF N1 <> N2 THEN GO TO 330
300 IF N2 <> N3 THEN GO TO 330
310 FOR C = 1 TO 1500: NEXT C
320 PRINT "YOU HAVE WON $";TL;" . . .
CONGRATULATIONS!":GO TO 340
330 PRINT "TOO BAD, SUCKER!!!": PRINT: GO TO 60
340 END
```

This program has several interesting features. Lines 170–190 generate three random numbers. Since RND in this case generates a number between 0 and 1, this number is multiplied by 10 and used as an argument in the INT function. The INT function converts the decimal number to one of the whole numbers between 0 and 9. For example, if the random number is .7362 the following happens:

```
N1 = INT(RND(?) * 10)
N1 = INT(.7362 * 10)
N1 = INT(7.362)
N1 = 7
```

The numbers are then displayed by lines 220–270 and checked for a match. By eliminating unmatched pairs in lines 290 and 300, it can be assumed that if line 310 is reached, all three numbers match and the jackpot has been won.

Part of the suspense of the game is to slow the presentation of the three numbers. The computer is delayed before printing each number with the FOR/NEXT loops of lines 220, 240, and 260, which must be performed 1500 times before the next number is printed.

A special trick is used to have the output from lines 230, 250, and 270 all printed on the same line. Lines 230 and 250 have a semicolon (;) after the TAB. A semicolon at the end of a PRINT statement forces the next output line to appear on the same line.

Predefined functions make programming easier and more efficient. It is worthwhile for a programmer to investigate the functions available on his or her computer and use them when appropriate.

Programmers can also define their own functions on any of these micro-computers except for the tape-recorder-based Radio Shack computer. This is done when an equation is repeatedly used. By defining the equation as a programmer-defined function, programmers can save coding time. In Step 10–Program #2, the random number computation could be predefined as follows:

```
25 DEF FNR(X) = INT(RND(X) * 10)
```

With the programmer-defined function FNR identified, lines 170–190 can be changed to the following:

```
170 N1 = FNR(?)
180 N2 = FNR(?)
190 N3 = FNR(?)
```

The ? should be replaced with the appropriate seed value used by your computer. This value is used as defined by the placement of X in line 25. The programmer can define several functions. In this program, the programmer can still define functions FNA to FNQ, and FNS to FNZ. Add line 25 to the program and change lines 170–190. Then RUN the program to verify that it works properly.

STUDY OBJECTIVES

50. Given a user's manual, correctly use the common BASIC functions and programmer-defined functions.
51. Define argument and seed value.
52. Demonstrate how to delay program output by using a FOR/NEXT statement.
53. Describe the effect a semicolon has at the end of a PRINT statement.

STEP 11

In the previous steps, data was stored and processed through the use of READ and DATA statements. With this organization, the first item must be READ before the second item. DATA statements are said to store data sequentially. Sequential storage means the data is organized in a predefined order. **Sequential processing** starts at the first item and continues without deviating until the needed item is found. In other words, item 3 is always processed before item 4 and after item 2.

Programs use sequential logic. LOAD and LIST Step 7—Program #1 with the emergency telephone numbers.

```
10 REM STEP 7 - PROGRAM #1
20 REM   EMERGENCY PHONE NUMBERS
23 ( CLEAR SCREEN )
25 PRINT "0 - STOP PROGRAM RUN"
30 PRINT "1 - AMBULANCE"
40 PRINT "2 - POISON CENTER"
50 PRINT
60 PRINT "ENTER 0, 1 OR 2"
70 INPUT A
75 IF A = 0 THEN GO TO 100
80 IF A = 1 THEN PRINT "555-2751"
90 IF A = 2 THEN PRINT "800-442-4571"
93 IF A < 1 THEN PRINT "INVALID RESPONSE": GO TO 50
95 IF A > 2 THEN PRINT "INVALID RESPONSE": GO TO 50
97 PRINT: PRINT "ENTER ANY LETTER TO CONTINUE"
98 INPUT XX$
99 GO TO 23
100 END
```

This program uses sequential logic. The series of **IF/THEN** statements checks the INPUT response in sequence for 0, 1, and 2. It then checks for a possible error condition. This technique works well for a few telephone numbers, but would mean numerous IF statements when working with large data bases.

Although data is often sequentially processed, another processing method is preferable for large data bases. It is possible to program a computer to directly access data. **Direct accessing** means going right to the requested data without processing data found before or after it. When using direct access techniques, it should take no longer to find item 500 than to find item 1.

Delete lines 80 and 90. Then enter the following statements:

```
10 REM STEP 11 - PROGRAM #1
21 N$(1) = "AMBULANCE DISPATCH: 555-2751"
22 N$(2) = "POISON CENTER: 800-442-4571"
96 PRINT N$(A)
```

RUN this program using options 1 and 2. What happens?

```
(OPTION 1)

0 - STOP PROGRAM RUN
1 - AMBULANCE
2 - POISON CENTER

ENTER 0, 1 OR 2
?1
AMBULANCE DISPATCH: 555-2751

ENTER ANY LETTER TO CONTINUE
?C

(OPTION 2)

0 - STOP PROGRAM RUN
1 - AMBULANCE
2 - POISON CENTER

ENTER 0, 1 OR 2
?2
POISON CENTER: 800-442-4571

ENTER ANY LETTER TO CONTINUE
?
```

The emergency telephone numbers are now directly accessed. To use direct accessing, each item in the data base must be uniquely identified.

Since computers work more efficiently with numbers, each item in the data base is given a unique number called a **subscript.** The telephone numbers in lines 21 and 22 are now identified by the variable name N$ and the subscripts (1) and (2).

Direct accessing is possible because each subscripted value of N$ has a different memory location. A subscripted variable is identified by a numeric variable or constant within parentheses. In this case, the numeric variable A, input by the user, identifies the desired telephone number in line 96.

Since subscripts are used to directly access a group of variables, these variables are often referred to as a **table** or **array** of values. Tables, or arrays, are very useful when large amounts of data must be repeatedly accessed.

Sorting numbers or names with a computer provides a classic example. A sort involves examining each item several times to determine the proper order. Storing the items in a table allows quick access to all items while sorting.

A sort program will follow these steps:

INPUT	PROCESSING	OUTPUT
1. Identify the number of Items to be sorted		
2. Enter each item	3. Sort items in ascending order or	
	4. Sort items in descending order	5. Display items in sorted order

This program will require more coding than previous programs. When writing large programs, programmers design their programs in sections, or modules. A program designed in modules is made up of interrelated sections that are written and tested separately. The following sort program uses modular design. Each of the above steps will be developed as a separate module.

479

Clear the memory and screen. Enter the following statements:

```
10 REM STEP 11 - PROGRAM #1
20 REM   SORTING NAMES AND NUMBERS
30 REM *** INPUT MODULE ***
40 ( CLEAR SCREEN )
50 PRINT "NUMBER OF ITEMS TO BE SORTED"
60 INPUT N: PRINT
70 PRINT "ENTER ONE ITEM PER LINE"
80 FOR X = 1 TO N
90 PRINT X;"- ";
100 INPUT N$(X)
110 NEXT X
```

Although these lines represent only part of the sorting program, this portion can be tested for syntax and logic errors.

RUN the input module using 12 to 15 entries. What happens?

```
NUMBER OF ITEMS TO BE SORTED
?12

ENTER ONE ITEM PER LINE
 1 - ?MARTHA
 2 - ?PETE
 3 - ?JOHN
 4 - ?SUE
 5 - ?HAROLD
 6 - ?SALLY
 7 - ?RANDY
 8 - ?DIANE
 9 - ?TODD
10 - ?DAVE
11 - ?MARY
::
```

APPLE: ?BAD SUBSCRIPT ERROR IN 100
COMMODORE: ?BAD SUBSCRIPT ERROR IN 100
IBM   Subscript out of range in 100
RADIO SHACK: ?BS ERROR IN 100

An additional statement is necessary when more than 10 subscripts are used. Enter

```
65 DIM N$(N)
```

The **DIMension** statement is used to allocate additional memory when more than 10 subscripts are needed. The numeric variable or constant within parentheses allocates enough space in memory for the specified number of subscripted variables.

Clear the screen. RUN the input module again using more than 10 entries. What happens?

```
NUMBER OF ITEMS TO BE SORTED
?12

ENTER ONE ITEM PER LINE
  1 - ?MARTHA
  2 - ?PETE
  3 - ?JOHN
  4 - ?SUE
  5 - ?HAROLD
  6 - ?SALLY
  7 - ?RANDY
  8 - ?DIANE
  9 - ?TODD
 10 - ?DAVE
 11 - ?MARY
 12 - ?JAKE
 ▨
```

Next enter:

```
120 REM *** MAIN MODULE ***
130 PRINT: PRINT "SORTING OPTIONS"
140 PRINT "   1) ASCENDING ORDER"
150 PRINT "      A, B, C . . . OR 1, 2, 3 . . ."
160 PRINT "   2) DESCENDING ORDER"
170 PRINT " Z, X, Y . . . OR 10, 9, 8 . . ."
180 PRINT
190 INPUT "SELECTION ";A
200 PRINT
210 IF A < 1 THEN PRINT "INVALID ENTRY":GO TO 180
220 IF A > 2 THEN PRINT "INVALID ENTRY":GO TO 180
230 IF A = 1 THEN GOSUB 1000: REM ASCENDING ORDER
240 IF A = 2 THEN GOSUB 1000: REM DESCENDING ORDER
250 END
1000 REM ASCENDING ORDER SORT
1010 PRINT "NOW SORTING BY ASCENDING ORDER"
1020 RETURN
2000 REM DESCENDING ORDER SORT
2010 PRINT "NOW SORTING BY DESCENDING ORDER"
2020 RETURN
```

Run the program.

The menu of the sort program provides the user with two sorting options: ascending (increasing) order or descending (decreasing) order. A special **algorithm** is necessary with each option and will be developed later. An algorithm is a set of codes written to perform a specific operation.

Both sorting algorithms are part of the main processing module. They are set off from the main module and are therefore called submodules or **SUB-routines.** BASIC translators allow subroutines within programs, which eliminates the need for GO TOs from the main processing module.

Two subroutines are referenced in this program. The subroutine to sort the table in ascending order starts in line 1000. The subroutine for descending order starts in line 2000.

Subroutines can only be referenced with a **GOSUB** statement. The general form for a GOSUB statement is

```
LINE NUMBER   GOSUB   FIRST LINE OF SUBROUTINE
```

The last line of a subroutine must be a **RETURN** statement. When a RETURN statement is encountered, control is transferred to the line following the GOSUB statement. Subroutines, like modules, are also useful in program design because they allow intermediate testing of program code.

In developing this program, the main module was tested without the sorting subroutines. All that was included in the test RUN were the REMarks and PRINT statements identifying the first lines of the subroutine and the required RETURN statements. The coding for these subroutines will be tested later.

The general rules for the use of GOSUB/RETURN statements are as follows:

1. The GOSUB statement contains the line number of the first statement of the subroutine.

2. Every subroutine must have a RETURN statement.

3. When the RETURN statement is encountered, control is transferred back to the statement following the GOSUB.

4. Subroutines can only be accessed with a GOSUB statement. An error will result if a GO TO statement is used to access the subroutine.

5. GO TO statements should not be used to transfer control outside of a subroutine.

Enter these lines:

```
250 REM ***OUTPUT MODULE ***
260 PRINT: PRINT "SORTED ITEMS"
270 FOR X = 1 TO N
280 PRINT X;"-_";N$(X)
290 NEXT X
300 END
```

RUN the program using five entries. What happens?

```
NUMBER OF ITEMS TO BE SORTED
?5

ENTER ONE ITEM PER LINE
  1 - ?TIM
  2 - ?SALLY
  3 - ?TERRI
  4 - ?NANCY
  5 - ?TODD

SORTING OPTIONS
   1) ASCENDING ORDER
      A, B, C... OR 1, 2, 3...
   2) DESCENDING ORDER
      Z, Y, X... OR 10, 9, 8...

SELECTION ?1

NOW SORTING BY ASCENDING ORDER

SORTED ITEMS
  1 - TIM
  2 - SALLY
  3 - TERRI
  4 - NANCY
  5 - TODD
▨
```

The input order should be the same as the output order because the sorting subroutines have not been added to the program. When the sort routines are added, any errors that occur are first assumed to be in these routines, since the input and output modules have already been tested.

This is a good example of how program modularity enables the programmer to isolate possible logic errors in a complicated program.

Enter the following lines:

```
1020 FOR A = 1 TO N - 1
1030 FOR B = A + 1 TO N
1040 IF N$(A) <= N$(B) THEN GO TO 1080
1050 D$ = N$(A)
1060 N$(A) = N$(B)
1070 N$(B) = D$
1080 NEXT B
1090 NEXT A
1100 RETURN
```

RUN the program using option 1. Enter five names: MIKE, MARTHA, WILLIAM, ALAN, AND MARY. What happens?

```
NUMBER OF ITEMS TO BE SORTED
?5

ENTER ONE ITEM PER LINE
  1 - ?MIKE
  2 - ?MARTHA
  3 - ?WILLIAM
  4 - ?ALAN
  5 - ?MARY

SORTING OPTIONS
  1) ASCENDING ORDER
     A, B, C... OR 1, 2, 3...
  2) DESCENDING ORDER
     Z, Y, X... OR 10, 9, 8...

SELECTION ?1

NOW SORTING BY ASCENDING ORDER

SORTED ITEMS
  1 - ALAN
  2 - MARTHA
  3 - MARY
  4 - MIKE
  5 - WILLIAM
☑
```

Subroutine 1000 contains the logic for the selection sort algorithm. The sorting algorithm uses nested loops to examine all the table values, two at a time.

Since the inner loop is completed before the outer loop is incremented, the computer will compare the first table value against all the others, then the second value against the remaining values, and so on, until all the items have been compared and placed in the proper order.

When an item is found to be out of order, it is swapped in lines 1050–1070 with the item it is being compared with.

Now enter:

```
2020 FOR A = 1 TO N - 1
2030 FOR B = A + 1 TO N
2040 IF N$(A) >= N$(B) THEN GO TO 2080
2050 D$ = N$(A)
2060 N$(A) = N$(B)
2070 N$(B) = D$
2080 NEXT B
2090 NEXT A
2100 RETURN
```

RUN the program entering the same names using option 2.
What happens?

```
NUMBER OF ITEMS TO BE SORTED
?5

ENTER ONE ITEM PER LINE
  1 - ?MIKE
  2 - ?MARTHA
  3 - ?WILLIAM
  4 - ?ALAN
  5 - ?MARY

SORTING OPTIONS
   1) ASCENDING ORDER
      A, B, C... OR 1, 2, 3...
   2) DESCENDING ORDER
      Z, Y, X... OR 10, 9, 8...

SELECTION ?2

NOW SORTING BY DESCENDING ORDER

SORTED ITEMS
  1 - WILLIAM
  2 - MIKE
  3 - MARY
  4 - MARTHA
  5 - ALAN
```

Writing computer programs can be made less complicated by organizing the data into tables and the program into modules. This technique makes programs easier to code and debug and also simplifies future maintenance and changes.

STUDY OBJECTIVES

54. Define sequential processing, direct accessing, subscript, table, array, and algorithm.

55. Describe the function of DIM, GOSUB, and RETURN.

56. Identify one advantage of using tables (arrays) to store large data bases.

57. Give the rationale for designing programs in modules.

58. Describe the rules for using DIM and GOSUB statements.

APPENDIX A

Start-Up Procedures for the Apple Microcomputer

The history of the Apple microcomputer is an often-told story. Two young men working out of a garage designed and built the original Apple computer. It was the first popular microcomputer to make extensive use of color and graphic displays.

The keyboard is built into the computer's housing with a television—usually color—and disk drives attached by cables. The early Apples also used tape recorders, but, this type of storage hardware has been phased out. Newer Apples rely on disk drives for storing programs and data.

A systems disk—with the operating system and one of two BASIC interpreters—must be placed in disk drive 1 before the computer is turned on. The disk drive does not have a separate on/off switch since it draws power from the computer. The on/off switch for the computer is in the back on the left side of the computer as you face the front. There is a separate on/off switch for the television.

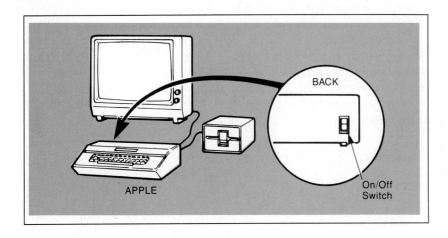

BACK

APPLE

On/Off
Switch

The computer will print a special message when first turned on. One of two symbols will also appear on the screen. A ⟩ means the Integer BASIC interpreter is being used, whereas a] indicates that the Applesoft BASIC interpreter is being used.

Read the message. Then enter NEW and press the Return key.

Once the computer is on, it will position a special symbol—called a **cursor**—on the screen. When entering data using the keyboard, the data replaces the cursor and the cursor moves over one space. The cursor for an Apple computer is the flashing box next to the ⟩ or].

Before starting to program the computer, take a closer look at the keyboard you will be using. Computer keyboards are laid out just like typewriter keyboards. In addition, there are special keys that allow the user to move the cursor—left, right, up, and down—or to delete characters already on the screen.

Enter the following into the computer using the keyboard:

PRINT "THE EARTH IS FLAT."

When you are done, the cursor should be located after the double quote.

Since the earth is not flat, the next step is to erase FLAT and type ROUND. The Apple will let you move the cursor to the left without erasing the sentence. The ⬅ key moves the cursor to the left. Since it moves the cursor without erasing what is on the screen, this is called **nondestructive cursor movement.**

Move the cursor on top of the F in FLAT and type ROUND.". The computer will overwrite FLAT with ROUND.

Since a science teacher might take exception to this sentence, ALMOST should be added before ROUND. Using the ⬅ key, move the cursor on top of the R in ROUND.

To add ALMOST to this sentence requires using a special combination of keys to edit the sentence. Press the ESC and D keys at the same time. The cursor will move up one line to allow you enough room to enter any additions to the line. Type a space, ALMOST, and another space, then press the ESC and C keys. This will move the cursor back to the original line.

Now move the cursor back over the R in ROUND by pressing the ESC and B keys for each letter. Since there are 5 letters in the word ROUND, this combination of keys must be pressed 5 times. You must press both keys each time. This is important because it indicates to the computer that it is to pick up the rest of the sentence starting with R. Move the cursor to the end of the sentence using the ➡ key. It should now look like this:

ALMOST
PRINT "THE EARTH IS ROUND."

If not, try again until it does.

To have the computer display or PRINT

THE EARTH IS ALMOST ROUND.

you press the Return key on the right side of the keyboard. When this key is pressed, the computer accepts that line into memory. Remember this when writing BASIC programs in STEPS 1 - 11. Mistakes are not entered into the computer until Return is pressed. Therefore, you always have a chance to correct mistakes by using cursor movement and other special keys.

Press Return, and THE EARTH IS ALMOST ROUND. should be displayed on the screen. You are now ready to start STEP 1 in BASIC on Microcomputers Step-by-Step.

APPENDIX B

Start-Up Procedures for Commodore Microcomputers

The Commodore PET was one of the first microcomputers on the market. It was followed by the Commodore CBM—Commodore Business Machine—a few years later. Both of these computers have a CRT and keyboard built into the computer's housing. The on/off switch is in the back on the left-hand side of the machine as you face the front.

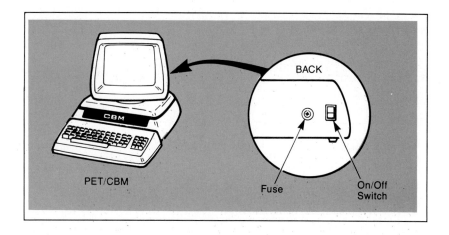

The difference between the PET and CBM is found in the character display. The PET will display upper-case letters and special graphic characters. The CBM was designed to work like a typewriter. Lower-case letters will be displayed when the Shift key is not pressed. When the Shift key is depressed, upper-case letters appear on the screen.

The VIC 20 and VIC 64 microcomputers represent another line of Commodore microcomputers. They have screen displays similar to the PET. The

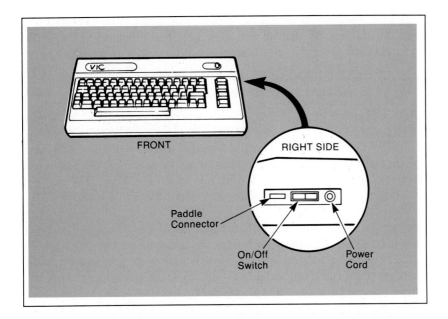

VIC 20 and VIC 64 have built-in keyboards. The user attaches a television with cables for use as output. The on/off switch for these machines is on the right side as you face the front. The television will have its own on/off switch.

The early Commodore computers had a tape recorder and small keyboard built into the computer's casing. Later models went to a full-size keyboard and attached the tape recorder to the back with a cable. Either way, the tape recorder does not have to be turned on. It draws its power directly from the computer.

Disk drives are attached to the computer with cables. They have a separate on/off switch located in the back on the left side as you face the drive.

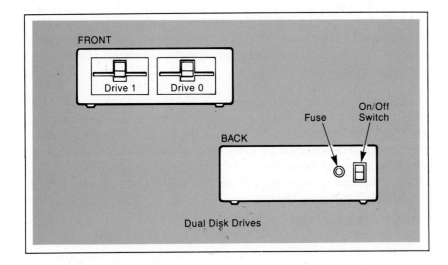

After the computer is turned on, a short message will be displayed on the screen. In addition, the display will show how much memory is available for data and BASIC programs. For example, a VIC 64 will display:

**** COMMODORE 64 BASIC V2 ****
64K RAM SYSTEM 38911 BASIC BYTES FREE

READY will appear on the screen when the computer is waiting for a command.

Once the computer is on, it will position a special symbol—called a **cursor**—on the screen. When entering data using the keyboard, the data replaces the cursor and the cursor moves over one space at a time. The cursor for Commodore computers is the flashing box under the R in READY.

Before starting to program the computer, take a closer look at the keyboard you will be using. Computer keyboards are laid out just like typewriter keyboards. In addition, there are special keys that allow the programmer to move the cursor—left, right, up, and down—and to delete characters already on the screen.

Enter the following into the computer using the keyboard:

PRINT THE EARTH IS FLAT.

When you are done, the cursor should be located after the period.

Since the earth is not flat, the next step is to erase FLAT and type ROUND. The ⌷INST DEL key erases one character at a time from the screen. Press this key enough times to erase FLAT. It should now look like this:

PRINT THE EARTH IS

If not, try again until it does.
Now type: ROUND.

Next, THE EARTH IS ROUND. needs to be enclosed in double quotes ("). But you don't want to erase the sentence to do this. Instead, most computers will let you move the cursor back to the beginning without erasing the sentence. The Shift and ⌷ keys move the cursor to the left without erasing what is on the screen. This is called **nondestructive cursor movement.** Move the cursor on top of the T in THE.

Use the Shift and ⌷INST DEL keys to insert a space for the double quote. Find the double quote on the keyboard. Usually, it is on the top of a key with another symbol or character underneath. If it is on the top of the key, this means you have to press the Shift key at the same time. If the Shift key isn't pressed, the bottom character will be printed.

Place the double quote in front of the T in THE by pressing the appropriate keys. It should now look like this:

PRINT "THE EARTH IS ROUND.

If not, try again until it does.

Now type a second double quote. Does it look like this?

PRINT " "HE EARTH IS ROUND.

Computers will overwrite what is already on the screen. Therefore, you first have to use the key for nondestructive cursor movement to move over the sentence.

Move the cursor back over the second double quote and type T again. The screen should now look like this:

PRINT "THE EARTH IS ROUND.

The ⊡ key will move the cursor to the end of the sentence. With the cursor at the end of the sentence, enter another double quote.

Does it look like this?

PRINT "THE EARTH IS ROUND."

If not, try again until it does.

All of the work that has been done so far has been on the screen. This line has not been sent to the computer yet. To have the computer display or PRINT

THE EARTH IS ROUND.

press the Return key on the right side of the keyboard. When this key is pressed, the computer accepts that line into memory. Remember this when writing BASIC programs in STEPS 1 - 11. Mistakes are not entered into the computer until Return is pressed. Therefore, you always have a chance to correct mistakes by using cursor movement and other special keys.

Press Return, and THE EARTH IS ROUND. should be displayed on the screen. You are now ready to start STEP 1 in BASIC on Microcomputers Step-by-Step.

APPENDIX C

Start-Up Procedures for the IBM Microcomputer

The IBM Personal Computer—PC—was one of the last entries into the market and IBM's first microcomputer. These microcomputers have the disk drive and computer in the same housing. One on/off switch—located on the right side of the computer as you face it—turns on both. The keyboard and CRT are attached by cables.

Before turning the power on, a systems disk—with the operating system and BASIC interpreter—must be in disk drive A. If the microcomputer has dual disk drives, drive A is on the left. The computer will default—assume—that a tape recorder will be used for storage if the systems disk is not in disk drive A when the power is turned on.

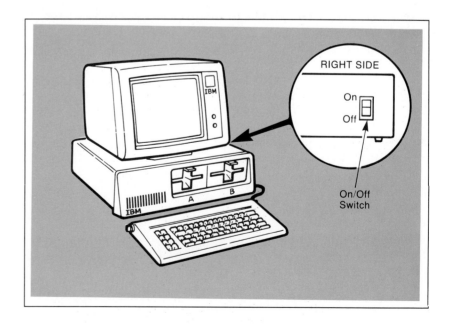

IBM microcomputers require the user to enter the current date when first turned on. At this time the following display will appear:

Current date is Tue X-XX-XXXX   (date will vary)
Enter new date:

Enter three sets of numbers representing the month-day-year and press the ⏎ key. Newer computers will then display:

Current time is X:XX:XX:XX   (time will vary)
Enter new time:

You have the option of entering time in hours:minutes:seconds or just pressing the ⏎ key.
Next the computer will display:

The IBM Personal Computer DOS
Version X.XX(c) Copyright IBM Corp. 1981,1982

A ⟩

Enter BASIC in upper- or lower-case letters and press the ⏎ key. This action will call in the BASIC interpreter. The computer will display:

The IBM Personal Computer BASIC
Version X.XX Copyright IBM Corp. 1981,1982
40956 Bytes free
OK

How much memory the computer has will determine the number of free bytes. OK will appear on the screen when the computer is ready.

Once the computer is on, it will position a special symbol—a **cursor**—on the screen. When entering data using the keyboard, the data replaces the cursor and the cursor moves over one space. The cursor for an IBM computer is the thin line under the OK.

Before starting to program the computer, take a closer look at the keyboard. Computer keyboards are laid out just like typewriter keyboards. In addition, there are special keys that allow the programmer to move the cursor—left, right, up, and down—and to delete characters already on the screen.
Enter the following into the computer using the keyboard:

PRINT THE EARTH IS FLAT.

When you are done, the cursor should be located after the period.

Since the earth is not flat, the next step is to erase FLAT and type ROUND. The ⌫ key erases one character at a time from the screen. Press this key enough times to erase FLAT. It should now look like this:

PRINT THE EARTH IS

If not, try again until it does.
Now type: ROUND.

Next, THE EARTH IS ROUND. needs to be enclosed in double quotes (").
You don't want to erase the sentence to do this. Instead, the IBM computer
will let you move the cursor back to the beginning without erasing the sentence.
The ⬅ key moves the cursor to the left without erasing what is on the screen.
This is called **nondestructive cursor movement.** Move the cursor on top of
the T in THE.

Another key is used to put the computer into an insert mode. Use the ⬚
key when inserting characters into a line. Press this key and watch the cursor
change in shape. Whenever the cursor is shaped like a box it means the computer is ready to insert characters.

Find the double quote on the keyboard. Usually, it is on the top of a key
with another symbol or character underneath. If it is on the top of the key, this
means you have to press the ⬆ key at the same time. If the ⬆ key isn't pressed,
the bottom character will be printed. Place the double quote in front of the T
in THE by pressing the appropriate keys. It should now look like this:

PRINT "THE EARTH IS ROUND.

If not, try again until it does.

Now type a second double quote. Does it look like this?

PRINT " "THE EARTH IS ROUND.

The IBM Computer will continue to insert characters in front of the T until
one of the cursor movement keys is used or the ⮐ key is pressed.

Erase the second double quote and move the cursor to the end of the sentence
using the ➡ key. With the cursor at the end of the sentence, enter another
double quote. Does it now look like this?

PRINT "THE EARTH IS ROUND."

If not, try again until it does.

All of the work that has been done so far has been on the screen. Nothing
has been sent to the computer yet. To have the computer display or PRINT

THE EARTH IS ROUND.

you press the ⮐ key on the right side of the keyboard. When this key is pressed,
the computer accepts that line into memory. Remember this when writing
BASIC programs in STEPS 1 - 11. Mistakes are not entered into the computer
until ⮐ is pressed. Therefore, you always have a chance to correct mistakes
by using cursor movement and other special keys.

Press ⮐ , and THE EARTH IS ROUND. should be displayed on the screen.
You are now ready to start STEP 1 in BASIC on Microcomputers Step-by-
Step.

APPENDIX D

Start-Up Procedures for Tandy Radio Shack Microcomputers

The Tandy Corporations's Radio Shack has several different microcomputer models. The first was the TRS-80 Model I, which is no longer in production. Several other product lines emerged after the success of the Model I.

Radio Shack designed the TRS-80 Color Computer for the home. It has a built-in keyboard with a color television and disk drive or tape recorder attached by cables. The on/off switch is located in the back on the left side of the computer as you face it. The television has a separate on/off switch.

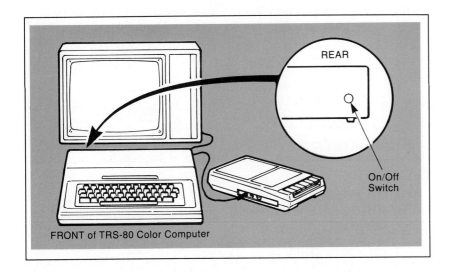

REAR

On/Off Switch

FRONT of TRS-80 Color Computer

One of Radio Shack's most popular models was the TRS-80 Model III. The TRS-80 Model 4 offers additional features and was designed to replace the Model III. Both computers have built-in keyboards and CRTs. Built-in disk drives, using floppy disks 5 1/4 inches across, are also available. The on/off

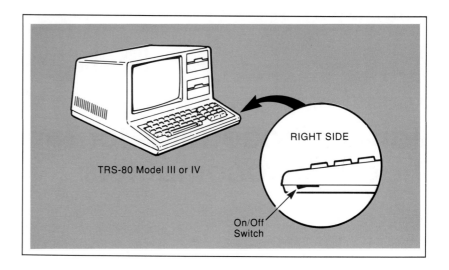

TRS-80 Model III or IV

RIGHT SIDE

On/Off Switch

switch for the Model III and Model 4 is located on the right side under the lip of the keyboard. This switch turns on the computer, CRT, and any built-in disk drives. Tape recorders can also be used for storing data and programs.

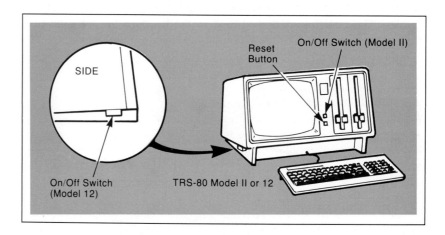

SIDE

On/Off Switch (Model 12)

TRS-80 Model II or 12

Reset Button

On/Off Switch (Model II)

The TRS-80 Model II and Model 12 were designed for business applications. The CRT and disk drives using 8-inch floppy disks are built into the computer's housing. Newer Model IIs and all the Model 12s have keyboards connected by cables. The on/off switch for the Model 12 is found on the left side of the computer. The on/off switch for the Model II is on the front between the CRT and disk drive. This switch will also turn on all the built-in equipment.

Radio Shack computers display special messages when first turned on. For example, the TRS-80 Model III, using a tape recorder for storage, will display the following message:

Cass:

The user's manual will explain in detail the purpose of these messages. Press the Enter key. The computer will then display:

Memory:

Press Enter again and the computer will display:

READY
〉

READY will appear on the screen whenever the computer is waiting for a command. The flashing box next to the > is called the **cursor.** When entering data using the keyboard, the data replaces the cursor and the cursor moves over one space at a time.

Before starting to program the computer, take a closer look at the keyboard. Computer keyboards are laid out just like typewriter keyboards. In addition, there are special keys that allow the programmer to move the cursor—left, right, up, and down—and to delete characters already on the screen.
Enter the following into the computer using the keyboard:

1 THE PLANET EARTH IS FLAT.

When you are done, the cursor should be located after the period.

Since the earth is not flat, the next step is to erase FLAT and type ROUND. The ⬅ key erases one character at a time from the screen. Press this key enough times to erase FLAT. The screen should now look like this:

1 THE PLANET EARTH IS

If not, try again until it does.
Now type: ROUND., and press the Enter key.
When the cursor erases a character, it is called destructive cursor movement. Some computers have cursor movement keys that allow the user to move the cursor over the line without erasing it. This is called **nondestructive cursor movement.**

Since a science teacher might take exception to our test sentence, ALMOST should be added before ROUND. To add ALMOST to this sentence, you must edit the line. Type: EDIT 1, then press the Enter key. This will put you in a special edit mode. You can now add to or delete from this line. However, the cursor must first be positioned in front of the R in ROUND by pressing the Space Bar. If you go too far and the R appears, use the ⬅ key to back up one space.
Next, press the ⎀I⎀ key. I stands for Insert. Type: ALMOST and a space. Now press the Shift and ⬆ keys. This will indicate that you are through inserting.
Press the Enter key and the rest of the line will appear. It should look like this:

1 THE PLANET EARTH IS ALMOST ROUND.

If not, try again until it does.

This line was not sent to the computer until Enter was pressed. When this key is pressed, the computer accepts inserted data into memory. Remember this when writing BASIC programs in STEPS 1 - 11. Mistakes are not entered into the computer until Enter is pressed. Therefore, you always have a chance to correct mistakes by using the ⌫ key. After pressing Enter you have to use the edit mode to make corrections.

Now delete PLANET from this sentence. Enter the edit mode again by typing EDIT 1. Using the Space Bar, move the cursor in front of the P in PLANET. Press the ⌑D⌑ key once. D stands for Delete.] P] will appear on the screen of all the computers except for color computers. This means P has been deleted from the line. Press the ⌑D⌑ key enough times to delete PLANET, then press Enter.

Double-check the correction by typing LIST and then pressing Enter. The corrected version of the line should be displayed under the edited version. You are now ready to start STEP 1 in BASIC on Microcomputers Step-by-Step.

The Hollerith Code for 80-Column Punched Cards

LETTER	ZONE PUNCH ROW	DIGIT PUNCH ROW
A	12	1
B	12	2
C	12	3
D	12	4
E	12	5
F	12	6
G	12	7
H	12	8
I	12	9
J	11	1
K	11	2
L	11	3
M	11	4
N	11	5
O	11	6
P	11	7
Q	11	8
R	11	9
S	0	2
T	0	3
U	0	4
V	0	5
W	0	6
X	0	7
Y	0	8
Z	0	9

NUMBER	DIGIT PUNCH ROW
0	0
1	1
2	2
3	3
4	4
5	5
6	6
7	7
8	8
9	9

SPECIAL CHARACTERS	ROWS
&	12
.	12,3,8
+	12,6,8
−	11
!	11,2,8
$	11,3,8
*	11,4,8
/	0,1
#	3,8
,	0,3,8
?	0,7,8

501

APPENDIX F

Comparison of BASIC Used by Popular Microcomputers*

SYSTEM COMMANDS/EDITING

Note: "✔" means the command is the same as the first column. "na" means this command is not available as such.

Description of Command	APPLE II Applesoft (disk)	PET (cassette)	TRS-80 Model III d = disk c = cassette	IBM
Loads a program	LOAD NAME	LOAD "NAME"	ᵈLOAD "NAME" ᶜCLOAD "N" a one letter name	LOAD "NAME"
Saves a program	SAVE NAME	SAVE "NAME"	ᵈSAVE "NAME" ᶜCSAVE "N"	SAVE "NAME"
Names a program	Automatic. Done when saving program	Automatic. Done when saving program	Automatic. Done when saving program	✔
Executes the current program	RUN	✔	✔	✔
Loads and executes a program	RUN NAME	Shifted RUN STOP (key). Loads and executes next program	ᵈRUN "NAME"	RUN "NAME"
Executes current program starting at line 500	RUN 500	✔	✔	✔
Halts a program or listing	Control C (2 keys)	Stop (key)	Break (key)	✔
Continues program execution halted by the previous command or key(s)	CONT	✔	✔	✔
Deletes current program in memory. (Sets all variables to zero and strings to null)★	NEW ★	✔ ★	✔ ★	✔ ★
Checks for recording errors after a program is saved.	na	VERIFY "NAME"	ᶜCLOAD? "N"	CLOAD "N"
To place multiple statements on a line	:	✔	✔	✔
Lists the entire program	LIST	✔	✔	✔

*Adapted from Johnston, Randolph P. *BASIC Using Micros.* Santa Cruz, CA: Mitchell Publishing, 1984.

Description of Command	APPLE II Applesoft (disk)	PET (cassette)	TRS-80 Model III d = disk c = cassette	IBM
LISTS program lines from line X to line Y	LIST X-Y	✔	✔	✔
Display program line X (used for editing)	LIST X	LIST X	EDIT X	✔
Deletes program lines from line X to line Y	DEL X,Y	na	DELETE X-Y	DELETE X-Y
Deletes the whole (specified) program from the storage device	DELETE NAME	record over old program	ᵈKILL NAME ᶜrecord over old program	KILL "NAME"
Clears the screen and puts cursor at top left	HOME	Shift CLR/HOME (2 keys)	CLS	HOME
Resets all variables to zero	CLEAR	CLR (key)	CLEAR	CLEAR
Returns amount of memory still available to use	FRE (0)	FRE (0)	PRINT MEM	FRE (0)
Deletes one character line being typed and moves cursor one space to left	na	DEL (key)	←	DEL (key)
Cancels line currently being typed	Control X (2 keys)	go to next line; type previous line number and press RETURN key	Shift—will restart current line, or use Break (key)	Control U

BASIC STATEMENTS

	APPLE II Applesoft (disk)	PET (cassette)	TRS-80 Model III d = disk c = cassette	IBM
For writing program comments (ignored by computer)	REM	✔	✔	✔
For writing on line comments	:REM	✔	:REM OR:'	:REM OR :
Assigns the value of Y to the variable X	X = Y	✔	✔	✔
Puts a ? on the screen and waits for the user to type a string value for A$	INPUT A$	✔	✔	✔
Establishes a list of data elements that can be used by READ statements	DATA 5, "Y", 12	✔	✔	✔
Assigns the next data element to A$	READ A$	✔	✔	✔
Starts READing from first data element again	RESTORE	✔	✔	✔
Prints string X = and then the value of the variable X	PRINT "X" = "; X (or ? means PRINT)	✔ (or ? means PRINT)	✔ (or ? means PRINT)	✔
Concentrates printed items (allows no space between strings)★	; no space after numbers and ★	✔ one space after numbers and ★	✔ one space after number and ★	✔ one space after number and ★
Separates items into Tab fields	, 3 Tab fields of 16,16,8	✔ 4 Tab fields of 10,10,10,10	✔ 4 Tab fields of 16,16,16,16	✔ 5 Tab fields of 14,14,14,14,14

BASIC STATEMENTS *(continued)*

Description of Command	*APPLE II Applesoft (disk)*	*PET (cassette)*	*TRS-80 Model III d = disk c = cassette*	*IBM*
(only in PRINT statement) Moves cursor to position X	TAB (X)	TAB (X-1)	TAB (X)	TAB (X)
(conditional branch) If the assertion X = 5 is true, execute the rest of the line. If the assertion is false, ignore the rest of the statement and jump to the next numbered line (Instead of a line number, any reasonable BASIC statement may follow THEN)★	IF X = 5 THEN 20 ★	✔ ★	✔ ★	✔ ★
Branches to line 400 (unconditional branch)	GO TO 400	✔	✔	✔
Executes all statements between the FOR statement and the corresponding NEXT, initially with X = 1, then with X = 5, X = 9, etc., until X = 20 at which time execution jumps to the line number after the NEXT statement. STEP size is one if not specified.	FOR X = 1 TO 20 STEP 4 . . . NEXT X	✔	✔	✔
BRANCHES to the subroutine at line 1000	GOSUB 1000	✔	✔	✔
Marks the end of the subroutine; returns to statement following most recent GOSUB	RETURN	✔	✔	✔
Halts execution (indicates in which program line)★	STOP ★	✔ ★	✔ ★	✔ ★
Halts execution with no message	END	✔	✔	✔

DEFINING VARIABLES AND THEIR RELATIONSHIPS

Negation	−	✔	✔	✔
Exponentiation	∧	↑	↑	✔
Multiplication	*	✔	✔	✔
Division	/	✔	✔	✔
Addition	+	✔	✔	✔
Subtraction	−	✔	✔	✔
Equal	=	✔	✔	✔
Not equal	<>	✔	✔	✔
Less than	<	✔	✔	✔
Greater than	>	✔	✔	✔
Less than or equal to	<=	✔	✔	✔

Description of Command	APPLE II Applesoft (disk)	PET (cassette)	TRS-80 Model III d = disk c = cassette	IBM
Greater than or equal to	>= ✔	✔	✔	✔
Logical "NOT"	NOT	✔	✔	✔
Logical "AND"	AND	✔	✔	✔
Logical "OR"	OR	✔	✔	✔
Real Variables (range: approx ±9.99999999 E + 37) [precision]★ Let A and B represent any letter. Let 1 represent any digit.	AB or A1 [9 digit]★	✔ [9 digit]★	✔ [7 or 16 digit]★	A or A1 [9 digit]★
Integer Variables (range ±32767)	AB% or A1%	✔	✔	✔
String Variables (range 0 to 255 characters)★	AB$ or A1$ ★	✔ ★	✔ ★	✔ ★

DEBUGGING AIDS

Branches to the Xth line number in the list (i.e., if X=2, branches to line 100)	ON X GOTO 300, 100, 500	✔	✔	✔
Branches to subroutine at the Xth line number in the list	ON X GOSUB 400, 100, 900	✔	✔	✔
(In error-handling routine) Causes return to the statement where error occurred	RESUME	na	✔	✔
Subsequent errors cause branch to error-handling routine at line 500 instead of message and program halt (i.e., if you think an error may occur, it branches to the error-handling routine	ONERR GOTO 500	na	ON ERROR GOTO 500	ON ERROR GOTO 500
Lists each line number as it is executed	TRACE	na	TRON (shifted @ causes pause)	TRON
Turns off previous command	NO TRACE	na	TROFF	TROFF
Returns the contents of memory location	PEEK (location)	✔	✔	✔
Changes the value of the memory location (ml) to 33	POKE ml, 33	✔	✔	✔

ARRAYS

Description of Command	APPLE II Applesoft (disk)	PET (cassette)	TRS-80 Model III d = disk c = cassette	IBM
Sets maximum subscripts for A; reserves memory space for $(X + 1)*(Y + 1)*(Z + 1)$ real elements starting with A(0,0,0)	DIM A(X,Y,Z)	✔	✔	✔
Sets maximum subscripts for A$, which may contain $(X + 1)*(Y + 1)$ string elements, each up to 255 characters	DIM A$(X,Y)	✔	✔	✔

FUNCTIONS

Description of Command	APPLE II Applesoft (disk)	PET (cassette)	TRS-80 Model III d = disk c = cassette	IBM
Defines a function FNA. In later use, the argument used with FNA will be substituted for X in the defined expression [i.e., FNA (5) returns 15].	DEF FNA(X) = X + 2*X	✔	^{d}✔ ^{c}na	✔

Returns
  sine
  cosine of X radians
  tangent
	SIN (X)
	COS (X)
	TAN (X)
		✔	✔	✔

Returns arctangent of X in radians	ATN(X)	✔	✔	✔
Returns −1 if X < 0, 0 if X = 0, 1 if X > 0	SGN(X)	✔	−	✔
Returns absolute value of X	ABS(X)	✔	✔	✔
Returns positive square root of X	SQR(X)	✔	✔	✔
Returns e (2.718289) to the power X	EXP(X)	✔	✔	✔
Returns natural logarithm of X	LOG(X)	✔	✔	✔
Returns largest integer less than or equal to X	INT(X)	✔	✔	✔
Returns random real numbers from 0 to 0.99999999 each time used	RND(1)	RND(TI)	RND(0)	RND(-1)
Returns number of characters in A$	LEN (A$)	✔	✔	✔
Returns number value of X, converted to string	STR $(X)	✔	✔	✔
Returns A$, up to the first non-numeric character, as a numeric value	VAL (A$)	✔	✔	✔
Returns leftmost X characters of A$	LEFT$(A$,X)	✔	✔	✔
Returns rightmost X characters of A$	RIGHT$(A$,X)	✔	✔	✔

Description of Command	APPLE II Applesoft (disk)	PET (cassette)	TRS-80 Model III d = disk c = cassette	IBM
Returns Y characters of A$, starting at character X	MID$(A$,X,Y)	✔	✔	✔
Operator used to concatenate strings	+	✔	✔	✔
Return ASCII code for first character of A$	ASC (A$)	✔ Has its own code for graphics	✔ Has special code for special graphics	✔ Has special code for special graphics
Returns ASCII character whose code is X	CHR $(X)	✔ Has its own code for graphics	✔	✔ Has special code for special graphics

GLOSSARY

abacus–an early form of calculator, developed in China, consisting of beads strung on wires

access mechanism–a structure holding all the read/write heads for a disk drive

accountant–person who records and organizes the financial figures for an organization, then produces reports reflecting the financial status of the company

accounting system–a manual or computerized system for recording and updating accounting data

accounts payable–records of the money owed by a company to its suppliers

accounts receivable–records of the money owed to a company by its customers

ACM–Association for Computing Machinery—an organization that supports professionals and students in the computer science and computer engineering areas

acoustic coupler–type of modem used to connect a computer or terminal directly to a telephone headset for data communication

activity log–a file that keeps a record of past online activities or transactions

AD–abbreviation for *automated drafting*

ADA–programming language developed for the Department of Defense as a standard for all armed services. It is patterned after PASCAL, is highly structured, and very complex

address–a unique number for each memory slot in a computer. Each slot will hold a single character

Aiken, Howard–pioneer in using electromechanical devices to perform calculations; developer of the MARK I computer

algorithm–set of program code written to perform a specific operation

alphanumeric field–a field containing any combination of letters, numbers, and special characters

American National Standards Institute–see *ANSI*

American Standard Code of Information Interchange–see *ASCII*

analog signal–continuous sound signal having a variety of frequencies, like those found in a voice or music

analysis systems–a system that processes marketing and sales data, producing reports used to plan marketing strategy

analytical engine–machine developed by Charles Babbage in 1834 that could mechanically compute any function. It had a memory unit and arithmetic/logic unit

animation–rapid display of slight variations of an image in order to simulate motion

ANSI–American National Standards Institute—a group that develops programming language standards for use by industry and computer manufacturers

applications node–a single but complete computer system that is part of a distributed data processing network and that does application processing—called *node*

applications package–a group of documents including a computer program with related manuals, user's guide, and run instructions

applications program–program written for a particular user's need, for example, payroll, inventory, scheduling

applications programmer–person who writes programs designed to control a specific IPO cycle

argument–the constant or variable used by a BASIC function

arithmetic/logic unit–the part of the processing hardware that performs calculations and logical comparisons

ARPA–Advanced Research Project Agency—a telecommunications network connecting research computers for the Department of Defense

array–a group of values assigned to a single variable name and organized for direct access using the associated subscript—also known as *table*

artificial intelligence–the ability of a computer to learn from experience by storing information and applying it to new situations

ASCII–American Standard Code of Information Interchange—a standard bit pattern using seven bits per byte, traditionally used on smaller computers

assembler language–machine language instructions written mnemonically to aid programmers

Atanasoff, John V.–pioneer who developed some of the theory behind the first all-electronic computer

audit–special review of the financial records and procedures of a company

auditor–a specially trained accountant who conducts audits

automated office–a business office where operations like mail, typing, copying, and scheduling are done on interconnected computer equipment

automatic drafting–abbreviated *AD*—the creation of detailed drawings by entering the data through a terminal or digitizer and using a database

auto-pilot–a computer that can help maintain a plane's altitude and speed without human intervention

Babbage, Charles–considered the "father of computing"; developer of analytical and difference engines

backup–an extra copy of data on a disk or tape that is kept in case of an emergency

bar code–machine-readable stripes found on consumer products that are read by a scanner and used for pricing and inventory

BASIC–Beginner's All Purpose Symbolic Instruction Code—a programming language developed in the 1960s at Dartmouth College. It is used extensively on microcomputers and in education and small businesses

BASIC statement–a single instruction found in a BASIC program

batch processing–processing data in groups

Berry, Clifford–graduate student who worked with John V. Atanasoff on the theories for an all-electronic computer

binary digit–see *bit*

billing–the generation of bills to a company's customers

bit–also called *binary digit*—the basic building block for data consisting of a 0 or a 1

block–a grouping of records on disk or tape to increase reading and writing speed

blocking factor–the number of records in a block on disk or tape

booting–loading the operating system into the memory after turning on a computer

bubble memory–memory unit using magnetized microscopic areas of a silicon chip to store bit patterns

buffer–a portion of memory set aside for temporary storage of data

byte–a group of bits that represents one character

CAD–abbreviation for *computer-assisted design*

CAD/CAM–linking product engineering and manufacturing by using both CAD and CAM machines to design and produce a product

CAE–abbreviation for *computer-assisted engineering*

CAM–abbreviation for *computer-assisted manufacturing*

cardpunch–computer hardware that produces output data on punched cards by punching a column of holes for each character

cardreader–computer hardware that puts input data into the computer by sensing the holes on punched cards

career path–a series of related jobs throughout a lifetime that allow a person to fulfill personal goals

cashless society–a futuristic idea that all sales, billing, checks, and transactions will be processed electronically without any exchange of money

CAT–abbreviation for *computer axial tomography*

CDP–Certificate in Data Processing—a recognized certification of competency in data processing

central processing unit–abbreviated *CPU*—the processing hardware that contains the control, arithmetic/logic, and memory units

character–a single letter, digit, or special symbol

chip–another name for *integrated circuit*

COBOL–Common Business Oriented Language—a programming language designed in the 1950s to handle business applications. It is the most widely used programming language

college major–the main area of concentration for a college student

college minor–a secondary area of study for a college student

column–vertical direction of a punched card representing one character. There are 80 columns on a punched card

COM–Computer Output Microfilm—output data produced as microfilm

command–instruction immediately followed by a microcomputer

communications control program–part of the systems software that aids a computer in transferring data to and from remote terminals or computers

communications line–line, cable, or devices that can transmit data for data communication

compiler–a systems program that translates a high-level program into machine language. The program is not run, just translated

computer–equipment used to process data

computer-assisted design–abbreviated *CAD*—a computer system used to create manufacturing designs for buildings, cars, and other products. The system would include a graphics terminal for output and possibly a light pen for input

computer-assisted engineering–abbreviated *CAE*—designing or engineering new products with the help of computers

computer-assisted instruction–using the computer in an educational setting to help students learn by means of drill and practice, tutorial, or simulations

computer-assisted manufacturing–abbreviated *CAM*—using programmable machines to control product manufacturing

computer axial tomography–abbreviated *CAT*—computer-controlled scanners used to display and analyze cross-sections of the body

computer center–the physical location of the computer system, housing the computer hardware, some input/output hardware, and related personnel

computer crash–a sudden failure of the computer to operate—also called *crash*

computer engineering–area of study that covers the design and development of computer hardware

computer-managed instruction–using the computer to assist with educational and administrative tasks such as scheduling, testing, and grading

computer operator–person responsible for the working of the computer and related equipment, who is capable of handling minor equipment emergencies and repairs

computer output microfilm–see *COM*

computer program–a set of computer instructions designed to perform a single job—also called *program* or *software*

computer programmer–see *programmer*

computer science–area of study that covers the working relationship between hardware and software

computer system–a collection of five components (people, data, hardware, programs, and procedures) that interact to satisfy a need

conference–a meeting, often lasting several days, where professionals meet to discuss aspects of a broad subject

consultant–independent computer professional temporarily hired by an organization to perform a given task

contract programmer–an independent programmer who is hired to write programs for a company but is not a permanent employee

control clerk–see *data control clerk*

control program–part of the operating system that manages the flow of data and programs through the computer

control totals–totals done independently of a computer to see if output is correct

control unit–the part of the processing hardware that uses the program to perform required operations by directing the arithmetic/logic unit

controls–procedures that help reduce illegal or accidental access or changing of data

core memory–an early type of memory unit using small ring magnets

correspondence print mode–a feature of some dot matrix printers where each line is printed over twice for added clarity

cost/benefit analysis–comparing all known costs of developing a system against tangible and intangible benefits. This helps to assess whether or not a project is worth starting

cost/performance ratio–a measurement of efficiency relating the cost of an operation to how well the operation is performed

cottage industry–earning a living by doing skilled labor at home

counter–a numeric variable used to keep count of sequences that are repeated

CPU–abbreviation for *central processing unit*

crash–see *computer crash*

CRT–cathode-ray tube—a televisionlike screen used to display information

cursor–the flashing box or line on a CRT that shows where the next character will appear

cylinder–the collection of tracks that can be read when the access mechanism is in one place

daisy wheel–a removable printing mechanism shaped like a daisy that has a character at the end of each petal

data–facts and figures

data administrator–a person responsible for the security and correctness of data

data base–a large collection of data

data communications–linking of one component of a computer system to the other via communication lines to transfer data between them—also called *data telecommunications*

data control clerk–a person who coordinates data flow through a computer center by checking users' data and later sending resulting reports back to user

data directory–an index of where scattered global data is located in a system. A data directory is available at each node

data entry operator–a person who enters data into the computer or onto a machine-readable medium

data entry shift supervisor–a person who manages or supervises data entry operators in a computer center or remote batch station

data librarian–person who identifies, maintains, and stores tapes and disks for a large computer center

data module–hardware having a hard disk, access mechanism, and read/write heads all sealed inside a case for protection

data processing–the act of converting data into useful information

data retrieval–accessing data from a file so it can be processed

data telecommunications–see *data communications*

data utility–a group of processing programs that helps to transfer programs and data between different types of hardware

database–an organized arrangement of a large amount of data or integrated files under the control of a database management system

database management system–abbreviated *DBMS*—special systems programs that allow data in a database to be accessed and maintained

database processing–organizing data into a database and using a database management system to access, update, and process it

DBMS–see *database management system*

debugging–finding and eliminating logic and syntax errors in a computer program

DEF–BASIC statement that defines the formula for a user-defined function

definition–the first step in program development. It consists of identifying the problem to be solved

delimiter–a symbol, like a comma or semicolon, that separates variables or data in BASIC

design–the second step in program development. It consists of designing the steps in a program by flowcharting or pseudocoding

detailed report–a printed form of output data containing an organized list of all available data related to a subject

diagnostic message–a phrase appearing when the BASIC interpreter finds a syntax error

difference engine–machine proposed by Charles Babbage that used a steam engine to compute linear equations

digital signal–a noncontinuous sound signal used in data transmission

digitizer–input hardware that converts a drawing into mathematical locations for input into a computer system

DIM–BASIC statement that defines the size of an array

direct access–the ability to retrieve records from a file in any order

disk–a circular platter with concentric tracks that is used as a machine-readable medium

disk directory–a list on a disk of all the files and programs kept on it. This list is updated and available every time the disk is used

disk drive–the hardware that spins a disk. The drive includes an access mechanism and read/write heads for storing and retrieving data

disk pack–a collection of hard disk platters stacked together to allow access and storage of large amounts of data

diskette–see *floppy disk*

distributed data processing–processing on many computers located at users' sites, instead of using one central computer

documentation–written support for a program, including manuals and a user's guide. Also, the fifth step in program development consisting of internal (i.e., REM statements) and external (i.e., user's guide) notes to a program

dot-matrix printer–a printer where characters are made up of small dots

downline loading–the transfer of software written elsewhere to a node via data communication

DPMA–Data Processing Managers Association—an organization that supports professionals and students in the data processing area

drill and practice–a computer-assisted instruction application where a problem is presented to a student, he or she answers it, the computer evaluates the results, and tells the student whether the answer is right or wrong

dummy value–a value entered for a variable that is not used later in a BASIC program

duplicate data–occurrence of the same data several times within a file processing system

dynamic display–the ability to take a graphic display and rotate, shift, or move it around the screen

EBCDIC–Extended Binary Coded Decimal Interchange Code—a standard bit pattern, traditionally used on larger computers, having 8 bits per byte

Eckert, J. Presper–co-developer with John W. Mauchly of the all-electronic computer (ENIAC) and the first commercial computer (UNIVAC I)

economics of scale–the cost savings due to having one large computer system instead of several smaller ones

edit–to update a text by adding, deleting, changing, or moving words and entire lines. This term is used in word processing

edit report–list of all verified updates to a data file

editing–having the computer check for errors in the input data

EDP–see *electronic data processing*

EDP auditor–auditor who specializes in reviewing a company's financial records and procedures kept on a computer

EDP controls–procedures used to prevent any illegal or accidental misuse of any component of a computer system

EDSAC–Electronic Delay Storage Automatic Calculator—completed in 1949, it had an early version of programmable memory

EDVAC–Electronic Discrete Variable Automatic Computer—completed in 1950, it was one of the first computers having a stored program in memory

EFT–see *electronic funds transfer*

elective–a college course that a student may or may not choose to take as part of the curriculum

electronic agenda–a person's daily schedule of meetings and work assignments kept on a computer

electronic cottage–people earning a living by working with computers at home rather than at an office or factory

electronic data processing–abbreviated *EDP*—an early term for computerized data processing used by accountants and auditors

electronic funds transfer–abbreviated as *EFT*—the handling of financial transactions through a computer rather than by exchanging cash

electronic mail–using personal data files to send and store messages in an office

electronic mailbox–the personal file or area on disk used to store messages in an electronic mail system

electronic spreadsheet–an applications package that allows the user to input rows and columns of data. Updating and resulting totals can be done by the program

electronics technician–a person who assembles hardware according to manufacturer specifications

END–BASIC statement that stops the program run

end-of-file mark–a small special area on a disk or tape that identifies the end of each data file—also known as *trailer label*

end-user operator–person who performs data entry as part of another job

engineer–a person with a college degree who creates new products or develops new manufacturing processes by using the latest technological advancements

ENIAC–Electronic Numerical Integrator and Calculator—built by John Mauchly and J. Presper Eckert, this was the first all-electronic computer

entrepreneur–a person who owns and runs his or her own business

entry-level job–a job having minimum or no work experience requirements. Relevant skills are taught on the job

environmental data–conditions of the environment, such as light, heat, pressure, and radiation measurements used as input into a computer

error log–a record of problems that users have with computer equipment or programs

exception report–a printed form of output data containing only that information which meets special conditions given by the user

expert system–a computer system containing a database and database management system that can draw new conclusions from the data and add them to the database—also known as *knowledge-based system* or *knowledge engineering*

Extended Binary Coded Decimal Interchange Code–see *EBCDIC*

facilities scheduling–a computer application that maximizes use of manufacturing machines by scheduling their set up and production times

Fair Credit Reporting Act of 1970–a law that gives consumers the right to see if the credit data stored about them is correct and to have it updated if incorrect

feasibility study–a research report determining whether a system is both financially and technically practical for the user at that time

field–a group of characters that represent a single piece of data. A customer's name, address, and phone number are all separate fields

fifth-generation computer–a computer now being developed that contains language translators and expert systems all under control of parallel processing hardware

file–a collection of related records; all information about a subject. For example, a student file is all information about all students in a school

file processing system–a computer application where each program accesses selected data files

first-generation computer–computers manufactured in the late 1940s and early 1950s containing vacuum tubes, having no memory units, and using magnetic drums as storage devices

fixed disk drive–a disk drive where the disk is permanently fixed within it. The access time is fast but the disk cannot be removed

floppy disk–A small, flexible disk used to store data—also known as *diskette*

floppy disk drive–hardware used to store data on floppy disk that accesses the disks through a window in its cover

flowchart–used by programmers to design the logic of a program by drawing specially shaped boxes containing descriptions joined by arrows

flowcharting template–a design tool that allows a nonartist to use standard symbols to represent program or system design—also called *template*

FOR/NEXT–BASIC statements that allow a series of statements to be repeated a number of times with a variable taking on specified beginning, ending, and incrementing values

format–(as applied to floppy disks) to establish tracks and sectors on a floppy disk before it is initially used

format–(as applied to programming) the layout of fields in a record

formulary–records of all the drugs and medicine in a pharmacy

FORTRAN–Formula Translator—a high-level programming language developed for scientific and engineering applications

fourth-generation computer–computer whose processing hardware is characterized by very large scale integrated circuits like a microprocessor

Freedom of Information Act of 1970–a law that allows an individual access to certain government-collected data

front end processor–a computer hooked to a larger computer in a telecommunication system that processes and edits some of the data before it gets to the larger computer

full-character printer–see *letter-quality printer*

function–a series of preset instructions available with a language translator that perform common operations

general ledger–record of all business transactions involving revenues and expenses

GIGO–meaning "garbage in-garbage out"—stressing the importance of having correct data

global data–data that is needed by more than one node in a distributed system. The data is either centralized or scattered around the system

GO TO–a BASIC statement that transfers control in the program to another statement

Goldstine, Adele–mathematician who was one of the early programmers of the ENIAC

GOSUB–a BASIC statement that directs program control to a subroutine elsewhere in the program. The subroutine contains a RETURN statement to bring control back to the GOSUB when finished.

hard copy–output data or information in the form of a printed report

hard disk–a large type of disk, usually consisting of several inflexible platters, to store data

hard disk drive–hardware used to read and write information on hard disk. The drive accesses hard disks through access arms containing read/write heads

hard sectored–a permanent sectoring of a floppy disk, indicated by several sensing holes around the inside of the disk

hardware–the input, processing, and output equipment or machines in a computer system

hardware communications specialist–a person who sets up and maintains communication lines and hardware

hashing routine–a mathematical formula used to convert the key field to a unique disk location for each record in a file

header–the first value in a data base that indicates how much data is contained in the data base

header label–a small amount of information put at the beginning of each file on disk or tape to help determine where the first record begins and the date the file was stored

hierarchy chart–a programming design technique that shows each module as a box with its logical relationship to all other modules in the program—also known as *structure chart*

high-level programming language–a people-oriented programming language, like COBOL or BASIC, that must be translated into machine language before it can be used by the computer

high-resolution graphics–a way of displaying graphic output using a large number of pixels per screen area, that is effective for drawing precise lines and curves

highlighting–increased or decreased intensity for one set of characters on a CRT that helps them stand out to the user

Hollerith, Herman–inventor who applied punched card technology to census data, thereby starting automated data processing

Hollerith code–a unique representation for each character by a combination of holes on a punched card

Hopper, Grace–a mathematician and programmer for the MARK I computer

hot line–a special phone number that users can call for help on hardware or software problems

hybrid network–an organization of computers in a distributed system where a ring of computers is connected and each has other computers clustered around itself

hypothesis–a scientist's formally stated idea about a subject that will be tested by experimentation

IF/THEN–BASIC statements used to perform actions based on a given condition

image processing–converting photographs into digital data so that the image may be transmitted to a computer for enhancement and printing

impact printer–a printer that produces output by having a hammer strike the paper through an inked ribbon

implementation–the point in systems development when all components are brought together, installed, and tested, and the users trained

increment–to increase the value of a variable

independent software–program capable of using only the data designed for it

indexed sequential file organization–a file that has records organized sequentially by a key field and an index to help directly locate records faster

information–knowledge derived by processing data, usually in the form of a printed report or CRT display—also called *output data*

information systems–an area of study covering the development and use of application programs and computer systems

information utility–a company that provides references and consumer information at standard rates to individuals and companies

informed user–a computer user who is aware of the components of a system, what it is capable of doing and not doing, and is comfortable with using computers to solve problems

INPUT–a BASIC statement that assigns incoming data to a variable name

input data–data read into the computer for processing

input hardware–equipment used to put data into the computer for processing, like a keyboard or bar code scanner

input/output port–see *port*

Institute for New Generation Computer Technology–a Japanese coalition of government and industry working to develop a fifth-generation computer

integrated circuit–a complete electrical circuit on a small silicon chip that is the basis for processing in third-generation computers

integrated software–programs capable of sharing data with other programs

intelligent copier–a copy machine that can accept and reproduce input from a word processor

intelligent terminal–terminal with limited processing ability—also called a *smart terminal*

interblock gap–a half-inch gap between blocks of records on tape that allows the machine to stop between blocks

interface–a device that converts data signals between different types of equipment

interpreter–a systems program that translates a high-level language one instruction at a time. Once translated, the instruction is followed even if the rest of the program is not correct

interrecord gap–a half-inch long gap between each record on a tape to help the machine distinguish records

inventory control–records of all stock acquired, stored, and sold by a company

I/O port–see *port*

IPO cycle–a three-step computer-related process consisting of:
   Input–information being put into the computer
   Processing–computer acting on the information
   Output–results of the processing becoming available

Jacquard, Joseph Marie–developed use of punched cards to identify weaving patterns on a loom

joystick–a lever used to control movement on a screen. Its motions are recorded as data. It is often used as input hardware for games

junior programmer–a person who is beyond the trainee stage who has yet to acquire a lot of programming experience

K–abbreviation for *kilobyte*

key–see *key field*

key field–one field that is used as a basis for organizing and identifying the records in a file

key-to-disk equipment–hardware that allows an operator to type on a keyboard and have data put directly on disk, usually a floppy disk

key-to-tape equipment–hardware that allows an operator to type on a keyboard and have data put directly on tape

keypunch–hardware that punches holes in punched cards by typing on a keyboard

kilobyte–abbreviated as *K*—a measurement of computer memory or disk capacity that is equal to 1024 bytes

knowledge engineering–see *expert system*

knowledge-based system–see *expert system*

language translator–a system that can translate one human language into another

lead programmer–a programmer who supervises the work of other programmers

LET–a BASIC statement allowing an internal value to be assigned to a variable name

letter-quality printer–a printer whose output is like that of a typewriter

light pen–penlike input hardware that is used to draw on a CRT. Its movements are recorded as data.

line number–a number before each BASIC statement identifying the order in which it will be performed

line position–a person working directly with a business customer or product

line printer–a printer that sets up and prints an entire line at a time, usually in lengths of 80 to 150 characters

linear–a program where statements are performed in order without stopping or deviating

LIST–a BASIC command displaying all or part of the program in the computer's memory

LOAD–a BASIC command copying a program from tape or diskette into the computer's memory

loading–copying of a program or data found on disk, tapes, or cards into computer memory

local data–data that is used and kept by only one node of a distributed system

logic error–programming code that is syntactically correct but produces incorrect or unintended results

LOGO–a high-level programming language used in education as a learning tool. Problem solving is done by graphically displaying geometric principles

loop–a series of statements that is repeated several times within a program

Lovelace, Ada Augusta–mathematician who helped explain the theory of the analytical engine and conceptualized the binary number system

low-resolution graphics–displaying graphic output by using a small number of pixels on a CRT screen. The display quality is rather limited when drawing curved lines

M–abbreviation for *megabyte*

machine language–instructions used by the computer itself. All instructions are reduced to bit patterns. It is not commonly used for application programming

magnetic drum–an early storage device that recorded data on tracks of a drum-shaped cylinder

magnetic ink character recognition–see *MICR*

mainframe computer–a large computer used by big businesses and organizations

maintenance programmer–a person who modifies programs already in use to reflect a change in a law or policy

major–see *college major*

management information system–abbreviated *MIS*–a collection of business systems, not necessarily computer related, that provides information to business people

management information system director–executive position which oversees all data processing managers and works with company executives to determine long range plans

management trainee–an entry-level managerial position with extensive on-the-job training

manager–a person who supervisors others and makes decisions based on company policy

MARK I–a computer having mechanical counters controlled by electrical devices, developed in 1944

mark-sense form readers–see *optical scanner*

materials management–inventory records of raw materials and finished goods of a manufacturing business

Mauchly, John W.–co-developer with J. Presper Eckert of the ENIAC (first all-electronic) and UNIVAC I (first commercial) computers

megabyte–abbreviated as *M*–a measurement of memory or disk capacity consisting of 1 million bytes

membrane keyboard–a keyboard with pressure sensitive keys that do not move when touched

memory unit–the part of the processing hardware where the program and data are stored before and after processing

menu–a list of available program options

MICR–Magnetic Ink Character Recognition—characters used by the banking industry that allow input hardware to read information directly from a check

microcomputer–a small computer, used in homes, schools, and businesses, with processing hardware that is based upon a microprocessor

microfiche–output data photographically reduced and put on a sheet of film for storage

microfilm–output data photographically reduced and put on rolls of film for storage

microprocessor–processing hardware on a small silicon chip. It is the basis for the processing power of the microcomputer

minicomputer–a medium-sized computer often used in research or to monitor a specific manufacturing process

minor–see *college minor*

MIS–see *management information system*

mismatch error–attempt in BASIC to put a numeric value into a string variable or vice versa

mnemonic–a memory aiding technique, like using letters to represent bit patterns, that is the basis of assembler languages

modem–modulator-demodulator—a device used to connect a computer or terminal to a telephone line for data communication

modular development–the design of a program as a set of interrelated sections that can be independently tested and modified

module–one section of a program that performs a single specific function

mouse–input hardware used to identify data on a screen

multiprogramming–capability of a computer to hold more than one program at a time while working on the program with highest priority

NC–abbreviation for *numerical control*

needs analysis–an itemized list of jobs for which users require help

nested loop–a program loop containing another loop

network–collection of computers connected by communication lines

NEW–a BASIC command that clears the program and data from the computer's memory

node–see *application node*

nondestructive cursor movement–using keys to move the cursor around the screen without changing information

nonimpact printer–printer that produces printed output without striking the paper through an inked ribbon. The image might be created instead by lasers, inkjets, or xerography

nonunique key–a feature of databases allowing information to be retrieved by key fields common to several records

numeric constant–numeric data which is limited to the digits 0 through 9, decimal point, and plus or minus sign

numeric data–data containing only the digits 0 through 9, a decimal point, and a plus or minus sign

numeric field–a field containing only numbers, a decimal point, and a plus or minus sign

numeric variable name–variable name in BASIC consisting of one or two letters or a letter and a number that identifies numeric data

numerical control–abbreviated as *NC*—the ability to program a machine to produce parts according to predefined measurements

numerical wheel calculator–an early form of calculator developed by Blaise Pascal consisting of wheels and cogs that displayed results in windows

OEM–see *original equipment manufacturer*

offline–input/output operations not under control of a computer (like reading a punched card and copying its contents onto tape for later processing)

offline telecommunication system–sending data via communication lines to a computer where it is processed only after all data has been received

one-way checks–also known as *truncated check flow*—a form of electronic funds transfer where a check would be sent only to the bank of first deposit and all other transactions would be done electronically

online–direct input and processing of information by a computer; results are immediately sent back to user

online telecommunication system–sending data via communication lines to a computer where it is processed as it is received

operating system–system programs that control the use of the computer's resources (like memory and input/output hardware)

operational system–type of marketing and sales system that provides clerical support by producing letters, orders, bills, etc.

operations personnel–people responsible for controlling the computer and related equipment

operations supervisor–a person who watches over the work of computer operators

optical characters–a standardized character set that can be read by both computer hardware and people

optical mark–mark made by a pencil on a designated area of paper, usually an answer sheet, that can be read by a scanner

optical scanner–an input device that uses light to read optical marks, bar codes, and optical characters

order entry–a type of operational system that accepts and processes customer orders

order of precedence–order that arithmetic operations are performed within a BASIC formula

original equipment manufacturer–abbreviated *OEM*—company that manufactures a finished product rather than selling unfinished work for other companies to complete

output data–the results of the IPO cycle, usually appearing as a printed report or on a CRT—also called *information*

output hardware–equipment that provides the processed information to the user, like printers or display screens

paging–to display information on a CRT by showing one screenful at a time, while allowing the user to decide when to display the next screenful

paperless office–a combination of online systems and automatic office equipment reduces or eliminates paper letters and reports in a business office

parallel method of implementation–a way of systems implementation that uses the old and new systems at the same time until the new system is thoroughly tested

parallel port–an I/O port that allows the entire bit pattern for a single character to be sent at one time

parallel processing–the ability of a computer to have several arithmetic/logic units and control units operating at the same time

PASCAL–a high-level programming language, developed in the 1970s, that is highly structured

payroll–a business application to pay employees while recording taxes, wages, and deductions for future reports

PEMDAS–acronym for the order of precedence in arithmetic operation for programming: *p*arenthesis, *e*xponentiation, *m*ultiplication, *d*ivision, *a*ddition, and *s*ubtraction

peripheral–any input or output devices attached to the computer

PERT–Program Evaluation Review Technique—a system that maintains data on the material, personnel, times, and order requirements for each step of a large process

piecemeal method of implementation–implementing a new system one part at a time while not adding a new part until the preceding part is tested

pilot method of implementation–implementing a new system by letting a few users test it out first before releasing the system to all users

pixel–picture element—one of a series or matrix of dots that makes up a visual display

pixel graphics–graphics that are formed by rows and columns of small dots. Resolution and clarity is limited

plotter–output hardware that draws continuous images by movement of pen on paper

plunge method of implementation–implementing a system by removing an old system and immediately starting up the new system

point of sale–abbreviated *POS*—a terminal combining a cash register with a machine-readable source document scanner that is connected to a computer

pointer–a field in the records of a database system that contains the location of the next related record

port–a plug or connector on a computer where input or output devices are attached—also known as *I/O port* or *input/output port*

POS–abbreviation for *point of sale*

pre-edit report–a report containing any updates to a data file that is hand checked for correctness before changes are made

preventative maintenance–routine procedures that help keep equipment in working order

PRINT–a BASIC statement that outputs data

print chart–form used to design printed report formats

printer–output hardware that produces information as a typed image on paper

Privacy Act of 1974–a law requiring the government to advise people what data is collected on them, what it is used for, and how it can be accessed

process control–using computer systems to monitor and control action output

processing data–data used by the computer to do the calculations and comparisons necessary to complete a specific job

processing hardware–the equipment that performs calculations and comparisons upon input data

processing programs–software within an operating system that translates the high-level languages and prepares machine instructions

production automation specialist–see *robotics engineer*

production data entry operator–see *data entry operator*

program–see *computer program*—also called *software*

program code–the statements that make up a computer program

program flowchart–a design technique that represents the logic of a program by a series of symbols and brief descriptions

program name–the name given to each program by which it is stored and retrieved

program/data independence–data required by a program is requested through a DBMS rather than directly accessed by the program

programmer–a person who writes the instructions for a computer according to set requirements

programmer/analyst–person who determines the users' needs and writes the appropriate programs

programmer trainee–a starting position for a new programmer in a company requiring on-the-job training

programming language–the instruction set for writing a computer program. Like human languages, each programming language has a different structure and vocabulary

project leader–individual who supervises the development of a new computer system or application package

project specifications–design instructions that detail the user's needs and project requirements

prompt–a short explanation to the user of what kind of data to input

pseudocode–used by programmers to design program logic by writing it in English-like phrases

punched card–data is represented by rows and columns of holes on a paper card. Each card has 12 rows and 80 columns

query system–an online application allowing a user to request information from a database

queue–a waiting line. In a computer, queues are used to hold data and programs waiting to be processed or output

quick-and-dirty system–systems development with little or no design, resulting in inefficient and incorrect systems

RAM–abbreviation for *random access memory*—the type of computer memory where programs and data are temporarily stored. RAM can be cleared and reused

R&D–abbreviation for *research and development*—an area of business or science that deals with the experimentation and designing of new products

random access memory–see *RAM*

random file organization–records in a file are organized by a hashing routine using a key field. Records are not in sequential order but in an order determined by a hashing routine

read only memory–see *ROM*

READ/DATA–BASIC statements that set variable names to a series of values given within the program

read/write head–the mechanism in a tape drive or at the end of a disk drive access arm that picks up or records data

record–a collection of related fields

record layout form–form used to design the format for records

reference search–use of keywords to have the computer look up related articles and books in a library

register–a limited storage area in the control unit for the program instruction or data currently being worked on

release–a version of an applications package

REM–a BASIC statement allowing internal program documentation

remote job entry–abbreviated *RJE*—submitting data for processing via input hardware located away from the computer

removable disk drive–a disk drive containing a movable access arm and read/write head that can be retracted to allow the disk pack to be exchanged

repetition–one of the three structured programming patterns. A sequence of instructions is repeated until a condition is met

research and development–see *R&D*

resolution–see also *high-resolution graphics* and *low-resolution graphics*—the clarity of letters and graphics. High resolution graphics means that minute details can be displayed clearly

response time–time elapsed between when the user request is sent to the computer and when the response comes back

RESTORE–a BASIC statement that resets the pointer back to the first DATA statement

RETURN–a BASIC statement identifying the end of a subroutine and initiating transfer of control back to the corresponding GOSUB statement

reverse video–a form of highlighting characters on a CRT by using opposite intensity patterns. For example, if a screen is green with white letters, a character in reverse video would be green with a white background

ring network–an organization of computers in a distributed system where each computer is connected to all or some of the other computers in the system

RJE–see *remote job entry*

robot–a computer-controlled mechanical arm that can be programmed to do repetitive and intricate movements

robotics engineer–engineer who designs robots for a variety of applications

ROM–abbreviation for *read only memory*—type of computer memory where preset instructions (like control programs and interpreters) are permanently stored

row–the horizontal direction on a punched card. A card has 12 rows

RPG–Report Program Generator—a high-level programming language first developed for producing standard reports that has now been expanded for general business applications

RUN–a BASIC command that has the computer follow the program instructions in its memory

salesperson–a person who sells a company's product or service

SAVE–a BASIC command that copies the program in a computer's memory onto tape or disk

scanner–input hardware that can read characters, marks, and bar codes as data

screen layout form–a form used to design the format of a CRT screen used for output

scrolling–method of displaying information on a CRT by adding new lines to the bottom of the screen and letting old lines roll off the top

second-generation computer–computer developed in the late 1950s that used transistors as part of the processing hardware. It contained core memory, used an operating system and was programmed in high-level programming languages

secondary storage–using tape, disk, or other media to permanently store data outside of a computer's main memory

sector–a division of a disk track used as a storage area and given a unique identifying number

seed value–number used by a random number generator to produce a series of numbers

selection–one of the three structured programming patterns. A choice of instructions is made based upon certain criteria

senior programmer–a supervisory programming position, where the person coordinates activities of programmers and is responsible for a programming project

senior systems analyst–experienced systems analyst who supervises the work of others

sequence–one of the three structured programming patterns. A series of steps is followed in a specific order

sequential access–retrieving records in the order they are found in a file, first to last

sequential file organization–method of organizing data by putting all records in key field order. Access can be slow

sequential processing–processing all items in the order they are found, from first to last

serial port–an I/O port that allows only one bit of a byte to be sent at a time

serial printer–a printer that types only one character at a time

service technician–a person responsible for keeping computer hardware in good working order by performing periodical preventive maintenance procedures and necessary repairs

simulation–a program that models or mimics a real-life situation, allowing the user to react without endangering life or property

slide rule–a calculating device having several calibrated rulers sliding along each other to match and compute values

smart terminal–see *intelligent terminal*

soft sectored–a sectioning of floppy disks done by the drive before the disk is initially used

software–see *computer program*—also called *program*

software communications specialist–person who develops the software for a telecommunications system

software engineer–a person with a 4-year college degree in computer science, who designs, writes, and tests systems software

software house–a person or company that designs, writes, and distributes software

solid object modeling–displaying a design in three dimensions

sound output–audible information in the form of words, music, beeps, sirens, and other noise

source document–form on which data is collected for computer input

speech-generated output–sound output in the form of computer-generated words

staff programmer–person who has enough experience to pass a company's programmer trainee and junior programmer positions

star network–an organization of computer systems where one computer serves as a central connecting point for all other computers in a distributed system

statistical package–application package with a series of mathematical equations allowing a user to analyze numerical data

STEP–part of the BASIC FOR statement that identifies the value by which the counter will be incremented

storage/cost ratio–a measurement of how costly storage is on disks. The ratio is calculated by dividing the number of bytes that can be accessed when the disk is in the drive by the cost of the drive

storage hardware–equipment used to record data for later use, like tape and disk drives

stored data–data that is saved on disk or tape for later processing

string–also called *string constant*—data that is any combination of letters, numbers, symbols, or spaces

string constant–see *string*

string variable–a string value that can change each time a program is run

string variable name–variable name in BASIC consisting of one or two letters or a letter and a number always followed by a dollar sign. It identifies string data

structure chart–see *hierarchy chart*

structured program–program designed and coded according to the principles of structured programming

structured programming–a method of programming where all program logic can be reduced to a combination of three patterns: sequence, repetition, and selection

structures–patterns of code used in structured programming

subroutine–an independent section of program code accessed in BASIC by the GOSUB statement

subscript–a variable or constant indicating a specific data value in an array

summary report–a report condensing all available information by calculating only totals and main trends of the data

supervisor program–one of the control programs of the operating system. It is usually the first program loaded in when the computer is turned on. It allocates memory and coordinates peripheral activity

support position–a job not directly connected to the company's product or service that might be in the personnel, data processing, or accounting departments

syntax error–program lines containing code that does not follow the rules (syntax) of a programming language

systems analyst–a person who puts together the computer system components by identifying needs, formulating requirements, and helping the user understand how the new computer system works

systems development personnel–people who design and maintain computer systems

systems flowchart–a representation using standard symbols on paper that outlines the components of a system and how they relate to each other

systems maintenance–the changes and additions of equipment and programs that keep a working system functional and efficient

systems programmer–a person who writes systems programs for an organization

systems programs–programs written to control the computer and related equipment (for example, programs that start and stop jobs or find data on disk and tape)

TAB–a BASIC function that skips to a specified column on screen or printer

table–see *array*

tablet–a special writing surface on which drawings are traced for input into digitizers

tape–a machine-readable medium in which data is stored as magnetic patterns on stripes of tape

tape/disk library–a fireproof room used to organize and store disks and tapes for a computer center

tape drive–storage hardware used to access information on tape. It runs the data tape over a read/write head

technician–a person with on-the-job training and minimum educational background who works with instruments, assembles parts, or oversees a manufacturing process

telecommunications–long distance communications including voice and data transmissions

teleprocessing–transferring data between terminals and/or computers using communication lines

teleprocessing system–a computer system where at least one of the five components is physically distant from the others

template–see *flowcharting template*

terminal–a keyboard and printer or CRT that is connected by communication lines to a computer and is used for input and output only. It can contain a limited memory but no control unit or arithmetic/logic unit

testing/debugging–the fourth phase in program development. It consists of eliminating all logic and syntax errors and trying the program with a variety of data

text editor–a program that allows documents to be written and modified on a computer. It does not allow computation as some word processors do

third-generation computer–computer developed during the 1960s that uses integrated circuits as the basis of processing. It normally has multiprogramming and online capabilities

timesharing–the ability of a computer to share its processing time by alternating work on several programs

top-down design–to develop a project by starting with a main idea and refining it until it is broken into workable and distinct modules

track–one of the concentric circles on a disk

trailer label–see *end-of-file marker*

training seminar–a meeting for professionals that concentrates on a single topic

transaction–the updating of data related to a business or computer application

transaction processing–processing each transaction as it takes place for faster accessing and updating of information

transfer of control–skipping from one line of a program to another

transistor–a small electronic component that can alter a signal in a predefined way. It is the basis of the second-generation computers

truncated check flow–see *one-way check*

turnkey system–a complete system with hardware, software, and procedures that is designed for use by people with little computer experience

tutorial–a computer-assisted instruction application, used in lieu of a textbook, that introduces new material to students and then quizzes them over it

Uniform Product Code–see *UPC*

UNIVAC I–Universal Automatic Computer—the first commercial computer developed in 1950 by John W. Mauchly and J. Presper Eckert

Universal Product Code–see *UPC*

UPC–Universal Product Code—a standard *bar code* on grocery items that helps with pricing and inventory—also called the Uniform Product Code

update–to keep a file current by adding, deleting, or changing records

user–anyone utilizing information generated by a computer

user friendly–software that is self-explanatory and easy to use

vacuum tube–a glass tube containing circuitry that was the processing basis for first-generation computers

vector graphics–graphics formed by drawing continuous lines on a screen. It characteristically produces clear and intricate drawings

vendor–organization that creates and/or sells a product

verb–one of many actions words that must begin a BASIC statement

verification–(data entry) when a person, rather than a computer, checks input data for correctness

verify–(programming) to have the computer compare what is in its memory to what it has just saved on tape or disk

vocational class–a class in which an employable skill is taught

vocational training–see *vocational class*

von Neumann, John–mathematician who developed the design for the first computer with the program stored in memory

Winchester drive–a disk drive using *data modules* instead of separate disk and access mechanisms

word processing–using computer technology to prepare letters, memos, and other documents

writing–the third phase in program development. It consists of using program code to express the design

BIBLIOGRAPHY

Bradbeer; DeBono; and Laurie. *The Beginner's Guide to Computers*. Reading, MA: Addison-Wesley, 1982.

Dorf, Richard C. *Computers and Man*. San Francisco: Boyd and Fraser, 1977.

Drucker, Peter. "Drucker's Anatomy." *Concepts*, Vol. 6, No. 4, Autumn 1982, pp. 2-7.

Friedrich, Otto. "Machine of the Year: The Computer Moves In." *Time*, Vol. 121, No. 1, January 1983, pp. 14-24.

Graham, Neill. *The Mind Tool*, 3rd ed. Saint Paul, MN: West Publishing, 1983.

Kent, E.W. *The Brains of Men and Machines*. New York: McGraw-Hill, 1981.

Kroenke, David. *Business Computer Systems*, 2nd ed. Santa Cruz, CA: Mitchell Publishing, 1984.

Luehrmann, Arthur and Peckham, Herbert. *Computer Literacy: A Hands-On Approach*. New York: McGraw-Hill, 1983.

Mehlmann, Marilyn. *When People Use Computers*. Englewood Cliffs, NJ: Prentice-Hall, 1981.

Morrison, Philip and Morrison, Emily, Eds. *Charles Babbage and His Calculating Engines*. New York: Dover Publications, 1961.

Rothman, Stanley and Mosmann, Charles. *Computers and Society*, 2nd ed. Chicago: Science Research Associates, 1976.

Rubin, Charles. "Some People Should Be Afraid of Computers." *Personal Computing*, Vol. 7, No. 8, August 1983, pp. 55-57.

Sanders, Donald. *Computers Today*. New York: McGraw-Hill, 1983.

Spencer, Donald. *An Introduction to Computers*. Columbus, OH: Charles E. Merrill Publishing, 1983.

Wood, Merle. *Computer Awareness*. Cincinnati, OH: South-Western, 1982.

UNIT A:

Welcome to the Computer Age

Arjani, K. A. *Structured Programming Flowcharts*. New York: Collegium, 1978.

Bernstein, M. K. "Hardware Is Easy - It's Software That's Hard." *Datamation*, Vol. 24, No. 11, November 1978, pp. 32-36.

Bohl, Marilyn. *A Guide for Programmers*. Englewood Cliffs, NJ: Prentice-Hall, 1978.

Bohl, Marilyn. *Tools for Structured Design*. Chicago: Science Research Associates, 1978.

Boraiko, Allen. "The Chip." *National Geographic*, Vol. 162, No. 4, October 1982, pp. 421-456.

Brechtein, Rich. "Comparing Disk Technologies." *Datamation*, Vol. 24, No. 1, January 1978, pp. 139-150.

UNIT B:

Putting Computer Technology in Its Place

Capron, H. and Williams, Brian. *Computers and Data Processing*. Menlo Park, CA: Benjamin/Cummings Publishing, 1982.

Cole, J. W. Perry. *ANSI FORTRAN IV with FORTRAN 77 Extensions,* 2nd ed. Dubuque, IA: Wm. C Brown, 1978.

Cooper, Doug and Clancy, Michael. *Oh! Pascal!*. New York: W. W. Norton, 1982.

Cortesi, D. and Cherry, G. *Personal Pascal: Compiled Pascal for the IBM PC*. Reston, VA: Reston Publishing, 1983.

Dijkstra, Edsger W. *A Discipline of Programming*. Englewood Cliffs, NJ: Prentice-Hall, 1976.

Dorf, R. C. *Robotics and Automated Manufacturing*. Reston, VA: Reston Publishing, 1983.

Freeman, David H. and Friedman, Roy. "Bar-code and Voice Recognition Ease Data-entry Problems." *Mini-Micro Systems,* Vol. 16, No. 7, June 1983, pp. 239-246.

Grauer, Robert. *TRS-80 COBOL*. Englewood Cliffs, NJ: Prentice-Hall, 1983.

Gries, David, Ed. *Programming Methodology*. New York: Springer-Verlag, 1978.

Hearn, Donald and Baker, Pauline M. *Microcomputer Graphics*. Englewood Cliffs, NJ: Prentice-Hall, 1983.

Inman, D. and Inman, K. *Assembly Language Graphics for the TRS-80 Color Computer.* Reston, VA: Reston Publishing, 1983.

Kenealy, Patrick. "Market Overview: Minicomputer Line Printers." *Mini-Micro Systems,* Vol. 16, No. 1, January 1983, pp. 131-140.

Kohl; Karp; and Signer. *The Genie in the Computer: Easy BASIC Through Graphics*. New York: John Wiley & Sons, 1982.

Lee, Iva H. *Data Entry*. New York: John Wiley, 1982.

Leeson, Marjorie. *Computer Operations*. Chicago: Science Research Associates, 1978.

Luehrmann, A. and Peckham, H. *Apple Pascal: A Hands-On Approach*. New York: McGraw-Hill, 1981.

Mallender, Ian H. "Color Non-impact Printers Hit the Market." *Mini-Micro Systems,* Vol. 16, No. 7, June 1983, pp. 217-224.

McCracken, Daniel D. "The Changing Face of Applications Programming." *Datamation,* Vol. 24, No. 11, November 1978, pp. 25-30.

McCracken, Daniel D. *A Simplified Guide to COBOL Programming*. New York: John Wiley, 1976.

Moritz, Fredrick G. "Conventional Magnetic Tape Equipment." *Modern Data,* Vol 8., No. 3, March 1975, pp. 51-55.

Noll, Paul. *The Structured Programming Cookbook*. Fresno, CA: Mike Murach and Associates, 1978.

Papert, Seymour. *Mindstorms*. New York: Basic Books, 1980.

Sammet, Jean E. *Programming Languages: History and Fundamentals*. Englewood Cliffs, NJ: Prentice-Hall, 1969.

Shelly, Gary and Cashman, Thomas. *Computer Programming: RPG II*. Brea, CA: Anaheim Publishing, 1976.

Spencer, Donald. *Introduction to Information Processing*. Columbus, OH: Charles E. Merrill Publishing, 1981.

Wanous; Wagner; and Lambrecht. *Fundamentals of Data Processing*. Cincinnati, OH: South-Western, 1981.

Ware, Willis H. "Handling Personal Data." *Datamation,* Vol. 23, No. 10, October 1977, pp. 83-87.

Weinberg, Gerald M. *The Psychology of Computer Programming*. New York: Van Nostrand Reinhold, 1971.

Welburn, Tyler. *Advanced Structured COBOL*. Palo Alto, CA: Mayfield, 1983.

Welburn, Tyler. *Structured COBOL*. Palo Alto, CA: Mayfield, 1981.

Welburn, Tyler. "Toward Training the Compleat COBOL Programmer." *Interface,* Vol. 1, No. 2, Spring 1979, pp. 40-42.

Whol, Amy and Carey, Kathleen. "We're Not Really Sure How Many We Have." *Datamation,* Vol. 28, No. 12, November 1982, pp. 106-109.

Yasaki, E. K. "Bar Codes for Data Entry." *Datamation,* Vol. 21, No. 5, May 1975, pp. 63-68.

Ackoff, Russell L. "Management Misinformation Systems." *Management Science,* Vol. 14, No. 4, pp. 147-156.

Alter, S. L. "How Effective Managers Use Information Systems." *Harvard Business Review,* November-December 1976, pp. 97-104.

Bateman, Wayne A. *Introduction to Computer Music*. New York: John Wiley & Sons, 1982.

Barcomb, David. *Office Automation*. Bedford, MA: Digital Equipment, 1981.

Burch; Strater; and Grudnitski. *Information Systems: Theory and Practice,* 3rd ed. New York: John Wiley & Sons, 1983.

Computer Crime: Criminal Justice Resource Manual. Washington, D.C.: Bureau of Justice Statistics, 1979.

Donelson, William S. "MRP - Who Needs It?" *Datamation,* Vol. 25, No. 5, May 1979, pp. 185-194.

Dorf, R.C. *Computers and Man,* 3rd ed. San Francisco: Boyd and Fraser, 1982.

Hilts, Philip J. *Scientific Temperaments: Three Lives in Contemporary Science*. New York: Simon and Schuster, 1982.

Jaffe, Merle. "Decision Support Systems for Manufacturing." *Infosystems,* Vol. 30, No. 7, July 1983, pp. 112-114.

Kindred, Alton R. *Data Systems and Management*. Englewood Cliffs, NJ: Prentice-Hall, 1973.

Lucas, H. J., Jr. *Why Information Systems Fail*. New York: Columbia University Press, 1975.

Machover, Carl and Blauth, Robert, Eds. *The CAD/CAM Handbook*. Bedford, MA: Computervision, 1980.

McCauley, Carole Sperrin. *Computers and Creativity*. New York: Praeger, 1974.

McLeod, Raymond, Jr. *Management Information Systems,* 2nd ed. Chicago: Science Research Associates, 1983.

Menosky, Joseph. "Video Graphics and Grand Jetes." *Science 82,* Vol. 3, No. 4, May 1982, pp. 25-32.

Mowe, Richard. *The Academic Apple*. Reston, VA: Reston Publishing, 1983.

Olson, Steve. "Computing Climate." *Science 82,* Vol. 3, No. 4, May 1982, pp. 54-60.

Palmer, Roger C. *Online Reference and Information Retrieval*. Littleton, CO: Libraries Unlimited, 1983.

Poppel, Harvey L. "The Information Revolution: Winners and Losers." *Harvard Business Review,* January-February 1978.

Rhodes, Wayne L., Jr. "Office of the Future, Fact or Fantasy?" *Infosystems*, March 1980, pp. 45-54.

Roberts, Jerome J. "Computer-generated Evidence." *Data Management*, November 1974, pp. 20-21.

Ryan, Frank B. "The Electronic Voting System for the United States House of Representatives." *Computer*, November-December 1972, pp. 32-37.

Schrage, Michael. "Computer Animation Comes of Age in a Studio on 'Dopey Drive'." *Smithsonian*, Vol. 13, No. 4, July 1982, pp. 86-95.

Stitt, Fred. "Computers for the Small Office: A Primer." *Architectural Record*, Vol. 170, No. 2, February 1982, pp. 47-51.

Tapscott, Don. "Investigating the Electronic Office." *Datamation*, Vol. 23, No. 3, March 1982, pp. 130-138.

Waterhouse, Shirley. *Office Automation and Word Processing Fundamentals*. New York: Harper and Row, 1983.

Young, George. *Kilobaud Klassroom*. Peterborough, NH: Wayne Green Books, 1983.

UNIT D:

Bringing People and
Computers Together

Bingham, John E. and Davies, W. P. Garth. *Planning for Data Communications*. New York: John Wiley, 1977.

Bohl, Marilyn. *Information Processing*, 3rd ed. Chicago: Science Research Associates, 1980.

Booth, Grayce M. *The Distributed Systems Environment*. New York: McGraw-Hill, 1981.

Carlson, Robert D. and Lewis, James A. *The Systems Analysis Workbook*, 2nd ed. Englewood Cliffs, NJ: Prentice-Hall, 1979.

Data Communications Primer - Student Text. IBM manual GC20-1668, White Plains, NY.

Date, Chris J. *An Introduction to Database Systems*. Reading, MA: Addison-Wesley, 1981.

Dolan, Kathy. *Business Computer Systems Design*. Santa Cruz, CA: Mitchell Publishing, 1983.

Glass, Robert L. and Noiseux, Ronald A. *Software Maintenance Guidebook*. Englewood Cliffs, NJ: Prentice-Hall, 1981.

Glossrenner, Alfred. *The Complete Handbook of Personal Computer Communications*. New York: St. Martin's Press, 1983.

Klee; Verity; and Johnson. "Battle of the Networkers." *Datamation*, Vol. 28, No. 3, March 1982, pp. 115-127.

Koberg, Don and Bagnall, Jim. *The Universal Traveler*. Los Altos, CA: William Kaufmann, 1976.

Kroenke, David. *Database Processing*, 2nd ed. Chicago: Science Research Associates, 1983.

Libes, Sol. *Small Computer Systems Handbook*. Rochelle Park, NJ: Hayden, 1978.

Magid, Lawrence. *Micro Decision User's Guide*. San Leandro, CA: Morrow Designs, 1982.

Martin, James. *Computer Data-Base Organization*. Englewood Cliffs, NJ: Prentice-Hall, 1977.

Martin, James. *Telecommunications and the Computer*. Englewood Cliffs, NJ: Prentice-Hall, 1976.

McGlynn, Daniel. *Simplified Guide to Small Computers for Business*. New York: John Wiley & Sons, 1983.

Meyers, Glenford J. *The Art of Software Testing*. New York: John Wiley, 1979.

Muchow, Kenneth and Deem, Bill R. *Microprocessors: Principles, Programming, and Interfacing*. Reston, VA: Reston Publishing, 1983.

Orr, Kenneth T. *Structured Systems Development*. New York: Yourdon Press, 1977.

Page-Jones, Meilir. *The Practical Guide to Structured Systems Design*. New York: Yourdon Press, 1980.

Remer, Daniel. *Legal Care for Your Software*. Reading, MA: Addison-Wesley, 1982.

Rothfeder, Jeffrey. "Networking the Workplace." *Personal Computing,* Vol. 7, No. 6, June 1983, pp. 79-87.

Sanders, Ray. "Managing Data Communications." *Datamation,* Vol. 24, No. 11, November 1978, pp. 43-47.

Scharer, Laura L. "User Training: Less Is More." *Datamation,* Vol. 29, No. 7, July 1983, pp. 175-182.

Shapiro, Neil. "10 Tips for Home Computer Care and Repair." *Popular Mechanics,* April 1982, pp. 112-115.

Spinner, M. *Elements of Project Management: Plan, Schedule, and Control*. Englewood Cliffs, NJ: Prentice-Hall, 1981.

Tanenbaum, Andrew S. *Computer Networks*. Englewood Cliffs, NJ: Prentice-Hall, 1981.

Thierauf, Robert J. *Distributed Processing Systems*. Englewood Cliffs, NJ: Prentice-Hall, 1981.

Weinberg, Victor. *Structured Analysis*. New York: Yourdon Press, 1978.

Weitzman, Cay. *Distributed Micro/Minicomputer Systems*. Englewood Cliffs, NJ: Prentice-Hall, 1980.

Yourdon, Edward and Constantine, Larry. *Structured Design*. New York: Yourdon Press, 1978.

Zaks, Rodney. *Don't! Or How to Care for Your Computer*. Berkeley, CA: Sybex, 1981.

UNIT E:

Looking Ahead

Burch, John G. and Sardinas, Joseph L. *Computer Control and Audit*. New York: John Wiley, 1978.

Cortada, James W. *EDP Costs and Charges*. Englewood Cliffs, NJ: Prentice-Hall, 1980.

Feigenbaum, Edward and McCorduck, Pamela. *The Fifth Generation*. Reading, MA: Addison-Wesley, 1983.

Framer, Dale F. "Confessions of an EDP Auditor." *Datamation,* Vol. 29, No. 7, July 1983, pp. 193-198.

Harris, Larry R. "Fifth Generation Foundations." *Datamation,* Vol. 29, No. 7, July 1983, pp. 148-156.

Holoien, Martin O. *Computers and Their Societal Impact*. New York: John Wiley, 1977.

Kling, Rob. "EFTS: Social and Technical Issues." *Computers and Society,* Fall 1976, pp. 3-10.

Krauss, Leonard I. and MacGahan, Aileen. *Computer Fraud and Countermeasures*. Englewood Cliffs, NJ: Prentice-Hall, 1979.

Levy, David. *All About Chess and Computers,* 2nd ed. Rockville, MD: Computer Science Press, 1982.

Markoff, John and Shea, Tom. "Information Utilities." *Infoworld,* Vol. 5, No. 13, March 1983, pp. 41-50.

McCorduck, Pamela. *Machines Who Think*. San Francisco: W.H. Freeman, 1979.

McKibbin, Wendy Lea. "Who Gets the Blame for Computer Crime?" *Infosystems,* Vol. 30, No. 7, July 1983, pp. 34-36.

McKnight, Gerald. *Computer Crime*. London: Michale Joseph, 1973.

Minsky, M. L. "Artificial Intelligence," *Scientific American,* September 1966, pp. 142–148.

BIBLIOGRAPHY

Mueller, Robert E. and Mueller, Erik T. "Would an Intelligent Computer Have a Right to Life?" *Creative Computing*, Vol. 9, No. 8, August 1983, pp. 149-153.

Negroponte, Nicholas. "The Computerized Global Village." *Concepts*, Vol. 7, No. 1, Winter 1983, pp. 8-11.

Parker, Donn B. *Computer Security Management*. Reston, VA: Reston Publishing, 1981.

Parker, Donn B. *Crime by Computer.* New York: Charles Scribner's Sons, 1976.

Personal Privacy in an Information Society. U.S. Government Printing Office, No. 052-003-00395, July 1977.

Rhodes, Wayne L., Jr. and Winkler, Raymond S. "Twenty-fifth Annual DP Salary Survey." *Infosystems*, Vol. 30, No. 6, June 1983, pp. 40-44.

Schefter, Jim. "Fifth-Generation Computers." *Popular Science*, Vol. 222, No. 4, April 1983, pp. 79-81.

Sheils, Merrill and Cook, William. "Machines That Think: And Man Created the Chip." *Newsweek,* Vol. 155, No. 26, June 1980, pp. 50-56.

Staples, Betsy. "Computer Intelligence: Unlimited and Untapped." *Creative Computing*, Vol. 9, No. 8, August 1983, pp. 164-166.

Swaine, Michael. "Knowledge Engineers' Handcraft Diagnostic Software." *Infoworld*, Vol. 5, No. 22, May 1983, pp. 11-12.

Toffler, Alvin. *The Third Wave.* New York: Morrow, 1980.

Turning, A. M. "Can a Machine Think?" *Mind*, 1950, pp. 2099-2123.

Weizenbaum, Joseph. *Computer Power and Human Reason: From Judgement to Calculation.* San Francisco: W. H. Freeman, 1976.

Wiener, Norbert. "Some Moral and Technical Consequences of Automation." *Science*, Vol. 131, May 1960, pp. 1355-1358.

UNIT F:

BASIC on Microcomputers Step-by-Step

Albrecht; Inman; and Zamora. *TRS-80 Level II BASIC*. New York: John Wiley & Sons, 1980.

Dwyer, Thomas and Critchfield, Margot. *A Bit of BASIC*. Reading, MA: Addison-Wesley, 1980.

Inman; Albrecht; and Zamora. *TRS-80 Advanced Level II BASIC*. New York: John Wiley & Sons, 1981.

Johnson, Randolph P. *BASIC Using Micros*. Santa Cruz, CA: Mitchell Publishing, 1984.

McRitchie, Margaret. *Programming in BASIC*. Toronto: Holt, Rinehart and Winston of Canada, 1982.

Osborne; Strasma; and Strasma. *Pet Personal Computer Guide*. Berkeley, CA: Osborne/McGraw-Hill, 1982.

Poole, Lon and Borchers, Mary. *Some Common Basic Programs*, 2nd ed. Berkeley, CA: Adam Osborne & Associates, 1978.

Presley, Bruce. *Guide to Programming: IBM Personal Computer.* New York: Van Nostrand Reinhold, 1982.

Shelly, Gary and Cashman, Thomas. *Introduction to BASIC Programming*. Brea, CA: Anaheim Publishing, 1982.

INDEX

NOTE: Italicized page numbers indicate figures. The photo essays are indexed by the following abbreviations:

C - The Chip: The Heart of the Computer
CS - Computers and Society: More Uses, More Users, More Questions
G - Computer Graphics: An Art, A Science, A Tool

H - Hardware: More and More for Less and Less
IC - The Computer Industry and Careers: Gold Rush of the 1980s
M - Micros: Selecting Your Own Computer